Debussy in Performance

Debussy in Performance

Edited by James R. Briscoe

Yale University Press

New Haven & London

Printed in the United States of America.

Library of Congress Cataloging-in-Publication Data

Debussy in performance / edited by James R. Briscoe.

p. cm.

Includes bibliographical references (p.) and index.

ISBN 0-300-07626-6 (alk. paper)

1. Debussy, Claude, 1862–1918—Criticism and interpretation. 2. Performance practice (Music)—19th century. 3. Performance practice (Music)—20th century. I. Briscoe, James R., 1949– .

ML410.D28D385 1999

780'.92—dc21 99-38223

CIP

A catalogue record for this book is available from the British Library.

The paper in this book meets the guidelines for permanence and durability of the Committee on Production Guidelines for Book Longevity of the Council on Library Resources.

10 9 8 7 6 5 4 3 2 1

To William W. Austin for articulating Debussy's primary place in the twentieth century

Contents

Preface

Musicians everywhere acknowledge the fundamental influence of Debussy in the twentieth century. Pierre Boulez, a leading composer and conductor of contemporary music, asserts in his *Notes of an Apprenticeship* that "modern music was awakened by Debussy." And Debussy has had an abiding influence on popular music and jazz: the leading jazz composer and performer Chick Corea notes that "Debussy is the most important classical composer in my life." Yet no comprehensive analysis of Debussy's own performance expectations, of the performance traditions surrounding his compositions, or of the internal and contextual evidence that can inform performers has hitherto been undertaken.

This book focuses on several important issues that are helping to energize Debussy scholarship today. First and perhaps foremost, several contributors inquire into the "esprit debussyste," as Richard Langham Smith terms it in his chapter on performance, where he calls on us to reach beyond the "urtext mentality" of too great a literalism. Claude Abravanel urges performers to adopt the symbolist mindset of Debussy, a point furthered by Louis-Marc Suter when he argues for the value of silence in performing Debussy's opera *Pelléas et Mélisande.*

Part II examines issues of Debussy's genres in performance. The evidence offered by the composer himself and by the earliest performers who knew him is the basic resource of these chapters. Questions about performance forces, flexibility of tempo, aspects of piano playing, performer license, and the interpretation of expressive indications are considered in my chapter on orchestral performance, in Cecilia Dunoyer's on Debussy and early Debussystes at the piano, in Stephanie Jordan's on Debussy's music for the dance, and in Brooks Toliver's on interpreting the songs. Fixing Debussy's intentions is no easy task, for the composer occasionally altered his expectations according to given circumstances, and he rewrote whole passages when a performance exigency was at hand. On occasion he performed works differently from the score indications. Rather than attempting to find a given "truth" of Debussy's intentions, these contributors have shown the range of values within which Debussy and those closest to him appear to have conceived his music. Historical sound recordings are considered extensively here, as throughout this book, such as those housed at the Bibliothèque Nationale and the Library of the French National Radio, in Paris, at the New York Public Library, and at the Library of Congress Sound Archives. The artistic context of Debussy performance is considered here, too, for example, in Stephanie Jordan's discussion of symbolism, cubism, and modernism in relation to dance performance.

Part III presents the viewpoints of particular interpreters, including the conductor Désiré-Emile Inghelbrecht, writing in 1933 on how not to perform *Pelléas et Mélisande,* and Pierre Boulez, who agreed to be interviewed for this book.

Part IV concerns score analysis. The structural elements of timbre, voice-leading, and the musical arabesque, as well as metric and phrase ambiguities are explored by Richard Parks, who focuses on Debussy's sonatas, and by Jann Pasler, who stresses the need for performers to consider texture and timbre in the piano music.

Several of the studies in this collection draw upon the memoirs of performers close to Debussy, such as the conductors Inghelbrecht, Gabriel Pierné, and Piero Coppola; the singers Jane Barthori, Mary Garden, and Maggie Teyte; and the pianists Marguerite Long, Alfred Cortot, and George Copeland. Some of these reminiscences have appeared previously in the invaluable collection by Roger Nichols, *Debussy Remembered* (1992), but here they are placed in a context of genre performance, performance analysis, and performance aesthetic. Many of the authors draw on Debussy's own letters and music criticism, which have only recently been published by François Lesure and others. Studies by Richard Parks, Roy Howat, Lesure, and Richard Langham Smith, among others, have provided important information about internal evidence in the music that affects performance choice, as well as about Debussy's own performances; the studies in this book are indebted to their pioneering work. Given this new interest in Debussy, as well as the ongoing publication of his complete works, the time is ripe for reflection on the issues raised in this book. The music of Debussy has been and will continue to be crucial in the evolution of contemporary music and music performance.

I am indebted to two former students, now scholars in their own right. Roberta Lindsey provided expert help in preparing the final copy and Andrew Simpson prepared the music examples.

Part One **The Spirit of Debussy Performance**

Chapter 1 Debussy on Performance: Sound and Unsound Ideals

Richard Langham Smith

There was in Debussy's playing a narcotic/erotic note, a sweet dreaminess like that of a woman's hand.
Karl Lahm

So-called period performances have been chasing musicologists more quickly than the boundaries of the discipline of performance practice have advanced. Even before musicologists have begun to put pen to paper, performers have rushed into the breach, warming up their late nineteenth-century conical silver flutes with the *Faune*'s C-sharps, and pressing into service some "authentic" pianos, even if documentation may show that they were of a type Debussy decidedly did not care for.[1] Before we are overtaken by a tide of performances claiming to be "historically informed," some serious consideration needs to be given to this composer's own performance ideals, seen in the context of those prevalent in his time. Why has so little been written on this subject, one might ask.

A perfectly legitimate response from those even moderately well read in Debussy's writings might be that this composer wrote precious little about such matters and that what there is has to be read with an inevitably speculative eye.

With regard to Debussy, the term "authenticity," outmoded when applied to the music of earlier times, may unashamedly be reverted to, for even in the composer's lifetime, performers identified a specific "esprit debussyste" and encouraged their pupils to try to find it. Notions of "historically informed" performances may thus be separated from similar notions in regard to the seventeenth or eighteenth centuries because there is no "lost tradition" in between. Or is there?

The present essay is founded on the principle that in the 1990s, when a lot more information is available on both desk and music stand, as well as on the compact disc player, a reconsideration of what we know about Debussy's own ideals of performance might valuably be made, and in particular, problem areas of contradiction can be probed. This is a fairly straightforward task of "police-station musicology" if you like: the sifting and juxtaposition of this widening body of evidence.

Better texts are currently in progress: above all, the "urtext" *Oeuvres complètes.* Also trickling out is a wealth of reminiscences of varying degrees of reliability, previously unpublished letters and articles by the composer, and, perhaps most important, recordings and player-piano transcriptions from Debussy's own day.[2]

With such a wide spectrum of sources, musicology must reexamine its methods, not least because as soon as early recordings of one sort or another are brought in as source material, danger signals should begin to flash. Recordings and piano rolls, of course, have to be treated with particular caution: what we deduce from them must take into account the technical limitations and idiosyncrasies of early recording as well as human fallibility. But while on one level they have helped the compilation of the Debussy urtext, on another they challenge the esteem given to the notion of an urtext edition by positivist musicology. How often is "musicologically informed" criticism based on the maxim "This was a good performance because it followed the urtext score, this was a bad performance because it didn't"? Is that so bad? Yes and no.

With regard particularly to the standard repertoire of the late nineteenth century, Robert Philip, in his pioneering work on early recordings, has neatly contrasted the performing traditions of the early with the late twentieth century as follows: "The performances of the early twentieth century are . . . volatile, energetic, flexible, vigorously projected in broad outline but rhythmically informal in detail. Modern performances are, by comparison, accurate, orderly, restrained, deliberate, and even in emphasis."[3] To summarize the dynamics of the process of change from the one to the other approach, Philip traces the gradual decline of a tradition in which a sparing use of a rather fast vibrato among both string players and singers gave way to a slower, wider, and more widespread use; in which the general avoidance of vibrato for wind players, except for those of the French school, gave way to a more widespread use; in which the use of portamento for both strings and singers gave way to its avoidance; in which a free approach to tempo gradually changed to a stricter approach, and so on. The musicologist must conclude that it was the former performing climate that Debussy knew and remind him or herself that he was dead before even the glimmerings of the latter tradition were felt.

Philip's unveiling of the detailed techniques of the performance practices of Debussy's day might profitably be approached in another way. Because Debussy himself was so fussy about the detailed notation of his scores (although he often seem to lose interest in precision at the proof stage), a dual approach that views the relationship between Debussy's printed scores and the recorded legacy might serve us well in situating Debussy's attitudes to performance in relation to the more general postromantic performing climate of his time. To put the question in a nutshell: Where did Debussy stand in relation to an interpretative tradition whose very essence was the licensing of riding a coach and four through the notational prescriptions of a score?

In this climate, composers' attitudes to their own scores were radically different, perhaps even the opposite, of what we expect today. Philip cites Mahler: a telling example of a composer in a pre-urtext mindset. On the one hand he produced immaculately notated scores; on the other he could claim that "all the most important things: the tempo, the total conception and structuring of a work are almost impossible to pin down. For here we are concerned with something living and flowing that can never be the same even twice in succession. That is why metronome markings are inadequate and almost worthless; for unless the work is vulgarly ground out in barrel-organ style, the tempo will already have changed by the second bar."[4] If Mahler as a conductor was as free as he liked with, say, Beethoven, then why shouldn't other conductors mess about with his own meticulously marked music?

Such a view might suggest that for most performers in the early twentieth century the notion of an urtext would have seemed ridiculous: Why go to the trouble of producing an impeccably notated score if it was assumed that any performer worth his salt would do what he wanted with it anyway? Mahler's view may seem extreme; Philip relates it to "Wagner and Bülow's kind of flexibility"[5]—but in fact a similar view was expressed by Debussy, with a metaphor that may make us smile in that it seems so typically French, and makes Mahler's reference to the "barrel-organ" style so typically teutonic. Writing to Durand in 1915, while working on an edition of Chopin, Debussy advises against the inclusion of metronome marks: "You know what I think about metronome markings: they're all right for one measure, like those roses which only last for a morning."[6] Clues about where Debussy stood as regards interpretational intervention can be had from a few of his letters. Surprisingly few more can be gleaned from his stint as a music critic.

Most important in this quest is to take Debussy's evolving aesthetic as the starting point, rather than to approach the issue from the other end. Whether he pulled triplets around or suggested bringing out "inner voices" are ultimately secondary questions. The basic level of the esprit debussyste must first be established.

From his earliest letters from the 1880s, written in Rome to such artistic mentors as Eugène Vasnier, Emile Baron, and Gustave Popelin, Debussy was apt to avoid any analysis of why a performance he had attended was in his opinion good or bad. He was content to affirm his approval or disapproval without going farther. On the few occasions when we can see through to ideals of performance, they are inevitably related to deeper ideas of how music should affect us.

A combing of the clues as to his ideas on performance that Debussy left us in his articles and letters reveals a polarity in his mind between realism and *rêverie.* His strong dislike of musical "realism" is a recurrent streak, developed at a time when he was faced with the task of assuming a stance as a critic.[7] These ideas were catalyzed by his disdain for Alfred Bruneau's opera *Messidor,* to a libretto by Emile Zola, which received its premiere at the Paris Opéra in 1897. Added to this were remarks made after his attendance at a rehearsal for Charpentier's *Louise* in 1900.

With regard to the former he confesses to the writer Pierre Louÿs that "life is too short" to attend such events and goes on to describe both Zola and Bruneau as "ugly" and "mediocre."[8] With regard to Charpentier a similar antipathy emerges again: "Note how Charpentier takes 'the cries of Paris,' which are wonderful examples of picturesque humanity, and like some wretched *Prix de Rome* turns them into chlorotic cantilenas with harmonies that, to be polite, I'll call parasitic. . . . And they call that life! Heavens above, I'd rather die on the spot—these are sentiments which are like a hangover when you've drunk your twentieth half."[9]

Debussy was clearly passionate about the falseness of Zola's naturalism and its transference into music because it was the polar opposite of his own approach. While Zola believed that the way to penetrate "reality" was "merely to observe," for Debussy such reality was less easily attained. For him, reality could be glimpsed only by engaging the imagination. *Pelléas* is the prime example of this procedure.[10]

Any speculations on the nature of the esprit debussyste must be founded in this aesthetic, which, curiously, has been approached copiously from every angle except that of a critical and penetrating reading of Debussy's own writings, although there is plenty of writing that confronts Debussy's music with the opposing concerns of literary symbolism and visual impressionism.[11]

Commentators have rightly seized upon the composer's response to Ernest Guiraud's question in his celebrated interview with Debussy about what constituted an ideal libretto: "Celui qui, disant les choses à demi, me permettra de greffer mon rêve sur le sien," freely translated by Lockspeiser as "the ideal would be two associated dreams" but perhaps more accurately rendered as that which, half-stating things, "allows me to graft my dream on to his" (the librettist's).[12] These ideas were already in germinal form during Debussy's early stay in Rome, as another, often cited letter to Eugène Vasnier shows. Speaking of his rejection of an initial plan for a setting of *Zuleima* after Heinrich Heine, as his initial *envoi* from Rome, he again touches on the question of "reality." He mentions the impossibility of being subservient to a rigid literary plan and speaks of his need for a libretto where "the sequence of external events is subordinate to an extended exploration of the sentiments of the soul—'des sentiments de l'âme.'" Reading further into Debussy's response to the "ideal libretto" question in the Guiraud interview, we find the composer expressing a preference for a setting without historical reference, "out of time, and with no distinguishable setting."[13]

One of the first works to fulfill these ideals was *La damoiselle élue,* a setting of stanzas from Dante Gabriel Rossetti's poem "The Blessed Damozel." The scenario for this poem, an imagined heaven studded with the mildly symbolic bric-a-brac of Pre-Raphaelitism, and not unrelated to the images of heaven in illustrated Victorian Bibles, was certainly the diametrical opposite of Zola's real-life scenarios. The Damoiselle's slow declamation clearly exemplifies Debussy's ideals of a distillation of human emotion: "des sentiments de l'âme." A performance of the piece in 1900 drew a revealing letter of gratitude from the composer to the singer of the Damoiselle, again stressing the idea of an escape from the material world. Debussy was moved by her ability "to abstract herself entirely from the material world so that it became supernatural." He went on to admire her delivery of the line "All this is when he comes," which distills the Damoiselle's longing for terrestrial love in this imagined paradise.[14]

For several reasons, 1901–2 may be identified as a crucial time in the crystallization of Debussy's aesthetic standpoint. Firstly, this was the stressful period when Debussy saw *Pelléas* go through the production machinery of the Opéra-Comique, after which it was dealt with by commentators of all positions. In addition, at this time he first took on the position of music critic for *La revue blanche* and later for *Gil Blas,* a job that necessitated the clarification of his own aesthetic standpoint. And finally, in retrospect we see that after this period his musical style suddenly advanced into new realms.

Two strands may thus far be identified in Debussy's credo as we go into this crucial period: firstly, the preoccupation with the dream, which must have been severely challenged as he saw *Pelléas* made flesh in a realistic manner far removed from his own inner vision of his opera;[15] and secondly, the concept of distilled and heightened human emotion—the search for "des sentiments de l'âme"—which Debussy had explored in *La damoiselle élue,* and in *Pelléas.*

In his public comments on *Pelléas,* Debussy gave us one or two further tantalizing insights into the basis of his aesthetic, the most telling (and frequently quoted) of which is his comment about "exploring the mysterious *correspondances* between nature and the imagination," whose application commentators have been tempted to extend well beyond the bounds of his opera.[16] With its Baudelairean overtones we may be tempted to append this idea to the two strands previously identified as being at the center of Debussyan ideals in general, and to extend its application to the period immediately following *Pelléas,* and in particular to the post-1900 piano works, with their evocative titles.

One figure whom Debussy seems almost to have envied as he formulated his own ideas was Paul Dukas. Debussy admired not only Dukas's opinions, developed in a vast corpus of articles mainly for the *Revue hebdomadaire,* but also his "intelligence at the service of complete understanding." This esteem he expressed in a letter of 1901 that was in part concerned with his approval of an article in which Dukas had stressed the difficulty of pigeon-holing Debussy in a climate where the public liked to identify composers as "pupils of Franck, pupils of Massenet or disciples of Wagner," and so on. Added to this, Dukas claimed, was that each of Debussy's pieces "brought something special, which marks, if not a sensitive transformation of his approach, at least an unexpected and different point of view."

Debussy may also have admired Dukas's probing of the nature of his relationship to symbolist poetry, an expansion of the composer's self-confessed preoccupation with the "*correspondances* between nature and the imagination." As Dukas wrote in his article:

> Whether he collaborates with Baudelaire, Verlaine, or Mallarmé, or draws upon his own sources for the subject of his works, the composer confirms himself above all care-

> ful to avoid what one might call a direct translation of feelings. What attracts him in these aforementioned poets is precisely their art of transposing everything into symbolic images, to make one word vibrate into multiple resonances. . . . The majority of his compositions are thus symbols of symbols, but expressed in a language in itself so rich, so persuasive, that it attains the eloquence of a new verb.[17]

Debussy's letter to Dukas clearly follows up ideas in Dukas's article. Even as, on the outside, he is appreciative of Dukas's ability to intellectualize his musical aesthetics, there is an anti-intellectual undercurrent in Debussy's response. After admitting that Dukas's piece on the *Nocturnes* is "practically a unique act of empathy," he adds that "having intelligence at the service of infinite understanding is a luxury to which you are accustomed." In a central sentence, clearly in response to Dukas's comments about Debussy's relation to poetry, Debussy confesses the he is "no longer thinking in musical terms, or at least not much, even though I believe with all my heart that Music always remains the finest form of musical expression we have." Possibly in a veiled attack on Dukas's own music, Debussy protests against music "manifesting an obvious inability to see beyond the work-table . . . lit by one miserable lamp and never by the sun."[18] Again he returns to the idea of taking people out of themselves into a land of dreams: "It is enough if music forces people to *listen* in spite of themselves, in spite of their little daily cares, . . . so that they think they have dreamt for a moment of a magic and therefore undiscoverable place."[19] Debussy's last phrase here is surely an important key to his kingdom.

If we are in danger of straying too far into compositional aesthetics which may not directly affect our notion of Debussyan performance ideals, a letter from the time of *Pelléas* brings us back to the question of interpretational intervention. Writing to André Messager after Henri Busser had replaced him as the conductor of *Pelléas* at the Opéra-Comique, Debussy accuses Busser of "ignoring the singers and throwing chords in front of their feet, without any attention to the harmonic logic." The idea here would seem to be twofold: firstly to give more time in the placing of chords so that the singers do not trip over them—perhaps those in the more recitativelike sections of the opera—and secondly to observe the inner logic of a progression of harmonies. After castigating Busser, Debussy identifies some of the points he admires in Messager, stressing his interpretative powers and raising interpretation as a wider question: "You knew how to bring the music of *Pelléas* to life with a tender delicacy that would be hard to find anywhere else, for it is incontestable that the interior rhythm of any music depends on who is performing it, just as this or that word depends on the lips that pronounce it. . . . So our impression of *Pelléas* was heightened by your personal intuitions and feelings from which came the sense of everything being put in the right place."[20] Debussy's stressing of the importance of the interpreter in bringing to life the "interior rhythm" of the piece, which he seems to consider of paramount importance, is an idea which recurs in subsequent letters to other correspondents. His mindset is certainly not of the noninterventionist interpreter, faithfully bringing to life the notational details of the score, although, we may note, he likes the sense of things being in their "right place."

Writing to Manuel de Falla in 1907, in response to a query about the interpretation of the dances for harp and orchestra, Debussy elaborates on a rhythmic problem: "What you ask me is difficult to resolve! You cannot show a rhythm exactly any more than you can show exactly the exact expression of a phrase. The best thing is to rely on your personal feeling."[21]

Debussy's concern with "personal feelings" guiding interpretation, "intuition," the impossibility of exactly notating rhythms and the respect for the "vertu" of harmonies may be tested by reference to the handful of recordings he bequeathed to us, and to a lesser, more speculative extent, by those of other performers who were coached by him.

A remarkable exemplification of some of the ideas which have been identified is found in the acoustic recording of the third of the *Ariettes oubliées,* "L'ombre des arbres," made by Mary Garden with Debussy accompanying her in 1904.[22] The poem could hardly better exemplify an exploration, as Debussy had put it, of "the mysterious *correspondances* between nature and the imagination." (See example 1.1.) The apex of the song, typical of Verlaine and of Debussy's response, is the moment of coincidence of the two images of the poem: the moment when the qualities of the landscape—the first preoccupation of the poem—are attributed to the "voyageur," a variant on the common anthropomorphic devices used by Verlaine. Across the line break "ce paysage blême / Te mira blême toi-même," a new chromatic phrase emerges from the middle register of the piano texture, rising to dominate the falling phrase of the vocal line and thus lead to the climax of the piece. Debussy's way of notating this has several subtleties, but his performance introduces still more. In the notation, the new phrase is not given a new phrase mark but is elided with the falling-fifth phrase which began the song and has insistently recurred at the same pitch: it is thus almost imperceptibly born of the first idea.

Over the whole phrase Debussy marks *un poco stringendo* and he gives the repeat and octave transposition of the phrase two crescendo marks as well as indicating a general crescendo over the vocal line. So far, Debussy's accompaniment (as pianist) has been hypnotically in time, with the recurrent triplet-duplet

Ex. 1.1. "L'ombre des arbres," mm. 13–20. Transcription of expressive devices as recorded by Mary Garden and Debussy, Paris, 1904.

rhythms (m. 2 of example 1) played exactly in time, without any hint of agogic alteration. In the recording, however, the *poco stringendo* is suddenly exaggerated, certainly not "un poco," and the four eighth notes are given agogic accentuation, suddenly accelerated, and delivered roughly in the following manner: dwelling on the second eighth note and rushing the last two.[23]

This type of melodic rubato was widely used at the turn of the century. In this case it effects a sudden injection of energy, raising the emotional pitch far above that suggested by the expressive markings in the score.[24] If these rhythmic variants are deliberate—and I would suggest that they are—then it may be concluded that Debussy was not averse to grafting the "expressive" performance practices common in his time on to his detailed, prescriptive-looking scores.[25]

Closer analysis reveals deeper links with Debussy's expressed performance aesthetics. His ideals of penetrating "des sentiments de l'âme" have already been brought out. Here Debussy's own rendering gives us the sudden intervention of a dynamic and expressive style into a performance whose prolonged stasis throws into relief the slightest expressive nuance above the score. Suddenly, in the passage quoted above, extreme expressive devices—both in composition and performance—are employed to heighten the key line of the poem, more attenuated than any other line, where the poet's "nature-rêverie" leads him to penetrate the "soul" of the "voyageur."

The recording yields one further insight. Given that the vocal portamento was an integral part of the singing style of the day, Debussy's line in this song climaxes in an interval in which he surely knew that the singer would utilize its most extreme form: the "full" portamento, beginning immediately on the top note, and slowly falling through the wide downward interval, in this case a diminished seventh. Four types of portamento of increasing intensity may be identified:

1. The use of a consonant as springboard for the next note, for example at m. 16, where the consonant of a word is sung on the previous note, in this case the "bl" of "blême": a device simply to increase the sense of line and clarity of diction.
2. The use of a vowel sound to bridge a relatively fast interval, for example an upward third. The portamento is subtle and not prominent, but again it joins the line. An example of this is the "ô voy-" of "ô voyageur" at m. 13.
3. The "goal" portamento, usually initiated on a beat after a long note which has been held at pitch, aiming at the "goal" of a strong beat, for example at m. 14.
4. The "full" portamento, where two notes, almost inevitably a high note followed by a low note, are joined by a slow and immediate portamento, as in the last bar of the vocal line of the song. Examples 1.1 and 1.2 show the cumulative effect of these unwritten devices, surely in the composer's mind.

Also of interest are further devices employed to retain the natural stress of the language, for example the shortening and lightening of the beginnings of reflexive verbs; and a refusal to let a legato line iron out diction. In "Il pleure dans mon coeur" this lightening of the beginnings of reflexive verbs happens twice, on the lines:

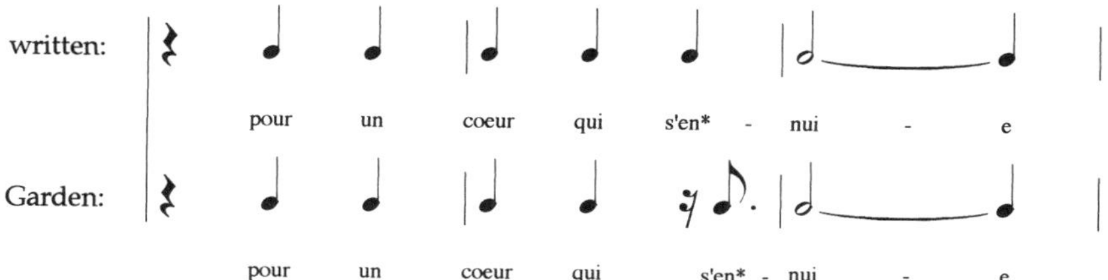

Comparison with subsequent early recordings in some way associated with the composer himself reveals that a similar approach to the composer's vocal lines of this time was commonplace, and it may tentatively be claimed to be central to the elusive esprit debussyste. Désiré-Emile Inghelbrecht, who left us a detailed analysis of points of technique in his essay on how not to perform *Pelléas,* advised singers to "say the text before singing it."[26] Sound advice! But as the century progressed, it seems to have been increasingly ignored in favor of "line," obscuring both speech-rhythm and differentiated vowel-sounds. (For more on this, see Inghelbrecht's essay, Chapter 8.)

Between the lines of Inghelbrecht's essay, which can claim to be near to primary evidence since Inghelbrecht had worked with Debussy as well as with several singers who had been coached by him, a point of balance between word and line may be distinguished. Quoting Mélisande's first words, he writes, "You have just heard me pronounce these words, pronounce them yourselves, in your mind, and recall Mary Garden singing them." All very well, but we must turn to our primitive recordings of a tiny extract from *Pelléas* and three songs to re-

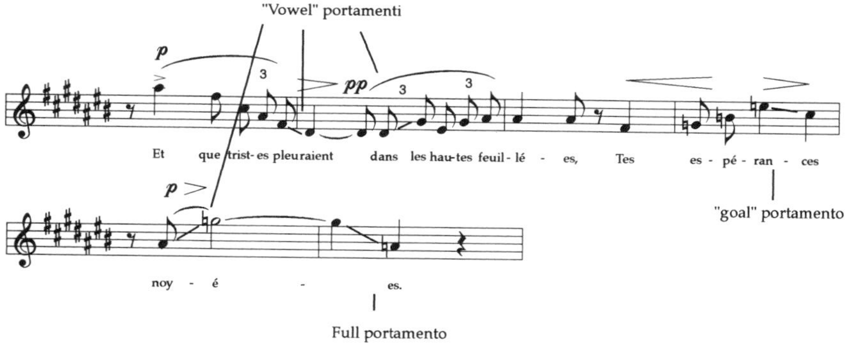

Ex. 1.2. "L'ombre des arbres," mm. 21–26. Hierarchy of cumulative portamento devices as recorded by Mary Garden and Debussy, Paris, 1904.

construct the musical context of Inghelbrecht's remark, echoed later when he continues (on the role of Mélisande) that it is "not enough for the singer to convey the word and the note," she must also, "by her look, convey the meaning of a phrase."[27] This, it seems, was an art which Debussy considered Mary Garden to have accomplished.[28]

Inghelbrecht cited various other interpreters of the roles from *Pelléas,* claiming them as exemplifying "le vrai," one of them being Hector Dufranne, creator of the role of Golaud. A letter from Debussy to Dufranne written in 1906 testifies to his admiration for this singer, and in keeping with what has already been put forward as an important priority in Debussy's credo, a penetration of the "sentiments de l'âme," encourages him to go still farther in this direction in a forthcoming revival at the Opéra-Comique: "You and Veuille [creator of the role of Arkël] are almost alone in having retained an understanding of the artistic conception which I attempted in *Pelléas.* . . . Please exaggerate the sad and poignant sadness of Golaud, . . . giving as much as you can the impression of everything he regrets not having said and done, and all the happiness which has now escaped him for ever."[29] The techniques Dufranne used can thus claim to embody that elusive esprit debussyste which Inghelbrecht stresses; moreover, he is the only interpreter from the original cast of *Pelléas* who bequeathed us extended excerpts of the role of Golaud. A brief examination of a series of historic remasterings reveals a good deal about changing performance styles. Act II scene 2 is the only scene common to them all.

Excerpts recorded 1928, conducted by Georges Truc, with Hector Dufranne as Golaud. Reissued on CD VAI audio, VAIA 1093, 1995. Dufranne, in a similar way to Mary Garden in "L'ombre de arbres," is slightly free in his interpretation of Debussy's notated rhythms, always because of the natural stress of the language. Slight portamenti or their absence are used to "soften" or "harden" the expression, an absolutely marked and rhythmic declamation being a special effect used for particularly telling phrases. In Act II scene 2, in the passage where Golaud describes how the horse had fallen on top of him, this effect is used to considerable effect: "cela ne sera rien" is uttered strictly in time; as Golaud recounts his accident, rhythms are tightened to lessen the contrast between the triplets and duplets which pervade the opera. This may throw some light on Ninon Vallin's remembrance of Debussy's insistence "that the duplets and triplets which so often feature in the melodic lines of Debussy's songs . . . had to be perfectly balanced."[30] "Balanced," our researches may suggest, did not mean metronomic.

Following Debussy's instruction "en animant peu à peu et sourdement agité," portamenti are introduced and the end of the first passage is highlighted by a loosening of the written rhythm and a considerable ritardando (example 1.3).

Excerpts recorded 1928, conducted by Piero Coppola, with Vanni-Marcoux as Golaud. Reissued on CD VAI audio, VAIA 1093, 1995. Even making excuses for Vanni-Marcoux's having an off-day, an entirely different approach is discernible here. The approach to the rhythmic values of the score is free to the point of extreme sloppiness. His breathing in the middle of the phrases indicates that he was out of sorts, but the rhythmic freedom suggests either that he had not re-rehearsed his part (he

*Reprint of Freach language VS, Fromont 1902.

Ex. 1.3. *Pelléas et Mélisande,* Act II scene 2, as recorded by Hector Dufranne, the creator of the role of Golaud, Paris, 1928 (*Example continues*)

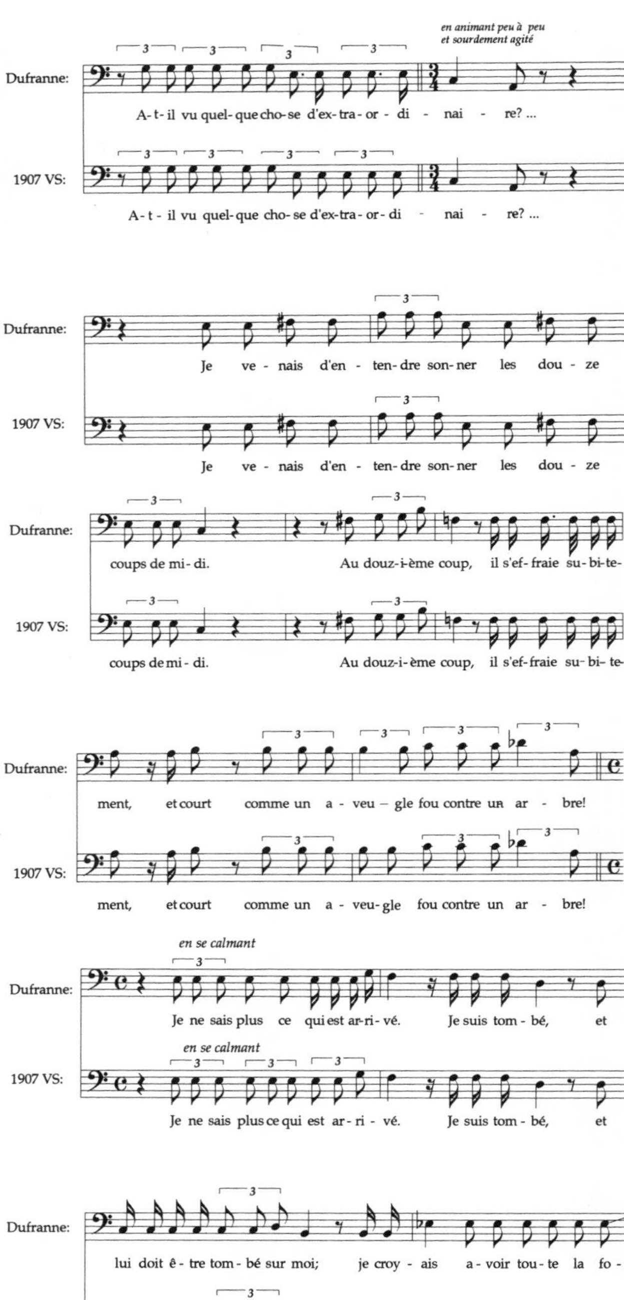

Ex. 1.3. (*Continued*)

Ex. 1.3. (*Continued*)

had first sung it in 1914, thirteen years before the recording) or that he took a free approach to Debussy's rhythms. Whatever the case, it pales beside Dufranne's version on every count. Examples of the rhythmic liberties are as follows:

These are just two of countless similar distortions (unless they were variants privately authorized by the composer, which is by no means impossible but, since the speech rhythm is distorted at least in the latter example, unlikely): Vanni-Marcoux's slapdash attitude to Debussy's text, off-day or not, is confirmed.

Complete opera, recorded 1942, conducted by Roger Desormière, with Henri Etcheverry as Golaud. Reissued on CD EMI Références CHS 7 61038 2, 1988. Etcheverry takes the opposite approach to that of Dufranne from the first note in Act I scene 1. Despite impeccable diction the musical notation is strictly adhered to with hardly any "nuance," forcing the language into the strict duplet-triple juxtaposition of Debussy's notation. There are no longer any portamenti, and in relation to the first recordings an entirely opposite, almost dehumanized effect is achieved.

Complete opera, recorded 1952, conducted by Ernest Ansermet, with Heinz Rehfuss as Golaud. Reissued on CD Decca Historic 425 965-2. Rehfuss takes a similar approach to Etcheverry, above, except for his poor diction (listen to the pronunciation of the word *d'extraordinaire* in Act II scene 2). This recording shows that even under an esteemed Debussyist like Ansermet, the tradition of Debussy's expression had not been preserved.

Complete opera, recorded 1953, conducted by Jean Fournet, with Michel Roux as Golaud. Reissued on CD Phillips Opera Collector 434 783-2, 1992. Roux, born in Angoulême in 1924, had made a specialty of the role of Golaud and was one of his most notable exponents during the 1950s. There is a clear move back toward a Dufranne-like interpretation: Debussy's rhythms are clearly absorbed, but the word-stress is allowed to predominate here and there. Unlike Dufranne there are no portamenti; and the line is not nearly as flexible and varied as Dufranne's, though it is commanding in a later interpretative style.

Complete opera, recorded 1962, conducted by D.-E. Inghelbrecht, with Michel Roux as Golaud. Reissued on CD Disques Montaigne TCE 8710. Under Inghelbrecht's direction the slight flexibility of Roux's approach becomes more pronounced: we seem to have come full circle and approach again the style of singing that Debussy obtained from both Dufranne and Garden.

Before moving away from vocal interpretation, the testimony—both literary and recorded—of one further singer may be mentioned: Claire Croiza. At the end of Debussy's life Croiza sang the part of Geneviève in a benefit performance of *Pelléas;* she also sang the Damoiselle in a staged version of the cantata, performing in *Le martyre de Saint-Sébastien* and giving the premiere of several early songs during the late 1930s.[31] The transcription of Croiza's master classes stresses time and time again the perfection of Debussy's notation and constantly advises the student to follow this exactly: "[Debussy] has caught the poet's rhythm so perfectly that the poem can be declaimed without changing anything in the rhythm. . . . The singer has only to follow the notation as closely as possible . . . musically everything must be rigorously exact, be sung with metronomic precision."[32] In this context Croiza's telling performance of the role of Geneviève in the extracts recorded with Dufranne in 1926 is illuminating. She gives a fine performance, but it is by no means metronomic! In the "letter scene" (Act I scene 2), she is never as rigorous as the later Golauds remarked upon above, even in the reading of the letter, which is marked "simplement et sans nuances." As with Dufranne, the rhythms of the score are clear, but there is considerable freedom, especially in the triplets. The opening words, "Voici ce qu'il écrit à son frère Pelléas," are delivered with a hurrying to the second syllable of the word *écrit* and a slight downward portamento, contrasting with a more deadpan delivery as she reads the letter. When Debussy begins to mark the nuances soon after this, they are faithfully observed, but as with Mary Garden's performance, there is a sense of the language dominating. Debussy's highlighting of the word *nuance,* implying that to sing "sans nuances" was a special effect, leads us conveniently into a further area of study. One line will suffice to illustrate this point, a line in which Croiza indulges in two successive portamenti, an upward "goal" portamento to the "glo" of "sanglote," followed by a full portamento downward to its final syllable (example 1.4).

Several of those who have bequeathed us memoirs of Debussy's coaching of his own music have stressed the importance he placed on the "nuance." These memoirs must, of course, be treated with considerable care since bruised egos and rose-colored spectacles are omnipresent. But corroborated evidence, as it were, may lead us to truths. For Marguerite Long and E. Robert Schmitz, two pianists who have left us both copious reminiscences and a recorded legacy, "nuances" were of paramount importance. Both stress that Debussy's dynamic range

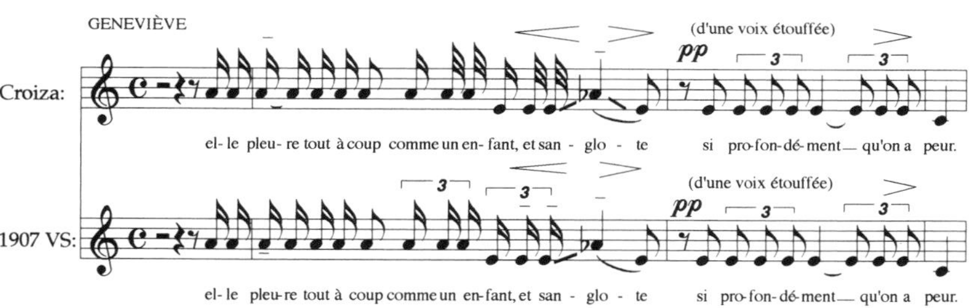

Ex. 1.4. *Pelléas et Mélisande,* extract from Act I scene 2, as recorded by Claire Croiza as Geneviève, Paris, 1928

was extreme,[33] and we should remember that the French word *nuance* clearly referred to sound quality and not rhythmic or agogic freedom.[34]

The concern Debussy showed for sound is testified to everywhere and occurs at every level from his playing (lid down) of his Aliquot strung Blüthner piano, especially shipped from England, to the exact nuances of a sung text.[35] The majority of those coached by him wax lyrical about his special sound as a pianist, which some relate to the Chopin tradition; most agree that his mature keyboard approach was extremely subtle and idiosyncratic and never over-forceful, although it could be strong and clear in a Toccata-like piece. This is an incontrovertible testimony: the subject of another article, perhaps, and a key to Debussy's "dream-world," but it is an area which will not be further probed.[36]

More puzzling is that many voices are raised in favor of a strict adherence to the markings of Debussy's scores in this respect, whatever their recorded legacy shows. Here, certainly, were arguments which undermine the slightly flippant assertion that if everyone was so free, why bother with an *oeuvres complètes?* Firstly there is Debussy's care in the marking of nuances, in the tradition of Chabrier followed, among others, by Albéniz. Secondly is his frequent advice to stick to what was written. "So many pianists, who play Debussy today," wrote Schmitz, "overlook his crescendo markings," presaging the concern of the *Oeuvres complètes* in documenting Debussy's post-publication ideas by considering scores which were "corrected" by the composer, such as those of Schmitz himself, their alterations "meticulous, in lavender ink."[37]

Not indicated on the printed score are further subtleties, some of them commonplace tips among pianists, such as Long's advice to play softly; Schmitz's recounting of Debussy's insistence, inherited from his teacher Mme Mauté, on practicing without the pedal; and Maurice Dumesnil's recollection of Debussy's recommendation that one note in an octave must always predominate: "octaves sound flat when played with the same volume in both hands."[38]

More interesting, because more contestable, is the question of rubato—the various types of deviation from the score that were the norm of the interpretative tradition. When the available recorded legacies of the contemporary commentators who were also the strongest performers are placed beside what they advised, a considerable gap appears: to put it bluntly, while they advocated performing in time, they themselves did not, taking considerable expressive liberties. "Musically, everything must be rigorously exact, be sung with metronomic precision, and the same is true whether of Debussy or Duparc," claims Croiza.[39] Long cites the amusing anecdote she claims was frequently recounted to her by Debussy: "A pianist, who had come to play some of his works to him stopped at a certain passage and said 'here, it's free, isn't it?' . . . Debussy, fuming, replied: 'There are people who write music, and people who edit it: and this man who does as he wants. . . . All I want is a faithful interpreter."[40] A reading of further passages, including those of Debussy himself, indicates that there is a line to be drawn, after all: the anecdote must be put alongside Debussy's remarks about rhythm and the evidence of early recordings.

Here then is our first major contradiction: Debussy on the one hand insisting that interpreters follow his markings yet on the other confessing that rhythms could not be exactly notated; on the one hand insisting on singers following exactly his rhythms and nuances and yet admiring above all those who took slight liberties. In his rich memoir, Maurice Dumesnil was charitable to Debussy when the latter accused him of not playing triplets exactly: Dumesnil thought he was playing in time, and could perceive no difference when Debussy demonstrated how they should be played. He concluded that Debussy must have had an especially perceptive ear, only to be reprimanded at the next attempt for playing too much in time![41]

To what extent do contemporary piano rolls clarify this point? First of all Debussy's piano rolls of preludes from Book I are illuminating, even allowing for all possible unfaithfulnesses in the Duo-Arte mechanism. Even taking into account the new set-up in a recent compact disc reissue, with a modern piano and digital recording, certain things are clear.[42] As in his accompaniment to "L'ombre des arbres," the rhythm in "Danseuses de Delphes" is mainly unwavering, although in the decrescendo in bar 10 a clear ritenuto is added where in the equivalent passage in bars 4–5 merely a slight placing at the cadence was made. The sound of the transcription bears out the praise bestowed on the duo-art system by several composers: the buried tenor melody line clearly stands out, retaining Debussy's legato playing of this line, and the chords sound carefully voiced and played with a penetrating rather than a surface touch where the pedal is allowed to "make the sound." Both of these features were corroborated by Long and Dumesnil, the former pointing out that "hands were not made to be up in the air at piano, but to *enter into it*,"[43] the latter remarking on the way Debussy "seemed to caress the keys by rubbing them gently downward in an oblique motion."[44] In the rolls of several pianists, including Debussy, some of the dynamic levels do not sound as quiet as the score indicates, possibly because the soft levels are difficult to obtain without affecting the simultaneity of chording: one clear weakness of the system. But as is well known, deliberately unsynchronised playing was a stock-in-trade expressive device among pianists of the time. Evidence suggests that Debussy himself employed this technique.

In his own piano rolls, even in “Danseuses de Delphes,” there are hints of an arpeggiated octave on the top, bell-like sonority, marked with a tenuto mark at m. 13, although Roy Howat has suggested that this was a technique specific to the recording system so that the pianist could achieve emphasis which would otherwise be lost.[45] But the hints in “Danseuses de Delphes” become overt in a passage from “La cathédrale engloutie” where arpeggiations are used liberally but not randomly. The climactic “peal of bells” gesture at m. 23 is given the special effect of having an upward arpeggiation on each octave. Before this, certain of the bell-like sonorities are also arpeggiated upward, though not so prominently, seemingly emphasizing the top note, and the chords “peu à peu sortant de la brume” also receive various degrees of arpeggiation (example 1.5).

Ex. 1.5. Arpeggiations in Debussy’s 1915 piano roll of “La cathédrale engloutie,” mm. 16–26. The printed score has no arpeggiations.

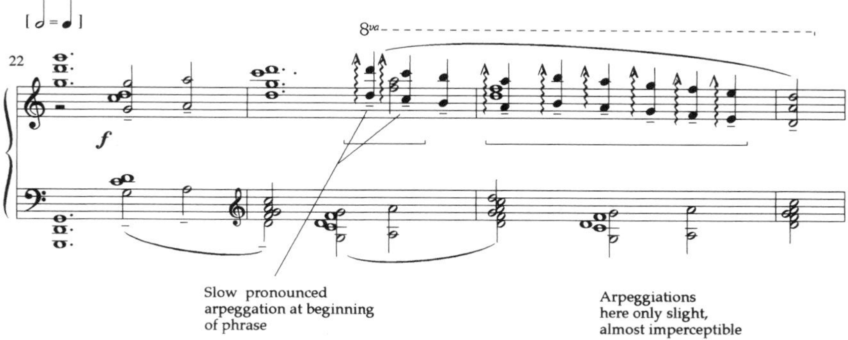

Ex. 1.5. (*Continued*)

Is this sloppy playing? An unreliable mechanism? I would suggest not. More likely is that it was just the normal interpretative freedom that a pianist trained by a so-called pupil of Chopin would carry forward into his or her playing even if, as a composer, this was counterbalanced by a more than usual respect for text. Before making further observations about the particular ways in which arpeggiation was applied, performances by two contemporary pianists may be profitably studied.

Performances by the American pianist George Copeland (1882–1971), who was active during Debussy's lifetime and who met Debussy and made a piano roll of, among other pieces, "Clair de lune," in 1915, show how Debussy's music, at least his more youthful music, could sound in the hands of an accomplished arpeggiator. Example 1.6 shows how Copeland's arpeggiation, like the well-used orchestral portamenti, the soft accent, and the delayed melody note, was used asymmetrically and with subtlety.

Copeland highlights unexpected chords within the gesture by two forms of his arpeggiation: the upward arpeggio and the playing of the left-hand chord in its entirety before that of the right. Several points emerge from the way this passage is arpeggiated. Firstly, in Debussy's arpeggiation in "La cathédrale engloutie," there is a dislocation or arpeggiation on the first chord of a new idea, as in mm. 15 and 20. Secondly, the repeats are arpeggiated differently, bringing out alternative highlights (or picking different flowers along the path, one might say). In addition, there is a general increase in dislocations at the beginning of the crescendo, giving a sense of tension building. In general, there is a sense that arpeggiations progress to synchronized playing rather than the reverse.

An earlier example from the same recording is perhaps even more interesting since it confirms a particular type of arpeggiation used by Debussy. In his roll of

Ex. 1.6. "Clair de lune," mm. 15–23, showing arpeggiations and manual dislocation as recorded by George Copeland in October 1915

"La cathédrale engloutie" we noted how Debussy arpeggiated the first chords of a new phrase: a "springboard" technique signaling the beginning of a harmonic period to the listener. Copeland uses a similar technique in "Clair de lune," where a descending chord pattern is given shape by gradually increasing the speed of arpeggiation to the point where it is almost synchronous, while at the same time using a slow diminuendo (example 1.7). Arpeggiation is being deliberately used to heighten the "vertu" of a harmonic progression.

Further tricks from early twentieth century pianistic traditions are in evidence in the playing of Schmitz, a remarkable testament being his piano roll, released in 1920, of "La fille aux cheveux de lin" (example 1.8). Two particularly important features emerge from Schmitz's playing: the melodic rubato and un-

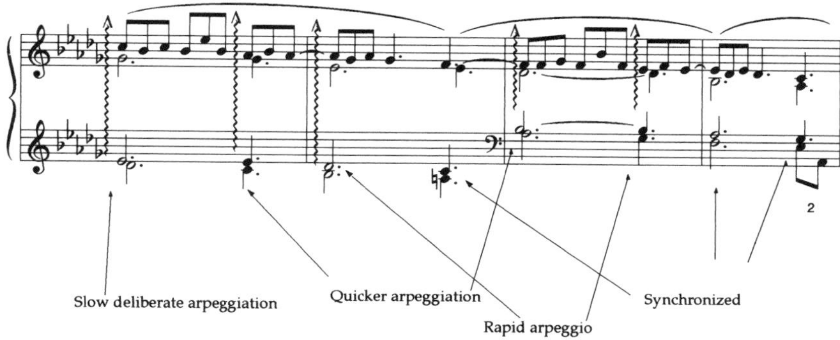

Ex. 1.7. "Clair de lune," mm. 5–8, showing arpeggiations and manual dislocation as recorded by George Copeland in October 1915

synchronised counterpoint, a common practice of which this is a striking example. This must be distinguished from another common practice, manual dislocation, which we have seen as an expressive device in example 6. In m. 11 of "La fille," Schmitz's manual dislocation is driven by a higher musical logic. The left-hand descending motive, on the wane, falls to join the bass. It has already been lingered upon, by stretching the sixteenth notes in m. 10, and further rhythmic attenuation would be inappropriate. Dovetailed with its decline is a new rising arabesque in the right hand, a movement Schmitz emphasizes by weighting the upbeat sixteenth notes which provide the most important opportunity for rhythmic expression in the piece. Here Schmitz plays these somewhat slowly and emphatically, partly to signal the new motive and also to leave scope for an accelerando up to the apex of the phrase. Consequently, the two dovetailed motives become unsynchronised.

Philip's study of tempo rubato in the second chapter of his book alludes extensively to the writings of Marguerite Long, who linked Debussy to Chopin: "Rubato . . . is as much a part of Debussy as of Chopin. This delicate rubato is difficult to obtain in both Chopin and Debussy. It is confined by a rigorous precision, in almost the same way as a stream is the captive of its banks. Rubato does not mean alteration of time or measure, but of nuance or élan."[46]

Here we are in the realms of contradictions again, for contrary to the oft-repeated imagery of piano pedagogy—streams being the captive of their banks, candle flames wavering, or firmly rooted trees waving their branches in the breeze—Philip shows what we all knew: that robbed time is robbed time, more usually lingering than lurching forward, dwelling on certain things but not making it up.[47] Perhaps the emphasis on a mythical equilibrium of rubato is ulti-

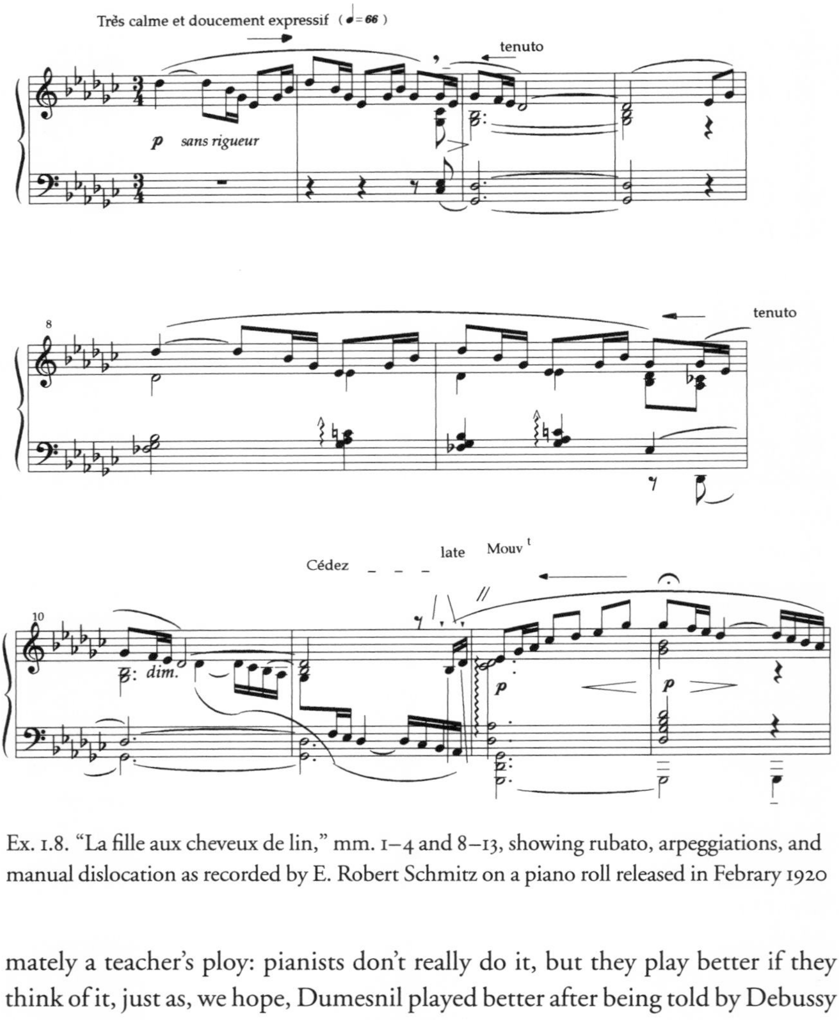

Ex. 1.8. "La fille aux cheveux de lin," mm. 1–4 and 8–13, showing rubato, arpeggiations, and manual dislocation as recorded by E. Robert Schmitz on a piano roll released in Febrary 1920

mately a teacher's ploy: pianists don't really do it, but they play better if they think of it, just as, we hope, Dumesnil played better after being told by Debussy to play triplets in time one minute, and to free them up the next.

"La fille aux cheveux de lin" could hardly be more inviting as regards rubato, the constant anacrusis of two sixteenth notes was precisely the type of figure to which pianists applied agogic variety ranging from a tightening of

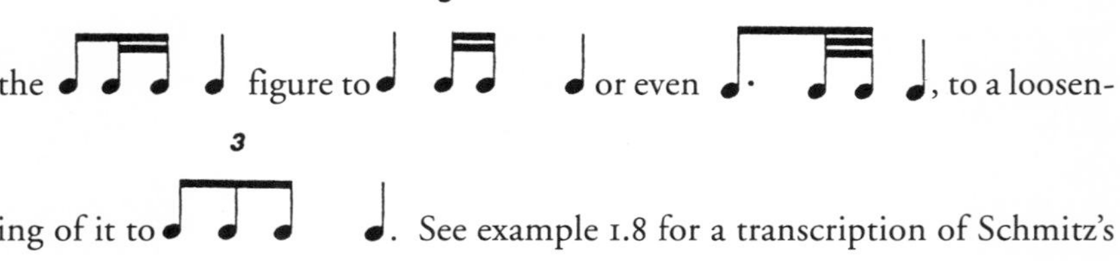

the figure to or even , to a loosening of it to . See example 1.8 for a transcription of Schmitz's rendering of the main theme, which makes an interesting comparison with that of Cortot, who in his two recordings of the piece plays the motive very strictly in time.[48] What is clear from this example is that the procedure, common among pianists of Debussy's day, of slightly lingering on one of a pair of notes bridging a beat (which we had seen Debussy using in "L'ombre des arbres) is not appropriate here because there is at first no harmonic context, and later, the motive does not have the tension between chord notes and accented passing notes which such rhythmic attenuations brought out.[49] Nonetheless, the recording is interesting if we bear in mind Debussy's comments on the impossibility of notating rhythms exactly.

Can we place any confidence in Schmitz's recordings as exemplifying the esprit debussyste? A difficult question to answer. What is clear, however, is that the techniques he employs—exaggerated expressive devices by today's standards—were also employed by Debussy, and that when Debussy urged his pupils to "follow the score" he was addressing those for whom such techniques were the lingua franca of pianism. His comments on precision were perhaps more of a "rappel à l'ordre." Had he been addressing performers already tainted with postwar, positivistic, teutonic, and Anglo-Saxon attitudes to the urtext edition, we might not altogether flippantly suggest that he might well have employed an opposite tactic. While on the one hand the Debussy *Oeuvres complètes* revisit the works, performance practice waits in the wings to put a spanner in them.

We may speculate on the way Debussy performance may go by learning from the early music revival. How unthinkable it is nowadays to hear baroque music without the host of expressive techniques which performance practice has rediscovered: the bulging string *messa da voce;* the encrustations of ornaments, often improvisatory in nature; the *trilli* of the music of Monteverdi's day; the *notes inégales* of French music. And how quaint and mechanical certain of the recordings of the immediate postwar years sound with their terraced dynamics, ungiving tempi, and mechanical bowings, sticking to the letter of the score. Maybe in twenty years' time it will be unthinkable for performers not to reopen the boxes of tricks which we can relearn through early recordings, using them to rediscover that esprit debussyste which seems to be lost, and which the *Oeuvres complètes* will not entirely help us to recover.

Chapter 2 Symbolism and Performance

Claude Abravanel

An artwork demands to be interpreted, for it functions in two dimensions at once: the one intellectual, the other emotional. This is particularly true for the art of music. While the intellectual aspect of a musical work can be represented by the score, its emotional aspect evades notation. One of the errors of musicians today is the belief that the intelligence alone can suffice in creating or interpreting a work. Certainly it is adequate for the structuring, but it cannot create music's essence. The creation as well as the expression of the intimate nature of a work belongs to the domain of musical intuition. The interpreter must know how to be in harmony with the spirit and style of the work in order to effect its reconstruction, which becomes a veritable re-creation in the course of performance.

For more than a century the music of Debussy has been played, analyzed, and discussed, and yet its mystery is still a major issue in our day. It possesses an undeniable vitality but remains extremely poorly understood—frequently even disfigured—by its performers. Research in musicology and theory without doubt have been fruitful and revealing, but they have focused on the technical side of the music, neglecting its affective dimension. Furthermore, such research has taken on an extremely complex cast, as it has centered almost entirely on a traditional conception of the music, whereas Debussy distanced himself radically from tradition and created an understanding of music that was founded on the objectives of musical symbolism.

The performance of a work depends on its interpreter. He or she will perform it according to the level and quality of culture he or she possesses and thus must find a way to understand it. To this end, I propose to offer certain clarifications concerning the art of Debussy in regard to its performance. One can obtain a comprehensive vision of Debussy's work using a certain approach: considering it not as a final creative work, present, fixed within a certain frame and constructed according to a known musical language, but as a work that is "becoming," a "creation" that comes to life freely and unforeseeably in the act of performance.

IMPRESSIONISM AND SYMBOLISM

The second half of the nineteenth century in France was marked by a profusion of aesthetic movements in the arts. Certain of these were unclear and poorly defined, which has been the source of substantial misunderstanding both at their creation and up to the present. Furthermore, art in general is loath to be confined to a rigid framework or definition that stems from intellectual reasoning alone. Every artist presumes to fashion, explain, and justify his or her art according to individual personality. For if one wishes to understand an artwork in order to present it correctly, one must disentangle and formulate precise aesthetic technical principles, while always recalling that they are a means and not an end. Not even the impressionist or symbolist movements escape these requirements. Regardless of numerous variations and even great divergence in their understanding of their art, the adherents of impressionism and symbolism nonetheless agreed on certain principles: reality is modified by the affective perception of the human being; the goal of art consists in describing that perception; and finally, a new technique must be created based on the fundamental element of each art. That is, the element of color exists as fundamental for painting, word for literature, and sound for music. If these common principles are found in every symbolist art form, each art by contrast differs in its essence.

Impressionism above all is an art of nature, one in which light is so important that objects which figure on the canvas have as their principal function its reflection. Impressionism is characterized by visual sensation. The object or landscape is recognizable, albeit modified. "The drawing is not the form; it is the manner of seeing the form," as Degas stated.[1]

Literary symbolism strives to reproduce the affective impressions of words or ideas. The visual object of painting is replaced by the literary description of a purely imaginary object, in such a way that it brings forth a symbolic interpretation. By joining together certain words in a more or less unexpected way, their customary signification disappears and they achieve a new dimension. Such a usage engenders various emotions in the listener or reader: "watery suns" (Baudelaire);[2] "full day trembling with the noon" (Verlaine).[3] As Mallarmé clarifies: "To name an object is to suppress three-quarters of the enjoyment of the poem, which is meant to unfold little by little."[4] Thus, symbolist poetry accustoms us to a usage of words in which the idea expressed largely surpasses the one that seems to be stated.

Musical symbolism (falsely termed "impressionism") aims at exactly the same goal, but its state of being is completely indeterminate. Sounds are neither landscape nor object nor idea; they have no signification if not that of producing affective and emotional states in the listener.

What is remarkable about symbolism is its admixture of the arts, a fusion that was cherished from Baudelaire onward. The arts are unified because they explain each other in reciprocal fashion. In effect, ordinary language turns out to be completely insufficient to describe the manifold nuances of color, verbal expression, or musical sound. The symbolist must continually apply an expression of sound to explain a color, an expression of color or luminosity to indicate a nuance of sound, or a sonority or color to give a word a particular affective state.

The poet René Ghil thus mixed all genres: "The Poem also becomes a veritable work of suggestive music which instruments itself: a music of evocative words, of colorful images that do no harm to the Ideas."[5] The painter Paul Sérusier advanced the same opinion: "Sounds, colors, and words possess a miraculously expressive value, quite beyond their literal value, beyond even the literal sense of the words."[6] And in a letter to Emile Baron on the subject of the symphonic suite *Printemps,* Debussy wrote, "I am struck by the idea of creating a work in a special color and of arriving at the greatest possible number of sensations."[7]

MUSICAL EMOTION

Symbolism in music is a phenomenon that belongs to the domain of emotion. It behooves us then to examine its affective quality. As Henri Bergson stated:

"Above all creation signifies emotion."[8] Emotion in the romantic is founded on an individualist conception, that the artwork not only sets forth the personality of its creator but also describes his or her particular emotion.

The symbolist, on the other hand, strives to represent in the artwork a neutral sensibility, depersonalized, which never imposes upon or does violence to the sensibility of the listener. Instead the symbolist sensibility gives the artist the liberty to graft onto the artwork his or her personal sensations. This sensibility has no dramatic emphasis or emotive exaggeration. Rather, it is characterized by a circumspection, a remarkable discretion. The performer of symbolist music thus is obliged to obey a sort of asceticism or refusal when presenting the emotions.

In an interview about *Pelléas et Mélisande,* Debussy spoke of the listener's emotions and about those of the characters in the opera. We can replace the word *character* by *work:* "Upon hearing a work, the viewer is accustomed to experiencing two sorts of emotions that are quite distinct: on the one hand, musical emotion, and on the other the emotion of the character; generally the viewer experiences these in succession. I have tried to make the two emotions become perfectly intermingled and simultaneous."[9] We must be quite precise in stating that the symbol in music gives birth to an emotion of a particular nature, one that has nothing to do with the feeling inherent in the personality of the composer or performer. This symbolist sensibility can be attained only by means of an inner hearing. In effect, the ear is the organ that perceives sound, and it acts in the same manner as all the other senses. Instead of speaking of "hearing" a sound, it is necessary rather to say "feeling" a sound. For the listener, this kind of auditory sensibility is the affective state that he or she experiences when hearing sounds. This sensibility can be committed to memory in the same way as are sensations that stem from the other senses. When concentrating on hearing sounds from the inner perspective, one can obtain the illusion not only of hearing them but also of feeling them. All musicians know this phenomenon. If great artists ever perform a work twice in the same manner, it is because they first hear what they play from within. They do not "think" of what they are performing, but they "hear" with fixed attention what they wish to play.

The last three measures of "Danseuses de Delphes," for example, consist of two chords followed by a single note, with all marked by a dash (—). This final note is also marked by a staccato dot. The first chord bears the indication of forte, the second pianissimo, and between these two chords there is the indication of a decrescendo that is impossible to realize at the piano.

It is evident that one might play what is notated in a standard way, but Debussy asks the player for something altogether different from a banal difference of volume of sound. He asks instead for a subtle distinction, to obtain a precise effect of sonority. In reality there is only a single chord that must resonate until its vibrations cease naturally. The forte is not a notation of volume of sound but of a sonority of expressive intensity (notated by the dash) that is prolonged for at least three measures. The chord played pianissimo is present only to prolong the evanescent sonority of the first chord, and the last note (for which the staccato dot suggests a light playing) continues the sonority of the preceding chord through to its disappearance, signaled by the fermata. Without an attentive inner hearing, without a precise sensibility of sonority, it would be impossible to obtain this acoustic effect.

It becomes evident that, not only for the performer but for any musician occupied with a symbolist music, inner hearing is revealed as the most efficient means, the most powerful instrument of "feeling" a work. Thanks to this concentrated hearing, the artist will be capable of understanding the structure of the work correctly, of discovering its sonorous colors, of feeling its rhythm. Equally, by this inner hearing the performer will end up filtering, choosing judiciously those emotions that will appear in the performance.

In this regard, it is significant to recall the critique Pierre Lalo wrote after the first performance of *La mer,* as well as Debussy's response. Lalo had reacted positively to the music of *Pelléas et Mélisande* but manifested reserve toward *La mer:* "It seems that Debussy wished to feel what he had not truly, profoundly, and naturally felt. For the first time upon hearing a picturesque work by Debussy, I have no impression of being in the presence of nature, but before a reproduction of nature. . . . I do not hear, I do not see, I do not feel the sea."[10]

Debussy did not take long to respond. In a letter addressed to Lalo he wrote:

> I have nothing to say if you don't like *La mer,* and I don't complain about that. . . . But I cannot keep you company when you take it as a pretext for claiming, all of a sudden, that my other works lack logic and hold up only through a tenacious sensibility and hard-headed search for the "picturesque" . . . a catch phrase by which people group things having nothing to do with what the phrase means, exactly. Really! My dear friend, if I don't feel music the same way as you, I am an artist all the same, and indeed I am nothing if not that. . . . You say—reserving the heaviest blow for the end—that you neither see nor feel the sea? That's a sizable claim . . . and you will have to concede that all ears don't hear in the same manner.[11]

It is clear that Debussy reproached Lalo for not hearing music in the same way as he. What is more, in grasping *La mer* as a "picturesque" work, Lalo more than showed that he did not understand the emotional signification of the work he had sought to "see" as if visually, as he had "seen" *Pelléas* on the stage of the Opéra-Comique without truly "hearing" it. Too, he was not able to "feel" *La mer,* which describes nothing other than emotions.

THE MUSICAL LANGUAGE OF SYMBOLISM

Musicians who have sought to write symbolist music have all believed it enough to introduce certain modifications to customary musical techniques to create a new style. Debussy alone understood that the traditional musical language could not accommodate the character of symbolism. At first a musical system seems to be erected as a complete edifice of erudite architecture, within which one may easily explain all musical problems. It might thus serve as a frame or a mold for the composer to fashion his or her work. But symbolist art demands a different conception of composition. Every musical symbol represents a unique world of sonority and affective states. This is why Debussy advanced a personal language, so poorly understood upon its appearance—a language that was never actually formulated in full; it was as if he invented it without perceiving the act of doing so. Moreover, he never intended to institute a system organized logically in the fixed sense, since for him every work possesses its exclusive theoretical system and particular structure. Thus it is appropriate to speak not of one technique but of multiple Debussy techniques, for a symbolist system that is valid for every work could not possibly exist.

Debussy's discussions with his composition professor Ernest Guiraud were recorded by Maurice Emmanuel. There he suggests that "there is no theory: it suffices only to *hear.* Pleasure is the rule."[12] This opinion, surprising if not shocking for the musicians of his era, has been explained in different ways. Seen from the perspective of symbolism, however, it may be understood as follows: theory, rules, the compositional order of a work surely exist, but they can never be determined a priori; they constitute themselves upon each new work and according to the will—the pleasure—of the composer.

Contrary to current opinion, Debussy did not abolish the musical language of his time; rather, he separated its elements and recombined them in different ways. He enlarged that language considerably and endowed it with new dimensions and possibilities; moreover, he employed different procedures of the classic language with special purpose.

Given that Debussy reconsidered the elements of music from the perspective of symbolism, it is therefore perfectly proper to speak of a performance that is particular to symbolist music. This may be understood as a projection, a path formed of emergence, unfolding, and disappearance. What proves completely remarkable is that this approach or model of thought, at once simple and natural, enables us to enter readily into the symbolist universe and explain its music. It can be applied equally to the emotional and technical aspects of the work. It furnishes a sort of key that is extremely useful for performers and theorists who wish to understand Debussy's music intimately.

SONORITY

Sonority holds a key place in the work of Debussy. The perception of music is based on sonorous phenomena. Sound contains the qualities of timbre and intensity, and it possesses special life through the resonance of its vibrations. They are given birth, develop, and disappear. Debussy explores and exploits these sonorous realities; and it is absolutely essential to understand them. This is why, for example, the music of Debussy only rarely surpasses a forte in dynamic level and moves about within the nuances of piano, for an attack that is too strong produces short vibrations that border dangerously on noise. This also is why Debussy considers a chord an aggregate of diverse sonorous "colors" rather than the sum of a homogeneous sonorous mass. The performer of this music must pay the closest attention to these needs for changing color and variable intensity, so as to produce the maximum variety of response to sonority. The performer must thus allocate the proper sonorous value to each section of the work, which gives the sonority a particular importance in the overall prospect of the work.

If we wish to observe the care and mastery with which Debussy incorporates the agent of sonorous color, we would do well to study the last four measures of the first movement of *La mer* ("De l'aube à midi sur la mer," mm. 138–41). For here is a remarkable use of orchestral sonority that allows the vibrations of the instruments to fade away naturally.

The woodwinds and then the horns play fortissimo (m. 138) and, with a crescendo, arrive at the three notes that Debussy accentuates markedly in m. 139; the resonance of the third accentuated note diminishes to the piano beginning m. 140 and disappears completely on the second beat of that measure. The strings, minus the contrabasses—as if to amplify the luminosity of sound—reinforce the sonority of the woodwinds at m. 139 and disappear from the texture along with them. With the exception of the horns, the brass and percussion enter only at the end of m. 139 and swell the volume up to the downbeat of m.

140, and then diminish in volume through to the piano of m. 141. We should observe the high tessitura of trombones and tuba which preserves the maximum of luminosity. At issue is not a description of the sea but a description of light upon the sea—"from dawn to noontime."

Too often in contemporary performances one hears this ending deformed by a crushing volume of massed sonority, punctuated by a noisy blow of timpani even when Debussy is quite careful not to provide any accent whatever for them (m. 139). It is certain that he intended to arrive not at a fortissimo in volume but at a maximal sonorous intensity. The most perfect performances of this ending, perhaps, are those of Ansermet and Toscanini.

Among the works for piano, very often a chord is spaced to facilitate playing it as an arrangement of distinct sounds from the piano. In "La cathédrale engloutie," for example, the parallel chords in two hands over the C pedal (mm. 28–40) engender intervals of parallel fourths between the hands, the special sonority that is easily heard and identifies this passage. But it is precisely this element of sonority, consisting of fourths embraced within other sounds, that gives these chords a mysterious and intentional transparency. One might displace the chords of the left hand a third lower, thus obtaining an opaque, quite heavy sonority, and thereby discover how quickly the mystery disappears.

"Reflets dans l'eau" is an example of a piano composition that contains only color and nuance. Theoretically, the work can be described as a universe of sonority in D-flat that is gradually transformed into E-flat, passing briefly through the tonal center on A and returning to its initial color. In this composition, however, the point is not a question of tonality or modulation, for these tonal centers are signified only by their dominants. One must thus consider tonality in this composition as "color," which creates in this work a matter of "luminosities." The luminosity of E-flat is prepared by a long crescendo that ends with the chord of E-flat at m. 56, which in fact is not the climax of the work. Rather, the climax occurs on the following chord at m. 57, expressed as the sole fortissimo of the piece. This is the emotional culmination that immediately propels the sonority of E-flat into a new, climactic color.

The long crescendo thus comprises not a massive augmentation of sonority but a growing luminosity, more and more intense and clarified. The great French pianist Yvonne Lefébure advised that one should begin the crescendo of m. 50 by a sonority veiled by the pedal, and then one should clear it little by little while playing in a more and more detached way (if always with pedal, mm. 54–55) up to the E-flat chord (m. 57), whose internal tones would be played less loudly than the outer voices to obtain an effect of transparency.

THE PLASTICITY OF MELODY

Debussy's melody is not a product of the Italian bel canto tradition. Rather, it is closest to French recitative in the aesthetic of Lully and Rameau. It is formed by motives of varying length, whose rhythms are adapted directly from the spoken language. These rhythmic motives are at the foundation of melody, which provides for large or small melodic intervals or for repeated notes. They are always to be sung naturally and without emphasis. Here is an astonishing plasticity, the rhythmic patterning for an extraordinary suppleness, that allows this melody the power of translating exactly the slightest affective signification of words.

The singer Jane Bathori, who had the opportunity to work with Debussy, made extremely judicious remarks in this connection. In her opinion Debussy's melody ought to be performed "by realizing rhythmic values with the greatest rigor," and she added, "It is a question of musical integrity, and you can never arrive at an exact expression without giving the duplets and triplets their proper value."[13]

Instrumental melody is of the same character: in the final analysis it is a "vocal" melody without words. The performer must seek to communicate through his or her playing the rhythmic and expressive plasticity of melody, as if there were a text to declaim.[14] Unfortunately, pianists and other performers do not always pay close enough attention to the rhythmic aspect of the work. In "Danseuses de Delphes," for example, the rhythm of the first phrase is notated as in example 2.1. But the rhythm of the second measure is not "felt" as that of the first, because the tie embracing the melodic motive prolongs it through to the first beat of the third measure. The peak of the crescendo occurs on the second beat of the last measure, which creates a weak-beat rhythmic ending. Too often one hears the rhythm of this phrase in a shockingly uniform manner, with a finish on a strong-beat cadence that completely alters the affective signification of the phrase (example 2.2.).

NOTATION

Considering the importance of nuance in symbolist music, it is apparent that its performance depends on a music notation that is much richer and more differentiated than traditional notation. Thus Debussy employs all known signs to

Ex. 2.1. "Danseuses de Delphes," mm. 1–4

Ex. 2.2. "Danseuses de Delphes," mm. 1–4, with an interpretation of rhythmic emphasis in error

indicate nuances, colors, and articulation signs (staccato, legato, and the like). He combines these in different ways, frequently adding a verbal explanation to make his intentions precise. The correct performance of this notation, while difficult, is essential for rendering the affective signification of the work.

For example, what shall we do with the incomprehensible crescendo in m. 18 of the prelude for piano "Des pas sur la neige"? From the musical point of view, it cannot be realized. Its presence in no way indicates an increase in the intensity of the sonority; rather, it shows a growth in luminosity.

In the first measure of Etude no. 5, "Pour les octaves" (example 2.3), what do all the diacritical signs indicate? Certain ones indicate the color or the manner of attacking the sound. Yet each possesses a particular significance that the performer must discover and perform, or else the work will become only a banal study in virtuosity.

One possible performance consists of hearing three levels within a single sound material: the notes *B* of the beginning, the chord in the left hand (on beat 2), and the descending motive in the right hand. The problem occurs in the left hand: the slur gives the impression of bounding from a trampoline. The chord, that is, transmits new elements to the sonorous material. If one accepts this three-part plan of sonorous material, all accents may easily be explained. The notes *b* with a circumflex accent are played "drawn out" but at the same time lightly, as the staccato dot indicates. The chord is to be stressed (with the sign of the dash and the light accent on the F-sharp), so that the chord may be colored differently. The articulation of the right-hand motive, as the third level in the

Ex. 2.3. "Pour les octaves," m. 1

material, poses no problem: the first and third notes are very light, the second is stressed. At issue here is a basic question of "orchestration for the piano."

SYMBOLIST TIME

Plato defined rhythm as "the ordering of movement."[15] In traditional music, musical movement consisting of melody, harmony, and rhythm directs itself consistently toward the cadence. Musical time in a work is thus punctuated by a series of melodies marked off by cadences.

Symbolist music is written within a completely different manner of time. Movement in music becomes the resonance of material sounding in time and space. It appears, then disappears. Sounds organized into such a material do not form a true melody; instead, they engender only melodic and rhythmic motives that are repeated and form a trajectory of sound composed of emergence, projection, and disappearance. Musical time is punctuated by differing sonorous events that are linked naturally if without cadences. That is why the symbolist work seems static: one hesitates forevermore to consider the sonorous moment as it appears and disappears.

For example, the first section of "Pagodes" (example 2.4, mm. 1–10) unfurls by means of the same sonorous material colored differently by the note *a* (mm. 5–6) or by the note *e* and *a*-sharp (mm. 7–10). The motives of the "melody" form two arches of lengths different in time, as in expanse of tonal space (mm. 3–4). This model is repeated three times (mm. 5–6, 7–8, 9–10). A new sonorous material appears only at m. 11.

In "La cathédrale engloutie," the "melody" (mm. 7–13) is a sinuous line within the constant sonority of *e:* the same motive appears three times, at mm. 8, 10, and 11, each likewise in the form of an arch.

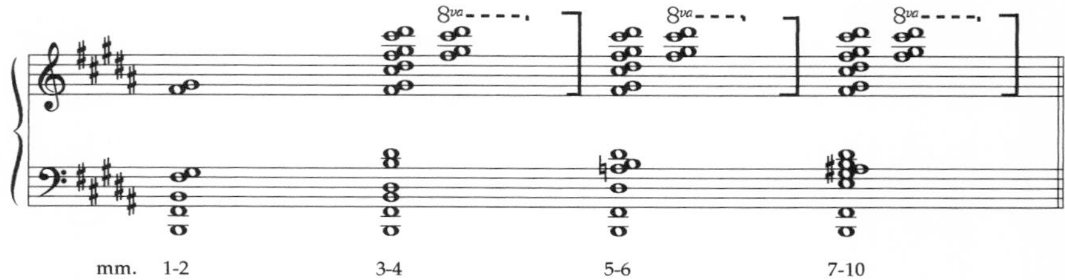

Ex. 2.4. "Pagodes," mm. 1–10

DEBUSSY'S COMPOSITION

Debussy expressed himself directly about certain works and thus provided precious instruction for the performance of his works. Too often it has been supposed that his claims are not to be taken seriously. But this is a worthless supposition, and we ought to consider Debussy's claims attentively, even when they overturn our long-standing notions. Moreover, when his remarks are interpreted according to symbolist objectives, they immediately appear to have a remarkable cohesiveness. In an interview published in the *New York Times,* Debussy is quoted as stating: "I do not know how I compose. . . . Of course, in the first place, I must have a subject. Then I concentrate on the subject, as it were—no, not musically, in an ordinary way, but just as my body would think of a subject. Then gradually, after these thoughts have simmered for a certain length of time, music begins to center around them, and I feel that I must give expression to the harmonies which haunt me. And then I work unceasingly."[16]

What is astonishing about this statement is its indication of the creative development of a work, from its intuitive birth, to its maturation during a period of incubation necessary to the interior emergence of the music, and finally to its written realization.

Couched in a language that is more poetic and above all more symbolist are the following reflections by Debussy, extracted from another interview: "Who will know the secret of musical composition? The sounds of the sea, the curve of the horizon, the wind in the leaves, or the cry of a bird lodges multiple impressions in us. Then suddenly, without the slightest assent, one of these memories pours out of us and expresses itself in the language of music. It carries its harmony within itself. No matter what effort one makes, one will not be able to find another harmony that is more appropriate or sincere. Only thus does a heart devoted to music make the most beautiful discoveries."[17]

And finally in a letter addressed to Robert Godet, Debussy disavows peremptorily that technique is the aim of composition: "That reeks of the workshop, and you can see the seams! The more of that I see, the more I am horrified by that intentional disorder that is nothing but an 'ear-deception.' The same goes for bizarre or amusing harmonies that are nothing but the playthings of high society. How much one must first seek after and then suppress to arrive at the naked flesh of emotion."[18] "The naked flesh of emotion": that celebrated expression of Debussy's that we must take at face value, that watchword of his musical universe, as well as the most intimate foundation of his art.

THE SYMBOLIST WORK

A work of music reveals a unique and complete universe, which is the result of a perfect fusion of the musical sensibility of the composer and the intellectual image of the work, without which the listener would not be able to understand it. Bergson described this phenomenon: "What is more constructive, what is more knowing than a symphony of Beethoven? But throughout the work of arranging and of rearranging choices, which proceeds along an intellectual course, the musician moves upward toward a point situated beyond the plan of the work to seek after acceptance or refusal, direction, inspiration: at that point is situated an indivisible emotion that the intelligence no doubt helped to explain in music, but which was itself more than music and more than intelligence."[19] This "point situated beyond the plan of the work" is simply the musical sensibility of the composer, his artistic intuition. The work is its expression.

The symbolist musical work has this that is peculiar to it: it represents a special quality of emotion couched within musical structures that are based in the natural phenomena of resonance. Above all it is an affective sonorous vision. It engenders a sonorous trajectory whose elements succeed each other and unfurl freely. The musical work is realized in a sonorous environment like a powder of sound cast into the light. An actual landscape does not decompose into independent objects; it is not simply a mosaic of houses, trees, or clouds juxtaposed beside one another. In like fashion a symbolist work does not consist of a banal assemblage of musical elements. On the contrary, the work presents us with an exquisite symbiosis of its elements. Its contours are often blurred, veiled, avoiding at any price a too precise and too realistic signification. It is a work of becoming. It seems to create itself spontaneously, gradually, and as the hearing unfolds, and its form is completely unpredictable.

Described in a conventional language, this work contains motives that are made up of sonorous material chosen by the composer. They develop in musical phrases that are in turn grouped into sections. A correct analysis of this music cannot proceed by a segmentation of form into the smallest melodic motives, as in classical and romantic music. Rather, it is appropriate to consider the work in its totality from a point that is at some distance, similar to the way the composer placed himself at "a point beyond the plan of the work," as Bergson put it. Then one may analyze its progression by adding together its diverse events and its sonorous moments without failing to perceive its totality.

The texture of a work presents a structural conception as original as it is ingenious. In order to exclude, if that is possible, the too-neat divisions of the musical plan, Debussy organizes the woven structure of sections in a polyphonic manner. In traditional music, by contrast, phrases are organized and delimited by their cadence.

Each section is formed of zones of sonority of different natures that are completely autonomous; these are arranged polyphonically. Each zone possesses its own sonorous material, motives, phrases, and rhythm, and develops in an independent manner. Accompanied melody is no longer at issue, but rather a melody that is woven freely into the pattern of the work. The performer of this music may bring into relief a motive or melody or even a rhythm according to his or her affective inspiration.

One finds a very clear example of this process in the first section of the piano prelude "Voiles." The sonorous universe encompasses all sounds heard in m. 1, until the section beginning at m. 22 (example 2.5). The first zone of sonority appears at the beginning (motive of thirds); the second is extended beginning at the fifth measure, with B-flat in the bass; the third zone begins at m. 7 with the three-note motive that later is transformed into chords; and the fourth zone (m. 21 to the beginning of m. 22) is comprised of only two sounds on the octave *d*.

This requires a search by the performer for particular sonorous color for each zone, whether in the dynamic level of piano or pianissimo. In any case these colors were indicated by Debussy himself: piano very softly (m. 1), pianissimo (m. 5), pianissimo again, expressive (m. 7), and pianissimo with a staccato dot for each note, which must signify a light touch (m. 21).

TITLES

In traditional music, the title of a work indicates something of its form and content, its subject. In symbolism, the matter is quite different, for the symbolist

Ex. 2.5. "Voiles," mm. 1–22

work must induce affective states in the listener that cannot be made precise by words, and which are different for each listener. Consequently, the work's title never represents its subject but only its object. By reference to this object the composer suggests the climate of his or her emotion to the listener. The listener reacts to the auditory perception spontaneously and without conscious process, without experiencing any need to analyze.

Thus it is absolutely clear—and it cannot be said often enough—that the symbolist work does not transmit a description of the title. The interpretation of the title is situated at an affective level and not on a realist one. The piano prelude "La cathédrale engloutie" is purely imaginary; it must "appear" within the sonorous universe of the composition so that the listener can "feel" the particular cathedral within him- or herself. The music is suggestion, decor, ambiance, sonorous vision; it is never concrete representation, reproduction, or the image of an actual cathedral.

From the beginning, the music of Debussy elicited many misunderstandings in this connection. Debussy himself continually raised his voice against the descriptive interpretation of his work. He attempted such a message, for example, by placing the title of his Preludes for Piano at the end of each work, in parenthesis and following three elliptical dots. Even the Etudes as well as the Sonatas must be viewed as symbolist works, despite the absence of titles.

The explanations of his titles that Debussy left us is framed in the purest symbolist style. A note on the Nocturnes, as reported by the important biographer Léon Vallas, provides the following commentary. "'Nuages': this concerns the unchangeable aspect of the sky with its slow and melancholy march of clouds, ending in a gray agony, quietly tinted with white."[20] Note the visionary description, unreal, of clouds in a nearly timeless span whose colors evoke the emotions: melancholy march, gray agony, quietly tinted. Certainly a landscape is not in question here, but the emotion that one finds evolving from the visual representation of the landscape.

In a letter to Georges Jean-Aubry, Debussy recounts Mallarmé's reaction upon hearing the composer play the *Prélude à l'après-midi d'un faune* at the piano: "I never expected anything quite like this. This music prolongs the emotion of my poem and established its scenario more passionately than color itself."[21]

Regarding the interpretation of Debussy's titles, nothing is more instructive than to compare "Soirée dans Grenade" and "La puerta del vino" for piano, as also "Les parfums de la nuit" from the orchestral set *Ibéria.* These three works have in common the subject of Spain, as an imaginary landscape, and share the rhythm of the habañera and the tone C-sharp or D-flat, which dominates their sonorous universe.

"Soirée" is one of the "prints" from the *Estampes;* "La puerta" is a prelude; and "Les parfums" are an image, from the orchestral *Images.* At issue is not a "dance" but an atmosphere evoked by the rhythm of the dance. The rhythmic pattern of the habañera, conventionally one measure long, is grouped into patterns of two measures and sometimes elongated into a third.[22] The signification is not parallel in all three works: in "Soirée dans Grenade," this change indicates certain important structural sections and brings about a sort of respiration in the musical discourse. For the prelude "La puerta del vino," the rhythm is intrinsic to the structure of the piece and at the same time brings an instability to certain of its sections. In "Parfums de la nuit," in contrast, the rhythm brings on an elongation of time, a relenting of rhythmic flow. Debussy intermixes these binary and ternary rhythmic structures in an astoundingly subtle fashion.

Whereas the sonorous universes of these three compositions depart from the same musical sound, those universes are very different from one another. "La soirée" and "La puerta" are based on a pseudo-moresque scale, albeit constituted in divergent ways. "Les parfums" employs a whole-tone scale for the most part. The C-sharp of "Soirée" is sometimes the tonic, at times the dominant, and at times the mediant of a chord. Its melodies are conceived as a "print" (a metaphor from the visual arts) and are neat and clear; they are all variants of the same motives.

The D-flat of "La puerta" develops into a rhythmic motive that is present throughout the work. Since Chopin the prelude has been an expressive evocation, which with "La puerta" is made up of "brisk oppositions of extreme violence and of passionate sweetness," as Debussy expressed it in his note at the beginning of the piece.

At the beginning of "Parfums," the C-sharp is simply one tone among the rest of a whole-tone scale. It develops into short melodic motives in a harmonically ambiguous climate, and is transformed slowly into the dominant tonality, only to arrive at the tonic of F-sharp major. At that point the relatively long melody evaporates into silence. The atmosphere Debussy suggests is one of lengthy anticipation followed by a release of tension.

Regarding this piece Debussy explained himself in a celebrated remark: "You just cannot realize how naturally the linkage occurs between 'Parfums de la nuit' and the 'Matin d'un jour de fête.' This seems not to be written down."[23] This grateful achievement bears witness to several symbolist processes: the dispersion of motives like drops of water from a wave, sonorous structures of long duration, extension of rhythmic unities, musical evanescence, and the marvelously subtle mixture of sonorities shared in common between two movements. For this reason the beginning of the "Matin d'un jour de fête," the final movement of *Ibéria* seems to be a sonorous variation of "Parfums de la nuit," its preceding movement. In fact, "Les parfums de la nuit" links without interruption to "Le matin d'un jour de fête," and the sonority of "Parfums" vanishes during the eight previous measures (mm. 124–31). The true beginning of "Matin" ("dans un rythme de marche lointaine, alerte et joyeuse") serves as a gradual introduction to the sonorous material of the march. Throughout this introduction one hears the true ending of "Parfums" (mm. 5–7) as an echo.

Otherwise the orchestration changes. The ending of "Parfums" is based on a melodic motive relegated to the flute, while the strings play the motive of the "distant march" at m. 2. Moreover this motive of m. 2 is the same thematically as the one which concludes the "Parfums," at m. 129 of "Parfums" but also m. 5 of "Matin d'un jour de fête."

"To believe that one can judge a work of art upon a first hearing is the strangest and most dangerous of delusions," as Debussy stated in an interview.[24] In reality the true understanding of a work demands a frequent attention that is as patient as it is profound, a contact on the part of the musician that is subtle and refined. Too few have the selflessness that is indispensable for embarking upon such a quest. Today interior, spiritual signification of artworks is sometimes absent; and we must call it back and proclaim in no uncertain terms the real essence of Debussy's music. The matter does not call for a disheartened and useless retreat; rather, it is a question of reintroducing emotion into an art that cannot exist without it. Nor is it a matter of minimizing the important advances of analysis that we now possess for understanding the technical aspects of this artwork: instead, it is imperative that we interpret this music through the lens of symbolism. Only then will we be able to appreciate the music of Debussy in its true worth.

—Translated from French by James R. Briscoe

Chapter 3 *Pelléas et Mélisande* in Performance

Louis-Marc Suter

INTRODUCTION

Side Questions

The circumstances of the composition, production, and dissemination of *Pelléas et Mélisande* have been well researched, and it is not necessary to recount them again other than to recall the many diverse ways in which this "lyric drama" has been performed. For example, I shall leave aside not only the work's external details, which have figured prominently in its realization since its first performances in 1902, but also its critical reception. I shall not consider Debussy's text in conjunction with Maeterlinck's, although it would be interesting to study the textual repetitions or omissions that reveal dramatic necessities perceived by the composer.[1] I shall leave for other studies the rhythmic connection of word and music as it evolved from the sketches to the definitive score and the several variations in the length of interludes up to the final notation.[2] Similarly, I shall set aside the wider problems of décor and scenic design, of such early, passing notions as scoring a woman's voice for Pelléas,[3] and of the debated orchestration with double basses or double basses and cellos for the low notes marking the scene at the grotto.[4] As to score variants, certain of these already belong to history and scarcely require a commentary here. For example, the episode concerning the sheep has been judged useless by some people. And yet it has proven appropriate and even indispensable, for it creates a pause between the scene of "grande innocence" and the final meeting of the lovers. In another example, Roger Desormière felt entitled to eliminate mm. *21* 17–20 (rehearsal 21, measures 17–20 following) from the interlude linking scenes 1 and 2 of Act I, in his 1941 recording. But since then, no conductor has allowed himself such a cut, which is unjustifiable. Other variants have tended to disappear from view but are perceptible here and there, such as the omission of the duplicated fragment "because custom wills it" done among others by Ansermet in his 1952 version or by Kubelik in his of 1971, but I shall abstain from commenting further on this subject. As for the many variants that remain up to the present, I shall pause neither over the details of certain notes nor on the question of whether to have the part of Yniold sung by a boy or a woman, just as I shall not spend time wondering whether to maintain in performance the fifteen or so measures when Golaud worries about Pelléas and Mélisande and their proximity to the bed in the bedchamber.

Essential Questions

My preoccupation here will rather be to get to the heart of performance problems in *Pelléas,* which seem always to have been Debussy's major concern. It is well known how demanding the composer was of himself and how elitist his attitude. As he wrote to the composer Ernest Chausson on about 3 September 1893, as the first sounds of *Pelléas* were humming in his head: "Truly music ought to have been a hermetic science, guarded by texts of such length and difficulty that it would certainly discourage the herd of people who use it as casually as they would a pocket handkerchief."[5] For some years he had imagined a distinctly personal relation between word and sound. As he wrote to his patron Eugène Vasnier on 4 June 1885 from the Villa Medici in Rome, "I would always prefer something in which, in some way, action would be sacrificed to the long-pursued expression of the feelings of the soul. That way it seems to me that music can become more human, stemming more from life, and thereby one can explore and refine one's means of expression."[6]

On 2 October 1893, he wrote again to Chausson and clarified the progress and new requirements of his musical thought:

> I was hasty in singing a victory song for *Pelléas et Mélisande* as, after one of those sleepless nights that always is a good counselor, I had to recognize that this wasn't it at all.

> The thing resembled a duo of Mr. So-and-So, or it doesn't matter by whom, and most of all the ghost of Old Klingsor, alias R. Wagner, appeared at the turn of a measure. So I tore everything up and struck out searching for a new chemistry of more personal phrases, and strove to become as much Pelléas as Mélisande. Thus I went searching for music behind all the veils she wraps herself in, even before her most ardent admirers! I've brought out something that might please you; as for the others it's all the same to me. Quite spontaneously I've made use of a means of expression that seems to me quite special, which is silence—Don't laugh! It acts as an agent of expression and perhaps is the only means of giving full value to the emotion of a phrase. And if Wagner used it, it seems to me that it was in an exclusively dramatic fashion, a little like the suspect dramas in the manner of Bouchardy, d'Ennery, and others.[7]

After *Pelléas* was virtually complete, on 13 October 1896, Debussy further refined his thought in a letter to the violinist Eugène Ysaÿe:

> Now I shall humbly submit to you the reasons why I am not of your opinion concerning a fragmentary performance of *Pelléas.* First, if this work is worth anything, it is above all in the connection of the scenic with the musical movement. It thus is apparent and even indisputable that this quality would disappear in a concert performance, and you could not hold it against anyone for not understanding the special eloquence of silences, with which the work is star-studded. Besides, the simplicity of means I've employed cannot realize its true significance without staging. At a concert performance they would throw in my face the American riches of a Wagner, and I'd seem like some poor soul who couldn't pay for any . . . bass tubas.[8]

Far from eliciting a smile, such statements highlight the priorities that Claude de France set for his lyric drama. Silence plays a fundamental role in the composition. But the nature and duration of silences are firmly connected to the rhythm of the drama in general, and above all to the libretto and thus to the musical dramatization of the text. Debussy allocates no passing or neighbor tones to the vocal line. An appoggiatura, an anticipatory note, or any other figuration can have an impact upon the delicate expression of feeling. Nothing like that occurs in *Pelléas:* Debussy without exception maintains the principle of "one sound to one syllable." Moreover, the "connection" between the musical thought process and the scenic vision of the composer of *La mer* is constant. One could not expound upon the one without evoking the other.

The present discussion is based on fifteen recordings of *Pelléas et Mélisande* (see the discography at the end of this chapter), as well as a concert performance of the work on 4 May 1995 at the Théâtre des Champs Elysées in Paris, by the Orchestre National de France under the direction of Charles Dutoit. It will be devoted to the essence of the work and to the rhythm of the score as it can be examined according to three fundamental means of expression: silence, verbal rhythm, and tempo linked to the dynamic of the drama. If I place the role of silence in the forefront of my discussion, it is because the degree to which silence is respected reveals the performer's understanding of the true spirit of the work. Even the slightest casualness in this regard is often linked to a general lack of rigor in the overall rhythm of the performance. I shall not attempt a comparative evaluation of the different versions of Debussy's lyric drama nor question specifics of any one performance. Instead, I have only one goal here: to present diverse reflections suggested upon hearing all these recorded productions and thereby to understand Debussy's most profound thought. In general, I must nonetheless note that I find the performances directed by Claudio Abbado, Pierre Boulez, and Charles Dutoit excellent.

AT THE HEART OF SILENCE

Silence occurs in divergent contexts in Debussy's drama. It can intervene within a character's solo passages or separate the replies of two characters. It can mark a pause between a part that is sung and an instrumental passage, or it can function with precise duration within an instrumental discourse. Finally, we may encounter a loosely measured silence between two passages that are reserved for the orchestra. Let us examine several particularly revealing examples of these five contexts, using PS for the pocket orchestral score and PR, for the piano reduction for voice and piano (both published by Editions Durand). The notation 4–3 *47*, for example, signifies the fourth to the third measure before rehearsal number *47*, while an abbreviation like *20* 2 signifies the second measure after rehearsal number *20*.

Silence Within a Character's Solo Passage

Three moments call for our attention here. First, shortly before the end of the first act, Pelléas and Mélisande are preparing to return to the castle; Pelléas sings two phrases without accompaniment (example 3.1). No matter what notational system is used—the pocket and vocal scores are equivalent—the dotted quarter rest separating the two fragments (m. 3 *47*) must not be unduly shortened. For "Descendons par ici" refers only to the general notion of possible motion along the path, while "Voulez-vous me donner la main?" is a personal invitation. Thus it is appropriate to separate the two utterances from each other. Moreover, this invitation itself begins with rhythmic values that correspond directly with the preceding silence, while it moves on in a slightly rushed manner, as if

Ex. 3.1. *Pelléas et Mélisande,* Act I, 4–2 before 47

Pelléas were suddenly startled by the boldness of his proposal. Mélisande will nonetheless refuse, only to accept the further offer of being helped "by the arm."

Second, in the last scene of Act III at mm. *54* 4–5, Debussy indicated a tempo "plus lent" and broke off the orchestral music. Golaud poses a double question that is separated by a quarter rest (example 3.2). This silence may not be abbreviated (and neither may the rest that ends the measure), for by itself it stands as testimony to Golaud's anguish. If one unduly places the "Non?" closer to what precedes, one makes the situation trite, significantly lessening the chance of increasing the tension when passing from the first to the second part of the passage in question.

A third example from Act V is relevant to this type of phenomenon. Several recordings reveal the same error in m. *5* 6, where Mélisande sings "bien" twice, separated by at least two quarter rests (example 3.3). Arkel's question places Mélisande's double reply in context. One observes that, in the piano reduction, Arkel's last note, and above all the note that sets Mélisande's first "bien," are shorter than in the pocket orchestral score. This shortening of the first "bien" gives more emphasis to the length of the silence separating the utterances of the adverb. Thus it is apparent that one may not shorten this silence in performance. Moreover, the first "bien" must link to Arkel's question and the second, slightly later, must immediately precede the playing resumed by the orchestra, which

Ex. 3.2. *Pelléas et Mélisande,* Act III, 4–5 after 54

Ex. 3.3. *Pelléas et Mélisande,* Act V, 5–6 after 5

makes all the more meaningful the ensuing sentences: "Pourquoi demandez-vous cela?—Je n'ai jamais été mieux portante." The worst reading to be heard in the various recordings gives a first "bien" followed by a single quarter rest and a second "bien" followed by the remaining quarter rest (if one can call it that!), a particularly unfortunate way of rendering Debussy's discourse banal.

Beyond the relation of silence, word, and sound, example 3.3 gives evidence of one of Debussy's several approaches to "measure." Here it is clear that the two utterances of "bien" do not possess a rhythmic function corresponding to their position in the measure. The first "bien" is not a downbeat any more than the second is an upbeat. On the contrary, in the piano reduction, the second "bien" assumes a greater importance than the first. The measure here is thus only an arithmetical cutting of time and does not have a rhythmic function. In other words, its true significance is not musical but relational, allowing the conductor, the instrumentalists, and the singer protagonists to preserve their musical guideposts. It already functioned thus in example 3.2, whereas example 3.1 showed an actual connection between the rhythmic and metric significance of the measure. A coherent performance of *Pelléas* must necessarily account for all these nuances.

Silence Within a Dialogue

Example 3.4 refers to mm. 6–2 *9* from scene 1 of the second act. Although the orchestra is heard in this passage, it plays no role in the two musical moments

Ex. 3.4. *Pelléas et Mélisande,* Act II, 6–2 before 9

that I shall discuss. Consider first m. 5 *9,* which appears as a counter-illustration of Debussy's conception of silence. In one of the recordings, Mélisande's "Non" at the end of the measure does not follow Pelléas's question immediately, thus effecting a silence between the two replies. Such a silence is not only misplaced but also ridiculous, since Mélisande's "Non" is categorical and immediate. In terms of characterization, one would say that Mélisande is experiencing a primary reaction at this moment. This quality of her "Non" is emphasized further by the orchestral commentary at m. 4 *9.* Here is proof that one may not introduce silence at this point or whenever the composer does not wish it. Soon afterward, at 3 *9,* the silence between the passage of Pelléas and the double "Oh" of Mélisande deserves scrupulous observation. In effect, Pelléas asks Mélisande a question that is embarrassing for her. If her double "Oh" intervenes too soon, Mélisande leaves us to presume that she has not listened to Pelléas's question and that she is expressing herself solely as a function of her ego. If on the other hand she replies only after the rest provided by Debussy, without extending the sixteenth note of the first "Oh," she shows clearly that she has heard the question but does not wish to proceed with it. Rather, she wants to turn the conversation to an incident that may be true or made up but is in any case irrelevant at this point in the drama. The two moments that we have just dealt with reveal, each in its own way, the psychological climate in which Debussy means to situate each protagonist in the drama, and particularly Mélisande.

Several recordings leave me unsatisfied at a critical moment in the last scene of the fourth act, at mm. 5–3 *38*. In question is the first statement by Mélisande following Pelléas's monologue just after the beginning of the scene (example 3.5). An important silence separates the entrances of the two characters present, a silence indicated among other means by a fermata on the first of two quarter rests. Despite her presence at the appointed rendezvous, Mélisande is divided in her feelings—sometimes she prefers light, sometimes darkness—and that must be marked by a first appearance full of shyness and nervousness. This is far from the virtually authoritarian assurance perceptible in one of the recorded versions I am considering. It is apparent that only a reasonably long silence can create this ambiguous atmosphere that, a little later, slips from brightness into shadow.

Silence Between the Voice and Orchestra

Two examples will suffice to show how important it is to observe silence when it occurs between the voice and the entrance of instruments. A first instance (example 3.6) occurs near the beginning of Act I at the very threshold of the encounter between Mélisande and Golaud. Golaud first states a fact (mm. 5–4 *7*) and then establishes a double relationship between the "petite fille" and himself (3–1 *7*). Between these two moments "he coughs" ("il tousse")[9] and then pauses a short time before resuming his soliloquy. This intermediary silence must not be shortened, precisely because of the double significance of the words that Go-

Ex. 3.5. *Pelléas et Mélisande,* Act IV, 5–3 before 38

Ex. 3.6. *Pelléas et Mélisande,* Act I, 5–1 before 7

laud sings: a personal reflection occurs before the silence, after which comes the first evidence of Mélisande's relationship to him and then his relationship to her. All these words precede the first question "Pourquoi pleures-tu?" (the question does not appear in example 3.6). Golaud's approach is slow; to his role of solitary hunter at the beginning of the scene will be added his protective mission for a being, Mélisande, who is as yet unknown. To curtail the moments of silence accompanying this change would alter its significance.

A second example illustrates a key moment in the last scene of Act IV, in which the doors are closed. Debussy shows this in several ways, including a prolonged silence at m. 8 *50,* between Pelléas's initial question and the second entrance of the orchestra (example 3.7).[10] The tempo is "plus lent" and could not be accelerated before the "serrez" at the end of the measure, which refers to the instruments only. The passage of three measures (9–7 *50*) shows rather well the sense of silence that Debussy desired, after the first statement by the orchestra at m. 9 *50.* Pelléas reacts immediately in surprise and responds similarly after the second announcement concerning the "noise" at m. 7 *50.* It thus is necessary for the intermediary silence at m. 8 *50* to be rigorously respected for the passage to gain

Ex. 3.7. *Pelléas et Mélisande,* Act IV, 9–7 before 50

its full meaning. A certain measure of time must pass between Pelléas's question and the confirmation of his foreboding.

Silence Within Instrumental Discourse

A single example may shed light on the sense of silence within instrumental discourse. In the first scene of Act II, at mm. *8*3–5, Mélisande concludes her passage by referring to her hair: "Ils sont plus longs que moi" (It is longer than I am tall). Meanwhile, the harp and string quartet suggest length by a descending movement that the harp alone echoes soon afterward (example 3.8). A first silence precedes the echo and a second silence follows, all in tempo "modéré." Although of equal length, these two silences mean different things. The first is inserted between two identical tritones, notated as diminished fifths and connected with what comes before, while the second separates the harp echo from the chord of D major—two harmonic worlds in stark contrast! This refers to the entrance of Pelléas at the second beat of m. *8*5. Mélisande's remark on the length of her hair is at once personal and general, but it is addressed to Pelléas only indirectly, while his cue two measures later begins anew the dialogue between the two characters. It is important for these two silences to be given their due in order to fully realize this moment in the drama.

Unmeasured Silences Between Measures

There are moments when Debussy indicates a silence with a fermata placed over a bar line. Clearly the length of this silence is left to the discretion of the conductor, but such a silence deserves observance, nonetheless.[11] Such is the case in the majority of performances; but there are unfortunate exceptions, such as at *36* in Act V. In that instance all the servants of the household fall to their

Ex. 3.8. *Pelléas et Mélisande,* Act II, 3–5 after 8

knees at the back of the room (example 3.9).[12] It is preposterous not to observe a pause that has great meaning in the drama, for it marks the transition from Mélisande's final agony to her death, signified in part by the tolling of the bell.

Thus, as in all preceding examples, silence is justified here as a function of dramatic circumstance.

VERBAL RHYTHM

If silence is a foundation stone in Debussy's construction of *Pelléas et Mélisande,* it is not the only one. Another of primary importance that joins physically with silence is verbal rhythm, the organization of language with respect to time. A comparison between the sketches of the work and the final version has revealed how Debussy refashioned the rhythm of his text to arrive at the optimum synthesis of verbal and musical rhythm.[13] But beyond the refining work of the com-

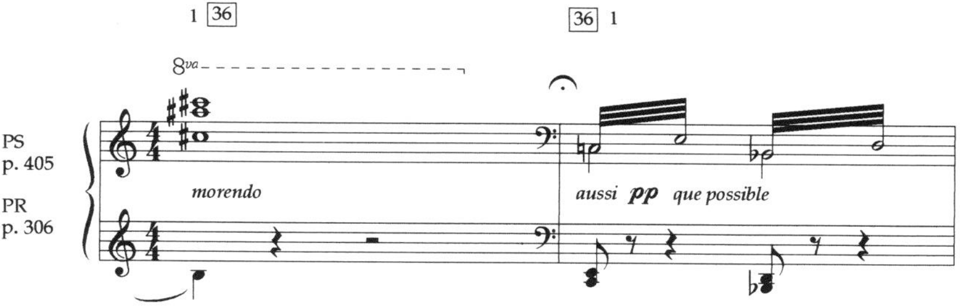

Ex. 3.9. *Pelléas et Mélisande,* Act V, 1 before 36 to 36, m. 1

poser, there is the matter of the performer's rendering. Let us focus now on two aspects of the relation of word to sound in performance.

The Harm of Excessive Lyricism

The numerous hearings of *Pelléas* undertaken for this study have revealed a flaw which happily is not frequent: an excess of lyricism, the consequences of which are often an alteration of the fundamental rhythm expected of the voice. Examples 3.10a, 3.10b, and 3.10c bear out this observation. The first scene of Act III offers Pelléas an opportunity to highlight his *beau chant*—his fine voice. But it is offered with the condition that he should not make too much of it and should not modify the rhythmic values allocated to certain sounds. Such an instance occurs in both examples 3.10a and 3.10b where, each time, the final two eighth notes become a dotted eighth followed by a sixteenth note. Such is also the case in example 3.10c, in which two eighth notes can become

Exx. 3.10a, 3.10b, and 3.10c. *Pelléas et Mélisande,* Act III, 1 before 8 to 8, m. 1; 3 after 9; and 2 before 13 to 13, m. 1

two sixteenth notes. At times, even, a quarter note is transformed into a half note and can distort a ternary measure into a binary one. Throughout his score Debussy shows the performer what he wants and, in like fashion, what is best to avoid.

Verbal Stress and Natural Musical Stress

Another aspect of the relation of word and sound, whose rhythmic importance is considerable, is the placement of the stress in the unfolding of a phrase. This is particularly notable when monotone cantillation is in question, such as abounds in Debussy's drama. A single but eloquent example can suffice to illustrate the problem. It is drawn from the first scene of Act IV (example 3.11), at mm. 2–1 3 on a monotone E recitative. Here Pelléas reports to Mélisande what his father has told him. Twice one hears the sentence "Il faut voyager" (You should go abroad), set in two different rhythms. With reference to example 3.3 above, it was noted that the bar line has nothing but an arithmetical significance for Debussy at times, although I have also observed the contrary in example 3.11, where the rhythmic sense is governed by metric units. That is the case now. The first utterance of the brief sentence suggests that the initial "Il" should be emphasized, although with a natural accent and no force other than that occurring from the placement of "Il" on beat three of the measure. By contrast, in the second utterance, where rhythmic values are a bit shorter and slightly raise the level of tension, the natural stress must fall on "faut," the first of three triplet eighth notes on the second beat. Thus the preceding "Il" would naturally be lighter. The repetition of this sentence shows the progression of the verbal expression, whereas one of the recordings studied here has Pelléas twice flatly accenting the first syllable of "voyager." Such a reading is double nonsense.

Ex. 3.11. *Pelléas et Mélisande,* Act IV, 2–1 before 3

TEMPO AND DYNAMICS

At times it is a delicate matter to speak of tempo and dynamics in *Pelléas* because, among other things, the pocket orchestral score and piano-vocal score show many differences among their indications. Only a critical edition will succeed—perhaps!—in bringing order to what can on occasion appear contradictory. So it is that on page 166 of the pocket score (m. *10* 7), one reads "plus lent," whereas in the corresponding measure of the piano-vocal score (page 127) one reads "au Mouvt (animé)." And again, at page 159 of the pocket score (m. *7* 5) the required nuance is piano, even though one observes a forte in the corresponding measure of the piano-vocal score, page 121.

This said, the parallels between the two scores are clearly more numerous than the differences, which ought to translate into parallel readings among performances. Even when all is clear in the score, such is not always the case. Thus, shortly after the curtain falls on the second scene of Act III, Debussy asks for progressive animation of the orchestral interlude up to the beginning of scene

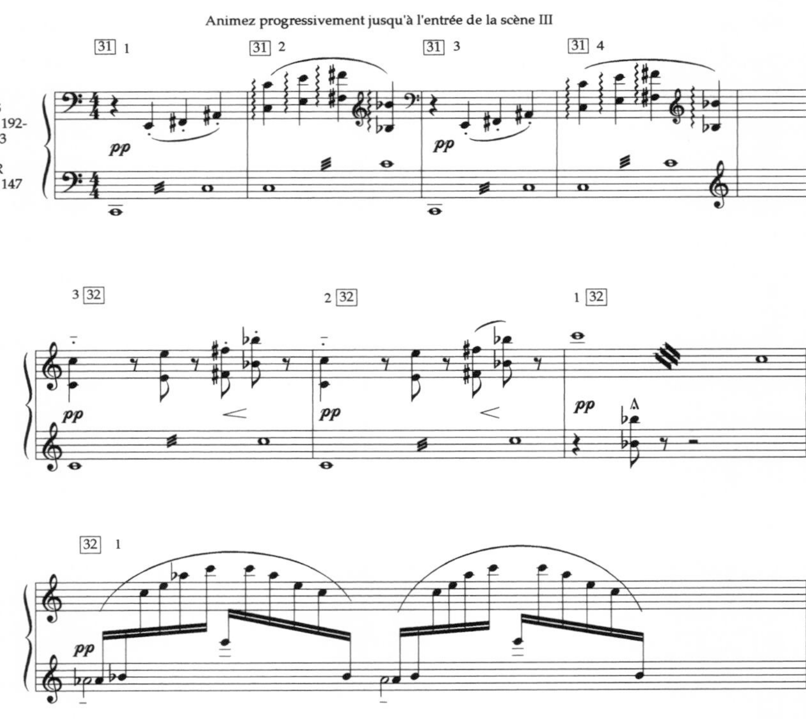

Ex. 3.12. *Pelléas et Mélisande,* Act III, 1 after 31 to 32, m. 1

3, cutting across seventeen or eighteen measures.[14] This animation should not end at m. 1 *32* and see the tempo fall back beginning at measure *32* 1, as was heard in one of the recordings. (See example 3.12, in which only the initial measures of the passage are transcribed.) Therein lies an error in the interpretation of the composer's indications.

THE REQUIREMENTS OF *PELLÉAS ET MÉLISANDE*

In the text of the booklet accompanying Pierre Boulez' 1970 recording, released after the presentation of *Pelléas* at Covent Garden in 1969,[15] the conductor comments on the "drame lyrique" of Claude de France and states among other things that "one of the principal characteristics of Debussy's music is fluidity of tempo." He then adds, "Yet, if one analyzes the text very carefully, and claims to discern its profound significance and to express it, numerous fluctuations prove necessary yet are not written down, for one would not be able to include them in an edition of the score without anesthetizing their subtle action. These are fluctuations that one must call upon to articulate the musical continuity and to give the combination of sound and word the inflections that characterize the suppleness of the dramatic action." But let no one be deceived: this "fluidity of tempo" and the "necessary . . . fluctuations" have nothing whatsoever to do with an unbridled liberty that would pretend to justify itself by the numerous expressive directions Debussy provides. The same attitude informed the conversation I had on 5 May 1995 in Paris with Gilles Cachemaille,[16] who sang the role of Golaud, as also my conversation with Pierre Boulez at the Nederlandse Opera of Amsterdam the following 7 August. Both the singer and the conductor exhibited a strong desire to approach the work in a spirit of rigor and discipline. According to both musicians, it is only after adopting this basic principle that one can make the work manageable, on one hand because of the demands of Debussy's score, and on the other as a function of particular circumstances and possible personal factors.

For Boulez as for Cachemaille, rhythm is of primary importance at any level. Thus one begins with the necessity of reciting the text metrically and with all desirable precision before singing it. This aids in the placement of the word and in the better understanding of each word's significance. But even when this approach is mastered, there still remains an uncertainty about finding the composer's true conception. I shall cite a single example from the end of Act III scene 3 at m. 2–1 *42*, as Golaud finishes addressing Pelléas "à propos de Mélisande." The repetition heard in "mais sans affectation d'ailleurs, sans affectation" can be understood in at least two ways. If the first words are undoubtedly addressed to Pelléas, the last two could signal either Golaud's internalization as he persuades himself of the rightness of his first statement or else a threat toward Pelléas in the event that the latter failed to observe the remonstrance of his half-brother. We see it all too well: the objective requirements of the score regarding nuance are not easy to read and can elicit much discussion, possibly fruitful, between the conductor and the singer.[17]

The middle approach to rhythm has an impact on the working out of each scene, as one seeks to establish its controlling tempo. But this tempo must have a flexibility and fluidity that will avoid both monotony of action and an undesirable fixation on the question by the listener. On this subject Boulez has made it a point to underline the basic difference between the precise forms of scenes in *Wozzeck* and the flexibility of forms in the scenes of *Pelléas.*

Finally, at the opposite end of the question of rhythm, there is the large rhythm that governs the work as a whole. In this connection it also is important to relate comments by Boulez, who made two recordings of *Pelléas* at an interval of more than twenty years. From one version to the other, the composer of *Le marteau sans maître* states that he has had no intention of rethinking his vision of *Pelléas.* Yet he claims that one's vision may evolve in spite of oneself, simply because over the years the man and conductor have aged, and because the circumstances of production changed: the version in the early 1970s was marked by the presence of the conductor as decision maker because of the death of Wieland Wagner shortly before, since the latter was intended to be stage director for the production. By contrast, the 1992 version undoubtedly resulted from a much more immediate collaboration with the stage director, Peter Stein, and thus implied a more finished realization. Boulez further mentions that rethinking each character, and recalling each musical moment anew, may lead at times to a "more radical" attitude, as in conceiving Golaud as "more deranged" and Mélisande as "more ambiguous"; in selecting a faster tempo, *scherzando,* better to highlight the theme in sixteenth notes that occurs just after the beginning of Act II; or even in deciding on a more violent tempo to underscore the apparent mental disorder of Golaud as he drags Mélisande about by her hair in the second scene of Act IV. It is apparent that such changes of tempo are directly reflected in the large rhythm of the work as a whole.

From all that has been discussed above, we might conclude that no matter how closely a performer endeavors to follow the composer in his final choices about musical creation and textual significance, the personal contribution of the interpreter can neither be avoided nor minimized. But it is a fact that, among all the versions of *Pelléas et Mélisande* either seen or heard, the few (hardly more than three or four) in which rigor and discipline have prevailed have impressed me most by the truth of their performance.

Debussy wrote to Eugène Ysaÿe, in the letter cited above, that he rejected the idea of concert performances or excerpts from the opera in concert. We should not regard this opinion as invalid just because the composer happened to make an exception when accompanying Mary Garden, who created the part of Mélisande, for the recording of the opening measures of the tower scene that begins Act III. It was therefore relevant to ask a performer his opinion of this issue, and Gilles Cachemaille was very clear: in the theater there is a twofold concern with acting or memorizing. Despite the assistance of the conductor, therefore, inaccuracies might occur. By contrast, these inaccuracies vanish when the score is before one's eyes, and one's attention is fully focused on the precision and vocal quality of the performance. On the other hand, in this second circumstance, it is sometimes annoying not to be able to accompany the vocal phrase with a gesture that occurs quite naturally on stage.

The major difficulty that any performer of *Pelléas et Mélisande* must master resides in the nature of the work and, finally, in the personality of the composer. As in certain other notable compositions, like *Jeux,* but also quite often in his piano music, Debussy demonstrates a loftiness of view conceived in utter liberty. This liberty corresponds only partially to a single, primary feeling driven by some compulsion that is little controlled, if at all. This feeling is a function of a conscious will choosing a deliberate path but also striving to explore new ones. Indeed, the nature of silence illustrated here is one such new path, with a striking and unexpected result.[18] Finally, in *Pelléas,* Debussy succeeds in achieving a remarkable synthesis of the varying forms liberty can take in human nature. The melodic and harmonic analysis of the score confirms this intuitive interpretation of the matter in every case.

It is therefore the mastery of freedom that defines the performance needs of *Pelléas et Mélisande* and compels us to devote ourselves to a strict discipline, including as one of its components the flexibility that makes every moment of the work come to life.

—Translated from French by Pierre-Eric Monnin and James R. Briscoe

DISCOGRAPHY

Here follows, in chronological order, the recordings consulted, with the names of the orchestras, conductors, and performers in the following order: Pelléas,

Golaud, Arkel, Mélisande, Geneviève, Yniold, un berger, un médecin. (Occasionally, not all singers will appear on the recording.) The list includes recordings that have never been made available to a general audience.

a. 1928. ? [Selections]. Georges Truc. Alfred Maguenat, Hector Dufranne, Armand Narçon, Marthe Nespoulos, Claire Croiza. Columbia 68518/23 or Columbia L2233/8. CBS (m) RL 3092. Reissued Pearl GEMM 145 (1979).

b. 1942. Orchestre de la Société des Concerts du Conservatoire. Roger Desormière. Jacques Jansen, Henri Etcheverry, Paul Cabanel, Irène Joachim, Germaine Cernay, Leila ben Sedira, Emile Rousseau, Armand Narçon. Choeurs Yvonne Gouverné. Gramophone DB 5161/80. Reissued RCA Victor LCT 6103 (1949). CD: CHS 7 61038 2.

c. 1952. Orchestre de la Suisse Romande. Ernest Ansermet. Pierre Mollet, Heinz Rehfuss, André Vessières, Suzanne Danco, Hélène Bouvier, Flore Wend, Derrik Olsen. Choeur du Grand Théâtre. Decca Historic Mono 425965-2 DM 02/London LLA-11 (LL592-LL595).

d. 1962. Orchestre de la Suisse Romande. Ernest Ansermet. Camille Mauranne, Heinz Rehfuss, André Vessières, Erna Spoorenberg, Hélène Bouvier, Hélène Morath, Oleh de Nyzankowsky, Derrik Olsen. Choeur "Motet" de Genève, dir. Jacques Horneffer. Decca/London A 4401. [Editor's note: the Nichols–Langham Smith source cited in note 3 indicates that the 1952 recording is the one listed here as recording *d,* and that the 1962 recording is the one listed directly above as recording *c.* Prof. Suter has verified his sources as given here.]

e. 1963. Orchestre de la Suisse Romande. Ernest Ansermet. Pierre Mollet, Heinz Rehfuss, André Vessières, Nadine Sautereau, Suzanne Danco, Annick Simon, Jean Chesnel. Choeur du Grand Théâtre de Genève, dir. G. Bria. Decca/London OSA 1379.

f. 1969. Orchestre de la Suisse Romande. Jean-Marie Auberson. Eric Tappy, Gérard Souzay, Victor de Narké, Erna Spoorenberg, Arlette Chédel, Anne-Marie Blauzat, Gregor Koubrak, Derrik Olsen. Choeur du Grand Théâtre de Genève, dir. Philippe Cart. Unpublished recording of the Radio de la Suisse Romande.

g. 1970. Orchestra of the Royal Opera House, Covent Garden. Pierre Boulez. George Shirley, Donald McIntyre, David Ward, Elisabeth Söderström, Yvonne Minton, Anthony Britten, Dennis Wicks, Dennis Wicks. Chorus of the Royal Opera, dir. Douglas Robinson. Columbia M3 30119. CD: SM3K 47265 Sony Classical.

h. 1971. Symphony Orchestra of Radio Bavaria. Raphael Kubelik. Nicolai

Gedda, Dietrich Fischer-Dieskau, Peter Meven, Helen Donath, Marga Schiml, Walter Gampert, Josef Weber, Raimund Grumbach. Chor des Bayerischen Rundfunks, dir. Josef Schmidhuber. Orfeo C 367942 I.

i. 1978. Berlin Philharmonic Orchestra. Herbert von Karajan. Richard Stilwell, José van Dam, Ruggero Raimondi, Frederica von Stade, Nadine Denize, Christine Barbaux, Pascal Thomas, Pascal Thomas. Chor des Deutschen Oper Berlin, dir. Walter Hagen-Groll. EMI CDS 749 350 2/Angel SZCX-3885. CD: CDS7 49350-2.

j. 1979. Orchestre National de l'Opéra de Monte-Carlo. Armin Jordan. Eric Tappy, Philippe Huttenlocher, François Loup, Rachel Yakar, Jocelyne Taillon, Colette Alliot-Lugaz, Michel Brodard, Michel Brodard. STU 71296/Erato 71296.

k. 1983. Orchestre de la Suisse Romande. Jésus Lopez-Cobos. Jérôme Pruett, Tom Krause, Jules Bartin, Faith Esham, Jocelyne Taillon, Eliden Arzoni, Jean Laine, Jean Laine. Choeur du Grand Théâtre de Genève, dir. Paul-André Gaillard. Unpublished recording by the Radio de la Suisse Romande.

l. 1988. Orchestre Philharmonique de Nice. John Carewe. Malcolm Walker, Vincent Le Texier, Peter Meven, Eliane Manchet, Carol Yahr, Un petit chanteur de Tölz, ?, Pierre le Hémonet. Choeur de l'Opéra de Nice, dir. Frank Meiswinkel. PV. 788093/94.

m. 1991. Vienna Philharmonic Orchestra. Claudio Abbado. François Le Roux, José van Dam, Jean-Philippe Courtis, Maria Ewing, Christa Ludwig, Patrizia Pace, Jean-Philippe Courtis, Rudolf Mazzola. Konzertvereinigung Wiener Staatsopernchor, dir. Helmuth Froschauer. DGG 435 344-2.

n. 1991. Orchestre Symphonique de Montréal. Charles Dutoit. Didier Henry, Gilles Cachemaille, Pierre Thau, Colette Alliot-Lugaz, Claudine Carlson, Françoise Golfier, Philippe Ens, Philippe Ens. Choeur de l'Orchestre Symphonique de Montréal. Decca/London 430 502-2.

o. 1992. Welsh National Opera. Pierre Boulez. Donald Maxwell, Kenneth Cox, Samuel Burkey, Alison Hagley, Penelope Walker, Neill Archer, Peter Massocchi, Peter Massocchi. Chorus of the Welsh National Opera. DGG 072 431-3.

Part Two **The Genres in Performance**

Chapter 4 Debussy and Orchestral Performance

James R. Briscoe

The orchestral compositions of Claude Debussy have exercised a major influence on musicians and audiences throughout the twentieth century. Pierre Boulez, for example, asserts that "the root of all modernism" in music may be seen in the *Faune.*[1] And yet no comprehensive view of Debussy's expectations for orchestral performance has previously been offered. In this essay, I seek to do so, taking for my primary works of study the *Prélude à l'après-midi d'un faune* (1894), the *Nocturnes* (1899), *La mer* (1905), and the three orchestral *Images* (1912).

In referring to his writings on the topic, we must beware of Debussy's irony and exaggeration. In addition, we need to verify and amplify his comments with those of contemporaries and, in interpreting his statements, remain focused on broad artistic values. I shall start with primary documents—Debussy's published and unpublished letters, music criticism, and interviews, as well as documents of his dealings with the conductors who were closest to him chronologically and professionally: Camille Chevillard, Gabriel Pierné, and Désiré-Emile Inghelbrecht. I shall also examine the approaches and views of the conductors who followed immediately afterward: Ernest Ansermet,

Arturo Toscanini, and Piero Coppola. Music critics and Debussy's close friend and first biographer Louis Laloy in particular offer further evidence of the composer's orchestral performance ideals. And finally, I shall refer to significant early practices in the performance of the orchestral works. Of particular interest is tempo and the attitude Debussy's earliest conductors took toward nuance and structural line.

For Debussy the authority of the score was considerable. The Canadian dancer Maud Allan discovered this when she commissioned the ballet *Khamma* and, in trying to speed up the slow composer, incited his antagonism. When Allan requested alterations to the score, he responded curtly in a letter of 1912, "Thus I composed it; thus it shall remain."[2] Even the smallest details were to stand as Debussy determined: to the conductor André Messager after the seventh performance of *Pelléas et Mélisande,* Debussy complained, "Martenot [the first harpist] added certain unexpected glissandos, which certainly appeared excessive!"[3] In 1902 Mme de Saint-Marceaux, who hosted a prestigious musical salon, proposed a chamber performance of *La damoiselle élue.* Messager was to direct and called for a reduced scoring. "It is a charming notion," Debussy replied to the proposal, "since you would direct, but the quartet is too feeble. Moreover, there are the two harps, and all the winds including bass clarinet."[4] Although he left the decision about the reduced scoring to Messager, he clearly if tactfully opposed it, and the socially desirable performance did not take place. On a few occasions, however, Debussy could be persuaded to alter a score, as with *Children's Corner,* arranged for orchestra by André Caplet, or the ballet *Jeux,* rearranged upon the impresario Diaghilev's urging.

We can relate the matter of score authority to an anecdote the pianist Marguerite Long told. "A pianist came to play for Debussy and insisted that his reading was to be free. Debussy later [told me in confidence], 'there are some who write music, some who edit it, and there is that person who does as he pleases.' I asked Debussy what he had said . . . he scornfully remarked, 'Oh, nothing. I looked at the carpet. But he will never tread on it again.'"[5] Even if Debussy might himself alter scores, he had little patience with others who presumed to do so without his approval.

Not all performers shared Debussy's belief in the authority of the score, including even the most prominent conductors in the years just following Debussy's death. Both Arturo Toscanini and Ernest Ansermet were champions of Debussy in the period 1920 to 1960, and both had studied with the composer. Toscanini, in his twenty-six years of conducting in America, played *La mer* fifty-three times, "Nuages" and "Fêtes" from the *Nocturnes* thirteen and fourteen times, respectively, and the *Faune* twenty-three times. Yet Erich Leinsdorf, who had been Toscanini's assistant at Salzburg from 1934 to 1937, later recalled, "Toscanini did a great deal of editing. . . . The belief that he followed punctiliously the letter of the score is quite mistaken. He made extensive corrections, even in *La mer.*"[6] The critic B. H. Haggin reported in his book *Conversations with Toscanini* that the conductor made many changes in *La mer* of what seemed to him miscalculations on Debussy's part, especially with regard to the clarity and forcefulness of lines. Haggin quotes Toscanini, "I tell Debussy are many things not clear, and he say all right to make changes."[7] We are not convinced, therefore, when Toscanini avowed an absolute stewardship of Debussy's score authority, "Is like reading the score, listening to my recording of *La mer!*"[8] Even so, the young Toscanini had conducted in and absorbed the musical atmosphere surrounding the composer, and on other occasions during his career he made a nearly religious point of following the score literally. As Haggin reported, Toscanini carefully conformed to Debussy's tempo relations indicated in the score of the *Faune,* at least where the three main sections were concerned.[9]

Ernest Ansermet likewise was scrupulous in his devotion to Debussy. He studied the scores closely, judging from his writings, and he coached with the composer at the end of Debussy's life on matters of tempo and interpretation. Nevertheless, Ansermet also found it appropriate to revise Debussy's score in a few details. He wrote, "In the final pages of *Ibéria* there are some glissando passages for trombone that come off better if they are reinforced by horns. So I add the horns. I cannot believe that accuracy is more important than good sense."[10]

Debussy frequently insisted that sets be performed in their entirety. This rule seems basic to performance practice today, but in the postromantic concert tradition of the composer's lifetime, audiences often heard only parts of orchestral sets. To his publisher Jacques Durand, Debussy observed in 1912 that the important conductor Camille Chevillard was "offering to play 'Gigues' but [didn't] speak of the other two *Images.* I believe that one should hear all three. Don't you think that we should leave that performance to [Gabriel] Pierné?"[11] But by the time of that letter Debussy had lost all confidence in Chevillard, calling him an "animal tamer" and an artist "whose soul is not adequate for something as virginal as the *Blessed Damozel.*"[12]

Further regarding the complete performance of sets, he wrote diplomatically to Pierné in 1907, "You know what a joy it would give me to hear you perform anything. But even so, I would rather await the chance of hearing *La mer* complete rather than hearing "Jeux de vagues" alone. . . . When you have three children you can scarcely afford to take only one to the Concerts Colonne. Put yourself in their place!"[13]

In 1890, desirous of establishing a niche in the Paris scene, the young Debussy had been asked by Vincent D'Indy to allow a portion of the *Fantaisie* for piano and orchestra to be heard. Debussy declined: "To play only the first part . . . can give a false idea. On reflection let me say that it is better to await a performance of the three parts for the premiere."[14] Ever the aristocrat, D'Indy pulled rank and scheduled only the first movement of the *Fantaisie* for performance at the prestigious Société Nationale. But just before the first rehearsal was to begin, Debussy entered the hall and surreptitiously removed the parts from the music stands. The "Christianly charitable" D'Indy, as Debussy put it in a later review, never forgot the audacity of the young composer, and they maintained a mutual antagonism throughout their lifetimes. The *Fantaisie* premiered only in 1920, two years after Debussy's death.

To be sure, conductors have consistently declined to play all five parts of the *Images* as a set, offering "Gigues" and "Rondes de printemps" as a pair or singly, though usually keeping *Ibéria* intact as a subset of three works. Debussy himself conducted the premiere of "Gigues" along with the other four sections of the *Images,* but perhaps it was not reasonable to expect subsequent performances to do so, in view of its length. Furthermore, the third of the *Nocturnes,* "Sirènes," was sometimes omitted in Debussy's day, whether for lack of a female chorus or because the chorus was incapable of performing the subtly difficult vocalises. The premiere of the *Nocturnes* by Chevillard at the Concerts Lamoureux in 1900 featured only the first two parts, for example. Since his day, however, Debussy's intention to hear the *Nocturnes* intact has generally been respected.

If he insisted that sets remain intact, Debussy was less convinced that an orchestra should play more than one of his compositions in the same concert. When his first publisher, Georges Hartmann, proposed that two be performed together in 1899, Debussy replied, "That's saying a lot . . . Do you really think it useful to play the *Afternoon of a Faun* before the *Nocturnes?* That appears to me to border on obsession—a faun running to perpetuity!"[15] However, in 1906 he relented, at least for the moment, writing to Durand: "Well, I find a certain interest in a program composed historically of my works, tho' I'm afraid they'll accuse me of scraping the bottom of my bureau drawers."[16]

As with most composers, Debussy insisted repeatedly that rehearsal time should be ample. His hopes in this regard remained largely idealistic—as they would be now. When the Société Nationale proposed a performance of two *Proses lyriques* with his recent orchestration, he complained to the singer Blanche

Marot, "[Two rehearsals are] stupidly insufficient."[17] The premiere of the opera *Pelléas et Mélisande* in 1902 required more than a hundred rehearsals, a luxury not often available. More usual was the premiere of *La mer* in 1905, again conducted by the "blustering time-beater" Chevillard. "I have just spent five hours over two days with Chevillard," Debussy wrote to the composer and conductor André Caplet, "and that is too much for one person! . . . Only 'Jeux de vagues' remains to be ironed out; the other two are nearly there. This is the moment that I hate with Chevillard—he's precious little as an artist."[18] In December 1910 Debussy was engaged to conduct the Vienna Konzertverein, where he was to lead the *Faune,* the *Nocturnes, La mer,* and *Ibéria* in a grand honorary concert. But as he reported to Durand, "They had assured me that they already knew *La mer,* having played it three times. But ah, you should have heard . . . it made me miss Chevillard!" Whereupon he canceled the performance of *La mer* and the *Nocturnes,* even at the risk of insulting his hosts and of missing the privilege of their performance in Vienna.[19] Recalling the incident in a Budapest interview soon afterward, a journalist asked him, "I understand there was a little incident surrounding your Vienna concert?" "No," Debussy explained calmly, "not really an incident. I simply couldn't permit the Philharmonic to play my symphony *La mer* because the musicians hadn't put the finishing touches on it."[20] By contrast, Debussy's conducting of *Ibéria* from the orchestral *Images* in 1912 occurred under nearly ideal conditions. The score had benefited from thirty rehearsals, prompting Debussy to promise, "I can assure you that, if the players don't stop of their own accord, I would not be the one to control them!"[21]

What can we learn about Debussy's expectations from his and others' comments on his own conducting? Apparently, he was extremely nervous about his own abilities. As he put it in a letter of 1908 to Victor Segalen, upon first taking up a baton to rehearse *La mer,* "It's not without heart palpitations that I climbed onto the podium yesterday. . . . You may be sure that I bring a real inexperience to the job of disarming those curious beasts called orchestral musicians, although they had a good enough will."[22] In a distinct minority among his observers, Debussy's respected biographer and analyst Louis Laloy considered him "an orchestral conductor with authority."[23] His friend the physician Pasteur Vallery-Radot was perhaps more informative, recording that "he directed [*La mer*] with simplicity, as if sketching rather than gesturing broadly, as if he were tracing letters in space, avoiding all effect so as to give a unity while still underlining the nuances."[24]

However, most observers found him inept as a conductor. The biographer Léon Vallas summarizes the many commentators who observed "a paradoxical dryness; [Debussy] was content to mark a straight beat with the baton and left index finger. . . . As to qualities of an excellent conductor, he possessed only one: an extreme finesse in hearing, making him sensitive to infinite details."[25] Less charitable observers saw him as clumsy and even rattled. When financial exigency persuaded him to conduct in Amsterdam, a Concertgebouw board member, Richard van Rees, recalled that "Debussy on the rostrum appeared clumsy and ill at ease. . . . He was a bad conductor, but the orchestra [for the *Nocturnes*] was very responsive and followed his indications attentively."[26] The outstanding conductor Vittorio Gui, whose performances Debussy admired, recalled, "He conducted as best he could, woodenly, mechanically, without fire and without really leading his forces. No calamities, but no poetic feeling." On one occasion, rehearsals in Turin had not gone well, and Gui remembered, "He was turning the pages of the score with the hand holding the baton . . . losing a beat[,] to the great confusion of the orchestra. I had to dash over with the excuse of being his translator . . . to quell that flood of natural disorder evident . . . especially in a group of Latins when the influence of a leader is not vouchsafed to them."[27]

Most embarrassing was Debussy's 1908 performance of *La mer* in London with the Queen's Hall Orchestra. No less acute an observer than the conductor Sir Henry Wood recalled the rehearsal: "I was [sitting beside] Madame Debussy, who called it 'the sea in lumps.'" And on a return visit in 1909, as Wood again reported on the concert, "There was a peculiar accident. In 'Fêtes' . . . Debussy suddenly lost his head, and his beat! . . . He tapped the desk [seeking to stop and start over] . . . but the orchestra refused to stop. The work was going beautifully—I never knew them more unanimous. The audience recorded their appreciation, and he was compelled to repeat the movement. . . . Debussy was nonplused and certainly did not understand the English mind."[28]

Debussy also conducted his orchestral works in Budapest, Moscow, St. Petersburg, Rome, the Hague, and Brussels. What we can extrapolate from reports of his conducting is that he relied on subtle understatement and extreme care over detail in rehearsals. Many commentators recalled that he had a remarkable acuity of hearing, which must have made it possible for careful rehearsal to make up for defects in conducting technique.

Lacking the ability to demonstrate his points, Debussy nonetheless was highly critical of other conductors. Regarding German conductors, Debussy could scarcely be generous, it seems. In 1903 he wrote ironically in *Gil Blas* concerning Felix Weingartner, "His gestures have an elegance that is almost geometrical. Then, suddenly—wild, incomprehensible gestures, which make the trombones roar and the cymbals go wild! It is most impressive and little short of miraculous."[29] Commenting on the conducting of Artur Nikisch in 1901, Debussy observed, "Monsieur Nikisch is an incomparable virtuoso: it seems that his virtuosity makes him forget that he also needs good taste!. . . . He takes the horns up to a climax for which there is no apparent reason. These are 'effects' for which there is no apparent justification."[30] And yet Debussy was able to extol the virtues of Hans Richter: "All this pantomime remains within the bounds of discretion: it is never distracting to the eye, nor does it come between the music and the audience."[31]

Debussy's opinion of French conductors varied. In a rare appreciation of Chevillard of 1901—before he became disgusted with him—Debussy wrote in *La revue blanche,* "Thanks also to Monsieur Chevillard for abstaining from the bullfight technique so common among international conductors these days. It is most disconcerting to watch banderillas being implanted in the mouth of the English horn, or the poor trombones petrified by the gestures of a matador! M. Chevillard is quite content to give the orchestra the assurance that he understands the music completely—a simple enough ambition but very difficult to achieve in practice."[32]

But Debussy's admiration for Chevillard rapidly declined, making one wonder whether an early currying of favor colored this particular review. Désiré-Emile Inghelbrecht, the conductor who was Debussy's protégé in orchestral conducting in the composer's last years, reports that "Chevillard, having just conducted the [orchestrated] version of the *Petite Suite,* asked Debussy if he were satisfied. 'Certainly, but I would have liked a bit more suppleness.' To which Chevillard replied with incomprehension, 'Suppleness? What the heck! *Faster,* or *slower?*'"[33] In a letter to his stepson Raoul Bardac, Debussy wrote, "Chevillard waves his arms about like a peddler, with a stiff back like a policeman on a bicycle, which scarcely constitutes . . . a vision of beauty."[34]

Reviewing Alfred Cortot in *Gil Blas* in 1903, when the young Cortot was trying his hand at conducting, Debussy wrote sarcastically, "M. Cortot of all French conductors has learned most from the pantomime customary among German conductors. . . . See how [his lock of hair] falls, sad and weary, at any hint of tenderness! So much so that it precludes any communication between M. Cortot and the orchestra."[35]

After the disliked Chevillard, Gabriel Pierné was most likely to conduct debut and subsequent performances during the composer's lifetime. Pierné had been a composition classmate at the Conservatoire but turned to conducting and concert management after 1900. He directed the first performance of *Ibéria* in 1910. Debussy wrote to André Caplet about the premiere, "The 'super-Spanish' rhythm of 'Par les rues et par les chemins' became 'left-bank' under the intelligent direction of our young Capellmeister, and the 'Parfums de la nuit' slipped quietly from beneath an awning, so as not to disturb anyone. . . . Today we need to work over 'Rondes de Printemps' . . . I really can't speak of the music, but the orchestra sounds like crystal, and it's as light as a woman's hand." A few days later he continued his performance critique: "Saturday morning. Rehearsal of *Ibéria.* . . . Things are better now. The young Capellmeister and his orchestra have consented to having less feet and more wings. Now 'Parfums' and 'Le matin d'un jour de fête' link perfectly and naturally. That seems like music that is improvised."[36]

The incisive articulation of rhythm and of the value of silences occupied Debussy's thought extensively. In writing about *Images* to Durand, he notes, "More and more I am persuaded that music, by its essence, isn't a thing that can flow into a rigorous, traditional form. Rather, it is a thing of colors and of rhythmicized time."[37] About *Pelléas* he wrote to Eugène Ysaÿe, "The special care with which one performs the silences is central to the work." As he expressed elsewhere, he preferred an orchestra "of clear sonorities" rather than an "opaque thick orchestra."[38] Commenting on the woodwind sonorities of the Moscow orchestra he guest-conducted, he wrote home to his wife, Emma, that "the woodwinds are excellent musicians, but their sound is heavy and they quack like ducks."[39]

Inghelbrecht likewise linked clear sonority with clear rhythm as fundamental in the performance of Debussy. In discussing "Fêtes" from *Ibéria,* Inghelbrecht focused on the need to maintain metric proportions, citing his own refusal to allow "showy pauses."[40] Furthermore, he argued against a "sort of hysteria among musicians [performing Debussy], caused by incessant string vibrato. This means of expression would otherwise be efficient if employed with more moderation, especially among basses and celli."[41]

Debussy foresaw that a large orchestra would be most appropriate for his orchestral music. Jann Pasler identifies a sense of "progress as boundless expansion" in the France of Debussy's time. She observes, "Paralleling the expansion beyond previously defined limits in the technological, economic, and political domains was a similar kind of musical progress. . . . The size of the orchestra had also increased dramatically by the end of the nineteenth century, eventually involving four woodwind instruments to a part and colossal brass, percussion and string sections."[42]

Debussy wrote to Maud Allan, who had commissioned the ballet *Khamma,* that "[the work] is precisely tailored to a complement of 90 players."[43] One is struck by the fact that such a large contingent was intended for a ballet pit orchestra. Writing in 1895 about the *Faune,* Debussy rhapsodized about the "humanity that thirty-two violinists bring to bear who've had to get up too early."[44] He exults over the performance of the Covent Garden Orchestra: "At Covent Garden . . . music is entirely at home. . . . The orchestra is huge and unfailingly pays attention."[45] Even the pristine Sirens in the third movement of the *Nocturnes* require a large complement to satisfy Debussy; writing to the conductor Doret in 1914 he asks him to take charge of placing the twenty-four choristers.[46]

In the earliest recordings, the cramped conditions of the recording studios still accommodated a full orchestra. Piero Coppola, the Italo-Parisian conductor who helped introduce Debussy's orchestral music to the world with the first recordings in the late 1920s, recalled that sixty musicians played for his 1926 version of the *Children's Corner,* orchestrated by André Caplet.[47]

The placement of the sections of the new, large orchestra onstage directly occupied the composer and his colleagues. In his written comment, Debussy was content with speculating fancifully, "The strings should make not a barrier but a circle around the others. Split up the woodwinds. Mix the bassoons up with the cellos, the clarinets and oboes with the violins, so that their entries don't sound like someone dropping a parcel."[48]

More pragmatic but nonetheless authoritative is Inghelbrecht's discussion of orchestral placement, which differs from the placement common today. In his foreword to the English translation of *The Conductor's World,* Sir Adrian Boult especially commends Inghelbrecht's insistence that first and second violins be set antiphonally. Inghelbrecht wrote: "Some orchestras place the celli at the edge of the platform, formerly held by the second violins to the right of the conductor. . . . They forget that the basses' tendency to predominate will thus become accentuated. . . . Piling first and seconds [violins] together does away with the effect of opposition, the result of their former placement." And with a nationalism piqued by World War II he adds, "This specifically Germanic distribution happened to come into favor in France after the Liberation [of 1945]."[49] Most notable in his seating charts is the placement of both the first and second violin sections at the front of the stage at the left and right, respectively. The cello section was seated to stage rear of the first violin section, the basses to the back of the first violins and cellos, and the violas to stage rear of the second violin section. The flutes, harps, and piano occupied the back of the main level to stage rear of the strings, and the remaining woodwinds filled the first raised tier, in the order, left to right, of bassoons, clarinets, oboes, and English horn. The brass occupied the second tier in the order, left to right, of tuba, trombones, French horns, and trumpets, slightly elevated above and behind the first tier; and the percussion occupied the third tier. Seen from the side, Inghelbrecht's seating of the Orchestre National formed a stairstep pattern. He also provided explicit directions for orchestra and chorus, in which the chorus occupied tiers behind the brass. When conducting the Orchestre National, Inghelbrecht customarily arranged the sopranos in a row left to right behind the percussion, the altos in a row behind the sopranos, and the tenors and finally basses similarly in single rows.

Norman Del Mar shows that the seating plan advocated by Inghelbrecht was also followed by "most of the past generation of traditionally minded conductors, such as Toscanini, Furtwängler . . . and Adrian Boult."[50] Daniel J. Koury confirms that the traditional seating plan had been present essentially throughout the nineteenth century. Koury cites Sir Henry Wood (rather than the German conductors faulted by Inghelbrecht) as the first documented conductor to employ the modern outlay with both first and second violins on the left of the stage, with the second violins located at stage rear of the first violin section.[51]

Regarding the state of instrument construction in the orchestras of Debussy's day, and the sonority to which Debussy was accustomed, scholars have affirmed that all the families of the orchestra arrived at their present construction by 1880. Even so, it is notable that French oboe players (and the makers they preferred) chose a "sweeter" sound than other national schools. French players of the French horn in Debussy's day and up to the present prefer instruments with a narrower bore and a smaller bell, which give a quieter sound.[52]

The sociology of orchestral personnel in Debussy's France and just afterward is notably liberal in that the orchestra contained a number of women—rare in those days. As Inghelbrecht wrote, "In the 1910s one felt a real national pride that our French orchestral school could be considered without doubt the finest in the world. In the Parliament of music, women have gained an appreciable number of seats during recent years. In the orchestral class at the Conservatoire, the post of concertmaster . . . solo cello, and the majority of string desks were occupied by the so-called 'weaker sex.' And it was the 'lady timpanists' who took it in turn to extract thunder and tempest from the copper basins in which once their ancestors had been content to cook jam for the family."[53]

On occasion, Debussy held up the banner of music "en plein air" with regard to the venue for orchestral performance. Writing in the modernist journal *Gil Blas* in 1903, he posited that "Concerts out of doors are one of the best opportunities for a musician to bring together all the resources of music. To have the natural scenery and . . . to make an orchestral commentary on the daily miracle of the sunset!"[54] Earlier in the same journal he had imagined, "a large orchestra augmented with the sound of the human voice. . . . Here would lie the embryo of music for the open air: new ideas flowing in broad lines from both the orchestra and voices . . . from the tops of the trees, through the light of the open air. . . . Any harmonic progression that sounded stifled within the confines of the concert hall would take on a new significance. Perhaps this is an answer . . . to ridding music of all those petty mannerisms of form and tonality—arbitrary questions with which music is unfortunately encumbered."[55] On the *Nocturnes,* he wrote to his first editor Hartmann, "I hope that will be music full of open sky that will shiver from the great wind of Liberty's wing (Lord, what a lovely phrase!)."[56]

Debussy was nonetheless ambivalent about music education for audiences, in whom he often revealed a lack of confidence. For example, he lodges a protest "against a prevalent custom each time a modern symphony is performed: a four-page thematic analysis is distributed among the audience. . . . I believe that it is dangerous to initiate laymen into the secrets of musical chemistry. . . . Most sensible people would simply put the program notes in their pocket."[57]

THE PERFORMANCE CRITERIA OF LINE AND NUANCE

As we see from this sentiment, Debussy insisted that the listener gain an overall perspective before being immersed in detail. The aesthetics of Debussy's orchestral music intersect with performance values on this central point: sensitivity to nuance must be present but must not obscure the central, structural line. Such a notion is of course present in any musical performance but seems to weigh especially heavily upon the thought of Debussy and his contemporary conductors.

Critics of Debussy agree that his orchestral music can be divided into two phases, which may be termed impressionistic and postimpressionistic, according to the commentator Louis Laloy, who was respected by the composer. Both phases intersect with the symbolist aesthetic in essential ways.[58] To the impressionist phase belong the *Faune* and *Nocturnes,* and to the postimpressionist *La mer, Images,* and *Jeux.* Laloy considered the *Faune* as "the most narrative" of all the orchestral compositions, and declared, "Here is a unity of character or of landscape . . . if in a less definite sense than the poets and painters experienced it."[59] Emphasizing that nuance of color seemed uppermost, and speaking in terms recalling the impressionism of the visual arts, Debussy wrote to Ysaÿe in 1894 about the *Nocturnes,* then in their formative conception as a solo violin and orchestra work: "This is a search for the different arrangements one can give to a single color, as for example the painters would do it, as an étude in grays."[60] The latter remark recalls his fascination at the time with Whistler and that painter's own Nocturnes as studies in color nuance.

For Laloy, the *Nocturnes* and *Pelléas* formed not only the taste of a generation but its heart. Calling upon the terms of impressionist painting with its emphasis upon nuance of color, he noted, "The *Nocturnes* are paintings not of objects or of actual beings, but of the reflections that their vibrations communicate into the air, their activity in a moving space. . . . It is possible that the *Nocturnes* are the masterpiece of impressionism."[61] The relation to performance of such an aesthetic may perhaps be broached through the critical view of Jean d'Udine, who in a review of the *Nocturnes* spoke of "spots of sonority[;] . . . harmonies replace lines in their unfurling."[62] Among the earliest conductors who recorded the *Nocturnes* and the *Faune,* Inghelbrecht, Walter Straram, and Piero Coppola appear to be closest to Debussy's thought and to hew the most closely to the interpretation Debussy and Laloy articulated, in which flexibility and a sense of narrative figure prominently. Although Laloy used the term "impressionist" to describe this sense of tone color nuance in performance, one could argue that it is not a visual impression but a musical symbol that is Debussy's main aesthetic intent. In the performance concerns considered here, especially conductors' approach to nuance and line, the debate among Debussy scholars over appropriate terminology—whether it is "impressionist" or "symbolist"—is peripheral.

A new direction emerges with *La mer* in 1905 and continues, speaking broadly, in the *Images* and *Jeux.* Reviewing *La mer* shortly after its premiere, M. D. Calvocoressi in the *Guide musical* observed, "The impression [is] that Debussy, who had studiously explored the domain of possible sonorities, here has considerably condensed the mass of his discoveries, and his music acquires an absolute harmonious unity that characterizes the masterpieces."[63] After hearing the work again in 1908, Calvocoressi affirmed that "the detailed and decorative side of Debussy's work subsides and the evocative force appears clearly."[64] Laloy found a classical procedure in *La mer:* "One finds here . . . the three movements of a classical symphony . . . and in the classical manner textural transpositions of the same idea."[65]

In a review of "Rondes de printemps" from the *Images,* Laloy wrote in 1910, "More robust than his previous manner, [the work develops] a single idea and moves about among fronds of melody."[66] In the *Revue S.I.M.* soon afterward,

Laloy continued this idea, describing the later manner of Debussy and pointing to Debussy's new emphasis: "Having previously made music capable of translating inexpressible impressions, Debussy disposes of them according to the wishes of his spirit."[67]

The conductors who performed the remarkable scores of the second phase in Debussy's day and just afterward were notably engaged in a search to communicate structural line. This is not to say that overall cohesion is not present in important early recordings of the *Faune* and *Nocturnes,* or that Debussy does not defend his interest in the central line. However, in the performance of orchestral works beginning with *La mer,* the main emphasis shifts from color and nuance to linearity. Commenting on Toscanini's many interpretations of *La mer,* Robert Marsh observes that "he keeps the orchestra integrated and holds the groupings of notes in a firm, singing line, so that no detail intrudes upon the complete form of the whole."[68]

Debussy had already set the stage for a sense of long-range structure in remarks on his stylistic conception, where he distinguished structure from the sensibility of the moment. Advising Ernest Chausson on a composition in 1893, Debussy suggested, "For one thing, I'd [be] free from a preoccupation with the inner parts of the texture." Such a counsel at first sounds incongruous with Debussy the contrapuntist, but here he apparently is urging Chausson to clarify his central idea.[69] To the young composer Raoul Bardac, Debussy offers, "Go ahead and collect your impressions, but don't be so hasty in noting them down . . . because music has this that is superior to painting: it can centralize its variations in color and light into a single prospect. . . . So often [the line is] overwhelmed by the richness or the banality of the frame."[70] Laloy found in *La mer* "an art of finesse but also a 'classic' art . . . that is distinguished from the impressionistic music of before, of the *Faune* and the *Nocturnes.*"[71] Continuing his critique, Laloy suggested that Debussy's sense of line intensifies with full maturity: in *La mer,* "One does not find the shimmering colors that make up the virginal charm of [the *Nocturnes*]. *La mer* has rather another character, a full-blown maturity . . . that is broader and larger. . . . No longer is there a pointillism, but there remains an impressionism of the emotions, translated into harmonies unique to the world." Debussy responds, thanking Laloy for his "delicate and rigorous comprehension. . . . You follow me step by step with a divination that grasps what in truth I cannot name."[72]

Drawing upon his wide studies of Debussy's writings, Richard Langham Smith finds that "purity was an ideal that shot through the whole of the Debussian aesthetic, not only his ideals of criticism, but also in his approach to composition."[73] Moreover, we may certainly add in the present context that the pure line which embodies the work's central idea consistently occupied Debussy's performance ideals.

DEBUSSY'S CONDUCTORS

Earlier in this study, we looked at the major conductors in the context of Debussy's expressed values at moments when their views stemmed or differed from Debussy's own. We now may consider them with regard to line and nuance while also summarizing their overall contributions to Debussy in performance. The role of Gabriel Pierné (1863–1937) as a conductor during the composer's lifetime was second only to Chevillard's. Pierné became chief conductor of the Concerts Colonne from 1910 to 1934, performing the premiere of *Ibéria* in 1910 and the first hearing of *Jeux* in concert in 1914. Thereafter he gave the first performance, which was in concert, of the ballet *Khamma* in 1924. Debussy appreciated the concert performance Pierné gave of *Jeux* but offered a telling remark on the need to project overall line: "You know me well enough to recognize that I have an affectionate response for all that you invested of yourself in the performance of *Jeux*. . . . But it also seemed to me that the several episodes lacked homogeneity! The link joining them is subtle perhaps but surely exists. You know that better than I. Besides, it was generally too loud."[74]

On the basis of all the available evidence, it appears that Inghelbrecht, of the conductors nearest to Debussy, drew the most closely to Debussy's thought in the early recorded performances. "Certain composers and Debussy in particular," wrote Inghelbrecht as if revealing his awareness of a unique kinship, "pose problems for the interpreter beyond the qualities of professionalism: they demand an understanding that says 'we are of the same blood, you and I.'"[75]

No particularly close acquaintance with the composer seems to have resulted when Inghelbrecht conducted the chorus for the premiere of *Le martyre de St. Sébastien* in 1911. However, the two collaborated actively in 1912, when the dancer Loie Fuller choreographed the *Nocturnes* and Inghelbrecht conducted. In succeeding months, Debussy would coach Inghelbrecht on the interpretation of the *Faune,* the *Nocturnes, La damoiselle élue,* and *Ibéria.*[76] When the conductor presented a "Festival of French Music" on 2 April 1913 at the Théâtre des Champs Elysées, the impresario Gabriel Astruc heard Debussy remark, "This is the first time I've heard my music really played," referring to *La mer.*[77] That reading seems to have benefited directly from Debussy's coaching, for in a score dedication the composer writes, "for D.-E. Inghelbrecht, remembering hours of study both tumultuous and charming. His friend, Claude Debussy, May 1913."[78]

A Parisian of German-Swiss ancestry and originally an orchestral violinist, Inghelbrecht (1880–1965) and his wife became close friends of Claude and Emma Debussy in the last few years of the composer's life. Inghelbrecht was among the handful of mourners who comprised Debussy's funeral cortège in 1918. The following year Inghelbrecht presented two concerts at the Théâtre des Champs Elysées that consisted of a complete performance of all Debussy's works for orchestra, an event apparently never repeated since.[79]

On the subject of placing an emphasis on broad line over nuance, Inghelbrecht wrote, "The slightest page of Debussy poses interpretive problems that supersede the scrupulous placement of [rhythmic] values and sounds. Here a hypertrophy of nuances, a crudeness of accents taken to excess might deform the creative thought."[80] There is no "ideal" Debussy early conductor if not Inghelbrecht, although he himself cited André Messager, whom Debussy particularly admired for his conducting of *Pelléas et Mélisande,* as an important influence. Of Messager, Inghelbrecht wrote, "I have never dared to modify in the slightest detail the dispositions of questions he offered in his conducting, forcing myself always to follow his example. Messager knew that joy, so rare, of having succeeded in satisfying Debussy." And so too, as he must have perceived, did Inghelbrecht himself.

Another conductor who had a similar relationship with Debussy, Ernest Ansermet (1883–1969), suggested that an overemphasis on nuance at the expense of larger line is misguided: "If the conductor will make what we call 'expression,' it would be quite wrong. [Debussy] must be a very quiet line, a pure line and equal, because the expression is in the line."[81] Ansermet is noteworthy—doubtless the most important after Inghelbrecht among the early generation of recorded conductors—for his sense of propelling the structural line: "The conductor," he argued, "must understand that musical time is not metric time. The conductor doesn't beat time; he beats the cadence." As many have, Ansermet found his famous colleague Arturo Toscanini remarkable in his Debussy conducting, but excessively fast in his tempi.[82] The practitioner of a compelling but not furious tempo, and generally firm on the adherence to Debussy's score indications (despite a few instances where he amended the scores slightly), Ansermet found in Debussy "the testimony to a perfect equilibrium of the head and the heart, of spirit and sense. Debussy's work . . . instills an order within us by communicating its own, interior order."[83]

Ansermet had begun a career in mathematics before transferring to conducting. In 1918 he founded the Orchestre de la Suisse Romande, remaining its only permanent conductor until his retirement in 1966. He was introduced to Debussy in 1910, following the composer's conducting of "Rondes de printemps" from *Images.* The acquaintance deepened, apparently, after Debussy observed Ansermet's artistic success with Eric Satie's *Parade* in 1917.[84] Ansermet spent an afternoon in 1917 with Debussy, then desperately ill with the cancer that would prove fatal, discussing the *Nocturnes* at length and especially the corrections Debussy had made; Ansermet also recalled that tempi in several orchestral works were discussed. Authorized or not, Ansermet's changes in *La mer* did receive Debussy's approval, according to Ansermet's biographer François Hudry. A further proof that Ansermet paid careful attention to Debussy's expressed desires comes in a letter written by Jean Roger-Ducasse. Ducasse owned the fair copy of "Gigues" from the *Images* in 1939, and he shared information on certain readings in the score with Ansermet.[85]

Gustave Doret, who premiered the *Faune* with Debussy's collaboration in 1894, considered Arturo Toscanini the "unique conductor of the world." Toscanini's links with French music are important, and he claimed to have discussed orchestral performance issues with Debussy. Doret described Toscanini's intensive rehearsal technique but straightforward performance manner, a pattern Debussy and his closest compatriots called upon: "For three-fourths of an hour," Doret recalled, "Toscanini repeated the same measure to draw attention to exact [rhythmic] values, rests, accents, dissecting the work so that the musical material might be pure and without the terrible approximations of our era, which he refused to admit at any price."[86] However one might admire his care in rehearsal, one must remember Toscanini's questionable editing of Debussy, despite his rationale that the changes improved clarity. Moreover, Simon Trezise, in his Cambridge Music Handbook on *La mer,* finds the work as Toscanini recorded it "a noisier, more brilliant work than seems justified by the authority of the score or the illuminating Paris recordings" of Coppola, Pierné, and Inghelbrecht in the early 1930s.[87]

Regarding Debussy's ideals of orchestral sonority, Gustave Doret recalled the *Faune* premiere and the composer's interpretation: "It was so immaterial, so subtle. . . . Constantly Debussy modified this or that sonority of the orchestra."[88] Quite independently, the conductors Toscanini and Ansermet employed the analogy of "washing" when they spoke of their approach to clarifying the sonorities in Debussy performances. Milton Katims, a violist in the NBC Symphony Orchestra under Toscanini, recalled, "If the clarity wasn't there, he would say, 'Is dirty—we wash!'"[89] Ansermet expressed the analogy in a somewhat earthier tone: "You have before you a nice lady. She is of very good appearance—nice clothes and so on—but you don't know if, under the clothes, the underwears are clean. I can tell you my effort is to make clean the underwears!"[90]

The conductor Serge Koussevitzky's contributions to American music are widely respected. Less recognized, however, is his dissemination of the new French music beginning with Debussy. The composer had first heard and eagerly applauded Koussevitzky as he conducted a Moscow orchestra. As Elliott Galkin suggests, under Koussevitzky "the Boston Symphony became the most French orchestra in America, the balance among the sections elegantly defined, the vibrato spare, the rhythmic qualities lilting." Virgil Thomson, who studied in Paris in the period immediately following Debussy, acknowledged how the Boston Symphony under Koussevitzky "makes their sounds like Paris orchestras, thin and utterly precise, like golden wire and bright enamel."[91] Galkin speaks of the Debussyan qualities of "clarity of texture, lightness of articulation, and dance-like phrasing," and beyond Koussevitzky, Galkin recognizes the French-American maestros Pierre Monteux, Charles Munch, and Jean Morel at the Juilliard school, and Paul Paray in Detroit. To Galkin's list one must add Pierre Boulez, a remarkable conductor as well as composer whose tenure in the United States has virtually reacquainted audiences with French traditions and Debussyan thought. The 1991 Deutsche Gramophon compact disc recordings by Boulez of Debussy's orchestral works stand as the most important contemporary recordings that trace from the Debussy ideal, especially where relatively animated tempi and attention to structural line are involved. In addition, one must acknowledge Charles Dutoit and his conducting in Montreal and elsewhere.

TEMPO IN THE ORCHESTRAL MUSIC OF DEBUSSY

Beginning with *La mer,* Debussy began inserting metronome markings, providing them consistently throughout the orchestral *Images* and ballet *Jeux* (with the exception of "Gigues" from the *Images*). Two aesthetic urges compelled him to do this. The first was his evolution away from the highly nuanced music of the *Faune* and the *Nocturnes,* in which the linear sense is less driving and the abundant nuances of tempo make set metronome markings inappropriate; the second was his desire to maintain an alert tempo that in turn would propel the structural line. He nonetheless would quip to Durand that "You know my opinion of these metronome markings: they are good for just one measure, as 'roses last the length of a morning.'"[92] His depreciation notwithstanding, he clearly intended the metronome markings as general guides to his music. (Table 4.1 at the end of this chapter sets out the tempo nuances and metronome markings of Debussy's music, as well as the recorded tempi of conductors in Debussy's circle and the generation thereafter.)

THE CONDUCTORS' SENSE OF STRUCTURE

Among the orchestral works, perhaps *La mer* has most often been the subject of structural analysis. We briefly may relate the conductors' tempi for "De l'aube à midi sur la mer," part I of *La mer,* to the structural goals identified by major analysts. Debussy once remarked on the piano *Images,* series 2, to his friend Georges Jean-Aubry that the pianist Ricardo Viñes "must be persuaded to work hard on them, for he does not understand their architecture in spite of his virtuosity."[93] Likewise, conductors might well be viewed in light of how they project a structural understanding. Structural analyses of *La mer* part I, "De l'aube à midi sur la mer," may be outlined briefly:[94]

	Introduction	Part I	Part II	Coda
Marie Rolf	m. 1	31, 76 transition	85, 123 transition	133
Laurence Berman	m. 1	31	85	133
Jean Barraqué	m. 1	Ia. 31	Ib. 85, IIa. 113 IIb. 123	133

Referring to the preceding outline and to table 4.1 below, we can relate directly to the three most important early conductors who have left recordings, Coppola, Inghelbrecht, and Ansermet. In the build-up to the arrival at part I and the sustaining of its tempo, they attend to structural significance closely. At part II (or for the analyst Barraqué, part Ib), Coppola and Ansermet approach Debussy's indicated tempo reasonably closely, if slightly under. The important subdivision of part II at m. 85, "Presque lent," is captured most sensitively by Inghelbrecht, and again it is Inghelbrecht joined by Coppola who most closely approaches Debussy's "Très lent" (80 = eighth note) at the coda.

Throughout the earliest recordings, one is struck by the corresponding sensibilities of moment and structural line. That is, the interpreters closest to Debussy allow for nuance, especially in slow and ad libitum passages most prevalent in the *Faune* and *Nocturnes,* but strive for an alert tempo close to Debussy's metronome indications or at least close in spirit to his expressive indications. Although such passages are prominent in "Fêtes" of the *Nocturnes,* it is not until *La mer* that a propelling sense of line is apparent in Debussy and heard in these closely attuned conductors.

Since 1950, with the exception of Ansermet, Inghelbrecht, and more recently Boulez, conductors' tempi have sagged noticeably. At the same time, the sense of the exquisite moment is too seldom conveyed for the early scores, and nuance becomes note-to-note tedium. Many recordings of the *Faune* are notorious in this regard. The remarkable art of the early conductors lay in balancing the aesthetic tendencies of nuance and of structural linearity in Debussy's music.

In sum, while Coppola, Ansermet, and occasionally the other conductors studied drew close to Debussy's intent and articulated his structure through careful tempi, it was Inghelbrecht who demonstrated both the constancy of the alert passages and the reduced, supple tempi of the slow sections. Inghelbrecht indeed seems to be "of one blood" with Debussy in "De l'aube à midi sur la mer" and elsewhere in the recordings studied here; such is Inghelbrecht's high place among the orchestral conductors. The appreciation of Debussy would be well served indeed if the 1984 Erato compilation of Inghelbrecht interpretations, originally recorded from 1955 to 1962 on long-playing record, were to be reissued on compact disc.

SELECT DISCOGRAPHY

Note: For many of these recordings, the playback speed has been adjusted mechanically to A = 440, thus reflecting the actual pitch and tempo of the recording. Most of the 78-rpm recordings and some early 33-rpm recordings were mastered at excessive speeds, evidenced by an elevated pitch level. In order to compare the tempi, the playing speed thus had to be corrected.

Images pour orchestre: Ibéria, no. 1, "Par les rues et par les chemins"

Coppola, Piero. 1930. Grand Orchestre symphonique. Gramophone W 1052/4.

Inghelbrecht, Désiré-Emile. ca. 1965. Orchestre National de la Radiodiffusion Française. World Record Club T428.

Monteux, Pierre. 195?. San Francisco Symphony Orchestra. RCA Victor LM 1197.

Munch, Pierre. ca. 1968. Orchestre National de l'ORTF. Nonesuch.

Pierné, Gabriel. 1935. Orchestre des Concerts Colonne. Odéon 123.738/40.

Toscanini, Arturo. 1953. NBC Symphony Orchestra. Arkadia CDHP 529.1.

La mer

Ansermet, Ernest. 1964. Orchestre de la Suisse Romande. Decca CD 433 711-2 LM.

Coppola, Piero. 1928. Grand Orchestre Symphonique. Gramophone W 1022/24.

Inghelbrecht, Désiré-Emile. 1955–62. Orchestre National de France. Pathé-Marconi (reissued Erato 1984).

Koussevitzky, Serge. 1938–39. Boston Symphony Orchestra. Pearl CD LC1836.

Munch, Charles. 1959. Boston Symphony Orchestra. RCA Victor.

Toscanini, Arturo. 1953. NBC Symphony Orchestra. Arkadia CDHP 529.1.

Nocturnes, no. 1 "Nuages," and no. 2 "Fêtes"

Ansermet, Ernest. 1949. Orchestre de la Suisse Romande. London LLP 44.

Coppola, Piero. 1928. Orchestre Symphonique du Gramophone. Gramophone W947/49.

Inghelbrecht, Désiré-Emile. 1934. Grand Orchestre des Festivals Debussy. Pathé PDT 16/17.

Inghelbrecht, Désiré-Emile. 1955–62. Orchestre National de France. Pathé-Marconi (reissued Erato 1984).

Monteux, Pierre. No date. Paris Conservatory Orchestra. RCA Victrola VICS 1027.

Munch, Charles. 1963. Boston Symphony Orchestra. Victrola VICS 1391.

Toscanini, Arturo. 1952. NBC Symphony Orchestra. Arkadia CDHP 529.1.

Wolff, Albert. 1930. Orchestra de l'Association des Concerts Lamoureux. Polydor 566.054/55.

Pierné, Paul. 1930. L'Orchestre des Concerts Colonne. Odéon 123.642/43.

Prélude à l'après-midi d'un faune

Ansermet, Ernest. 1957. Orchestre de la Suisse Romande. Decca CD 433 711-2 LM.

Coppola, Piero. 1927. Orchestre Symphonique du Gramophone. Gramophone W 837.

Inghelbrecht, Désiré-Emile. 1955–62. Orchestre National de France. Pathé-Marconi (reissued Erato 1984).

Pierné, Paul. 1930. Orchestre des Concerts Colonne. Odéon 123.689.

Straram, Walter. 1930. Orchestre des Concerts Straram. Columbia LFX 30.

Toscanini, Arturo. 1953. NBC Symphony Orchestra. Arkadia CDHP 529.1.

Wolff, Albert. 1929. Orchestre des Concerts Lamoureux. Polydor 566 000.

Table 4.1. Debussy's Tempo Expressions as Interpreted by Major Conductors

	Prélude à l'après-midi d'un faune Debussy	Coppola	Wolff	Pierné	Ansermet	Inghelbrecht	Toscanini
		1927[a]	1929	1930	1957	1955–62	1953
m. 1	*très modéré*	94 (pulse)	96	87	90	95	114
3		94	98	86	90	95	114
11		92	100	87	93	96	112
21	*légèrement et expressif*	95	104	91	96	99	110
31		100	104	98	99	103	114
37	*en animant*	103	100	103	104	104	119
44	*toujours en animant*	106	104	115	111	111	137
51	*ler mouvt.*	94	98	92	90	94	100
55	*mème mouvt. et très soutenu*	54	59	58	49	45	47
63	*très expressif et très soutenu*	57	59	62	53	90	88
74		120	120	116	94	84	86
79	*mouvt. du début*	114	120	116	92	94	93
86	*ler mouvt.*	120	122	112	98	100	95
90	*dans le mouvt. plus animé*	68	65	69	49	98	120
94	*dans le ler mouvt. avec plus de lanqueur*	89	90	86	89	93	90
96		89	90	86	90	95	90
103	(*a tempo*)	94	85	80	93	90	116
106	*très lent et très retenu jusqu'à la fin*	88	75	70	90	80	85

(*Table continues*)

Table 4.1. (*Continued*)

	Nocturnes: "Nuages" Debussy	Coppola	Wolff	Inghelbrecht	Toscanini	Ansermet	Monteux	Munch
		1928[a]	1930	1934	1952	1949	195-	1963
m. 1	*modéré*	84	79	98	126	79	75	78
43		90	85	104	133	83	75	82
57		85	83	104	130	85	77	83
63	*un peu animé*	92	80	106	142	95	79	85
80	*primo tempo*	84	75	95	132	80	76	76
94	*plus lent*	80	72	90	123	75	69	75

	Nocturnes: "Fêtes" Debussy	Coppola	Pierné	Inghelbrecht	Toscanini	Ansermet	Monteux	Munch
		1928[a]	1930	1934	1952	1949	195-	1963
m. 1	*animé et très rythmé*	148	154	153	157	149	150	151
27	*un peu plus animé*	152	158	154	162	153	157	155
33		153	157	156	162	153	155	156
70		154	158	147	162	152	156	150
102		164	159	147	160	153	143	146
116	*modéré mais toujours très rythmé*	120	115	117	175	143	126	126
132	*un peu rapproché*	137	117	119	175	143	127	126
174	*primo tempo*	146	148	150	178	147	145	146
190–[m. 194]	*de plus en plus sonore et serrant le mouvt.*	153	148	151	169	145	147	169
208	*meme mouvt.*	158	152	149	169	145	145	147
244		138	153	147	160	141	137	160
252	*un peu retenu*	106	112	97	124	128	97	124
266	*a tempo*	144	145	152	168	145	149	168

	La mer, part I: "De l'aube à midi sur la mer" Debussy	Coppola	Koussevitzky	Inghelbrecht	Toscanini	Ansermet
		1928[a]	1938	1955–62	1953	1964
m. 1	*très lent* (116 = quarter note)	82	77	83	102	108
23	*animez peu à peu jusqu'à l'entrée du* $\frac{6}{8}$ [m. 31]	108	87	122	135	118
31	*modéré, sans lenteur (dans un rythme très souple* (116 = eighth note)	108	113	119	122	120
54	*au mouvt.* [preceded by *un peu animé*]		112	124	140	119
59	*cédez un peu*	97	95	108	91	98
77	*a tempo*	105	108	117	117	118
85	*très rythmé* (104 = quarter note)	96	94	89	80	100
98	*au mouvt.* (*un peu plus mouvementé*)	99	90	92	93	94
105		103	104	60	80	80
119	*presque lent*	88	68	54	61	90
122	*très modéré* (104 = quarter note)	82	74	80	72	101
133	*très lent* (80 = eighth note)	77	65	71	67	68

(*Table continues*)

Table 4.1. (*Continued*)

	Images: Movement 1, "Par les rues et par les chemins" Debussy	Coppola	Pierné	Ansermet	Inghelbrecht	Toscanini	Monteux	Munch
		1933[a]	1935	1949	1955–62	1953	195-	1959
m. 1	*assez animé (dans un rythme alerte mais précis)* (eighth note = 176)	172	160	156	166	164	140	165
98	*a tempo*	171	160	156	161	164	137	170
122	*meno mosso, poco a poco*	165	136	153	153	150	131	160
139	*librement expressif*	165	140	147	151	147	130	160
178	*modéré bien rythmé* (eighth note = 144)	142	157	136	137	138	128	162
186	*a tempo* (eighth note = 132)	140	134	116	124	132	112	153
212	*expressif et souple* (eighth note = 132, *pour commencer*)	137	127	116	123	129	120	134
234	*primo tempo* (eighth note = 176)	170	162	149	162	160	143	166
272	[recapitulation, truncated]	178	167	160	164	164	153	172
313	*a tempo* (*sans presser*)	170	146	154	153	160	144	158

[a]Date of recording.

Chapter 5 Debussy and Early Debussystes at the Piano

Cecilia Dunoyer

If the music of Claude Debussy still mystifies our minds and ears at the close of the twentieth century, we can only imagine what a disconcerting effect it must have had on Debussy's contemporaries. In her journal the sophisticated Marguerite Baugnies de Saint-Marceaux noted on 21 February 1908: "[Ricardo] Viñes plays the piano—a new thing by Debussy, *La lune qui sur le temple fut* or some similar title. This master composer presents to his audience in all seriousness the harmonies that a cat walking on the keyboard would have created. Truly, he is pulling our leg [Il se paie notre tête]."[1] A more humble and awed reaction to Debussy's art were the words of Jules Massenet, "Debussy is the enigma," as well as those of Marguerite Long, one of the few pianists contemporary with Debussy who performed his works to the composer's satisfaction: "Little by little, I was entering the enchanted forest."[2]

This chapter delves into aspects pertaining to the performance of

Because of the general availability of Debussy scores, discussions of scores and tempi will not be accompanied by music examples. However, having the scores at hand while reading this chapter is recommended.

Debussy's piano music from an essentially historical perspective. I begin with Debussy as a pianist and interpreter of music, referring to the many recollections by Debussy's contemporaries. In addition, a recent compact disc reproduction of Debussy's Welte-Soehne piano rolls recordings of November 1913, produced by Kenneth Caswell, greatly enhances our appreciation of Debussy's own performances. This remarkable recording bears witness to the composer's keen and highly personal pianistic style.[3] The extensive collection of published letters provides a diary of Debussy's candid thoughts about musicians of his time, especially about early performances of his music. The famous Italian pianist Alfredo Casella summed it up: "Himself so incomparable an executant, Debussy was extremely exacting of the interpreters of his works. Rarely indeed have I ever seen him fully satisfied with a performance. He detested almost all the greatly celebrated 'virtuosi.'"[4] "A faithful interpreter is all I need" he retorted when an artist of "great genius" was suggested to him for the role of Mélisande.[5]

His unforgiving attitude toward the pianists of his time is sometimes so extreme that it borders on the humorous, while still giving important clues about his aesthetic intentions. A study of the performances and writings by the early "Debussystes" on this most elusive repertoire constitutes the second part of this chapter. These pianists include Walter Rummel, Marguerite Long, Ricardo Viñes, Alfred Cortot, George Copeland, and E. Robert Schmitz, who were the first to introduce Debussy's music to more or less receptive audiences. All had personal or professional contacts with the composer. Their recordings in the early days of the phonograph established a historical foundation for performances of this music.

Debussy's evaluation of himself as a pianist was hardly more forgiving than his evaluation of other pianists. In an interview in February 1914, Debussy admitted: "I am not a great pianist." When his interviewer argued that people believe "your Preludes when you perform them, are a . . . revelation!" Debussy retorted: "Let them talk. . . . It's true that I can adequately perform some of the Preludes, the easiest ones. But the others . . . make me quiver."[6] More revealing, however, are the innumerable and concurring accounts of Debussy's playing, on the one hand, and the marvelously well-preserved recordings of it, on the other. It is those two sources that undoubtedly give genuine insights into Debussy's conception of his own piano music and show how unique was his technical approach. "His hands were large, bony, with square finger tips; his playing was sonorous and sometimes very tender and singing."[7]

Debussy's accomplishments as a pianist are worth noting. While still at the Conservatoire in the days of Antoine Marmontel (from 1872 to 1879), between the ages of ten and seventeen, Debussy performed such works as J. S. Bach's

Chromatic Fantasy and Fugue, Beethoven's Sonata Op. 111, Weber Sonatas, Chopin's Sonatas in B Minor and B-flat Minor, Chopin's F Minor Concerto, Chopin's Fantaisie and G Minor Ballade, Mendelssohn's D Minor Concerto, and so on.[8] Soon, however, Debussy's gifts led him toward his own discoveries and a very personal style as pianist. Two of his classmates, Raymond Bonheur (1861–1939) and Gabriel Pierné (1863–1937), described their friend at the piano: "We all know what an incomparable player he was of his works, always expressing an extraordinary feeling of life and movement. . . . But it was when he would play a sketch of a piece in progress, still caught up in the heat of improvisation that he was truly prodigious."[9] And in Pierné's words: "In the piano class of Marmontel he would astonish us with his bizarre playing. I could not tell whether it was out of natural clumsiness or shyness, but he would literally throw himself into the keyboard and exaggerate all musical effects. He seemed to be in a rage at the instrument, acting with impulsive gestures. . . . These faults would gradually taper off and he would occasionally achieve effects of quite gorgeous tenderness. With all his faults and good qualities, his playing remained something highly unusual."[10]

Other accounts, one by Debussy's friend Léon-Paul Fargue, described how compelling the composer's improvisational style was: "Debussy would sit at the piano . . . and start to improvise. Anyone who knew him can remember what it was like. He would start by brushing the keys . . . then he would sink into velvet. . . . He gave the impression of delivering the piano of its sound." Mary Garden, Debussy's first Mélisande, also spoke highly of Debussy's improvisations: "After dinner . . . for an hour or so he would improvise. . . . I have never heard such music in my life, such music as came from the piano at those moments. How beautiful it was. . . . Debussy never put those improvisations down on paper."[11]

An improvisatory feeling was the single most important characteristic of Debussy's playing style and hence a quality we must seek most when interpreting his music. The composer confessed with great delight, referring to a rehearsal of *Ibéria,* that it was the improvisational quality of the passage in question that he found so appealing. In a letter to his close friend André Caplet, dated 26 February 1910, Debussy wrote: "You cannot believe how naturally the transition from 'Parfums de la nuit' and 'Le matin d'un jour de fête' flowed. *It sounded as though it was improvised.*"[12]

This improvisational quality is quite evident upon hearing Debussy's performance of five of his Preludes from Book I recorded for the Welte-Soehne piano rolls in November 1913. Four of those five Preludes ("Le vent dans la plaine" was the exception) were given their first public performance by Debussy at the Société Nationale on 25 May 1910. From the opening measures of "Danseuses de Delphes," we hear what appears to be a spontaneous and effortless flow of musical ideas emanating from the instrument. Debussy's velvety touch truly creates a sound that seems to float away from a piano "without hammers." The sensual chords gently envelop the simple melodic line in a homogenous halo of harmony. The tempo is utterly satisfying: it neither drags nor shows any trace of impatience. Keeping in mind that overall tempo is unreliable on piano rolls because the playback depends on the speed at which the roll is set, we can hear that Debussy's tempo in this recording is quite a bit slower than that indicated in the Durand score. Instead of quarter note = 44, it is closer to eighth note = 63 (performance time is 2 minutes, 58 seconds).[13] His overall pulse is fairly consistent. Debussy ever so slightly relaxes the end of phrases and imperceptibly pushes ahead on the strings of descending eighth-note chords. Pedaling is such that the harmonies are kept clear, hardly ever overlapping.

The same compelling balance is found in his performance of "La cathédrale engloutie," discussed below. "La danse de Puck" is exactly *capricieux et léger.* Debussy is so absolutely at ease technically that we are hardly aware of the notes or the mechanics of piano playing. The subtleties in pedaling, a remarkable lightness of touch, and tempo flexibility are mastered to such a degree that one can only be charmed by the whimsical, elusive, and delicious fantasy of Puck, the sprite from *A Midsummer Night's Dream.* The tempo is swift. Although Debussy opens in a comfortable eighth note = 144–52, the rest of the Prelude favors the tempo of the first *pressez* at m. 14. *Au mouv't* sections are consistently eighth note = 192–200, until the last ten measures, where the *retenu* and the *plus retenu* three measures later slow the "Danse de Puck" to eighth note = 132–38 (performance time is 2 minutes, 10 seconds). As to pedaling, Debussy establishes a sharp contrast between the seven-measure opening dotted rhythm played without pedal and the rest of the piece, which bathes in an atmospheric wash of sound. The dynamic level throughout is understated, so that individual chords remain clear, even though pedaling is generous.

"Minstrels" is playful, awkward; it stops and starts spontaneously. The performance sounds rhythmically clumsy occasionally, which makes it more difficult than usual to indicate a specific metronomic pulse (roughly quarter note = 104 to 116, with an overall performance time of 1 minute, 42 seconds). Is it a technical shortcoming on the part of Debussy, or rather a deliberate interpretative choice? I opt for the latter, for the composer did indicate "nerveux et avec humour" on the score, and his performance emphasizes just that. That he might have been nervous in the recording studio is feasible. However, Debussy showed great control in the other works recorded on the same roll, proof that he was able to overcome nerves. The crude buffoonery of these music-hall performers is what amused Debussy and clearly what he wanted in his performance of this Prelude, which Marguerite Long described as exhibiting the flavor of a Toulouse-Lautrec.[14]

In "Le vent dans la plaine," the lightness and evenness of the fast pianissimo sixteenth notes is dazzling. Debussy's pulse is impeccably consistent throughout (quarter note = 126), hardly even wavers on the *Cédez* moments (performance time of 1 minute, 55 seconds). It is as even as "Minstrels" was awkward, which supports this opinion that rhythmic clumsiness there was indeed deliberate. His foot is as light as his fingers: the occasional melody is heard clearly, never blurred or intruding in any way on the atmosphere already created by the harmonic background. As Alfredo Casella wrote: "No words can give an idea of the way in which he played certain of his own *Preludes.* Not that he had actual virtuosity, but his sensibility of touch was incomparable; he made the impression of playing directly on the strings of the instrument with no intermediate mechanism; the effect was a miracle of poetry."[15]

The most revealing aspect of Debussy's recording of *Children's Corner* is his choice of tempi. Every movement seems faster than one is accustomed to hearing nowadays. Again, for the reader's reference, I shall indicate timing and approximate metronome markings for each movement. "Doctor Gradus ad Parnassum" opens swiftly at quarter note = 160. The several *retenu* measures are hardly slower, and instead yield subtly to the next section. The "en animant peu à peu" coda picks up speed, ending at an exciting quarter note = 200. This performance is concluded in 1 minute, 46 seconds, making it the fastest known to this study. Cortot's recording is a close second at 1 minute, 52 seconds! (Of the early Debussystes here discussed, Cortot is the only one to have recorded *Children's Corner.*) Here Debussy is more generous with pedal than usual: this "Doctor Gradus" is far from Clementi's infamous collection of finger exercises and études of the same name, and closer to a wash of C major sounds strategically accented with augmented chords and other harmonic touches of color.

"Jimbo's Lullaby" starts slowly (half note = 44) and gently moves along to settle at half note = 60 at the *un peu plus mouvementé,* m. 39. After the *retenu* (m. 61), the ending indicated *1o tempo* is actually still half note = 60. The timing is 3 minutes, 3 seconds, compared to Cortot's faster lullaby of 2 minutes, 25 seconds. There appear to be greater discrepancies of tempi between different performances of this movement of *Children's Corner* than in any of the other pieces in the set, which makes Debussy's Welte-Soehne roll an all the more welcomed reference here. The pedal indication by Debussy at m. 9 ("les 2 Péd.") is worth noting, a rare instance of such markings. The pedal-release symbol does not appear until the end of m. 14.

"Serenade of the Doll" is another example of a surprisingly fast tempo, compared to contemporary and older recordings of this piece. Interestingly enough, both Debussy and Cortot play this "Serenade" in 1 minute, 46 seconds. "Léger et gracieux," as indicated on the score, well describes Debussy's beautiful interpretation of the "Serenade." His touch is so delicate that the accompaniment does not seem as fast as quarter note = 184–92, and the melodic material, gently brought out like clear magical bells, is in keeping with the *allegretto ma non troppo* tempo indication at the top. Debussy's pedaling must account for the delicious sheen on every single note, and the roundness of the sound overall, which is never dry or staccato. Cortot, by comparison, is much more present in his attack, more percussive. As respectable as his recording is, it does not have the fairylike, elusive quality of Debussy's.

"The Snow Is Dancing" exhibits a frequent tendency with Debussy to incrementally accelerate throughout the piece. Starting at quarter note = 116, this movement gradually picks up speed to end at quarter note = 138–44. Here too, Debussy's control of the constant sixteenth-note background is remarkable: one observes an evenness not only of meter but of touch and dynamics, especially. The balance between long notes and bits of melodic material, and the constant "snow dancing," is always clear. The performance time is 2 minutes, 6 seconds, while Cortot's is 2 minutes, 20 seconds.

"The Little Shepherd" is played as simply as the title suggests. There are two distinct and consistent tempi: the opening melody and all its corresponding sections are at quarter note = 112–16, and the *plus mouvementé* passages are quite agitated at quarter note = 192. Pedaling is light and never interferes with the simple narration of the story. The overall time, faster than most recordings, is 1 minute, 46 seconds. Cortot plays the piece in 2 minutes, 12 seconds: he takes many more liberties with rubati and uses a more declamatory style.

The "Golliwog's Cakewalk" recording is very much in the spirit of Debussy's interpretation of "Minstrels": clumsy, rhythmically awkward, indulgent rubati at the *cédez,* and as crude as the "Serenade of the Doll" was delicate. The overall pulse is quarter note = 100–104, and his timing is 2 minutes, 42 seconds. Different interpretations of "Golliwog's Cakewalk" do not vary in tempo as much as the rest of *Children's Corner.* Cortot's time, for example, is 2 minutes, 35 seconds.[16]

Debussy's recording of *Children's Corner* exhibits faster tempi as a whole, to be sure. As mentioned above, although we must keep our perspective as to the authenticity of overall tempi when playing piano rolls, we can feel confident that relative tempi within and between pieces are dependable. Moreover, I believe that since every aspect of Kenneth Caswell's reproduction of the Welte-Soehne rolls was handled with such care, musical knowledge, and sensitivity, we can assume that the tempi are as close to authentic as one could hope for.

Finally, mention should be made of the four songs Debussy recorded with Mary Garden in 1904. These are the only acoustical recordings Debussy made, and as such, they are treasured. In all fairness to the performers, and as a pianist myself, I have strong reservations about making a fair assessment of these performances from the recordings. More than ninety years old, these reproductions of the composer's interpretations are so faded and blurred by scratches and extramusical background noises that they hardly do justice to the artistry of both singer and pianist. That said, what little we can hear of Debussy's playing is quite consistent with the lightness of touch and clarity exhibited on the Welte-Soehne rolls, and thus, the 1904 engravings confirm the findings described above.

Not only do the Welte-Soehne rolls give us a moving appreciation of Debussy the pianist, but they also reveal significant divergences from the Durand 1910 edition of Debussy's piano music, which until recently had been pianists' only source, in spite of the fact that its numerous mistakes and misprints were a constant cause of frustration. These musical differences include dramatic tempo changes, as in the famous case of "La cathédrale engloutie," as well as added chords, notes, and accidentals, and changed figurations and even harmonies.

But we shall never know for sure whether the variants on the piano rolls are spontaneous improvisations on Debussy's part or definite corrections to be made to the printed score. For example, two variants are found in "Danseuses de Delphes" and "La cathédrale engloutie."[17] The first, from "Danseuses de Delphes," is textural. In the Durand score, the left-hand off-beat chords that start at m. 6 suddenly vanish at mm. 8–9. Yet Debussy's Welte-Soehne performance clearly has a much fuller and lower-sounding chord at mm. 8–9 than the score indicates. Interestingly enough, later in the piece, at mm. 16–17, the corresponding texture played by Debussy is reflected in the Durand edition, suggesting that the composer's intentions were what he recorded on the roll as opposed to the printed score. This suggestion is indicated in the *Oeuvres complètes.*

The problem of the time signature and tempo in "La cathédrale engloutie" has engulfed many a pianist and critic. The choice of tempo has offered an endless dilemma ever since the printed edition came out. The problem stems from the misleading $\frac{6}{4} = \frac{3}{2}$ time signature. Every pianist has struggled with the fact that if the tempo of the $\frac{6}{4}$ bars is satisfying, the $\frac{3}{2}$ bars are deathly slow. If the $\frac{3}{2}$ bars move comfortably, the $\frac{6}{4}$ bars are rushed and hasty, which is inconsistent with Debussy's indication at the top: "Profondément calme." The Welte-Soehne roll puts this insoluble dilemma to rest in revealing that Debussy unequivocally plays the $\frac{3}{2}$ bars as though they were $\frac{3}{4}$, and precisely as though m. 7 were preceded by half note = quarter note, m. 13 by quarter note = half note, and m. 22 by half note = quarter note again. Charles Burkhart discussed this issue in an article on the composer's rolls and subsequent recordings of other pianists[18] Debussy's revealing tempi relations, indicated in the *Oeuvres complètes* as well as in Schirmer's recent edition,[19] make such indisputable musical sense that surely they need not be justified further. For the skeptics, let us add that other pianists, such as Alfred Cortot and George Copeland, opted for Debussy's solution, both having heard Debussy play. Gina Bachauer, who studied with Cortot, also follows this model. But there are great artists renowned for their French music affinities, in particular E. Robert Schmitz, Walter Gieseking, and Robert Casadesus, who went to extraordinary pains to make the $\frac{6}{4} = \frac{3}{2}$ work literally. Because of their great artistry, the result is not "deathly," especially in the case of Gieseking, but it appears not to be the "Cathédrale" Debussy envisioned.

Again, the key issue here is tempo relations between the $\frac{6}{4}$ and $\frac{3}{2}$ sections and not the actual overall tempo, which ranges from quarter note = 60 for the six opening and closing measures, to half note = 80 at the *un peu moins lent,* m. 47 (overall performance time is 4 minutes, 56 seconds). Noteworthy interpretative choices on the part of Debussy include his moving along at m. 7, when *doux et fluide* push the half-note pulse to 69. At m. 16, *peu à peu sortant de la brume* pushes the tempo farther, to quarter note = 72. It is not until m. 30 or so that it slows down again progressively to a quiet half note = 60 at mm. 40–46. In the faster section alluded to above (mm. 47ff), Debussy highlights the five chords marked by "-" (m. 63) by playing them distinctively slower (half note = 60). The last section, *au mouv't* (m. 72), is back up to a pulse of half note = 72–76.

Finally, one last testimony to Debussy's tempo intentions in "La cathédrale engloutie" is the orchestration of the work in 1917 by Debussy's long-time friend Henri Büsser, which proves to be consistent with Debussy's tempi relationships.

For the many piano works for which Debussy performances do not exist, Roy Howat, editor of the Preludes in the *Oeuvres complètes,* admits:

> One of the worst and most mystifying problems we had to face in the editing task was the virtually complete loss of Debussy's own printed piano scores, from which he played at concerts and other occasions such as the Welte sessions. Some vanished even during his life, as presents or to pay debts, but the worst loss was after his death. . . .

One of his only traced printed piano scores is of the second book of Preludes, which Debussy gave in May 1913 to the pianist Fernand Lamy. This was only a month after the book's publication, but already it reveals a few dozen corrections inked in Debussy's meticulous hand. From that, and from similarly annotated orchestral scores that survive, we can guess the probable density of corrections marked in other scores, now lost, which he had used for much longer.[20]

Debussy was extremely meticulous and precise in his musical indications, and therefore he expected nothing short of faithful readings on the part of his interpreters. But there are three subjects about which Debussy relied on performers' common sense and musical intelligence: fingering, pedaling, and exact tempo, as indicated by metronome markings. About the latter, he expressed his point of view in no uncertain terms to Jacques Durand, in a letter dated 9 October 1915: "You know what I think about metronome marks: they're right for a single bar . . . only there are 'those' who don't hear music and who take these marks as an authority to hear it still less! But do what you please."[21] The very few metronome markings reluctantly indicated were usually encouraged by his publisher.

Pedaling in Debussy's music is an essential and much debated topic. The composer's own feelings about it are described again in a letter to his publisher, dated 1 September 1915: "He [Chopin] recommended practicing without pedal and, in performance, not holding it down, except in very rare instances. It was the same way of turning the pedal into a kind of breathing, which I observed in Liszt when I had the chance to hear him in Rome. I feel Saint-Saëns forgets that pianists are poor musicians, for the most part, and cut music up into unequal lumps, like a chicken. The plain truth perhaps is that abusing the pedal is only a means of covering up a lack of technique, and that making a lot of noise is a way to drown the music you're slaughtering!"[22]

The closest Debussy comes to pedaling advice is to use it as "a kind of breathing." Any discussion of pedal is intimately connected to one of pianos, and especially so in the case of Debussy because of the nature of both his music and the instruments of the period. "Pedaling cannot be written down, it varies from one instrument to another, from one room, or one hall, to another" he explained.[23] French pianos at the turn of the century were very different from the highly resonant contemporary American Steinways, which is not to say that our Steinways are inappropriate for Debussy's music. Rather, it is a reminder that we must be aware of and sensitive to Debussy's sound aesthetic when playing on our modern instruments. "Faites confiance à vos oreilles" was his overriding advice (trust your ears).[24] Even if the composer had indicated specific pedaling instructions (which he did not), they would have to be carefully reconsidered and adapted to suit *his* sound.[25]

Debussy wanted very clear sonorities, "de la clareté avant toute chose," never muddy nor fuzzy, and he strongly disliked "making a lot of noise." Creating color in sound is central to his aesthetic, as evidenced by his orchestrations, and pedaling is a means to this end. Also, the long sustained bass notes in his piano scores are to be interpreted as a sort of pedaling indication.

This brings up the topic of the third (or middle) pedal, which did not exist on European (French or German) pianos of the time. For some, this mere practical limitation is a determining argument against using the middle pedal at all in Debussy's piano music. I believe Debussy would have used the middle pedal if it had been available to him, for it offers a new range of possibilities that are particularly well suited to Debussy's music. As Cortot described: "He made use of the pedal and especially of a blend of both pedals with infinite artistry."[26] Cortot's words echo those of Casella: "He used the pedals in a way all his own."[27] It is, after all, a distinction of great composers to exceed the possibilities of the instruments of their time—Beethoven is a celebrated example from a century earlier.

Because Debussy's pianos were not as sonorous and had less sustaining power, long pedals were more appropriate then, even though the composer in no uncertain terms warned pianists not to overdo it. On the contemporary Steinway, such long pedals may obliterate the clarity and harmonic subtleties of this music. The bass in particular is overpowering compared to the turn-of-the-century Pleyel, Erard, and even their German contemporaries like Bechstein and Blüthner, so that long pedals must be understood as half and quarter pedals and all shades in between. Debussy expected the foot to be intimately attuned to the ear and a rich sound palette. He advised performers, for instance, "to depress the pedal before starting to play, so that the overtones would vibrate immediately upon contact."[28] The middle pedal, used ingeniously, greatly enhances not only the coloristic possibilities of the instrument but also the control of dynamic layers. Debussy made his "layered conception" clear when he notated all of the Preludes from Book II and *Images* II over three staves, instead of the customary two. The clarity of the various "layers" of musical material is compelling in Debussy's own recorded performances, which never rise above moderate dynamic levels and illustrate the importance Debussy attributed to the "beauty of the sound."[29]

The pianos that Debussy actually owned are of great interest. Although most pianists in France were attached to French pianos, beginning with Chopin, Debussy apparently made exceptions. In his memoirs, Casella wrote of a week when he and Debussy read through much two-piano music, including a transcription of *Ibéria:* "For our rehearsals, he had the Bechstein upright moved from his studio into the living-room, beside the grand piano."[30] Maurice Dumesnil, who played for Debussy at the latter's home on the Avenue du Bois de Boulogne, described how "in the middle of the room the black Blüthner grand stood, free of music, books or photographs."[31] Debussy was particularly fond of this Blüthner (Aliquotflügel) because it had an extra set of strings set on top of the others, which, although not touched by the hammers, would vibrate sympathetically and enrich the sonority. This would produce an effect similar to, and even richer than, that of depressing the pedal before starting to play, which Debussy recommended. The Blüthner, now in the Musée Labenche in Brive, was purchased in Jersey in 1904, according to Dolly de Tinan, Debussy's stepdaughter. Raoul Bardac, her brother, was also positive about the presence of both the Bechstein and the Blüthner in Debussy's home.[32] Debussy's instruments of choice were apparently German. Nevertheless, other accounts allude to a Pleyel upright which had been given by the "manufacturer, always generous towards artists."[33] This is confirmed by George Copeland, who also played for Debussy and described a room which had a Pleyel upright piano.[34]

As to fingerings, composers rarely give specific instructions. But Debussy makes it clear that they are not his responsibility and prints on the first page of Volume I of his *Etudes:* "Our old Masters,—I mean 'our' admirable clavecinistes—never indicated any fingering, trusting without a doubt the ingenuity of their contemporaries. Doubting that of our modern virtuosos would be out of place. . . . Let us find our own fingerings!"[35] Nevertheless, Debussy is usually very specific about which hand is supposed to handle which note, or group of notes. Examples abound where the composer indicated *m. d.* or *m. g.* (r. h. or l. h.), especially when such indications affect a phrasing or a musical inflection. In the Etude "Pour les agréments," at the bottom of the page, Debussy even writes "take the note over with the right hand, without sounding it." Such directions are akin to fingerings in that they advise the performer on how to distribute the score between the hands, which ultimately reflects the composer's musical intentions. In some of the sketches of the Etudes, Debussy did indicate occasional numerical fingerings, specifically in "Pour les tierces" and "Pour les notes repétées."[36] In the letter to Jacques Durand cited above, Debussy wrote: "I'll see you again and be able to play you these Etudes, which are giving your fingers such a fright. . . . I may say there are certain passages which sometimes bring mine to a halt too. Then I have to get my breath back as though I'd been climbing a flight of stairs. . . . In truth this music wheels above the peaks of performance!"[37]

Debussy was unusually pleased with his Etudes, a sentiment he very rarely expressed about any of his compositions: "I've invested a lot of passion and faith in the future of the *Etudes.* I hope you will like them, as much for the music they contain as for what they represent," he wrote to his publisher, Durand, on 28 August 1915.[38] Some of the Etudes had been premiered on 21 November 1916 by George Copeland, and on 14 December 1916 by Walter Rummel. Even so, Gabriel Fauré, then director of the Paris Conservatoire, asked Debussy in a letter dated 25 April 1917 to perform his Etudes at a concert of the Société Nationale at the end of May. "It is in my name and in the name of all your friends that I take the liberty to make such a request! But you know what joy you would cause if you accepted."[39] On 29 April Debussy replied: "My hesitation in answering your kind letter, dear *maître* and friend, stems from the humble reason that I do not know how to play the piano well enough anymore to risk a performance of my *Etudes.* . . . In public I get a special phobia: there are too many keys; I don't have enough fingers anymore; and suddenly I don't remember where the pedals are! It is sad and perfectly nerve wrecking. Believe me, I am not being a bad sport, for I would have particularly liked to please you."[40]

Debussy's last public performance as a pianist was on 5 May 1917 at the Salle Gaveau, when he played his Violin Sonata with Gaston Poulet and accompanied Rose Féart in some of his songs. Eighty years later, our only ears into Debussy's pianistic genius are through such comments as Igor Stravinsky's "How well that man played!"[41] Stravinsky was referring not only to Debussy's own music but also to the now famous sight-reading by both composers of *Le sacre du printemps* in piano-duet version.

There is no doubt that Debussy's extremely high artistic standards and occasionally cynical temperament did not allow him objectively to assess, much less praise, others' attempts to perform his works. "Debussy was the most violent of all the critics I ever met," wrote Harold Bauer, a Francophile American pianist and the contemporary of Marguerite Long, Ravel, and Cortot.[42] But of all performing artists, it seems as though pianists were prime targets for comments that expressed great sarcasm at best—"He did not miss a note, it was awful!" he exclaimed upon returning from a pianist's recital—and utter disgust at worst: "We are so often betrayed by those so-called pianists! Believe me, you cannot imagine to what extent my piano music has been deformed, to such a degree that I often hesitate to recognize it!" complained a letter to Varèse dated 12 July 1910.[43] In all of his correspondence, few kind words can be found toward pianists. The only known exceptions include comments addressed to Long and Walter Rummel. Debussy's most enthusiastic response to a pianist, however, is found in a letter sent from Saint-Jean-de-Luz on 27 September 1917 to Durand about Francis Planté, then seventy-eight years old: "Let me tell you about F. Planté who came to Saint-Jean-de-Luz recently and gave two concerts. . . . This man is prodigious. He played—very well—the 'Toccata' [from *Pour le piano*], *Feux Follet* by Liszt, marvelously well, too. He will play, at the second concert: 'Reflets dans l'eau,' 'Mouvement' and asked for my advice."[44] However, in Saint-Jean-de-Luz that same summer Debussy wrote to his friend Désiré-Emile Inghelbrecht: "Here we are in the delightful Basque country. . . . There are a lot of famous pianists in the area including R. Viñes, J. Nin, Mme. M. Long, etc. . . . but I have the advantage of staying in an outlying part of the town, so I don't hear them."[45] In the same vein he had confided to Jacques Durand (from Eastbourne, 26 July 1905) twelve summers earlier: "It's a charming, peaceful spot. . . . What a wonderful place to work . . . ! No noise, no pianos, or only delightful mechanical ones"[46]

Curiously, most of the early Debussystes wax eloquent on their personal connections, if not intimate friendships with Debussy, who never reciprocated those claims. If Debussy tended to exaggerate his contempt for pianists, they, in turn, tended to overstate their intimacy with the composer. Whether it be through Viñes's diaries, Long's book, or Copeland's writings, one is led to believe that Debussy felt only pride, gratitude, and delight toward these performers. It is not so. The only two pianists toward whom we can document Debussy's genuine satisfaction are Walter Rummel and Marguerite Long.

Walter Rummel (1887–1953) was a pianist and composer born in Berlin of a German father and an American mother. His childhood was spent mostly in Berlin, except for three years in Washington, D.C., between 1901 and 1904. By the age of twenty-two, Rummel decided to settle in Paris, "yielding to the attraction of the modern school of Debussy and Ravel."[47] Rummel does not figure much in any of Debussy's biographies even though he seems to have been one of the few pianists chosen by the composer. "He had a pianist friend, Walter Rummel, who used to come to him and play the Bach chorales," reminisced Ernest Ansermet in an interview about his meeting with Debussy in 1917.[48]

Following a recital by Rummel, Debussy wrote on 28 June 1917:

> Cher ami, you have forgiven me, I am sure, for not coming to congratulate you at the end of your last recital? . . . One does not congratulate a sunset, nor does one congratulate the sea for being more beautiful than a cathedral! You are a force of nature . . . and, like her, you move from the grandest to the smallest apparently without effort. This is why you can understand the soul of the great Sebastian Bach as well as that of the little Claude Debussy, in such a way that, for a moment, they appear to be

on the same level in the mind of the audience. . . . For this and everything else, may you be thanked profusely, my dear friend, and believe in the affection of your old friend C. D.[49]

Charles Timbrell's ongoing interest in Rummel has brought to light valuable information that suggests Debussy actually showed Rummel a great deal of esteem. Unfortunately, of the six pianists discussed here, Rummel is the only one who did not leave behind any recordings of Debussy's piano music. Hence, we are all the more curious about this "prince of virtuosos," as Debussy dubbed him in a letter to Godet on 31 October 1917. Rummel's playing can be heard, however, on a number of recordings (made in 1943 for the most part) of Chopin, Liszt, and his own numerous Bach transcriptions of Chorale Preludes, as well as the B-flat minor Prelude and Fugue (*Well-Tempered Clavier,* Book I).[50] From these we can hear a musician with a strong temperament who had a wonderful control of sonorities and rubato in Chopin, a lyrical approach, and an effortless technique. His playing of Bach expresses quiet serenity with a limpid singing tone that would probably have pleased Debussy. Nevertheless, we should be hesitant to draw conclusions about his playing of Debussy's music from these recordings. I would venture that some of the liberties Rummel takes with Chopin and Bach's scores (especially at the end of the Prelude and Fugue, where he adds low basses and thickens chords) are not particularly in agreement with what we know of Debussy's rigorous expectations of performers. Since we will never be able to assess with our own ears his interpretations of Debussy, and since Debussy respected him so highly, we shall focus on a number of significant facts and circumstances surrounding the two musicians.

Rummel shared with Debussy a passionate interest in French music of the past, which culminated in his editing two anthologies, one of seventeenth-century French songs and the other of troubadour songs. Even though Rummel was a composer, his musical taste was very much for the past. He did not play any contemporary music except for Debussy, which makes his keen interest in championing it all the more intriguing. All told, Rummel performed the premiere of at least ten Debussy piano works, including five Preludes, "Ce qu'a vu le vent d'ouest" (Book I, no. 7), "Ondine" (Book II, no. 8), "Hommage à S. Pickwick Esq." (Book II, no. 9), "Canope" (Book II, no. 10), and "Les tierces alternées" (Book II, no. 11).[51]

On 14 December 1916, Rummel gave the first public performance of two (and possibly four) of the *Douze Etudes.*[52] From the letter quoted below, we can infer that one of them was "Pour les octaves." With his first wife, Thérèse

Chaigneau, he also premiered the two-piano piece *En blanc et noir* on 22 January 1916. Outside of France, Rummel was responsible for the American premiere of four Preludes (of which no. 7 was a world premiere) from Book I on 26 July 1910 in Stockbridge, Massachusetts. And finally, he gave the only known public performance in Debussy's lifetime of the entire set of Preludes, Book II, at the Aeolian Hall in London on 12 June 1913. Four of the twelve were the premieres listed above. In addition, Rummel often performed the two sets of *Images* and soon added *L'isle joyeuse* and *Estampes* to his repertoire.

Of great interest in the relationship between Debussy and Rummel are a number of letters which display a warm and friendly tone. That Debussy addressed him as "Mon cher Rummel" is worth noting, as the "Mon cher" was reserved for only a chosen few. Later, Debussy addressed him as "Cher ami," also a mark of respect. On 5 September 1916, two months before the premiere of the Etudes, Debussy candidly shared with Rummel his state of mind: "Cher ami . . . I am reduced to playing solitaire or to trying to play the *Etudes,* and I am more successful at the former than the latter. Are you still working on your tennis? This princely game, where one needs at the same time passion and self-control, must suit you perfectly."[53]

The following is an important letter concerning a correction in the Etude "Pour les octaves." Dated 3 December 1916, it precedes by about ten days Rummel's premiere of the work: "A propos of 'Pour les octaves': on page 19, 2nd bar, there's an E[-flat] which isn't in the right place. Besides, it's awkward to play, at least for me. If it doesn't trouble your left hand too much, could you take it down an octave. . . . The same correction goes for the parallel passages."[54]

According to Roy Howat and the *Oeuvres complètes,* this is the only postpublication correction known of to the Etudes. The Etudes went into print soon after completion (Debussy usually clung to a manuscript for a long time, allowing many finishing touches and retouches), a habit that explains in part why they contain more mistakes and misprints than other works. Debussy's premature death prevented him from correcting later reprints, which he had been able to do with the *Images* and the Preludes.

The only shadow in this seemingly flawless record of Debussy's approval is a letter apparently turning down Rummel's request for a recommendation. It is dated 30 September 1916:

> Cher ami, If I have put off answering you for so long, it is because what you ask of me is very delicate. Not that the grounds are lacking, far from it, one would be able to write enough about that to fill volumes. But the question is, how to go about it? I cannot recommend you to dilettantes as the best pianist of modern times—that would

> look like a prospectus. . . . Very simply, I am sincerely grateful to you for having reawakened in me the appetite for music at a time when I fully believed I would never again be able to compose. And especially: one must pay homage to your prodigious understanding of music from Bach to Mussorgsky—by way of Debussy—I cite this name only for euphony. . . . To come back to what you ask me, I don't think it's possible to do it now. . . . My apologies and my friendship.[55]

Rummel's name comes up in other accounts of Debussy's home life, confirming the words cited just above. Debussy's stepdaughter, Dolly de Tinan, remembered that "Debussy was visited by . . . interesting people, among whom were Stravinsky, Walter Rummel, . . . Edgar Varèse, Falla." Pasteur Vallery-Radot, the doctor who treated both Debussy and Ravel at the end of their lives, called Debussy a loner who had nevertheless a small number of friends for whom he cared greatly. He further described the dinners after which "we would repair to the *maître*'s studio and Rummel would sit down at the piano, while Toulet and Debussy broached a bottle of amazing whiskey."[56]

What Rummel and Marguerite Long (1874–1966) have in common is the fact that their contact with Debussy spanned the last years of his life. And although Long did make some recordings of Debussy's music, they are extremely few. They include only "Jardins sous la pluie," "La plus que lente," and the two Arabesques. It is regrettable that the two pianists who succeeded in earning Debussy's approval neglected to record his music.

Long's meeting with Debussy came relatively late in her career. Already an established artist and professor at the Paris Conservatoire since 1906, championing such French music as Fauré's yet "undiscovered" piano music, Long seemed to shy away from playing Debussy's music and admitted being awed by it. Moreover, she disliked what she heard from other pianists, while admiring Debussy's own performances. Much as *Pelléas et Mélisande* had been "the biggest bewilderment of her life," Long felt that Debussy's piano music was beyond her reach: "The notes are not difficult but the realization puzzles me, it escapes me." When in 1914 the composer suggested that she work with him, she seized the opportunity. Long's husband, Joseph de Marliave, reported in a letter to Long's sister Claire that Debussy's wife, Emma, had contacted Long with these words: "He has no performers with whom he is happy; male pianists do not understand a thing about his music. We went to hear you recently: you are the only one who could play it well."[57]

Long and Debussy's work together was inaugurated on 27 May 1914, when Debussy agreed to participate in a benefit concert organized by Long and to accompany Rose Féart in two of his songs. A few weeks later, Long played *L'isle joyeuse* for him for the first time, at his home on a hot Sunday afternoon in July.

Their work was tragically interrupted, though, with the outbreak of war and the death in August 1914 of Long's husband. Long retired from the stage, and it was not until 1917 that she resumed her collaboration with Debussy, after he had just heard her, to his delight, at a concert of the Société Musicale Indépendante. Debussy's enthusiasm for Long's playing on this concert spilled over in the following letter to his friend Roger-Ducasse: "Cher ami, you already know what a huge success your two Etudes have had, especially the one for repeated notes which was encored. In my humble opinion, I have rarely heard such a stunning handling of sonorities. . . . The fingers of Madame M. Long seemed to multiply and you sure owe her an enthusiastic 'encore.' Your happy old friend C. D."[58]

The summer of 1917 brought the two musicians together in the southwestern coastal town of Saint-Jean-de-Luz, where the Debussy family was spending several months. There, Long worked with Debussy on much repertoire: *Images* I, *Estampes,* several Preludes, some Etudes, and *Pour le piano.* Believing Debussy had revolutionized piano music, Long wished to learn Debussy's way, his own technique: "His hands were deep into the keys, but always gentle, creating a wide range of colors. Without any harshness, ever, his sound was always full and intense, yet keeping to the dynamic range between pianissimo and forte. Within that range, he never lost the subtleties of his harmonic palette."[59] What Long remembers most about Debussy's titles is that they ought not to be taken too literally. "More sun, please!" he exclaimed when she played "Jardins sous la pluie," claiming that the music evoked children playing in the Luxembourg Gardens *after* the rain, while everything still sparkled. And Long's performance of "Jardins sous la pluie" does sparkle indeed more than it drizzles.

At a tempo of half note = 112–20, this last movement of *Estampes* is stunning by its speed, evenness, and clarity. Played in barely three minutes, it is the fastest performance I know. Pedaling is crucial in that it merely highlights important melodic notes but never drowns passage work in washes of sound. The cadenzalike descending arpeggios at m. 118 indicated as *rapide,* for example, are played without pedal; the following trills are also free of pedal. Whenever possible, Long holds on to long bass notes with her fingers rather than with pedal, ensuring therefore a *pp* as well as a light and clean sixteenth-note accompaniment. *Net et vif,* as indicated in the score, is what Long strove for and accomplished, while making the listener keenly aware of the subtleties of Debussy's harmonic palette.

The last time Long visited Debussy was on the eve of her performance of the two Etudes "Pour les cinq doigts" and "Pour les arpèges composés" at the Société Nationale. That night she played both pieces for the master, who was by then very ill and could not attend this concert of 10 November 1917. Debussy died on 18 March 1918, but Long's intimate friendship with his inconsolable widow continued. Emma Bardac Debussy wrote: "I looked for this intimate photograph of you—taken by me 'at our home.'. . . . I have lost too much to be consoled. . . . You will feel, I hope, all the affectionate recognition I owe you for what you allow me to listen to so marvelously."[60] And a year later, upon the tragic death of their daughter, Chouchou: "It is too, too cruel, too unfair. Forgive me, dear friend, I am in such pain . . . but you loved her and will be able to understand my dreadful agony."[61]

The many letters from Emma Debussy to Long testify not only to their enduring friendship but also to the esteem Debussy had for Long: "I remember the unique way you had of interpreting the innermost thoughts of the one who appreciated your art so much," Emma wrote around 1920.[62] After the December 1919 premiere of the Fantaisie for Piano and Orchestra, entrusted to Long and André Messager (who had conducted the premiere of *Pelléas et Mélisande*), the composer Gustave Samazeuilh echoed the same sentiment: "And those who remember how much, in the last years of his life, Debussy appreciated the way she could translate the unique fantasy of his music, will not doubt for a moment that the choice of Mme Marguerite Long . . . would have answered his wish."[63] Emma's letter following this premiere reiterated: "I am so *sure* that the beloved Master would have approved of your interpretation and lauded once again your incomparable and fairylike virtuosity."[64] This same letter ends with Emma's wish to give Long the manuscript of the Fantaisie. This gift is confirmed by Long in her book.

Long's recordings exhibit an extraordinary clarity, grace, and vivacious quality. Her playing is direct, elegant, and of a certain classical balance without ever being cold. The first Arabesque is as limpid as a mountain spring. Long keeps to a pulse of half note = 80–84 in the outer sections, observing accurately every *rit.* the composer indicated, with grace (performance time of 3 minutes, 10 seconds). Her touch is exquisite in that it is extremely light, fairylike and yet always ringing. Her skillful pedaling gives a beautiful luster to her sound, without ever blurring melodic lines or harmonies. Even arpeggiated left-hand accompaniments are pedaled ever so slightly. Occasionally, the ascending arpeggios are pedaled while the returning, descending arpeggios are dryer, with an almost *détaché* finger articulation. Her subtle variances in sound are all contained within *p* and *pp*—with only one *mf* reserved for two measures in the middle section. The second Arabesque is as whimsical as the first was flowing. Here Long's pulse of quarter note = 132–38 is steady throughout. Her *staccato* is never sharp but rather delicate and graceful. Long saves longer pedals and a slower tempo (104–8) for an utterly different sonority at the *meno mosso,* m. 82, which sets up, by contrast, the flirtatious mood of the coda, mm. 90–end (performance time of 3 minutes, 3 seconds). And finally, it comes as no surprise that Long's recording of *La plus que lente* resembles in mood and sound quality that of Debussy. Their performance times are identical: 3 minutes, 24 seconds!

In these recordings, Long comes across as a master of the pedal; but the wide range of touches and articulations are also characteristic of her style. "Mme Marguerite Long brings to [Debussy's music] . . . a remarkable refinement in sonorities which would have thrilled Debussy," wrote Florent Schmitt in *Le courrier musical* in January 1920. It is those specific attributes which undoubtedly struck the master when he himself wrote of Long: "I have rarely heard such a stunning handling of sonorities." Debussy cared deeply about refinement in the details, rather than grand gestures. And when Debussy added "The fingers of Madame M. Long seemed to multiply . . ." he was referring to her dazzling ability to handle multiple touches with ease and subtlety, as much as to her virtuosity. We have to cherish these few pieces and regret all that she did not record.

Two other celebrated early Debussystes who were contemporaries of Long are Ricardo Viñes (1875–1943) and Alfred Cortot (1877–1963). Viñes was France's adoptive son, as his family settled in Paris for good in 1887. Even though Debussy casually told his friend Victor Segalen that Viñes's playing was "too dry,"[65] Viñes remains the most passionate and committed early champion of both Debussy's and Ravel's music. Francis Poulenc, who was a pupil of Viñes's, described his teacher in most colorful terms: "He was some kind of a strange hidalgo with an enormous mustache, a brown sombrero in true Barcelona style and button boots with which he used to kick me on the shins whenever I was clumsy at the pedals." And pedals were an important part of Viñes's teaching, as Poulenc continues his description: "No one could teach the art of using the pedals, an essential part of modern piano music, better than Viñes, who somehow managed to extract clarity from the very ambiguities created by the pedals."[66]

Viñes had an insatiable intellectual curiosity, and his phenomenal memory enabled him to learn French, English, German, Greek, and Latin, as well as to perform new music from memory, a feat rarely attempted in those days. His burning urge to share his passion with others was what fueled his desire to perform in public the new French, Spanish, and Russian piano music during the first decades of the twentieth century. His legendary virtuosity made it possible for him to tackle with ease such difficult and utterly new works as Balakirev's *Islamey,* Mussorgsky's *Pictures at an Exhibition,* and Ravel's *Jeux d'eau.*

Viñes's diaries enable us to follow his connection with Debussy, even though he tends to overstate his successes. What he cannot inflate, however, is his genuine passion for Debussy's music: "Sunday 28 [Jan. 1897], at the Concerts Colonne to hear the *Prélude à l'après-midi d'un faune.* It is the most gorgeous thing I've heard in my whole life."[67] Viñes was the earliest Debussyste, premiering *Pour le piano* on 11 January 1902 at the Société Nationale. Other world premieres of Debussy's major works include *Estampes* on 9 January 1904, *Masques* and *L'isle joyeuse* on 10 February 1905, *Images* I on 5 February 1906, *Images* II on 21 February 1908, five Preludes from Book I in January and February 1911, and three Preludes from Book II on 5 April 1913. In addition, he performed with Debussy the two-piano transcriptions of *Nocturnes* on 21 April 1903 and that of *Ibéria* on 19 June 1913.

In return, Debussy dedicated "Poissons d'or," the third piece of *Images* II, to Viñes, a significant gesture since this was the only dedication Debussy ever made to a musician, except for Chopin (the *Douze Etudes*) and the "Hommage à Rameau." It is again disappointing to have only "Poissons d'or" and "Soirée dans Grenade" engraved on record among all the Debussy works that Viñes championed. His recordings of Scarlatti, recorded in 1930, show extreme delicacy and purity. His Albéniz recordings are fantastically rhythmic but light-footed, effortless, spirited, and exhibiting great ease.

If Viñes's "Soirée dans Grenade" seems rather hurried, it may be because it needed to fit on one side of a 78-rpm record, according to Emile Vuillermoz. Whatever the reason, what is missing from Viñes's recording compared to Debussy's Welte-Soehne roll is that extraordinary languorous atmosphere. With Viñes, there is never a moment when one is spellbound by the atmosphere of an evening in Spain that Debussy so successfully re-created. Debussy's rhythmic control holds the piece together through rubati and tempo changes handled with great subtlety, and neither Viñes nor Copeland come close to the composer's recording. Not only is Viñes's recording much faster overall, but there are hardly any tempo changes or rubati. Although the basic pulse in Debussy's performance ranges between eighth note = 60 and 100 throughout the piece, the pace is consistent between corresponding sections. When he indicated at the beginning "Commencer lentement," he meant it: the first five measures are slower (eighth note = 60–66) than the rest of the piece, which settles on eighth note = 72–80 at the entrance of the left-hand melodic line at m. 7. Except for the *retenu* of mm. 15–16, the slow tempo of the opening measures only returns at the end of the coda (mm. 130–end), several measures after the composer indicated *mouv't du début.* This consistency between the opening and closing of

"Soirée dans Grenade" is very fulfilling and makes it convincing that there is nothing erratic about the composer's handling of tempi. Viñes's tempo is startlingly faster than Debussy's: the opening moorish theme is played at eighth note = 138, and the *retenu* of mm. 15–16 is ignored as are all the other *retenu* moments in the piece. The middle section, *tempo 10* (m. 67), specifies "avec plus d'abandon": here, Debussy's pulse picks up from eighth note = 88 and remains at 100 until the transitional measures, which precede the last *tempo giusto* (m. 92). Debussy's handling of the *tempo giusto* sections is quite distinctive. Not only is it much faster (eighth note = 160 at peak) than the rest, but the sixteenth-note chords rush at first and then relax subtly on the rolled chord just before the end of the measure. Viñes accelerates the *tempo giusto* sections disproportionately and does not relax them at all at the end of the measure as Debussy does. No matter how rushed, how much the pulse accelerates or holds back, there is never a hint of haste or agitation in Debussy's performance, which exudes a feeling of whimsical nonchalance, yet never stalls. If time seems to be suspended occasionally, it is always in the middle of measures, not on the downbeats. Debussy never delays a downbeat, so that even though it feels as if we have all night in Grenada, the musical pace moves forward. If mood is everything, then Viñes's hurried performance missed it all (performance times are 5 minutes, 26 seconds, for Debussy, and 3 minutes, 50 seconds, for Viñes).

The composer's pedaling is discreet. The moorish left-hand melody in the opening is enunciated simply, without notes overlapping. Harmonies, as always, are heard unblurred. Passages more generously pedaled include mm. 52–60, where Debussy holds the open fifth in the bass. The corresponding passage, mm. 98–106, is also more pedaled; here Debussy chooses to bring out the right-hand motive and succeeds in keeping it clear while creating a heavy-pedaled texture. Debussy's sound is expressive, his touch elegant and never harsh.

Viñes's "Poissons d'or" on the other hand, is dazzling (performance time of 3 minutes, 12 seconds). The lightness and clarity of the figuration as well as the control of dynamics in the opening pianissimo, the subtle shades of color and the elusive character of this work are all handled admirably. Debussy, however, was also concerned with the architectural balance of the performance, as evidenced in a letter of 10 April 1908: "With regards to the new *Images,* we will have to gently convince Viñes that he needs to practice them a lot! . . . He does not feel the architecture clearly yet and, in spite of his indisputable virtuosity, he distorts its expressive intention."[68] Debussy attributed the poor reception of this set of *Images* to Viñes's casual approach, referred to at the beginning of this chapter.

Alfred Cortot was a leading figure in French musical life at the turn of the century, and remained in great esteem until his death. He showed a strong affinity toward German music both as a pianist and as a conductor. At home and abroad he conducted Wagner operas, which he had memorized and could play through at the piano. Debussy, who had a certain aversion to anything German (except pianos!), unleashed an infamous tirade against Cortot in a review of a concert for *Gil Blas* dated 6 April 1903: "Of all French conductors, Cortot is the one who has learned most from the pantomime customary among German conductors. . . . He has Nikisch's lock of hair . . . and we find this most attractive because it waves passionately at the least nuance in the music. . . . Then, at the warlike passages, it proudly stands on end again, and just at this moment M. Cortot bears down on the orchestra, and threatens them with a menacing baton. Just like the banderillero tantalizing the bull!"[69] Debussy does admit later on in his review that "It is right to add that M. Cortot is a perfect musician. . . . He is young and has an open-minded love of music."

Cortot's German taste did not exclude French music, however, which he played and taught to countless disciples throughout his long life. His commitment and genuine interest in the repertoire was immortalized in his comprehensive book *La musique française de piano,* in which Cortot discusses the piano works of Debussy, Ravel, Fauré, Franck, Chabrier, Saint-Saëns, D'Indy, Maurice Emmanuel, Dukas, Florent Schmitt, Déodat de Séverac, Roussel, Satie, Pierné, Samazeuilh, and "Les Six." Considering how much contemporary music Cortot played, it is curious that he never played for Debussy. And of the six pianists discussed here, he is the only one not to have done so, as far as is known. It may have had something to do with his interest in German music, and in particular Wagner, an interest which was incompatible with Debussy's strong feelings on the subject.

Nevertheless, Cortot premiered Debussy's Fantaisie for Piano and Orchestra on 7 December 1919 in Lyons, under the direction of Georges Witkowski at the Grands Concerts. (Long premiered the work on the same night, at the Salle Gaveau, in Paris, with André Messager.) Although Cortot did not premiere any of Debussy's solo piano works, this music held a prominent place in his repertoire: he gave the first complete New York performance of Preludes, Book I, in January 1920 and the first Montreal performance the following month. Reissues of his extensive recordings from 1928 to 1930 make his interpretations of *Children's Corner* and the Preludes, Book I, widely available, as well as his performances with Jacques Thibaud of the Violin Sonata and Debussy's charming arrangement of "Minstrels" from the Preludes, Book I, for violin and piano.

Cortot's style was very different from Long's and Viñes's, and from Debussy's, too. His playing is rich and heavy, and exhibits a huge range of color. It has neither the simplicity and refinement nor lightness and clarity associated with Long and Viñes, and may be considered a little indulgent. His artistry is undeniable, even though there occasionally may be more Cortot than Debussy in his interpretations of the Preludes: dynamic swells, rubati, separation of the hands, although often compelling, may be stylistically questionable. It is noteworthy that his choice of tempi, however, is usually very similar to the composer's. After Debussy's death Cortot went to play the Preludes for his widow, Emma. Debussy's ten-year-old daughter Chouchou was there. When Cortot asked her whether his playing was anything like her father's, she replied with hesitation: "Yes, perhaps, yes. . . . But Papa listened more carefully." It is well known that Debussy loved the presence of his daughter when he played. Ninon Vallin, one of Debussy's best sopranos, recalled: "He liked to have his little daughter present at all the lessons he gave me."[70] So what Chouchou may have sensed was that some of Cortot's liberties got in the way of Debussy's clarity of ideas.

The last two pianists discussed here are younger than the trio of Long, Viñes, and Cortot, and share an American connection with Rummel. George Copeland (1882–1971) was a native of Boston who emigrated to Europe and after a time in Paris lived in Italy. E. Robert Schmitz (1889–1949) was a Frenchman who later emigrated to the United States. Both are lesser figures in the world of Debussy's early pianists, but their contributions deserve mention.

Copeland was one of the first pianists to introduce Debussy's music to American audiences, at a recital on 17 April 1906 in Boston: "Passepied," "Clair de lune," and "Prélude" from *Pour le piano* were performed. Copeland was so struck by this music that he continued to study all the works of Debussy available at that time. Notably, Copeland gave the world premiere of two Etudes, "Pour les arpèges composés" and "Pour les sonorités opposées," on 21 November 1916 at Aeolian Hall in New York. In addition, he made his own transcription for piano solo of the *Prélude à l'après midi d'un faune,* which he recorded in 1933. According to Copeland, Debussy himself was delighted with it. Indeed, this transcription captures extraordinarily well the hauntingly mysterious atmosphere of this work as well as its remarkable subtleties of color and texture. Copeland's masterful command of the piano does not make one miss the orchestra for a single instant: at times it sounds as though there are two pianos, but all within a Debussyan dynamic range. Copeland's immersion into Debussy's music led him to meet and play for the composer in 1911 in Paris. His claim that Debussy said "I never pay compliments. I can only say that I have never dreamed that I would hear my music played like that in my lifetime," however, could be an exaggeration of Debussy's positive response.[71]

Like Viñes, Copeland gained the esteem and friendship of many French and Spanish composers of the period for his vivid interest and commitment to their music. Ravel, Granados, Falla, Nin, and Villa-Lobos all heard their works successfully performed by Copeland. And it was Copeland who claimed that Debussy's answer to why so few people were able to play his music was: "I think it is because they try to impose themselves upon the music. It is necessary to abandon yourself completely, and let the music do as it will with you—to be a vessel through which it passes."[72]

It is fortunate that Copeland recorded so much of Debussy's music over the years, including *Suite bergamasque, Pour le piano,* "Ondine," "Canope," "General Lavine," "Bruyères, "La cathédrale engloutie," "La terrasse des audiences," "Minstrels," "La puerta del vino," "Danse de Puck," "Et la lune descend sur le temple qui fut," "The Little Shepherd," "Hommage à Rameau," and his transcription of *Prélude à l'après-midi d'un faune.* The earliest recordings were made in March 1933 on a Mason and Hamlin piano. Other recordings were made on Steinways in 1950 and as late as 1962, when he was eighty. Overall, Copeland's playing tends to be rather matter-of-fact and rough-edged, his tempi are too fast, and his dynamic range louder than Debussy's wish. He does not possess the wide variety of touches, of color, and the overall subtleties so characteristic of Debussy and Long. Perhaps because of the Mason and Hamlin, I find the quality of sound of the 1933 recordings more satisfying. Copeland honors the tempo relations preferred by Debussy in "La cathédrale engloutie," and his performance times range between 4 minutes, 50 seconds, and 5 minutes, 5 seconds, as he recorded the piece several times (very close to Debussy's 4 minutes, 56 seconds). "Soirée dans Grenade," though, is hasty compared to Debussy's unhurried and sensual interpretation and does not exhibit nearly as rich an imagination (performance time of 4 minutes, 15 seconds). Copeland's transcription of *Prélude à l'après midi d'un faune* remains one of his best recorded moments by far.

E. Robert Schmitz worked with Debussy over a period of two years, as accompanist to the singers who coached with Debussy, and when he learned the solo piano music. Schmitz's notable contribution to Debussy performance is his book *The Piano Works of Claude Debussy,* published in 1950. His years of firsthand experience with the composer, his sensitivity and articulate understanding of the music, which he loved, make up a helpful guide, even if it is a little outdated. What is rather curious about Schmitz is that his recordings of both books of Preludes (engraved in 1947) in no way reflect the intimate understanding of the composer's aesthetic that his book suggests. Schmitz's own playing sounds labored, academic, square, and utterly devoid of the fantasy, the humor, the richly imaginative and "impalpable quality" of Debussy's music. There is a certain restlessness in fast-note passages, although they are always very clean and polished. This aspect is unlike Copeland, who tends to be casual about wrong notes. Schmitz's "General Lavine," to which Debussy indicated "spirituel et discret," is too fast and has none of the playfulness contained in the music. It is neither spirited nor discreet! His performance of "La cathédrale engloutie" does not show any awareness of Debussy's tempo relations but instead follows the inappropriate indications in the score. The result is the inevitable "funereal speed" to which Dolly de Tinan referred. And yet Schmitz's writings show a distinct understanding of Debussy's intentions. Even before his 1950 book, his article in *The Etude* points to many pertinent aspects of performance practice in Debussy's piano music: "Crescendos in those days were one of Debussy's obsessions in piano playing. He liked slight crescendos, a *ppp* increasing into a mere *pp*. Such tiny changes were meaningful and important to his art." This is an extremely important point. The range of delicate shadings in Debussy's playing is perhaps his single most distinctive characteristic, one which, to me, was best matched by Long. With regards to sound, Schmitz observed astutely: "Debussy regarded the piano as the Balinese musicians regard their gamelan orchestras. He was interested not so much in the single tone . . . as in the patterns of resonance which that tone set up around itself."[73]

Some may ask why Gieseking, Casadesus, and other celebrated interpreters of Debussy's repertoire do not figure here. I deliberately narrowed this study to early Debussystes, that is, the first generation of pianists who championed his music. Born in 1895, Walter Gieseking was a whole generation younger than Long, Viñes, and Cortot. And yet until recently, he was the earliest pianist whose recordings of Debussy's music were not only widely available but considered authoritative, in France in particular. When I was a child, my teachers in Paris recommended Gieseking's recordings of the Preludes over everyone else's. What earned him this recognition were his undeniable clarity, his legendary shades and control of pedaling, and an infinite range of colors. The greatest compliment came from Dolly de Tinan, who described Gieseking as "one of Debussy's first and finest interpreters." She further reminisced: "My mother was struck by the playing of this artist, which resembled as faithfully as could be that of the composer."[74]

In the end, it was perhaps Marguerite Long who best captured in words what Debussy's music meant to pianists: "We could never hear nor play the piano after Debussy in the same way as we did before him."[75] However many ways Debussy's contemporaries attempted to describe the composer's playing or to emulate it, the common thread was that he had a manner all his own. "He played . . . like no other living composer or pianist," wrote Casella.[76] Pedaling played a large part in his sound. Many commented on that specific aspect, which Viñes in turn taught as "an essential feature of modern piano music." The feeling of improvisation was also part of this unique manner: "It was like hearing a poet reciting some of his own delicate lyrics,"[77] an impression repeatedly shared by Casella ("a miracle of poetry") and other musicians.

Aesthetically, Debussy might have felt more kinship with the early eighteenth-century French composers, namely the *clavecinistes* Rameau, Couperin, Daquin, and Chambonnières, than with any other musicians except Chopin. Debussy paid homage to them in the preface to his *Douze Etudes* and in the most venerable ways throughout his correspondence and other writings: "So? Where is French music! What happened to our old clavecinistes, where there is so much real music!"[78] In an interview for *Comoedia* (4 November 1909), Debussy reaffirmed his beliefs: "I sought above all to rediscover being French. The French tend to forget too easily their innate qualities of clarity and elegance." And Debussy found those qualities in the music of his eighteenth-century ancestors. George Copeland recalled from his time with Debussy: "Perhaps the composer whom he most admired . . . was Rameau, whose genius, compounded of delicacy, charm, and restraint, he regarded as being in the true French tradition."[79]

As a pianist, Debussy did not follow in the footsteps of romanticism as did Ravel, whose technique was indebted to Liszt, Saint-Saëns, and Mendelssohn. With all his startling discoveries, Debussy looked back two hundred years to a very different aesthetic. Clarity, concision, elegance, simple and natural declamation are recurring ideas in Debussy's writings about his own music and about what he considered to be French music.

SELECT DISCOGRAPHY

Note: For a complete discography of the 78-rpm recordings, the reader is referred to Margaret Cobb, *Discographie de l'oeuvre de Claude Debussy* (Geneva: Minkoff, 1975). Recordings are of Debussy's music unless otherwise indicated.

Claude Debussy

"Danseuses de Delphes," "La cathédrale engloutie," "La danse de Puck," "Minstrel," "Le vent dans la plaine," "La plus que lente," "La soirée dans Grenade," the entire *Children's Corner,* and *D'un cahier d'esquisses* were recorded for M. Welte and Soehne, in Paris, 1 November 1913. Also, four songs with Debussy accompanying Mary Garden: "Mes longs cheveux," "Green," "L'ombre des arbres," and "Il pleure dans mon coeur," were recorded in Paris, 1904 (G&T 33447; G&T 33449; G&T 333450; G&T 33452)

Compact disc produced by Kenneth Caswell (Austin, Texas, 1991)

Walter Rummel

Chopin: Waltz in C-Sharp Minor, op. 64, no. 2 (DGG 68063); Waltz in A Minor, op. 34, no. 2 (DGG 68063); Waltz in A-Flat Major, op. 69, no. 1 (DGG 68064); Waltz in G-Flat Major, op. 70, no. 1 (DGG 68064); Mazurka in a minor, op. 17, no. 4 (DGG 68279); Mazurka in A Minor, op. 68, no. 2 (DGG 68279), all recorded in 1943

J. S. Bach: Chorale-Preludes transcriptions by Walter Rummel, recorded in 1928 (Gramophone P-858)

J. S. Bach: Prelude and Fugue in B-Flat minor, Book I, recorded in 1942 (DGG 67933)

Compact disc Dante Productions HPC027 (Vanves, France, 1995). This disc contains fourteen of the twenty-two sides that Rummel recorded on 78 rpm between 1928 and 1943.

Marguerite Long

"La plus que lente" and "Jardins sous la pluie," recorded in 1929 (Columbia LFX 24)

First and second Arabesques, recorded in 1930 (Columbia LF 55)

The above recordings were reissued on long-playing record, Pathé Marconi 2 C 051–16349, in the 1950s.

Compact disc Pearl GEMM CD 9927 (Wadhurst, England, 1991)

Ricardo Viñes

"Poisson d'or," recorded in 1930 (Columbia LF 41)

"Soirée dans Grenade," recorded in 1930 (Columbia D 15245)

Alfred Cortot

Children's Corner, recorded in 1928 (HMV DB1248–49)

Two Preludes, "La fille aux cheveux de lin" and "Le vent dans la plaine," recorded in May 1928 (HMV DB1249)

Violin Sonata in G Minor and "Minstrels" arranged for piano and violin, with Jacques Thibaud, recorded in 1929 (HMV DB1322–23)

Preludes Book I, recorded in 1930 and 1931 (HMV DB1240–44)

Compact disc Biddulph Recordings LHW 006 (London, England, 1991)

George Copeland

"Ondine" and "Canope," from Preludes, Book II (Victor 1643); "Bruyères" and "Général Lavine eccentric," from Preludes, Book II (Victor 1644); "La cathédrale engloutie," from Preludes, Book I, and "La terrasse des audiences au clair de lune," from Preludes, Book II (Victor 7962); "Clair de lune," from *Suite bergamasque,* and "Soirée dans Grenade," from *Estampes* (Victor 7963); *Prelude to the afternoon of a Faun* (trans. Copeland) (Victor 7964), all recorded on 21 March, 1933

"Menuet," from *Suite bergamasque,* and "Sarabande," from *Pour le piano* (Victor 14201); "Voiles," from Preludes, Book I, and "La puerta del vino," from Preludes, Book II (Victor 14904), all recorded between 16 and 24 April 1936

"Clair de lune," from *Suite bergamasque,* "Minstrel" and "La cathédrale engloutie," from Preludes, Book I, "Prelude," from *Pour le piano,* and "Hommage à Rameau," from *Images* I, all recorded in 1950 on a Steinway (recordings available at the University of Maryland International Piano Archives)

Suite bergamasque, "Et la lune descend sur le temple qui fut" and "La puerta del Vino," from Preludes, Book II, recorded in 1962 by the producer Peter Bartòk, on privately issued long-playing records (known as Subscription Recordings GC 1, 2, and 3, some of which are also available at the University of Maryland International Piano Archives)

E. Robert Schmitz

Preludes Book I, recorded in 1947 (RCA Victor M1031)

Preludes Book II, recorded in 1947 (RCA Victor M 1138)

Reissues in 1955 of Preludes Book I and Book II (RCA Camden CAL 179 and CAL 180)

Chapter 6 Debussy, the Dance, and the *Faune*

Stephanie Jordan

Attending London's music-hall Empire Theatre in 1903, Debussy mused on his ideal ballet, one in which "spirituality" did not give way to the "tactical exercises of strictly disciplined Pomeranian regiments," as seemed to him the case at the Empire. The occasion nonetheless inspired him to develop clear and unconventional ideas of his own, which he discussed in an article for *Gil Blas* later that year. In it he describes a language of dance where

> the mysterious lettering is inscribed in the winged grace of a dancer's leg and the rhythmic tension through her body evokes in turn the delicacy of a flower and the tenderness of a woman.
>
> The vibration of impatient or angry feet can express love or hate more clearly than the conventional gestures through which one normally translates these feelings. . . . To this unreality one adds the dreamy imprecision of a decor of shifting lighting effects rather than precise lines. Music must provide the design, like a shadow, enhancing the silent fluttering of gauze dresses with a frou-frou of compatible sonorities.[1]

I would like to thank Millicent Hodson for her helpful comments as a reader of this essay.

Dance continued to interest Debussy, and on a number of occasions he expressed admiration for Serge Diaghilev's Ballets Russes.[2] Yet in 1913 we find him writing disparagingly of its new, avant-garde choreography. He had just seen a rehearsal of his own *Jeux,* choreographed by Vaslav Nijinsky. The ballet suggested amorous encounters between three tennis players, two women and a man, searching for a lost ball in a park at twilight: "I am no scientist and am therefore ill-equipped to talk about dancing; these days one has to be something of an anatomist to talk about this otherwise light-hearted subject. Before I wrote a ballet I had no clue what a choreographer was. Now I know: he's a man who is very good at arithmetic. I am not very learned in that subject, but I do remember one or two lessons from school. This for example: one, two, three; one, two, three; one two, three, four, five; one, two, three, four, five, six; one-two, three; one, two-three (*a little faster*) . . . and then one adds it all up."[3]

Debussy's negative impressions of Nijinsky are well known. Yet there are good reasons for reassessing the Debussy-Nijinsky relationship, given the important status of the work in which they were involved. *Jeux,* for instance, turns out to be the only ballet that Debussy completed by himself, including the full orchestration, and it is now recognized as a seminal score of the twentieth century. Nijinsky himself has recently undergone radical reassessment as a choreographer, particularly after the reconstruction by Millicent Hodson and Kenneth Archer in 1987 of his *Le sacre du printemps* (1913). The other Debussy work that Nijinsky set, as *L'après-midi d'un faune* (1912), is now considered one of the most innovative ballets of the century.

At the premiere, Debussy kept his feelings about Nijinsky's *L'après-midi d'un faune* quiet. According to Stravinsky, he consented to the use of his score begrudgingly and under extreme pressure from Diaghilev.[4] Indeed, in 1913 he congratulated Nijinsky on the success of the London performances, although the message could be read as sarcastic: "Thanks, my dear Nijinsky, for having sent me that telegram, whose words flame like the gold of victorious trumpets! Thanks to your peculiar genius for gesture and rhythm the arabesques of my *Prélude à L'après-midi d'un faune* have been endowed with a new charm. Congratulate the English on having understood it."[5] A year later, interviewed in Rome, Debussy was unequivocal: "*L'après-midi d'un faune* as a Russian ballet was a grievous disappointment to me. . . . I will spare you a description of the terror I felt at the dress rehearsal, when I saw that the Nymphs and the Faun were moving across the stage like marionettes, or rather, like figures cut from pasteboard, always presenting themselves frontally, with stiff, angular gestures, stylized on some grotesque archaic model!"[6]

The *Faune* will be the main focus of this essay. It has continued in the repertory over the years, and Nijinsky's own notation score has recently been decoded. Set by a number of choreographers, *Faune* has also become Debussy's most famous ballet score.

The Nijinsky pieces are situated within the context of Debussy's checkered career in ballet.[7] He had talked about ballet projects in the 1890s with the writers Paul Valéry (*Orphée*) and Pierre Louÿs (*Daphnis and Chloë*), but neither of these projects went any further. Later a number of projects were started and abandoned, left incomplete or with no musical score. These included *Masques et bergamasques* (1909) on a commedia dell'arte theme (intended for Diaghilev's Ballets Russes), for which Debussy unusually raced to write the libretto himself; *No-ja-li* (1914), with a libretto by Georges de Feure, planned for the London music hall; and *Crimen amoris* (1915), later retitled *Fêtes galantes,* based on poems by Verlaine and commissioned for the Paris Opéra. For his other ballet scores, Debussy relied on colleagues to complete the orchestration. Thus Charles Koechlin assisted him with *Khamma* (1913), commissioned by the "barefoot" Canadian dancer Maud Allan (but in fact never danced by her). The ballet told of the Egyptian dancer Khamma, who, begging the god Amun-Ra to deliver her city from the besieging enemy, wins her appeal through an ecstatic dance but falls a sacrifice at its climax. André Caplet was engaged to complete the orchestration of *Le martyre de St. Sebastien* (1911), a fantasy play by Gabriele D'Annunzio that included sung, mimed, and danced episodes, and originally lasted some five hours. It starred the statuesque Ida Rubinstein in the title role, a dancer already well known from her appearances with the Ballets Russes. Caplet also finished the orchestration of the ballet *La boîte à joujoux* (1919), which Debussy had written in 1913 as a ballet for marionettes and which premiered after his death.

We should bear in mind that Debussy's career developed at a time of great change in the tradition of music for dance. Composing for the ballet was becoming less a job for opera-house hacks and more an undertaking for serious composers. There also was the sense that dance could develop as a more serious art form if it was supported by good music. Entrenched ideas about ballet music were shifting away from standard dance rhythms and short numbers to embrace contemporary, complex music; existing scores (performed as written or arranged for the ballet); and musical structures of large proportions. In their separate fields, Isadora Duncan and Diaghilev led the way forward to change and innovation in musical matters. In 1914 Michel Fokine, the first Ballets Russes choreographer, outlined in a letter to the *Times* (London) his five principles for choreography, the fifth proclaiming that while dance should not be a slave to music neither should it demand so-called ballet music. Every kind of music was potentially suitable, provided that it was expressive of the subject matter of ballet.[8] Two years earlier, Hugo von Hofmannsthal had written to Richard Strauss encouraging him not to think that he had to write "ballet music." Although Nijinsky was the first choice for choreographer of Strauss's *The Legend of Joseph,* the score was eventually set by Fokine: "I fear it is the idea of ballet, of the need for accentuated rhythms which has misled and confused you. Therefore I must make myself the spokesman of Nijinsky, who implores you to write the most unrestrained, the least dance-like music in the world."[9]

The notion of musical interpretation as the prime reason for a dance was also in the air, especially among the pioneers of modern dance like Duncan and Allan. The work of the Swiss music pedagogue Emile Jaques-Dalcroze, however, had considerable influence too on both modern dance and ballet cultures: his method offered a more precise means of negotiating with musical structure and a clear analysis of meter and beat in relation to phrase. Dalcroze's teaching at his center in Hellerau, Germany, included exercises in moving in parallel and in counterpoint to musical structure, as well as freer interpretation of music.[10] Demonstrations and lectures on his method in St. Petersburg stem from January 1911, where it is likely that Diaghilev and Nijinsky would have heard about his work.[11] In 1912 Diaghilev and Nijinsky visited Hellerau, whereupon the Ballets Russes dancer Marie Rambert was invited to use her Dalcroze knowledge in helping with the choreography of *Sacre.* It is important here to bear in mind that the creation of *Jeux* overlapped that of *Sacre.*

The year 1912 was also the one in which Diaghilev turned to contemporary composers in France, commissioning scores from Maurice Ravel and Reynaldo Hahn as well as Debussy, and at one point encouraging the setting of a ballet to Debussy's "Fêtes" from the *Nocturnes.* Yet Debussy was not a born collaborator, and more than one writer has commented that his individualistic attitude did not suit the teamwork that Diaghilev promoted.[12] Debussy had a tendency to belittle his colleagues and to denigrate libretti he did not write himself. With one exception, his ballets were commissions, not concepts that he originated for himself, and many of them were probably accepted for the practical reasons of money and publicity. This was the case, for instance, with *Khamma* and *Le martyre,* although he did acknowledge to D'Annunzio that "the very thought of working with you gives me a kind of *advance fever.*"[13] He had difficulty agreeing to Rubinstein's demands "to detach the dances from the rest of the work,"[14] while the collaboration with Allan was a disaster. He disliked the plot: "Have you considered the influence a ballet scenario might have on a ballerina's intelligence? In *Khamma*—which I hope to play for you soon—one feels a curious vegetation invading the brain, so the dancers are forgiven."[15] He fell out with Allan, unable to produce his score on time and unwilling to meet her demands for modification.

Whatever Debussy's opinion of *Faune* and *Jeux,* there is information to suggest that Nijinsky was a choreographer of rare musical ability and some musical schooling. Too often musicians have tended to denigrate Nijinsky's choreography and to dismiss it as part of the myth surrounding him—the ravings of a genius dancer who worked painfully slowly, unable to communicate his thoughts in rehearsal, and who later suffered a mental breakdown. Yet, biased in his favor though she may have been, his sister Bronislava Nijinska recounts in her memoirs not only that they both studied the piano at the Imperial Ballet School but also that as a child "he could play any musical instrument that he came across. Without any lessons he had been able to play his brother's accordion, clarinet, and flute."[16] She also recalls his "unusual talent of being able to hold perfectly in his memory a piece of music he had heard only a few times."[17] Thus he quickly memorized the parts of *Jeux* that Debussy had played for him on the piano. Marie Rambert recalls Nijinsky's close attention to the written score of *Sacre.* And although Stravinsky's attitude to Nijinsky and comments about his choreography for *Sacre* were probably the most instrumental in setting up the negative view of Nijinsky's musicality, Stravinsky later recanted. Nijinsky's dance notation of the *Faune* demonstrates a clear, analytical, and rhythmically acute mind.

Nijinsky's ballet is about a faun (originally danced by Nijinsky himself) who first appears lying on a high rock, playing a flute, the signature instrument of Debussy's score. Seven nymphs glide into view, but he continues to play, as if his music has conjured them into view. Suddenly he stops and takes notice as the chief nymph begins to disrobe for bathing in the stream below (the decor by Léon Bakst shows a waterfall beneath the rock). The faun descends to approach the nymphs, and they scatter. When the chief nymph removes her third veil, he is left alone with her and dances with her, but the others soon return and she escapes. Left alone with her veil, he picks it up, returns to his lair, and stretches out along it in orgasmic climax. The implication is that he then sleeps and dreams. The early flute playing might also have represented his dreaming and fantasy. Perhaps the whole episode lies in the faun's imagination. At the time of the premiere, there was considerable controversy over the faun's orgasm. However, the musical and choreographic climax of the ballet probably comes earlier, during the dance of the chief nymph and faun.

A number of structural markers have been regularly noted by analysts of the music, and they are all identified in some way in the choreography:

Mm. 1–29: Motto flute melody beginning on C-sharp. The faun plays his flute. Nymphs enter.

Mm. 30–36: A cadence and a new musical idea on the clarinet. The faun stops his flute playing and starts to watch the nymphs. The chief nymph removes two veils.

Mm. 37–54: A new melody and the timbre of the melody transferred to oboe, with a quickening in tempo. The chief nymph bathes in the stream. She removes her third veil.

Mm. 55–78: Cadence, new key of D-flat major, and another new melody, moving to musical climax. The duet for the chief nymph and faun.

Mm. 79–93: Return of opening flute material, varied and not at original pitch. The faun is alone and he moves toward the veil the chief nymph has left behind. Other nymphs return briefly to taunt him.

Mm. 94–105: The opening flute material and another variation, but at the same pitch as at the start of the piece. The faun is now left entirely alone.

Mm. 106–10: Coda to final cadence in E major. The last moments of the faun on the rock.

Debussy's score has resisted easy analysis, and there are many different views on the respective importance of these marking points. Nijinsky encourages us to hear the music broadly as A (bars 1–54), B (bars 55–78), and A1 (bars 79–110). First comes the conjuring up of the nymphs, ending as he lays down his flute (he also marks the point when they start to arrive, bar 21); next the central duet, which is marked by extremes of stillness and zig-zagging pursuit of the nymph; and finally the return to the faun's solitude.

Different versions of the ballet exist, including a recent reconstruction from Nijinsky's own score and a number of memory-based versions. They do not entirely agree, even about the relation of the structural outline to the music. I have based my analysis here on the film of the reconstruction from Nijinsky's notation directed by Jill Beck, using students from the Juilliard School. This was undertaken in 1989, the year Ann Hutchinson Guest and Claudia Jeshke completed the decoding of Nijinsky's notation. This notation was completed in September 1915, and Guest and Jeshke believe that the ballet is likely to have remained unaltered from the 1912 premiere. As well as the Juilliard film, resources for analysis include the Labanotation score written by Guest and Jeshke and a monograph that documents the process of decoding and reconstruction.[18] This documentation claims that the reconstructed version was "more sensitive, eloquent" than the memory-based versions, softer and smoother in dynamics, more varied in its musical relationships and generally more in harmony with the tone of Debussy's score.[19]

Yet one of the most remarkable features of this piece, one that was frequently alluded to at the time of the premiere as well as later, is the tendency toward disjunctive relations between music and dance. Nijinsky himself knew well that he was experimenting musically and drew attention to this in an interview before the premiere. His choreography, he claimed, would not relate "very tightly to the music."[20]

Observers at the time viewed the style with a mixture of concern and admiration. Just arrived from the Dalcroze school, Rambert was originally shocked by "the discrepancy between the impressionistic music of Debussy and Nijinsky's absolute austerity of style,"[21] while Fokine praised Nijinsky for the moments of stillness, "resisting any movement despite the apparent demands of the agitated measures of the music."[22] Hofmannsthal found that the music faded into the background as a secondary element:

> There are seven or eight minutes [in fact ten or eleven minutes] of a severe, earnest, rhythmically restrained pantomime to a piece of music by Debussy, which is well known to all. But this music is by no means the key to this ballet, as perhaps Schumann's *Carnaval* is the key—and a sure-fitting key—to the ballet *Carnaval*. *Carnaval* always seems to flow on as an improvisation on the music. But with the severe inward strength of Nijinsky's short scene, Debussy's music seems to fade away gradually till it becomes merely the accompanying element—a something in the atmosphere, but not the atmosphere itself.[23]

In later years writers could see the full force of innovation in Nijinsky's work, setting it within the historical tradition of musical-choreographic practice. Richard Buckle noted a freer relationship than had ever existed before, and later posited that "a step had been taken which might lead to dancing without any musical accompaniment at all."[24] Edwin Denby considered *Faune* the "first ballet choreography set clearly not to the measures and periods, but to the expressive flow of the music, to its musical sense."[25] Denby's view is not so much that there is disjunction but rather that there is a new kind of relationship between music and dance.

But in the 1914 interview in Rome, Debussy had spoken only of the extreme disjunction and of his unhappiness about the way his music had been misused: "Imagine if you can the discrepancy between a sinuous, soothing, flexible musical line on the one hand, and on the other a performance whose characters move like those on Greek or Etruscan vases, ungracefully, rigidly, as though their every gestures were constricted by the laws of plane geometry. So profound a dissonance can know no resolution!"[26]

Recall his earlier reference to "stiff, angular gestures." Debussy was commenting on the predominantly two-dimensional style of *Faune,* in which the dancers moved in grooves across the stage, feet parallel, hips and faces toward the wings and upper bodies twisted toward the audience. The limb shapes are often angular, indicating the joints at elbows and wrists and, in the case of the faun, at the knee and ankle, so different from the soft curves of classical ballet. The whole body posture is often stopped in stillness or held above a bent-legged walk. Thus, at the climax of the work, when the faun abruptly turns to meet the chief nymph face to face, they stand absolutely motionless for an exaggerated amount of time (mm. 55–56), then she slowly bows down (m. 57), both hold again (mm. 58–59), and finally she slowly rises and arches back (mm. 60–61). Energy is pent up within the body—she clutches the last veil to herself—but lines of tension also strain to pass from one to the other. The effect is the opposite of the easy flow and long, never-ending lines of the music. The lines on the tunics of the nymphs continue the geometry of the choreography. Otherwise, Bakst's contribution reveals its symbolist leanings and is closer in spirit to Debussy's music than to Nijinsky's choreography.

The sculptor Rodin commented that the faun was "like a statue" at the start of the work, lying back on one arm playing his flute, and again emphatically still. Then came movements "forward and back in a rhythm sometimes deliberate, sometimes jerky, tense and angular."[27] Many of these staccato movements have no equivalent dynamic in the music. There are the frequent little starts in the faun's role, a turn of the head as if to indicate listening, a stretching of the neck to signify alertness, or more pronounced accents as he laughs or abruptly confronts a nymph. In m. 48, he suddenly swivels to face a nymph, who reacts in fright, throws up her hands, and switches direction to bound away into the wings. Most strikingly, just before the chief nymph drops her third veil, the others react suddenly like sparks (mm. 52–54). The faun starts toward the nymphs, the veil drops like a portcullis, two accompanying nymphs gesture frantically—they had hoped to catch the veil—and then depart. The handling here is interesting: the last of the three veils is dropped to its own, different music; it is given special treatment, and the sharp shocks of this very brief episode enhance the contrast of sustainment and stillness that follows in the duet. During this central duet, the faun leaps once (m. 62), passion let fly for one moment. A number of writers emphasized this single jump.[28] It stands out like a blasphemy, just after the extreme sustainment and stillness, and comes out of nowhere—certainly nowhere in the music.

Sometimes, but not with any consistency, musical effects do clearly coincide with the dance. Buckle noted that "certain musical scurries suggest little encounters and furtive disappearances among the trees."[29] The dancer Lydia Sokolova recalls that "for every lift of the hand or head there was a corresponding sound in the score."[30] And, in fact, some of the nymphs do scurry in to musical flourishes, from m. 24 and also when they taunt and confront the faun at the end of the ballet. Debussy's music repeats itself in sequence at a number of points, and Nijinsky matches this: the playing of the flute and the raising of the instrument as the melody swells (mm. 3 and 13); the lifting of a bunch of grapes (mm. 17 and 18); the dropping of the first two veils, accompanied on both occasions by the nymphs turning in pairs and throwing their arms into angular positions over their heads (mm. 31–33 and 34–36); the zig-zag pursuit of the chief nymph during passages of rushing triplets (mm. 68, 70–73). At other times, there are effects of anticipation or echo (as when the first three nymphs run forward and back to greet the fourth, after the melodic flow has settled, m. 25). Walking nearly always fits the musical pulse, although this is not at all emphatic: the musical pulse is often hard to hear in any case. It is revealing that Sokolova remembers the feeling of "walking across the music: "The dancers had to be musical as well as rhythmical and it was necessary to relax and hear the music as a whole: it had to trickle through your consciousness, and the sensation approached the divine. One walked and moved quite gently in a rhythm that crossed over the beats given by the conductor."[31]

To me the musical and choreographic style of *Faune* appears varied; even in the version reconstructed from Nijinsky's notation, it mixes harmonious relationships with disjunction. Clearly, different viewers perceived different effects of balance. Beck, for instance, noticed more harmony than Debussy did. In this respect, however, more important than the visualization or counterpointing of musical structure is Nijinsky's stretching the boundaries of stylistic coherence—as Rambert observed, there is "an absolute austerity of style" opposing "impressionistic music." An understanding of the artistic context in which the work was made throws light upon the issue of tension and coherence between music and dance and upon Debussy's reaction to Nijinsky's choreography.

The art movement in which Beck situates Nijinsky's work rather more confidently than I would is symbolism, a movement from late nineteenth-century France that spread to other countries, including Russia: "In its sense of being outside normal time, *Faune* approaches the Symbolist ideal of art being its subject, rather than describing its subject. With our concentration fully absorbed and our sense of real time aborted, *Faune* can be experienced in a fantasy state. It can be mesmerizing. When this happens, watching *Faune* is a state of mind more than it is about a state of mind."[32]

Now, Debussy's aesthetic was bound up with artistic movements of the nineteenth century, particularly symbolism, and to some extent the related Pre-Raphaelite and art nouveau movements. Symbolism was the movement that reacted to the art of realism and naturalism in a celebration of feeling, dreams, and the unconscious. Its ideas were couched in terms of artifice, ambiguity, and mystery. The features of fluidity, curved lines, and organic forms from nature are all characteristic, as are muted tones and a spare language that included silence. The movement took much inspiration from the Wagnerian Gesamtkunstwerk principle of a synthesis of the arts in the theater: an organic meeting of contributing art forms. Thus in 1893, explaining his opera *Pelléas et Mélisande,* Debussy spoke of not wanting music restricted to "a more or less exact reproduction of Nature, but rather to the mysterious affinity between Nature and the Imagination. . . . The drama of *Pelléas*—which despite its atmosphere of dreams contains much more humanity than those so-called documents of real life—seemed to suit my purpose admirably. It has an evocative language whose sensibility is able to find an extension in the music and in the orchestral setting."[33]

Most of the writers with whom Debussy was associated, certainly for theater projects, were linked with the symbolist movement. Debussy's opinions about an ideal kind of dance also betray a symbolist attitude, one in which dance is shrouded in its own mysteries rather than in concrete literary ideas. Dance was, in fact, for some symbolists, the art form that best fulfilled their metaphysical ideals, the dancer embodying "the marriage of concrete form and divine Idea, with no mediation of reason."[34] Thus the particular attraction of many symbolists, including Debussy, to the performances of the American dancer Loie Fuller, to her style of veiled allusion, the sensual image play of colored light on yards of billowing silk. But the symbolists were also delighted by the early Ballets Russes of the Fokine period. The critic Camille Mauclair wrote of "this dream-like spectacle beside which the Wagnerian synthesis is but a clumsy barbarism, this spectacle where all sensations correspond, and weave together by their continual interlacing. . . . The collaboration of decor, lighting, costumes, and mime, established unknown relationships in the mind."[35]

We recall Debussy's musings in 1903 as he watched the ballet at the Empire Theatre in London. The allusions to flowers, tenderness, and female sensuality recur in Debussy's description of the Ballets Russes ballerina Tamara Karsavina in *Jeux* (whom he admired despite the "arithmetical" choreography). In the same ballet, he also saw Ludmilla Schollar, in true symbolist vein, "playing so artlessly with the shades of the night."[36] Orledge's speculation that Debussy might have warmed to Allan had he seen her is an interesting one; Orledge takes his lead from the symbolist tone of *Khamma*'s coauthor, William Leonard Courtney: "When she dances she strikes upon the harp of life, and sets us dreaming. She is, above all, the interpreter of strange, half-remembered thoughts."[37]

The much younger Nijinsky developed his artistic sensibility at a time of critical change in the arts, and a number of writers have situated him securely within what they call modernism (as opposed to symbolism), indeed as the first modernist ballet choreographer. Modernism is seen by these writers according to the terms of Roger Shattuck, as embracing a number of "-isms" that sprang up around the time of the *Faune* premiere, like futurism, cubism, and simultanism. All of them represented arts of juxtaposition rather than transition, revealing the jerky reality of subconscious thought processes and seizing upon a new kind of unity and coherence of experience through divergence and collage.[38] At the time of the premiere of *Faune*, some were already noting the links between Nijinsky's work and the newest developments in the arts around him.[39] Thomas Munro has skillfully analyzed the distinctions between the artistic sensibilities of composer and choreographer within *Faune:*

> Debussy . . . had produced his art in the rosy afterglow of the romantic era, with its love of softly curving forms and rich mellow textures. . . . By Nijinsky's day, a strongly anti-romantic trend had asserted itself. It was evidenced in painting and sculpture by cubism, with its hard, bare, geometrical shapes and its love of drab, harsh or monotonous coloring. It was shown in the new tendency to glorify archaic and primitive sculpture, such as that of the early Greeks. . . . Nijinsky's angular conception of the Faun was thus in keeping with advance-guard trends of his own generation and even of the 1890's.[40]

By the time of *Faune,* Nijinsky had already begun to educate himself in the arts, especially the visual arts, and he had had the opportunity to acquaint himself with the latest artistic movements, the fauves, cubists, and futurists, in both Russia France, as well as with indigenous Russian experimental art. Gauguin was a favorite painter. Nijinsky was undoubtedly reviewing his notions of the human mass while he saw natural shapes and dimensions distorted in abstract visual art and the various moves toward it.

The story is told that before *Faune* was choreographed, Diaghilev took Nijinsky to the Louvre to see Greek art, whereupon Nijinsky hung back, more intrigued by the harder-edged Egyptian paintings. Interviewed in London when the ballet premiered there, Nijinsky recalled that it was "simply a fragment drawn from a classic bas-relief"—he had spent time finding inspiration from the Greek art in the British Museum.[41] But Nijinska adds a more subtle statement from Nijinsky: "I want to move away form the classical Greece that Fokine likes to use. Instead, I want to use the archaic Greece that is less known and, so far, little used in the theatre. However, this is only to be the source of my inspiration. I want to render it in my own way. Any sweetly sentimental line in the form or in the movement will be excluded."[42] The hard, "primitive" archaic interest, as Munro points out, links Nijinsky with the progressive modernist artists of his time.

Interviewed before the Paris premiere, Nijinsky and Diaghilev, who, with the designer Bakst, originated the subject (and possibly other aspects) of the ballet, came straight out with a cubist explanation: *Faune* was cubist theory applied to choreography, concerned as it was with "a quasi-geometrical linear reality."[43] Whether or how much this was a publicity stunt is hard to tell, but it is easy to see a relation to cubism in the angular approach to the body, the breaking up of its natural planes in order to achieve the two-dimensional effect, and in the constantly fragmenting phrases and asymmetrical regroupings of dancers.

Of course, art movements do not start and finish neatly, and terms for them are often shorthand fictions that are convenient for scholars. Symbolism and the ensuing modernism are linked movements. Indeed, according to some definitions, modernism embraces symbolism. Some of Nijinsky's devices, for instance, came straight from symbolist theater: the bas-relief style, the use of two-dimensional movement and staging, the monotone tendency, the sparse movement and long pauses. More subtly, the new modernism continued the quest for the symbol, the essential image, promoted by the symbolists after earlier attempts at statement and mirror images of reality. Perhaps the main distinction is the shift toward a new expression of objectivity in a crisis period of displacement and lost harmony. As Joan Acocella suggests, "Symbolism . . . contained equally weighted values of subjectivity and objectivity. Modernism shifted the balance, taking subjectivity for granted and making the question of aesthetic value hang on objectivity alone."[44]

The new art places fresh emphasis on mass, solidity, the capturing and controlling of an often-fractured physical object. The abstracted, broken object (see, for instance, Picasso's work from *Les demoiselles d'Avignon* [1907] onward) also distances the viewer: it encourages a more analytical attention. Thus, stylized to the point of petrification, and spare—"everything. . . . reduced to its bare essentials"—the choreography of *Faune* leaves space for the audience, and, with the dancers withholding projection, the viewer feels like a voyeur.[45]

Most important to a consideration of the musical and choreographic aspect of *Faune* is the dissociation of sensibilities between music and dance (as between design and dance), which also contributes to this new objectivity. *Faune* speaks of the death of the Wagnerian Gesamtkunstwerk, the symbolist ideal of synthesis of the arts. It is as if Nijinsky preempts Brecht's repudiation of the Wagnerian principle, although Brecht used distancing techniques to encourage analytical attention for very different polemical reasons: "The process of fusion extends to the spectator, who gets thrown into the melting pot too and becomes a passive (suffering) part of the total work of art. Witchcraft of this sort must of course be fought against. Whatever is intended to produce hypnosis, is likely to induce sordid intoxication, or creates fog, has got to be given up. *Words, music, and setting must become more independent of one another.*"[46]

Nijinsky's *Faune* was a major step toward such independence. The faun is a statue at the start, separated ironically from the music by his own absolute stillness as he holds the flute to his lips. Nijinsky immediately signals that he is giving space to the music. Twice he returns to stillness with the flute to the lips, between the plainest, simplest, stylized raising of the flute with the upward movement of the melody. Likewise in this objective context, the climactic moment of stillness between faun and chief nymph is a moment of shock that draws attention to a device, the switch from the visual to the aural; as much as the music swells from pianissimo and envelops us with its "witchcraft," the stillness and then very slow bowing and rising of the nymph dissociates us from it, pulls against its emotional power. On other occasions, a gentle melodic trace leaves a nervous jerk or shower of gestural sparks unclouded and revealing their "real" physical energy. *Faune* is a dual experience. Viewers at the time were clearly captured by the charismatic performance of Nijinsky and the nymphs, and when seduced by that, the music may have seemed to fade away (as it did for Hofmannsthal), but the juxtaposition of choreography with music operates in bracing dialogue with this. *Faune* looks forward to the future of a Merce Cunningham aesthetic where music and dance are completely independent, and we experience each with a new clarity and objectivity.[47] Perhaps its statement about music is *Faune*'s most important modernist statement. It may also help us understand better the reason for Debussy's acute discomfort with *Faune.*

This is by no means the end of the complexities surrounding *Faune.* Nijinsky's wife, Romola, tells us that Nijinsky and Diaghilev spent hours searching for a piece of music, and "they totally failed to find what they wanted. Finally there was Debussy's *L'après-midi d'un faune.* Nijinsky was enchanted. Yes, the feeling, the atmosphere, was exactly what he wished, but the music was too circular, too soft for the movement he had conceived. In everything, except its lack of angularity, it was the very thing he wanted, so finally, *faute de mieux,* he decided to use it, realizing that the musical movement would not be the same as his own plastic expression. . . . Naturally it could not echo the ideas that Nijinsky wanted twenty years later."[48]

Was the choice of Debussy therefore a compromise all along; did the disjunction between music and dance just happen faute de mieux? Romola Nijinsky is a notoriously unreliable source, but her account is supported by the following description of a private studio performance of *Faune* that took place some years after its premiere. One Jean Bersier of Paris described it to Thomas Munro: "For music, there was a string quartet with piano. Someone proposed the Debussy music, but Nijinsky indicated his distaste for it. He or someone else then proposed Borodin. A score was found and played without rehearsal to his satisfaction. The exact composition is not known but it was more accented, staccato, and violent than Debussy."[49] This must surely have been a rough sort of experiment! However, it does suggest that Nijinsky's ideal music was more percussive, more staccato, indeed more in tune with the style of his own choreography.

Only a year after the premiere of *Faune,* Nijinsky produced *Jeux* and *Sacre,* both of which Nijinsky saw as representations of modern man. Again, viewers were alert to the links between the ballets, cubist art, and the primitive roots of cubism. Jacques Rivière commented on the new emphatic statement about the body, the medium laid bare in *Sacre,* "Motion . . . is constantly made to return to the body; it is tied to it, caught and pulled back by it."[50] Rivière refers to the machine precision, the angular, percussive style and disjunctive relationship between body parts. He sees this style as a counter to the aesthetic of impressionist painting and to the indistinctness and mystery of Loie Fuller's style—and he adds, "Quite naturally, she has been led to illustrate Debussy's *Nuages.*"[51] What clearer statement could there be of a mismatch between the aesthetics of Debussy and Nijinsky?

Jeux, like *Faune,* embodied differences in sensibility between music and choreography, although musicians would nevertheless acknowledge the advance in Debussy's musical style in the later piece. Henri Quittard, perhaps mindful of *Faune,* wrote, "No doubt people would have been content just to listen to the music. Composer and choreographer take absolutely no notice of each other in this ballet. Just as well for the music."[52] The musical-choreographic relationship in *Jeux* did differ from *Faune* in one important respect: the rhythm and pulse of the score became a base for the stressed movements of sport incorporated into the choreography. Some viewers commented on the dense visualization of every note of the score.[53] Yet the force of the dance pulse was of an entirely different magnitude from that of the music. Debussy wrote that Nijinsky had, "with his cruel and barbarous choreography . . . trampled my poor rhythms underfoot like weeds."[54] Hence Debussy denigrated the approach sarcastically as school-level arithmetic after he had heard the dancers counting in rehearsal. It could well have been the counts and visualization of rhythms that persuaded Debussy to lay all the problems at the door of Dalcroze: "The man [Nijinsky] adds up demisemiquavers with his feet, checks the results with his arms and then, suddenly struck with paralysis all down one side, glares at the music as it goes past. I gather it's called the 'stylization of gesture.' . . . It's awful! Dalcrozian, even—I consider Monsieur Dalcroze one of music's worst enemies! And you can imagine the havoc his method is capable of causing in the breast of a young savage like Nijinsky!"[55]

The Dalcroze name had become something of a catchword for rhythmic exercises and counterpoint in dance by this time. Debussy appears to have seen an element of counterpoint within the body here. Hodson, who reconstructed the lost choreography of *Jeux* in May 1996, notes that there is a moment when the dancers divide the music into three contrapuntal lines.[56] Yet it is possible that Debussy, so removed from the Nijinsky aesthetic, held the received and limited view of Dalcroze's work, seeing or choosing to see here only an unrelenting "mathematical" visualization of his musical structures.

Valentine Gross has suggested that the creation of *Jeux* to a piano score was of vital importance, for the piano is more percussive than the orchestra, and Nijinsky had no way of hearing the brilliant shimmering of what Debussy described as his orchestra "without feet" until just before the premiere.[57] *Sacre* was also created to piano, but here the music held much more of its character in piano reduction, and, crucially, Stravinsky's music was at least as strong and percussive as the choreography itself. As one critic commented, here was real balance and fusion between music and dance, as in "a new compound result."[58] Here at last too, the sensibilities of music and choreography were at one with each other.

Unperturbed by Debussy's distaste of his settings of *Faune* and *Jeux*, Nijinsky also choreographed the "Golliwog's Cakewalk" and planned, though never realized, a setting of the *Chansons de Bilitis*. Debussy's music has proved popular with many other choreographers too. Yet the *Prélude à l'après-midi d'un faune* stands out as by far the most popular of all his scores, with settings by choreographers as diverse as Serge Lifar (1935), Jerome Robbins (1953), Jiri Kylian (1986), Maurice Béjart (1987), and Marie Chouinard (1987). Many of the *Faune* settings, like the most famous reworking by Robbins, *Afternoon of a Faun,* have made some reference to the original ballet.

In the Robbins ballet, a male dancer in practice clothes is seen sleeping, stretching, and posing narcissistically in a dance studio (the audience "fourth wall" is the studio mirror), until a woman walks in (m. 31). She too limbers up, self-absorbed, and then they dance together (at the musical climax again, from m. 55), still admiring themselves but also developing a sensual involvement with each other. The man kisses her (m. 103), the spell is broken, and she leaves (m. 106); he returns to sleeping. The outline of the ballet is similar to that of the original Nijinsky piece, although the woman arrives at a later point than the nymphs and then remains onstage until later in the score. Some of the man's movements recall Nijinsky's faun gestures: the legs bent in parallel position, with elbows pressed behind the body, the arching back before he returns to sleep. Most important, by keeping such references, the aura of the famous 1912 theater piece remains strongly in our minds. Yet Robbins's languorous movement is closer in spirit to Debussy's music than was Nijinsky's ballet.

The Nijinsky aura is so strong that postmodern choreographers have been eager to develop from it in deconstructive essays. In Marie Chouinard's solo *L'après-midi d'un faune,* she is a woman playing the faun, dressed in a heavily padded costume with male genitalia attached; Hellmut Fricke-Gottschild's *The Late, Late Afternoon of a Faun* (1992) includes taking time out of performance to explain his role to the audience.[59] Both pieces examine the discourse of desire provoked by the original ballet; both, again, make some reference to the original movement.

It is interesting to speculate on how Debussy might have reacted to such developments. In his own time, it is clear that he had some feeling for the art of dance, although we know that he was unhappy about the manner in which choreographers used his music, including *Faune,* the ballet that has been most applauded. *Faune* is an example of a musical text that has been separated radically from its author's aesthetic and artistic context and has taken on new meanings when choreographed. Debussy's score was never given the symbolist choreographic setting he might have hoped for. Freed from his control, it has been appropriated as a luscious backcloth soundscape, as an excuse for oppositional treatment, and as the reminder of a notorious theater production of long past.

Chapter 7 Thoughts on the History of (Re)interpreting Debussy's Songs

Brooks Toliver

Is it possible to define authenticity in the performance of Debussy's songs? At first glance, the prospects look good. For one thing, we seem to have a general sense of the aesthetic ideals guiding the earliest interpreters; critics of modern recordings lament the loss of such "Gallic" traits as clear diction, lightness of touch, and gracefulness.[1] For another, an ever larger number of early recordings have been reissued on compact disc. In short, we have guiding principles and the material on which to base them; it should only be a matter of filling in the details.

Upon closer scrutiny, three issues call into question anything as sweeping and solid as an authentic performance tradition. First, as has been noted elsewhere, the stylistic diversity of Debussy's songs discourages broadly defined performance ideals.[2] Second, the idiosyncrasies of early recording technology often threaten to eclipse aesthetic principles. Third, although certain performance traits are common throughout the early recordings, on the whole these recordings are arguably more diverse than uniform, a circumstance that further challenges the applicability of our guiding principles.

Such complexities ultimately enrich rather than thwart a discussion of performance practice, however, provided that one follows a carefully delimited plan. Accordingly, I have adopted these priorities: while not entirely avoiding the first two issues, I focus on the third; to that end, I first define authenticity as a set of specific style traits preferred by Debussy. I arrive at those traits by examining some of the recordings that most likely exhibit his influence, namely, those with Debussy himself accompanying Mary Garden, as well as some by Maggie Teyte, Jane Bathori, Ninon Vallin, and Claire Croiza. A study of other, stylistically contrasting recordings then offers up a different sort of authenticity, one ironically defined by interpretive freedom.[3] I cap this study with a quick look at yet a third performance practice, that of modern times, which is probably based less on the other practices than on an abstract idea of how Debussy's songs ought to sound.[4]

In 1904 Debussy and Mary Garden recorded selections from *Ariettes oubliées* (along with "Mes longs cheveux" from *Pelléas et Mélisande*).[5] Their renditions diverge markedly from those of the later twentieth century. To begin with, Garden and Debussy outpace many subsequent interpreters. Indeed, their tempi are such that, were the pitch level not where it should be, one might suspect mechanical distortion. Examples: Garden/Debussy complete "Green" in just 1 minute, 34 seconds (thus averaging dotted quarter note = 75), compared to Gérard Souzay/Dalton Baldwin (1961) at 2 minutes, 10 seconds (dotted quarter note = 54), Frederica von Stade/Baldwin (1970s) at 2 minutes, 7 seconds (dotted quarter note = 55), and Benita Valente/Lydia Artymiw (1989) at 2 minutes, 2 seconds (dotted quarter note = 57). Given the limited usefulness of such comparisons, I pass over them quickly, alerting the reader to two ancillary points. First, a few interpreters have contradicted the trend just identified: early recordings with Francis Poulenc as accompanist occasionally reveal tempi exceeding those of Garden/Debussy, as have more recently some of Valente/Artymiw.[6] Second, if modern interpreters do not always go as fast as Garden/Debussy, they have nevertheless picked up the tempo over most of their precursors, as the previous comparison suggests. This forms part of a larger development toward a crisper style that I shall touch upon later.

The fast tempi of Garden and Debussy go hand in hand with a tendency toward unyielding forward motion; they keep rubato to a minimum while generally downplaying—and occasionally ignoring altogether—the shifts in tempo that Debussy himself indicates in the score. The opening of "Green" provides an excellent example of the relative avoidance of rubato: Garden delivers the tripartite statement of "des fruits, des fleurs, des feuilles" undramatically (mm. 5–7), entrusting whatever surge might belong there to the sequentially rising melody itself. By contrast, Souzay (1961) intensifies the line; he contracts "des fruits, des fleurs," hesitates, and then pounces to the high A-flat of "feuilles." Where Garden itemizes fruits, flowers, and leaves, Souzay prioritizes them. As for instructions in the score, Debussy foregoes his own indication of ritard in m. 75 of "Il pleure dans mon coeur," as does Garden at "qui ne bat que pour vous" of "Green" (in the last beat of m. 11).

If Debussy and Garden approach rubato with caution, they do not avoid it entirely. In fact, they embrace one type that I find in no recent recording, which is the staggering of vocal and pianistic attacks: Debussy adheres to the pulse while Garden holds back or rushes ahead. To take one case among many: in "Il pleure," Garden drags behind Debussy for the entire two phrases of "O bruit doux de la pluie / Par terre et sur les toits!" (mm. 23–27). I call this "rubato" because of its expressive power: it creates the effect of softly falling rain. Furthermore, it recalls nineteenth-century descriptions of rubato, whereby the right hand (in this case the vocal part) ebbs and flows while the left (here the piano) observes the beat more strictly; one of Chopin's students, Wilhelm von Lenz, recalled Chopin delineating just such an approach to expressivity: "'The left hand,' I often heard him say, 'is the conductor, it must not waver, or lose ground; do with the right hand what you will and can.'"[7]

In his recent book on the history of rubato, Richard Hudson offers a context for what we find in the Garden/Debussy recordings.[8] Hudson explains that this loose synchronization constitutes the original style of rubato (hence he calls it "earlier rubato"). In the nineteenth century it gradually gave way to "later rubato," in which the tempo fluctuates throughout all musical layers simultaneously.[9] Debussy occupied a transitional place in this historical progression: although his recordings with Garden exemplify earlier rubato, the verbal indications of "rubato" that he included in both his own scores and those of Chopin that he edited suggest the later form.[10] The discrepancy resolves in light of Hudson's observation that earlier rubato had stronger associations with vocal music, and thus hung on longer in that sphere. This view obviously does not contradict another, that the earlier rubato of the Garden/Debussy recordings reflects the taste of the singer more than the composer.

The understated expressivity that thus far characterizes the Garden/Debussy interpretations extends to other parameters as well. Dynamic extremes are held in check (I base this not on the actual recording volumes, obviously, but on vocal and pianistic timbres), and Garden's voice is relatively thin and vibratoless. Also, she avoids overtly expressive diction, favoring instead the natural inflections of the French language. This complements the undramatic phrasing of "des fruits, des fleurs, des feuilles," where Garden does not dwell on the beauty of individual syllables so much as string the latter into smooth, isosyllabic chains. By contrast, modern interpreters tend to sculpt each syllable; at the same line of "Green," von Stade unfurls her words, lingering ever longer on the "f"s of "fruits," "fleurs," "feuilles." This leads to a mini-climax on the last word which recalls Souzay's own (and indeed, he enunciates very much like von Stade).

Two other characteristics of the Garden/Debussy recordings demand our consideration, so thoroughly do they contradict contemporary performance styles. The first involves a flexible treatment of pitch: Garden regularly arrives at pitches by scooping and descends via portamenti.[11] Such practices obviously signal a bygone vocal style, but this circumstance should not rule out a quest for particular meanings; Why does Garden scoop and slide at some moments and not others? Scooping emphasizes words central to a poetic verse or the poem as a whole; Garden scoops both notes of "pleu-re" in "Il pleure sans raison" (mm. 38–41), a line that both begins the second half of "Il pleure dans mon coeur" and arrives at the heart of the melancholic poet's conundrum.[12] Garden's portamenti answer to a variety of demands related to declamation (linking or extending sounds), emotion (sighing), or character (conveying gracefulness or elegance).

The final characteristic transforms many of the preceding points into a general principle: Garden and Debussy do not adhere literally to the score, offering instead an imprecise, even inaccurate, performance. To take an extreme example: in the first measure of "L'ombre des arbres," Garden can be heard clearing her throat, a common practice in introductions dating at least as far back as the early nineteenth century.[13] She then enters approximately an augmented second too low (D rather than E-sharp) before unceremoniously sliding up to the correct note for the second syllable (example 7.1).[14] Although we have witnessed modern interpreters taking minor liberties, their adherence to the score—and particularly to pitch—distances them from the attitude evidenced here.

Should these observations be taken as guidelines for an authentic performance practice? Certainly a performing duo could duplicate the Garden/Debussy interpretations (complete with Garden's throat-clearings and missed notes) and feel some sense of historical prerogative. What is missing thus far is an understanding of the causes behind the effects; Do the latter result entirely from aesthetic principles, or do other, less idealistic concerns "taint" them? Also unclear is the prevalence of these effects; Do they recur consistently in the early recordings, or do they remain the property of Debussy and select singers under his guidance?

Let us begin with the issue of aesthetic versus other determinants and ask

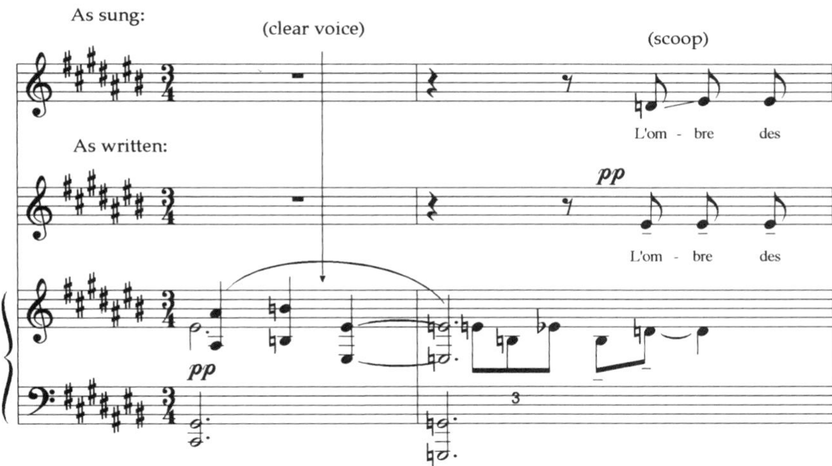

Ex. 7.1. Transcription of excerpt from "L'ombre des arbres," mm. 1–2, as recorded by Mary Garden and Debussy, 1904

specifically how the recording process might affect our findings. In fact, most of the traits I attributed to the Garden/Debussy recordings *could* result from that process.[15] The relative dynamic sameness of those recordings might reflect the inadequacy of acoustic recordings in capturing extreme high and low volumes.[16] We must immediately consider a counterargument regarding the high end: singers were generally counseled to step back from the recording horn rather than sing at a lower dynamic level. Thus the inability of recording equipment to handle high volume need not have dictated performance style.

Recording limitations might account for Garden's light voice, constrained vocal timbre, plain diction, and quick and relatively consistent tempi. In the first case, acoustic recordings entail the loss of harmonics, which in turn adversely affects resonance and deemphasizes vibrato. On the other hand, many of Garden's contemporaries attest to her relatively small voice, especially in its upper range. Regarding timbre and diction, the implication is that early recording technology simply could not capture the breathy tones and sculpted syllables that we find in modern recordings.[17] The arguments related to tempo are more intricate. While maximum recording lengths varied among companies, 78-rpm recordings generally set the limit at between three and four minutes. This would seem irrelevant to the Garden/Debussy recordings, which all fall under three minutes. Yet scholars of early recordings point out that the psychological pressure of conforming to time constraints may well have caused unnecessarily rushed performances; J. B. Steane has compared interwar recordings made in studios to those in concert halls (where the recording process was presumably less obtrusive) and has found that performers tended to adopt a quicker pace in the former.[18]

Thus far I have identified one-to-one correspondences between specific recording conditions and the resulting sound of the Garden/Debussy recordings. General attitudes toward the recording process may have insinuated themselves into the final product as well. Steane's comparison supports a common observation that an audience was crucial to an inspired performance. Nellie Melba's advice to singing students in 1926, even if not read literally, nevertheless reinforces the centrality of an audience to the singer's muse: "Remember that when you sing, the act of singing is not complete until it has carried its message to the listeners. Think of them. Speak to them, telling them the story contained in the song or aria you are singing."[19] Furthermore, the physical and mental discomfort of recording (as amply chronicled by the performers), coupled with a frequent dissatisfaction with the results, might have contributed to the hasty and loose air of these recordings. Debussy had implied his own dissatisfaction in previous years, when writing disparagingly of military bands: "It's [like] the cry of a phonograph but louder."[20]

The preceding discussion serves less to sort out technical versus aesthetic factors than to identify the problems in doing so. Hard and fast conclusions are even less advisable, given the probability that a particular performance trait may reflect both types of influences. For instance, the untidiness of the Garden/Debussy recordings may well have something to do with the placement and demands of the recording horn, and yet a looser approach to performance seems to have an aesthetic basis as well, as we shall see.[21] Rather than forcing completion on this topic, let us move forward to another issue raised earlier regarding the extent to which the Garden/Debussy traits turn up elsewhere. This puts us on firmer ground; slippery issues of *why* a given performance trait arose, though not completely disappearing, temporarily cede to the more verifiable investigation of who did what and when.

The recordings of Teyte, Bathori, Vallin, and Croiza make for a logical next step: despite the considerable time separating them from both Garden's recordings and Debussy's death, they carry authoritative credentials; Debussy admired all four singers and, in several instances, is known to have worked with them. Owing to the preponderance of her recordings and her extensive interaction with Debussy as his second Mélisande, Teyte will form the core of this study, with the other three entering into it whenever they have something to add. Stylistic links between the Garden/Debussy recordings and those of this second group of interpreters surface along these lines:

1. *Tempo.* All four singers reinforce the tendency toward fast tempi. Teyte, Vallin, and Croiza outpace most contemporary—and many subsequent—interpreters, if they do not actually equal the brisk tempi of Garden. Bathori does in fact approach Garden's speed; although we cannot make direct comparisons among their recordings, her renderings of *Fêtes galantes* II and *Chansons de Bilitis* outpace other versions markedly enough to suggest that she adheres to the same aesthetic as Garden.[22]

2. *Timing.* Teyte, Vallin, and, to a lesser extent, Croiza display the flexible interaction with their accompanists noted in the recordings of Garden and Debussy. I hypothesized that the latter occasionally fell out of synchronization for expressive purposes. Teyte avoids extended passages of this, but the principle remains in place on a smaller scale: in "Clair de lune" (*Fêtes galantes* I), she jumps ahead of Cortot at "Ils n'ont pas l'air de *croire*" to convey urgency (m. 17) and, for solemnity, arrives an instant late at the termination of "Les grands jets d'eau sveltes parmi les mar-*bres*" (mm. 27–30).[23] At other times, she and her accompanists simply seem unconcerned with the synchronization so prized by later interpreters.

The fact that Bathori accompanies herself effectively disqualifies her from this particular discussion but simultaneously raises some interesting questions. With the exception of moments when she staggers voice and accompaniment for expressive purposes (as at the end of "C'est l'extase," where the lagging melody conveys languor on a warm evening), she is far more precise than the others. Does this constitute a perfection that the singer/accompanist duos found harder to attain? Does it reflect the ideal of a later age? Or is it simply an acceptable extreme on the precise/imprecise spectrum, one particularly suited to a singer accompanying herself? As with earlier questions, I shall not force an answer.

3. *Pitch.* All the singers but Vallin continue Garden's free treatment of pitch in the form of portamenti and scoops. In the case of Teyte, the portamenti often seem more important than the framing notes, so leisurely does she descend; a relatively common technique consists of her crisply attacking the high note (where Garden would be more inclined to scoop), descending via a prolonged portamento, and then, at the last moment, scooping "up" to the bottom note. The length of the fall seems less relevant than the text: the maneuver often serves to accentuate the end of poetic lines. Like Garden, Teyte often uses such techniques for illustration as well; her half-step slide suggests time slipping away in

the second line of "Le jet d'eau": "Tes beaux yeux sont las, pauvre amante / Reste longtemps *sans les* rouvrir" (mm. 2–7).[24]

4. *Phrasing and Diction.* I noted that Garden passes subtly through the opening phrases of "Green," rather than building to the mini-climax of m. 7. The same understatement defines the others' approach to phrasing; Teyte is slightly more inclined than Garden to rush to a high point, yet this in itself seems a businesslike handling of such moments compared to later interpreters' tendency to anticipate these arrivals by a dramatic hesitation.

Teyte exhibits the same light voice and undramatic diction as Garden. Could this reflect the fact that neither singer was French? Undoubtedly it does; one disposed to pronounce "un conseil de goûter le charme" as "*da* goûter *lay* charme" (Garden, "Beau soir," mm. 21–22, 1929 recording) cannot be expected to tease every timbral nuance out of French poetry. At the same time, it is surely this understated delivery—if not the actual pronunciation—that Debussy preferred, given his high estimation of the sopranos he chose as his first and second Mélisandes. Furthermore, Bathori and Vallin, both native French speakers, reveal a similarly restrained diction.[25]

A brief comparison of Teyte to the baritone Pierre Bernac both exemplifies the distinction between earlier and later diction and suggests widely differing expressive results. Although Bernac's recordings do not greatly postdate Teyte's (those I have selected date from 1950), he nevertheless stands at the head of a more modern style of song interpretation. This is evident, among other ways, in his exacting prescriptions for correct performance. These are to be found in his book *The Interpretation of French Song* (1970), whose very existence suggests the attempted reconstruction—more than continuation—of a tradition. In his instructions for "La grotte" (*Trois chansons de France,* 1904), Bernac uses the word "mysterious" three times in two paragraphs.[26] Certainly "mystery" has a central place in these lines by Tristan Lhermite, and particularly in Debussy's setting of them (I excerpt the final stanza):

L'ombre de cette fleur vermeille
Et celle de ces joncs pendants
Paraissent être là-dedans
Les songes de l'eau qui sommeille.[27]

Bernac prescribes this approach for the end of the song: "In the beautiful curve of the voice: ['Et celle de ces joncs pendants / Paraissent être là-dedans'] no *diminuendo* coming down. This makes it possible, after a quick deep breath, to be more mysterious in speaking of the dreams of the water that slumbers ('les songes de l'eau qui sommeille')." His own recording of the song, along with a later one by his protégé Souzay (1961), exemplify his instructions and separate this approach from Teyte's; the hushed tone with which Bernac and Souzay treat the final line (mm. 19–21), together with their penchant for caressing syllables, have little place in her interpretive language.[28] Teyte, too, sometimes strives for mystery, but mystery of a different sort, and herein lies the crux of the issue: she employs restraint as an expressive device, whereby the mystery lies in the counterpoint between the suggestiveness of these lines and the enigmatic understatement with which she delivers them. To put it another way, Bernac, followed by many later interpreters, often gives the impression of narrating a mystery to children. Teyte is a child herself, and her naïveté in the face of profundity is reminiscent of another childlike enigma, Mélisande; both women *live* rather than describe mystery.

Questions of recording limitations aside, most of this chapter has gone toward establishing what performance traits Debussy might have condoned. I now gauge the common currency of those traits over a field of interpreters less closely connected to the composer than Garden, Teyte, and the others. Among the least far removed are mezzo-soprano Eva Gauthier, soprano Marie Louise Edvina, contralto Jeanne Gerville-Réache, and baritone Charles Panzéra, all French speakers whose contact with the composer, however tangential or brief, is documented or at least plausible.[29] More distant are several historically significant singers, French-speaking or not, whose careers overlap with Debussy's but who had little or no contact with the composer and did not specialize in the mélodie repertoire; these include the French tenor Edmond Clément, the American soprano Lillian Nordica, the Australian soprano Nellie Melba, the German-American soprano Elisabeth Rethberg, and the Italian soprano Claudia Muzio. Farthest removed from the composer are those singers active in the first era of electric recordings (1925 to the birth of the long-playing record in 1948); among them are Lily Pons, Bidu Sayão, Hugues Cuénod, Dorothy Maynor, and Jennie Tourel.

One could reorder these singers by countless criteria: nationality, primary repertoire (at the very least, opera versus song), voice type (Lily Pons demonstrates a coloratura approach to Debussy—including added trills in "Fantoches"—that suggests a performance tradition distinct from that of other voice types), decade, and so forth. One might even trace chains of influence originating with particular teachers, with French tenor Jean de Reszke, for instance, who taught Gauthier, Edvina, Sayão, and even Teyte. I acknowledge a variety of approaches as a way of clarifying my own, which leads in a different, philosophical direction: I question whether the interpretive freedom of these recordings as a whole disqualifies them as authentic.[30]

In limited ways, these interpreters *do* reveal some affinities with the previous group. Portamenti are common among most of them, along with the other types of flexible treatment of pitch. The "earlier rubato" involving loose synchronization between singer and pianist (or orchestra, in the case of arrangements) also marks the recordings as a whole. Finally, although understatement cannot be said to characterize the singers as a whole, they do tend to avoid what I earlier referred to as the sculpted or caressed syllables of later interpreters. In other words, their diction has less to do with accentuating the beauty of the French language than with capturing—or attempting to capture—natural speech inflections.[31] Most of these traits are inherent in the early recording era as a whole (a fact that makes them no less relevant to Debussy's songs) and thus begin to disappear toward mid-century as part of a general shift in aesthetics. For instance, the portamenti with which Pons renders "Green" in 1938 have disappeared when she returns to the song in 1950. Also, it is hard to find a singer and accompanist after 1940 willing to sacrifice precise synchronization for expressive effect.

Other traits turn up haphazardly at best. As mentioned earlier, only Panzéra follows the crisp tempi and attendant understatement of Garden, Teyte, and the others; the rest generally adopt slower tempi and indulge in a great variety of expressive liberties. Muzio's operatic sob on (of all words) "au" of "nous au tombeau" ("Beau Soir," mm. 37–39) comes to mind, as does Sayäo's similar treatment of "prier" and "pleurer" in "De fleurs" (mm. 69–71). Both would likely have displeased the composer, who advised Bathori at the end of "La chevelure": "Above all, no romantic shudder."[32] And yet these represent but minor liberties in view of what the other recordings exhibit; below I sketch three of the more flagrant violations of Debussy's edict that the performer should adhere to the score.[33]

1. Pons rewrites the melody of "Il pleure dans mon coeur" at "par terre et sur les toits" and "de ne savoir pourqoui" (mm. 25–27 and 59–61, 1938 recording) to parallel the descending line in the piano that both accompanies and precedes it (mm. 21–22 and 54–55; example 7.2).

2. In Nordica's rendition of "Mandoline," an unidentified harpist replaces the opening grace note to G with an arpeggiated chord of fourths and fifths; the final two measures—which should repeat the opening—are missing entirely. Nordica herself drastically alters tempi and vocal timbre to cajole, flirt, and convey irony. All three attitudes figure into mm. 18–25, where she slows to scoff affectionately at Clitandre (m. 18), and then, after rushing through the melisma

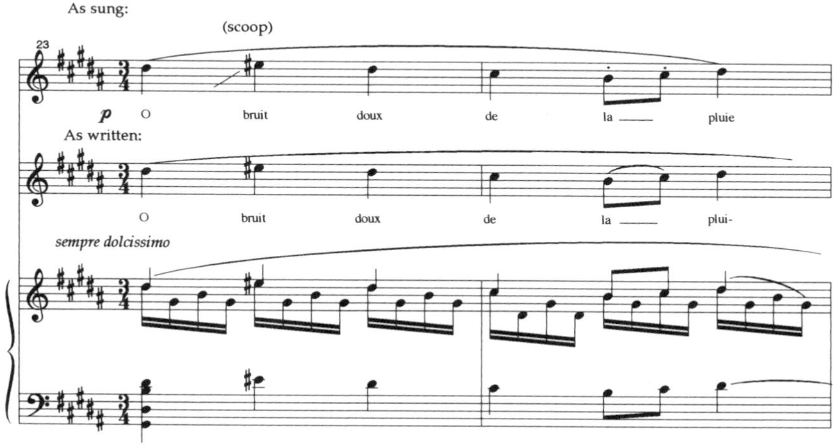

Ex. 7.2. Transcription of excerpt from "Il pleure dans mon coeur," mm. 23–27, as performed by Lily Pons and Frank La Forge, 1938

(mm. 19–21, on "Cli-*tan-dre*"), nearly grinds to a halt as she mocks the tender verses of Damis (mm. 22–25).

3. Clément and his unidentified accompanist in "Green" carry loose synchronization to a level that can only be considered mannered: the accompanist, who rolls most chords, anticipates or trails Clément by as much as half a measure. Measures 34–36 exemplify these licenses along with three others: altered

rhythms, pitches, and meter (example 7.3). Tempi go by the wayside in other ways as well: the Clément performance takes more than forty seconds longer than that of Garden/Debussy, and the andantino beginning in m. 40, which even the breakneck Debussy observes, passes unnoticed. Also striking—if not unheard of—is Clément's octave displacement, which raises the final words (beginning at "dorme un peu," m. 54) to his "tender" range.

At what point have these performers crossed the line into unsanctioned territory? The question may seem gratuitous, given the quotations that ostensibly demonstrate Debussy's disapproval. Despite his ire at specific licenses, however,

Ex. 7.3. "Green," mm. 34–36, as performed by Edmond Clément and an unknown pianist, 1925

I believe Debussy accepted interpretive liberty as a principle; had he faced the task of defining an authentic performance practice, he might even have included it. Before building a context for that claim, I shall support it with some examples. As an accompanist, Debussy has already suggested as much by ignoring his own markings and avoiding the sort of precision a modern interpreter would consider mandatory. From this perspective, Clément's "Green" could be seen as but a somewhat eccentric elaboration on Debussy's own performance style. That Debussy took liberties in the performance of his own works does not in itself give others permission to do so. But he did apparently abdicate his authority on more than one occasion, as when he pronounced Teyte's departure from the score superior to what he had written.[34]

What is more, Debussy's preferred singers themselves do not seem to have maintained a literal sense of fidelity to the composer, judging by the works and words of their later years. Teyte's recordings of the 1930s and 1940s may well replicate earlier performances under Debussy's tutelage, but this undoubtedly had more to do with taste than allegiance to a concept of historical accuracy. She suggests as much in her musings on "tradition," from which I quote: "There are academic teachers of tradition, who will not exercise imagination of any kind, and the vandals who imagine they are doing Mozart a service by stripping him of all his charming ornaments and embellishments."[35] One of her collaborators, Alfred Cortot, lived out the freedom inherent in those words when he inserted a piece of paper in the piano strings to add a percussive edge to "Le faune" (in the 1936 recording). In her 1929 recording of "Beau soir," Garden seems unconcerned with upholding the style that characterized her earlier work with Debussy; she adopts the most sluggish tempo I have found for the song (2 minutes, 55 seconds), forcing accompanist Jean Dansereau to slow his already leisurely pace by almost half when she enters in the fifth measure. The long pauses between measures and before meaningful words and phrases, the unnotated ritards, and the sudden and dramatic accelerandi further contradict the tendencies we have come to expect from Debussy's disciples.[36]

Interpretive freedom as a principle nevertheless can be "authenticated" from several angles. To begin with, Debussy composed with an awareness of it; most important in the following complaint is not what he wanted but what he expected: "People imagine they can do anything they like with modern music—old music is a religion to them, a fetish; people respect and revere every measure of it, but with modern music they think they can take any liberties."[37] But Debussy's attitude toward interpretive freedom amounts to more than a grudging surrender to the inevitable; he depended upon it. For one thing, he saw no way of notating certain crucial nuances, and thus had to rely on the interpreter to "complete" the score; this attitude sounds clearly in his skepticism regarding pedal and metronome marks.[38] More significant, he understood that such freedom guarded against artistic stagnation. Debussy's well-known fear of repeating himself in successive compositions formed part of a larger distaste for artistic repetition in general; as he allegedly explained to a puzzled Camille Chevillard, the first conductor of *La mer:* "I don't feel music the same way every day."[39] Although the remark may seem to tell us nothing about the prerogative of performers, it argues against the ideal of a single, perfect interpretation.

The fluidity that Debussy evidently desired in a performance tradition also helped preserve the magic and secrecy of music. I read this in the many comments that effectively relinquish his tight control over performance parameters in favor of the elusive principle of "taste."[40] I read it as well in his assault on the phonograph; on the surface, he takes a slightly different tack, arguing that recordings "domesticate" music by making it accessible: "In a time like ours, when the genius of engineers has reached such undreamed of proportions, one can hear famous pieces of music as easily as one can buy a glass of beer. It only costs ten centimes, too, just like automatic weighing scales! Should we not fear this domestication of sound, this magic preserved in a disc that anyone can awaken at will? Will it not mean a diminution of the secret forces of art, which until now have been considered indestructible?"[41] If Debussy does not directly concern himself with performance-practice issues, the implication is nevertheless there: a codified practice exposes music's secrets by holding her in place for all to apprehend.

A final and ironic imperative for interpretive freedom goes as follows: Debussy's aesthetic creed involved transforming musical traditions to such a degree that performers may well have reworked his transformations in order to remain faithful to the concept. Debussy interpolated folk songs into his music in ways that fundamentally transgress their character (this in spite of his condemnation of the practice in others' music);[42] the whole-tone version of "Keel Row" that opens "Gigues," for instance, projects an uncertainty out of keeping with that sunny tune. Likewise, his appropriations of Javanese gamelan music, profound or not, hardly define fidelity to a tradition. This argument requires several leaps in logic, foremost among them that of equating the reworking of preexistent styles with transforming the works of a specific composer. At issue, however, is not the soundness of the logic but the possibility that performers subscribed to it. We have already recognized their obligation to dress up the score; I merely suggest that they felt it yet more strongly in Debussy's oeuvre.

Throughout this study, I have invoked modern recordings purely for the perspective they offer on what came before, not as objects of study in themselves. Without changing that priority significantly, I close by focusing more closely on the relation of modern to older performance styles. Although the idea of a modern tradition, no matter how sliced, coheres scarcely any better than did that of an early tradition, one can nevertheless witness the consolidation of certain tendencies around mid-century, tendencies that survive, albeit modified, to the present. Among the first recordings to exhibit them are Bernac/Poulenc (1950), Lucienne Tragin/Poulenc (1954), and Flore Wend/Odette Gartenlaub (1954). I list the tendencies below, and elaborate on them where necessary:

1. *Increasingly swift tempi.* We have seen that, with the exception of Bathori's, recordings made in the decades immediately following Debussy's death adopt slower tempi than the composer's own recordings with Garden. Following this "sag," tempi begin to pick up; by the 1980s and 1990s, many interpreters seemed intent on recapturing the speed Debussy evidently preferred. A selective history of timings for "Beau soir" makes the point:

Year	*Performers*	*Time*
1929	Garden/Dansereau	2′55″
1935	Muzio/[orch.]	2′45″
1940	Maynor/Sandor	2′37″
1941	Teyte/Cortot	2′30″[43]
1950	Bernac/Poulenc	2′00″
1961	Souzay/Baldwin	2′24″
1970s	Souzay/Baldwin	2′15″
1980s	Benita Valente/Artymiw	2′10″

2. *Banishment of portamenti, reduction of scooping;* related to this trend is the following one:

3. *Ever greater precision in pitch, rhythm, and in the synchronization of singer and accompanist.* These and the previous traits signal an aesthetic shift that goes beyond Debussy's songs.[44] At the same time, it is fair to guess that most interpreters view them as correct for the latter. Given the overwhelming evidence that Debussy would have disagreed, it is worth our while to ponder how such precision arrived at its position of authority. The trend may well represent the privileging of biography over the aural record and, within that, may reflect an image of Debussy that best applies to his late life and works. The Debussy who taught Maggie Teyte the "pedantic and precise method of approach" to his music, who praised Rameau as "controlled and clean," and who told Pierre Monteux that he wanted nothing shimmering, everything exactly in time (I paraphrase), is not

the immortal Debussy; rather, it is the man who lived and worked in fastidious privacy near the Bois de Boulogne, who could not give lessons with an errant thread on the carpet.[45] The claim does not depend on finding contrasting anecdotes from Debussy's earlier years (although there is indeed evidence that Debussy was not always so prim); more to the point is that this common understanding of the composer's character finds its closest artistic correspondence in the terse and declamatory style of his late songs. One example suggests just how specific to his later works Debussy's twentieth-century outlook might be: his insinuation in 1901 that portamenti belong in sentimental, popular songs, however problematical it may be in view of the recordings we have studied, could at least be *imagined* as representing the views of one soon to compose the second set of *Fêtes galantes;* regardless of whether Debussy would have classed his "Romance" ("L'âme évaporée") as a popular song in 1901, an early recording of it without portamenti is inconceivable.[46]

4. *Increasingly expressive diction.* Throughout this study I have suggested that modern diction differs from that of earlier this century. To summarize those observations: more recent singers tend to caress syllables in a way that may add to the beauty of the language and certainly helps shape the melodic line but that departs from the more restrained and speechlike diction of Debussy's singers.[47] Although the modern trend may reflect the enhanced capabilities of recording technology, the implication that Debussy's singers would have sounded this way under better circumstances ("live" or in the presence of more sensitive equipment) is unlikely.

Symbolist poetry undeniably deals in the sensuous beauty of raw sound, a fact that surely lies behind—and partially justifies—the modern trend in diction. In light of this, the absence of such diction in early recordings would validate a separate study. Here I offer some brief speculation as to that absence. The sensuous delivery of poetry by force encourages a like (that is, sensuous) interpretation of its subject matter. This in turn limits the range of character portrayal open to the interpreter. For example, it is hard to convey childlike vulnerability when one is cooing seductively. This, more than any personal idiosyncrasy, may explain why Anna Moffo has missed the mark, according to many critics, in her rendering of *Chansons de Bilitis;* as Robin Bowman puts it: "The singing personality in the first *Bilitis* is incongruous[ly] presented as a worldly-wise seductress rather than a girl in her early teens registering some of the earliest explicit promptings of her sexuality."[48]

The tendency toward monochromatic sensuousness in modern recordings may also explain why the early interpreters come across as more colorful in their depiction of poetic imagery. In a word, many images are denied modern interpreters because they threaten to disrupt the overriding atmosphere: it would be hard to reconcile Teyte's playful illustration of heartbeats in "Green" with the silky beauty of a modern interpretation.[49] Modern interpreters do not shun all word painting; few avoid trembling at "frissonnez" ("Le jet d'eau"), for instance. But the fact that "frisson" is fair game where other images are not is telling in this regard; whatever its immediate meaning (shudder, shiver, tremble), it easily conjures up eroticism. Moffo's pointed delivery of "frisson" at the end of "La chevelure" may lie behind the previously mentioned criticism of her seductiveness. In the same way, it contradicts Debussy's insistence at this moment on "no romantic shudder."[50]

5. *Uniformity.* Uniformity increasingly characterizes modern recordings of Debussy's songs. By this I mean both that the traits itemized above recur with great consistency and that interpretive freedom, though still practiced, takes subtler forms. These dual trends are not limited to modern interpreters, for we find even the older singers responding to the changing aesthetic: in Pons's 1950 recordings, the sassy "la"s with which she had earlier filled in the final melisma of "Mandoline" (mm. 58–60, recording of 1938) have disappeared, along with the portamenti.[51]

Here we are faced with a discrepancy similar to the one surrounding the change in diction: in an age that values fidelity to the composer's intentions, uniformity contradicts the premium Debussy placed on interpretive freedom. The discrepancy gapes wider in light of the fact that uniformity has clearly been construed as an act of fidelity: the distance from the composer's time has encouraged a more studied kind of interpretation; ground rules have replaced intuition, and with them has come the notion of a single, correct performance (to which the modern interpreter wisely conforms).[52] The development is rich in irony: where we previously noted earlier interpreters ignoring Debussy's specific wishes in pursuit of an authentic spirit (interpretive freedom), we now confront modern interpreters discarding that general precept in quest of what are evidently supposed to be authentic style traits but that, as we have seen, often are not.

I began this study by questioning the pursuit of an authentic performance practice for Debussy's songs. That question, initially practical, grew increasingly philosophical: if authenticity lies in a specific style, then we glimpsed it in the recordings of Garden, Teyte, Bathori, Vallin, and possibly Croiza; if it consists of an attitude, then we found it in the artistic liberties of contemporary and subsequent interpreters. Although I have not adequately sketched post-1950 trends to pass judgment on them, I suspect that they, too, could be authenticated as rather abstract translations of Debussy's perceived character into musical fact.[53] I make such points lightly, for ultimately, the process of looking for answers proves more useful than settling upon any particular one. And this is undoubtedly the way it should be, given that we face a composer who was ambivalent about aesthetic absolutes and, what is more, one who was inclined to feel his music differently every day.

SELECT DISCOGRAPHY

Note: I name only those sources consulted for this chapter. For a more comprehensive list of historical recordings, see Margaret Cobb, *Discographie de l'oeuvre de Claude Debussy* (Geneva: Minkoff, 1975), 79–93. General references (such as *Ariettes oubliées*) indicate a complete cycle.

1904 Mary Garden, soprano; Claude Debussy, piano: "Green" (Gramophone 3077F-11,33451); "Il pleure dans mon coeur" (Gramophone 3074F-11,33449); "L'ombre des arbres dans la rivière" (Gramophone 3077F-11,33449)[54]

1909 Nellie Melba, soprano; Melba, piano: "En sourdine," *Fêtes galantes* I (Victor C-6697-1)[55]

1911 Lillian Nordica, soprano; [accompanist unknown]: "Mandoline" (Columbia 74027)

1911 Jeanne Gerville-Réache, contralto; [orchestra unknown]: "Air de Lia," *L'enfant prodigue* (Victor 88281)[56]

1913 Nellie Melba, soprano; Gabriel Lapierre, piano: "Mandoline" (Victor C-13899-1); "Romance" (Victor C-13899–2)

1917 Eva Gauthier, mezzo-soprano; [pianist unknown]: "Fantoches" (Victor 69669-1); "Romance (L'âme évaporée)" (Victor 69669-2)[57]

1920 Marie Louise Edvina, soprano; [pianist unknown]: "Noël des enfants qui n'ont plus de maisons" (HMV 2.033.072)[58]

1925 Edmond Clément, tenor; [pianist unknown]: "Green" (Green Label Pathé 3165)[59]

1928 Charles Panzéra, baritone; Orchestre du Gramophone, Piero Coppola, conductor: "Noël des enfants qui n'ont plus de maisons" (Pathé 723 BFR 80-2)[60]

1928 Ninon Vallin, soprano; [pianist unknown]: "Green" (Odéon 188595)

1929 Jane Bathori, mezzo-soprano; Bathori, piano: *Chansons de Bilitis* (Columbia D 13086 and LF 50 ["Le tombeau des Naïades"]); "C'est l'extase langoureuse" (Columbia LF 50)

1929 Mary Garden, soprano; Jean Dansereau, piano: "Beau soir" (Victor 1439 A)[61]

1930 Jane Bathori, mezzo-soprano; Bathori, piano: *Fêtes galantes* II (Columbia D 15196)[62]

1930 Claire Croiza, mezzo-soprano; Francis Poulenc, piano: "Il pleure dans mon coeur" (Columbia D 13084)

1932 Claire Croiza, mezzo-soprano; Ivana Meedintiano, piano: "Le jet d'eau" (Columbia LFX 109)[63]

1932 Ninon Vallin, soprano; Grande Orchestre, Gustave Cloëz, conductor: "Air de Lia," *L'enfant prodigue* (Odéon 123708)[64]

1935 Claudia Muzio, soprano; [Lorenzo Molajoli, conductor]: "Beau soir" (Columbia BQ 6001)[65]

1936 Maggie Teyte, soprano; Alfred Cortot, piano: "Claire de lune," *Fêtes galantes* I (Gramophone OEA 3146, DA 1472); "Le faune" (Gramophone OEA 3150, DA 1473); "La flûte de Pan" (Gramophone OEA 3152, DA 1474); "La grotte" (Gramophone OEA 3155, DA 1475)[66]

1938 Lily Pons, soprano; Frank La Forge, piano: "Green," "Mandoline" (Victor 1905);

1940 Dorothy Maynor, soprano; Arpad Sandor, piano: "Beau soir" (Library of Congress LCM 2141)[67]

1940 Lily Pons, soprano; Frank La Forge, piano: "Il pleure dans mon coeur" (Victor BS-051214-1)[68]

1940 Maggie Teyte, soprano; Gerald Moore, piano: "Le jet d'eau" (Gramophone JG 180)[69]

1941 Maggie Teyte, soprano; Gerald Moore, piano: "Green" (Gramophone OEA 9246, DA 1893)[70]

1942 Elisabeth Rethberg, soprano; [orchestra unknown]: "C'est l'extase," "Il pleure dans mon coeur" (ANNA Records 1040–41)

1943 Lucienne Tragin, soprano; Francis Poulenc, piano: *Ariettes oubliées* (Pathé COLC 317)[71]

1944 Maggie Teyte, soprano; Gerald Moore, piano: "Beau soir" (Gramophone OEA 10141, DA 1838); "Romance" (Gramophone OEA 10140, DA 1838)[72]

1947 Bidu Sayäo, soprano; Mile Charnley, piano: "De fleurs" (Columbia 12878 D)[73]

1949 Jennie Tourel, mezzo-soprano; Erich Itor Kahn, piano: *Cinq poèmes de Charles Baudelaire* (Columbia ML 4158)

1950 Lily Pons, soprano; Frank La Forge, piano: "Fantoches," "Green," "Il pleure dans mon coeur," "Mandoline," "Romance" (Columbia ML 2135)

1950 Pierre Bernac, tenor; Francis Poulenc, piano: "Beau soir," "La grotte" (also called "Auprès de cette grotte sombre") (Odyssey 32 26 0009)

1954 Flore Wend, soprano; Odette Gartenlaub, piano: *Proses lyriques, Chansons de Bilitis, Trois ballades de François Villon* (Haydn Society HSL 106)

1961 Gérard Souzay, baritone; Dalton Baldwin, piano: "Beau soir," "Green," "La grotte" (DGG 138758)

1970s Elly Ameling, soprano; Mady Mesplé, soprano, Michèle Command, soprano, Frederica von Stade, soprano, Gerald Souzay, baritone; Dalton Baldwin, piano: *Debussy Mélodies* (complete: EMI France 2C 165-16.371–16.374)[74]

1972 Hugues Cuénod, tenor; Martin Isepp, piano: *Cinq poèmes de Charles Baudelaire* (Nimbus 2127)

1989 Benita Valente, soprano; Lydia Artymiw, piano: "Beau soir," "Green" (Centaur CRC 2220)

Part Three **Interpreters on Debussy**

Chapter 8 How Not to Perform *Pelléas et Mélisande*

Désiré-Emile Inghelbrecht

Désiré-Emile Inghelbrecht (1880–1965), a Parisian of German-Swiss extraction, began his career as a violinist but soon became a conductor of great renown. In the 1910s a close friendship developed between Inghelbrecht and Debussy, and Debussy discussed performance aspects of his scores with the conductor, who directed the chorus in the 1911 premiere of Debussy's *Le martyre de Saint Sébastien.* Inghelbrecht founded the Orchestre National in 1934, with whom he gave a concert version of *Pelléas et Mélisande.* Numerous recordings of Debussy's orchestral music followed from this ardent disciple of Debussy.

"Comment on ne doit pas interpréter *Carmen, Faust, Pelléas*" (How Not to Perform *Carmen, Faust, Pelléas*) is a collection of three *causeries,* or "chats," in Inghelbrecht's term, that was first published by Editions Heugel in Paris in 1933. In his preface Inghelbrecht expresses a concern that artists have formed bad performance habits for the older two operas, and today's artists are in the process of forming more for *Pelléas,* habits that will soon become ingrained thanks to the advent of the phonograph recording. Inghelbrecht's stated intent is to defend performance as a living entity, and he repudiates the idea that these works should become monuments set in stone, bad habits and all. At the same time, he argues that, for *Pelléas* especially, the "esprit debussyste" emanating from the composer might yet be recollected, from the vantage point of 1933, and communicated to younger generations.

From the beginning of these chats, you will have been surprised to see *Pelléas* associated with *Faust* and *Carmen* as a masterpiece of our lyric theater. As is evident from the essentially musical point of view, [Gabriel Fauré's] *Pénélope,* [Paul Dukas's] *Ariane et Barbe-bleue,* and [Vincent D'Indy's] *Fervaal* have contributed as much as *Pelléas* to elevating French lyric art to the level of German opera. But the derivation of the lyric theater of D'Indy, Dukas, and even Fauré separates *Pelléas* from their three contemporary masterpieces. This is because Debussy's score, so French in its essence, is the immediate offspring of Bizet and Gounod. The drama of Maeterlinck is as specifically theatrical (all musical value aside) as Barbier's *Faust* or Meilhac and Halévy's *Carmen.*

Even so, you will nonetheless still be surprised that *Pelléas,* so early in its existence, should be associated with *Carmen* and *Faust* as the victim of false traditions. To be sure, from the point of view of popularity one cannot yet confuse the three scores or the three plays underlying them. But must one not recognize that all three, from their outset, were received, argued, discussed, and criticized in the same manner? And were they all not similarly impressed by an elite upon the masses? For considering that *Pelléas* came to life twenty-seven years later than *Carmen* and forty-three years after *Faust,* it clearly has not had to wait as long to achieve the popularity of its elders.

We certainly recognize that the "bad traditions" of singers and conductors have not had time to taint *Pelléas* to the point of affecting the musicians themselves, as has occurred in *Carmen* and *Faust.* But the danger is latent nonetheless, although not of quite the same sort. For *Carmen* and *Faust,* the ill effects wrought upon the spirit of the author have been the consequence, above all, of the bad taste of inferior performers and of professional inability. One observes here a lack of taste, of culture, and of a spirit of observation among directors or indifference toward these works that have enjoyed such success in the repertoire.

For *Pelléas* there is another problem. At issue above all is the incomprehension of the "esprit debussyste," a misunderstanding that is as common as the lack of understanding of Mozart's spirit. The majority of performers scarcely differentiate the study and performance even of markedly opposing works in their repertory. They imagine—often in the best of faith—that their "personality" will level out all differences thanks to their talent. As Faure said so clearly, in his fine book on singing, "They put the servant in the place of the master—the music."[1] It's that simple!

In bad interpretations of Debussy, as in those of Mozart, we see not just a professional inability, ever seeking to "work out some difficulty." Rather, we recognize the innate inability of the artist to discover the true thought of the composer and to adapt him- or herself appropriately. What is necessary to succeed is instinct and sensibility more than knowledge and talent.

Everything we shall say relative to *Pelléas* could be adapted to all of Debussy's work, much as what one can say about *Don Giovanni* could be adapted to all of Mozart's music.

We shall not bother with the thrashers about in music who get wrought up and are bent upon unduly obscuring "La fille aux cheveux de lin," only to justify some absurd theory of performance. We shall focus instead on the real servants of music, whose probity cannot be doubted but who nonetheless cannot resist modifying what the composers have written. For this is an illness, consistent with professional habits, and it cannot be ignored for long. This illness affects us all.

An illustrious director laughed when he discovered certain variations of tempo marked in the "March to the Scaffold" in [Berlioz's] *Symphonie fantastique,* variations indicated by such puerile indications—as if the work were choreographed—that one conductor had penciled in naively, convinced of his spectacular genius: "crescendo!! . . . grandioso! . . . avanti! . . . échevelé! [wild] . . . FORMIDABLE!!!"

But the same director who had criticized his colleague had not hesitated earlier to publish manuals written specifically to sanction modifications of tempo, nuance, and even orchestration in the symphonies of Schubert, Beethoven, and Mozart.

How then can one be surprised when here in Paris a composition professor (now deceased) recalled to his students the time when, as a conductor, he did not hesitate as he approached masterpieces to "skim the fat," as he would say, from the orchestra of [Gluck's] *Orfeo* or to "lard up" that of *Don Giovanni*!

I have always considered Nikisch to be one of the greatest conductors who ever existed, if not the greatest.[2] Nonetheless, if, as has been claimed, he truly argued that personality in performance could extend even to the adaptation of nuance and tempi left us by composers, then on this point and despite my veneration for his memory I would dare to disapprove.

What would one think of a painter who tried to foist off on the public a reproduction of a Rubens in which he deliberately diminished the brilliance of color or a copy of a Monet in which the features had been outlined more firmly? It is only through an absolute respect for the text and the thought of Debussy that perfection was attained on the first evenings of *Pelléas.* Thus we forever owe the most complete thanks to the genius of Messager.[3] If his *unequaled* performances might have been fixed thus on the phonograph, how they would cause those traditions to collapse in which we pretend to dress up this unique masterpiece!

From the first measures of the score, mystery envelops us and the problem of interpretation is posed.[4] All my life I shall remember the first time I heard this at the debut. For my first experience ever, when listening to music, I believed that the first performance was priceless. I would give a great deal to discover once again that impression of sorcery.

The problem that is posed here, in the perfect equilibrium of the first four measures, was resolved by Messager, thanks to his rare instinct for "neither too much nor too little." And yet this has nothing to do with knowledge or learning but depends solely upon sensibility. It is a little like the grasp of the hand that opens the heart of a friend to us. Meanwhile others bully us while yet others lack . . . support . . . and make us uneasy.

The first four measures of *Pelléas* contain the whole problem of the *Nocturnes,* of the *Faune,* of "Parfums de la nuit," or of "Jeux de vagues." In like fashion, the few measures marking the entrance of Donna Elvira [in *Don Giovanni*] pose the problem of the symphonies or the *Requiem* of Mozart.

For the music of Debussy, the most common error of performance consists in making the instruments *enter,* as when marked entrances occur in a symphony of Saint-Saëns or Beethoven.[5] However, in Debussy the instruments must frequently *be insinuated.* One must also be aware of the constant issue of continuity among the "neighboring territories," among the underlying voices of this music, which has wrongly been called pointillist.

These, above all, are the essential errors that have held back the majority of conductors on the edge of that mysterious forest where we are about to discover Golaud, lost . . . but singing. For he is going to sing too much, whatever he has got to tell us, if he exaggerates the "r" sounds to an extreme: "Je ne pouRRRai plus soRRRtiRRR de cette foRRRêt." In the same fashion, just before being killed by his brother, Pelléas might roll off, "On a bRRRisé la glace avec des feRRRs RRRougis."

Let us hasten to note that we are not questioning the care taken by singers in pronouncing the consonant well. But why emphasize one rather than another? And since it is a question of "grammatical liquid dentals," how can one get caught up forevermore in the "r" without thinking of the "l" which has such an importance, for example, in Mélisande's passage at the window:

Mes longs cheveux descendent jusqu'au seuiL de La tour;
Les cheveux vous attendent tout Le Long de La tour,

Et tout Le Long du jour.
Saint DanieL et Saint MicheL,
Saint MicheL et Saint RaphaëL.

[My long hair falls to the foot of the tower;
My hair awaits you the length of the tower,
And the length of the day.
Saint Daniel and Saint Michael,
Saint Michael and Saing Raphael.]

I think further about another place in the score where the importance of the letter "l" is suggested:

Vas-y avec n'importe qui. Dépêche-toi. Demande à Pelléas d'y aller avec toi.
Pelléas? Avec Pelléas? Mais Pelléas ne voudra pas.
Pelléas fera tout ce que tu lui demandes. Je connais Pelléas mieux que toi.

[Go there with anyone at all. Hurry. Ask Pelléas to go with you.
Pelléas? With Pelléas? But Pelléas won't come.
Pelléas will do whatever you ask him. I know Pelléas better than you do.]

About this moment I reminded Dufranne that many singers of Mélisande and Golaud tend to pronounce the name "Pèléas" rather than "Pelléas." But as Dufranne exclaimed, "There are two 'l's' even so, and two fine ones!"[6]

"In this composition," continued the unforgettable creator of the role of Golaud, "the more one subdues one's pride the better one succeeds. The rarity of such a submission of one's mastery can be explained easily: it is the responsibility of the great."

Neither do I pretend that one must not *sing Pelléas,* only that it must be sung differently from *Faust* or *Carmen.* This is the crux of the matter. Given the precise rapport of musical rhythm to text, here as in the majority of modern works, performers would gain a great deal by speaking the text at times, before adding Debussy's melody, which is intended to render the word poetic.

For example, we might better understand the first words of Mélisande, the mysterious young girl whom Prince Golaud has just discovered weeping at the water's edge. Scarcely has he so much as touched her shoulder and begun to question her, than she trembles and seeks to flee. He speaks again, and she cries out, if virtually without voice: "Ne me touchez pas! Ne me touchez pas!" And then, just afterward, "Ne me touchez pas, ou je me jette à l'eau!" [Don't touch me or I'll throw myself in the water!] As we pronounce these words, we can virtually hear Mary Garden *singing* them.[7]

At the debut performances, the creative genius of Mary Garden knew how to resolve the mysterious problem of "neither too much nor too little," which is posed imperiously on each page. Whatever might be the high value as "singers" of those artists who attempt the roles in this work, they must above all adapt their personality to the "esprit debussyste." We might add here that, more than elsewhere, the disposition toward plasticity should enter in a singular way into the question, and singers do not consider that disposition often enough.

I recall a woman who was brought in one day to audition as Mélisande. Her robust frame linked her less to Tom Thumb than to . . . Tom Canon. Moreover, in her manner she conceived the role in such a way, it would appear, that she tended to bring out its comic element. I must report that when she succeeded at that, with her first "Ne me touchez pas," she murmured the thing in a voice charged with meaning! I quite soon interrupted the audition, suggesting that my visitor might stick with roles better suited to her aesthetic and her charms.

I would be pressed to the point of absurdity to find another example of so complete an incomprehension of Maeterlinck's character.[8] Such examples happily are encountered infrequently, above all from the point of view of plasticity. But they still occur often enough that excellent singers still fail, in terms of the visual effect and even of vocal color, to differentiate Mélisande properly from other heroines in the repertory. One simply cannot simper or pout in the castle of the old King of Allemonde!

Although she might still remain perplexed by the disappointed hopes of life on earth, Mélisande is already the sister of the *damoiselle élue.*[9] She has fled from a previous life that she keeps hidden, and from where the halo crowns her as it does her celestial sister.

Where does she come from? Where was she born? . . . "Oh! oh! far from here . . . far . . . far away . . . " And if the singer has admirably translated the inaccessible quality of this distance, it will not suffice for her to convey only the word and the note. By the fixity of her gaze, she will illustrate the clairvoyant precepts of Faure relative to physiological influences, in order to triumph over certain difficulties of interpretation. And still further, after Golaud's question, "Qu'est-ce qui brille ainsi au fond de l'eau?" [What is glistening in the depths of the water?] a feminine and even childlike reflex of curiosity will make her exclaim, almost gaily, "Où donc?" [Where?] And soon after, her "Ah!" will plunge us again into her sadness.

We shall find many other similar examples, and they are what differentiates this study from those on *Faust* and *Carmen.* For *Pelléas* we must view all at once the issues in question. The matter is no longer to compare two manners of singing a piece, but of singing a phrase. Sometimes, even, we must compare two manners of pronouncing one word, one syllable. In the following discussion I may occasionally ignore the score order, in seeking to make a point of comparison or an association of ideas.

A room in the castle (where one encounters Arkel and Geneviève): one discovers, in reading the score, that Debussy never intended to offer posterity the Air of Geneviève any more than the Cavatina of Yniold, or even the Stanzas of Arkel, wishing instead to recall Mélisande's smile as part of the scene. Geneviève says, "Voici ce qu'il écrit à son frère Pelléas." [Here is what he writes to his brother Pelléas.] And then she reads Golaud's letter, *simply and without nuances,* as Debussy explicitly indicated. But that is exactly what singers used to proclaiming Werther's letters—which ought to be sung piano, as well—fail to do.[10]

Simply listen—as they say in Switzerland—to the fate of this "letter of Geneviève" at the hands of the majority of singers who have recorded it, and then someday try to hear Rose Féart read the same letter, but as Debussy wrote it.[11]

"Qui est-ce qui entre là?" says the old king. "C'est Pelléas. Il a pleuré." [Who is entering there? It is Pelléas. He has been weeping.]

This entrance Jean Périer fixed in performance admirably and definitively by advancing simply, without gesture, holding in his hand the letter from Pelléas's friend Marcellus, who is about to die and who is calling on him to come.[12] And Roger Bourdin adopted this fine tradition, changing nothing.[13]

However, I have witnessed certain singers of Pelléas who break away from it sharply and deliver an unanticipated *verismo* rendering of the entrance, wild and frantic, striking with their fist the letter and their forehead in turn, then crying out at length, "Grammp'Père!" One finds this *verismo* approach as well in certain recordings.[14] And then one comes upon the true Pelléas when one hears our Roger Bourdin.

The curtain comes down again, and the admirable interlude, evoking the magic of the String Quartet of Debussy, allows us to read to the depth of Golaud's heart, where there is an immensity of love for the mysterious girl he has brought home. Then we find ourselves before the castle. Let us not be too exacting about the fast pace of the orchestra. Certain difficulties must be dealt with, such as in the immense curtain of gauze in the foreground, earlier destined to give the illusion of sea mists that haze over the terrace. [Ed. note: Inghelbrecht's text appears to be unintelligible in the preceding passage because of a publishing error.]

The maternal solicitude of Geneviève does its utmost to welcome the newcomer Mélisande to the somber gardens where one never greets the sun. Pelléas appears. Sounds rise up confusedly from the sea. "Quelque chose sort du port" [something is sailing from the port], says Mélisande. The light of a beacon pierces the falling darkness. In the orchestra, other lights glimmer that we do not yet see. Mélisande recognizes the sails of the ship that brought her there, but she seems to see it but poorly, for she does not sing well in the key! And she adds, "Il fera peut-être naufrage!" [Perhaps there will be a shipwreck!] And yet one is not afraid at all. Finally, after the several measures needed to complete this scene, we have learned that it is not Golaud but his younger brother who soon will become Mélisande's lover.

It only takes a flute playing too loudly or an indiscreet harp to distort the decor of "La fontaine dans le parc."

If at this point the two characters just stand and sing loudly the first of their three duets, Debussy's and Maeterlinck's language becomes immediately unintelligible. What is more, if they adopt this interpretation to cater to the wider public, lovers of bel canto, not only will they have misrepresented the conception of the authors, but they will not achieve their goal. For the public will always prefer the duet from *Cavalleria rusticana!*

Pelléas must give us the impression of an oppressively hot day: "Qu'on étouffe aujourd'hui, même à l'ombre des arbres." [How stifling it is today, even in the shade.] And meanwhile, Mélisande should be able to freshen the atmosphere by her first few words, when she notices the fountain, "Oh! l'eau est claire." [Oh, how clear the water is.] But then a little further on, she must give us the impression of solitude and silence: "Comme on est seul ici . . . on n'entend rien." [How alone one is here . . . one hears nothing.]

A few pages farther along, there are ten measures that can suffice to demonstrate to the singers that they must not commit the folly of "chirping out" the role of Mélisande, who "n'est plus une enfant" [is no longer a child], as Golaud soon will say. "Ses cheveux ont plongé dans l'eau" [her hair is dipped into the water] that she cannot reach. She says a few words in a silence that is barely troubled by the dripping water. And suddenly Pelléas questions her. She is caught unaware and slips into a lie just at the moment when, the dialogue having become too embarrassing, she seizes as a pretext that "quelque chose se passe au fond de l'eau" [something moved at the bottom of the water], to escape by the diversion.

I assure you that she is not acting as a girl of eleven and a half; she is certainly a full-grown woman, admirably a woman. She is the young wife of a husband who is already old, the beloved of a handsome young man. A woman with ruses, a woman who knows how to lie—and how!

Admirable artists, charming comrades who have so generously accorded me their collaboration, have rightfully reproached me: it seems that I rendered their task awkward at times in making them listen to a recording containing bad examples of singing. In addition, I abused their capacity to take their work seriously, offering amusing anecdotes.

Thus I have waited until the end of this "demonstration" to remark on the windfall of a Pelléas full of fine imagination. After the affirmative response of Mélisande to his question, "C'est au bord d'une fontaine aussi, qu'il vous a trouvée?" [He also found you beside a fountain?] he continues with a discreet wink of the eye, "Que vous a-t-il dit?" [What did he say to you?] It's a small thing but worth considering!

Finally, Mélisande symbolically allows her wedding ring to fall into the water, and she is quite disturbed. The singer must know how to distinguish her concerns, so interestingly confused: "Non, non, nous ne la retrouverons plus, nous n'en trouverons pas d'autre non plus." [No, no, we shall not find it again; we shall not find another either.] These are to be distinguished from the useless problems that she will now offer her companion: "Je croyais l'avoir dans les mains, cependant." [Yet I believed that I had it in my hands.] And yet now this figure who was so recently the strongest character will implore, with all her feminine submission, the support of her accomplice, asking, "Qu'allons-nous dire à Golaud, s'il demande où il est?" [What shall we say to Golaud if he asks where it is?] Pelléas, in all his candor, responds, "La vérité . . . , la vérité." And yet the truth will be the last thing Mélisande will tell Golaud when we find her at his bedside.

We have just left the two charming lovers, quite concerned over the loss of the ring, and of two minds about how to explain the matter to Golaud. We find him now reclining on his bed and recounting his inexplicable accident while hunting. Ah, how admirable the orchestration is, which weighs as heavily as those woods the sick man believes he has on his chest! And oh, Mélisande's foreboding of the terrible interrogation! And how she seeks all the more to postpone its coming, for this moment at least, and turn aside the inevitable result! What child has not encountered so terrible an anguish? "Voulez-vous boire un peu d'eau? Voulez-vous un autre oreiller? Fermez-les yeux et tâcher de dormir." [Would you like to drink a little water? Would you like another pillow? Close your eyes and try to sleep.]

What admirable music comprises these last two measures! And too, there is also all the disquietude that will no longer attend the poor little Mélisande at the moment of her death, because then her child will have been born. Which of the two, poet or musician, has better conveyed the delicacy of soul of this young woman who is about to become a mother? Have they not completed each other's artistry admirably? And yet Catulle Mendès maintained that one must not set poems that are too good for musical treatment![15]

We must linger over each of the phrases that come next. Here, when Mélisande wishes to go away with Golaud to flee the danger she foretells. Or there, when Golaud says of Pelléas, "Il est jeune" [he is young], with all the love of youth and all the regrets that come from a distance! And still further, when the flute recalls the scene at the fountain, Mélisande remembers that she has seen the sky "pour la première fois, ce matin" [for the first time, this morning]. And then, and then, the discovery that the ring is lost, just at the moment when Golaud is evoking the coming year so tenderly, with his hope for the child that she will bear him. It is then that he takes in his hands the little hands of his wife, "ces petites mains qu'il pourrait écraser comme des fleurs" [those little hands one could crush like flowers].

"Tiens . . . où est l'anneau que je t'avais donné?" [Wait . . . where is the ring I gave you?]

As there is no complete recording, I cannot illustrate the stupid fermata that certain performers of Golaud's role have sought to institute as a tradition—on the high note, naturally—sought so successfully that it would have been recorded had it not been for friends who saw to it that it wasn't! But you will find at this moment all the trouble and falsehood of Mélisande, observed previously at the fountain.

All the rustling of the muted orchestral strings over the shimmer of the cymbal, the distant oboes sounding like miniature trumpets, that impression of a harmonica suggested by flutes and clarinets . . . all this makes one sense the night, the sea smells, and the salt air. For already here are the premises of that sea—Debussy's admirable *La mer*—that he would soon write. "Il faut pouvoir décrire l'endroit où vous avez perdu la bague, s'il vous interroge." [You must be able to describe the spot where you lost the ring if he questions you.] We might recall the few measures that lead to these two words, "Entrons-y." [Let's go in.] And we remember as well the story of the beggars asleep in the cave who made Mélisande utter a cry of terror.

In a tower of the castle, Mélisande sings at the window as she combs her loosened hair. We are at the renowned Tower Scene, as it has become known.

The harps play too loudly, even more so in the recording, first because there is only one, and then because those minor clergy in the order of orchestral conductors find certain instruments to be "deluxe." And among these are numbered the harps. When one is called for, they want to make sure you know all about it, and the instrument has to drown out everything else. That makes a rich display. The conductors exhibit them like the butcher displays his treasures on Saturday afternoon. But for conductors who have a habit of following the natural orchestration, the harp of the orchestra follows the principle of the simple and is the equivalent of a pinch of salt in a good pastry or a pinch of sugar in new green peas.

In certain recordings I have heard, there is nothing to be said about the Tower Scene. In the theater you have a personage offstage: the violinist responsible for giving the note to Mélisande, who always seems to refuse it and to take the note above. It's a question of good taste. Thus on one recording things are fine up to the arrival of Pelléas. But from there everything goes wrong. I have observed also that the singers of Mélisande were superior to their counterparts . . . with regard to the microphones.

As I mentioned previously, the care brought to the articulation of the letter "l" singularly favors the legato realization of the Tower Song. The singer must also take care to prepare her "b" if she truly wants to make us experience that "Il fait beau, cette nuit." [How lovely it is tonight.] You see thus that all the consonants are important, and that there is more than the famous "r!"

—Donne-moi du moins ta main ce soir . . . avant que je m'en aille . . . Je pars demain.
—Je ne te donne pas ma main si tu pars.
—J'attendrai, j'attendrai.
—Je vois une rose dans les ténèbres (here she sings a bit off pitch . . .).
—Ce n'est pas une rose. J'irai voir tout à l'heure. Mais donne-moi ta main d'abord.

[—At least give me your hand this evening . . . before I go away. . . . I'm leaving tomorrow.
—I won't give you my hand if you leave.
—I'll wait, I'll wait.
—I see a rose in the shadows (here she sings a bit off pitch . . .).
—It isn't a rose. I'll go see at once. But give me your hand first.]

Here is what I wished to come to. Pelléas does not sing slightly out of tune. Rather, he sings a third low by design. You all know what has been said, in matters of singing, with regard to "touched-up roles." When an author offers a role to an interpreter whose voice does not have the precise range required, he might consent to change certain notes in the extreme range of the role. That occurred for *Pelléas,* and Debussy himself indicated what "touching up" he might offer an artist *he* was supporting.

But on the other hand, when an interpreter is eager to sing a role, he must sing it as it was written; he does not have the right to adapt it for his vocal means. Above all, recall that the author is not there to defend himself, despite the more or less debatable "permission" the interpreter has received from whoever has fallen heir to the composer.[16] The case becomes significantly more serious when recording is at issue, especially when other artists have offered brilliant proof of their capacity to sing the text without deforming it. And to the responsibility of

Ex. 8.1a. *Pelléas et Mélisande,* Tower Scene, Act III

Ex. 8.1b. *Pelléas et Mélisande,* Tower Scene, Act III

the singer is added, one must note, that of the recording company!

If we heard Bourdin sing these short fragments, immediately after hearing a certain disk in question, and simply compared the texts transcribed here, we would quickly perceive how much lyricism is stifled by the inadmissible touching up, in my opinion, a singer has been authorized to fix in the recording.

I hasten to add that, this point apart, I appreciate the values and taste of the artist in the recording. I can only deplore the fact that he allowed such a sacrilege to occur. (See examples 8.1a and 8.1b.)

This second example will transport us for an instant to the second act. We remark upon an error common to many a Mélisande, who, in the effort to adhere to the meter, separates into two fragments the phrase "Il y a quelqu'un derrière nous." Here is an example, as Steinlen would say, where traces of the "métier" must be concealed by its very perfection.[17]

And finally, since I am in the middle of grumbling and cannot hide what I am thinking, I would say that the orchestra here in the recording is scandalously bad, to the point of anticipating or pulling back the singer on one occasion or at times more. One might offer the proof: with the disk on the turntable and the text in hand, here is what one will hear (example 8.2):

Ex. 8.2. *Pelléas et Mélisande,* Tower Scene, Act III

Is the lack of professional awareness not as bad here for the conductor as for the singer in this case?

The last example brings us back to where we were in the third act (example 8.3).

as written:

et ils m'ai - ment, ils m'ai - ment plus que toi!

alteration:

et ils m'ai - ment, ils m'ai - ment plus que toi!

Ex. 8.3. *Pelléas et Mélisande,* Tower Scene, Act III

How complicated life is, and how impossible you are going to find me. This is what they call in the army "a bad spirit."

I have reproached the singer for not singing "the note." Can you argue that, should another sing *the note,* I would still not be content? So here I have a measure that a singer's story reminds me of, which delighted my dear friend Rose Féart. She had so admirably "said" the letter of Geneviève and was then, at the inauguration of the Théâtre des Champs-Elysées, an Agathe in *Freischütz* that no Vienna or Berlin star could make me forget.

In the opera troupe we had a certain Mediterranean tenor who excelled in *Benvenuto Cellini* in delivering up an admirable "Trommppe le trommppeur mmême . . . ," which one took pleasure in having him repeat under all sorts of pretexts. One day Durec, in whom scene design has lost a wonderful artist, reproached our tenor for being too passive in singing a love duet in some old work I now forget. "But good heavens," exclaimed Durec, "at least move your arms a little!" "Well, look here," retorted the other, "I am a tenor with my voice, and not with my arms!"

Thus you can hear in recording this same fragment of the third act sung by this *tenor with the voice.*[18] He will speak vehemently to you of the "châveux" (for "cheveux") of Mélisande, and when he emphasizes the words "toute la nuit, toute la nuit," you will certainly wish to add, thinking of the unfortunate Mélisande, "Poor little woman!!!" At least we can pay our respects to the disk for having spared us this bit of theater.

To the first of these gentlemen, who lacked "certain notes," we would bring to mind the great Faure declaring in all humility that, when asked by Verdi himself, he was able to resist the temptation of singing certain magnificent roles that he would have been happy to interpret, had his voice not denied him the tessitura.

And to the other gentleman, as to many other singers and conductors in the second rank who shamelessly dare to launch into such works, we dedicate the sage advice of a laborer full of good sense: "There are some things you can't get mixed up in!"

To the last words of Pelléas, "Tu es ma prisonnière cette nuit . . . toute la nuit . . . toute la nuit" [you are my prisoner tonight . . . all night . . . all night], Mélisande responds simply and in her charming lover's faltering, "Pelléas, Pelléas" (example 8.4).

Ex. 8.4. *Pelléas et Mélisande,* Tower Scene, Act III

One might observe that the rhythm of the second "Pelléas" is exactly a metrical doubling of the first, as with Pelléas's two expressions of "toute la nuit" (exnple 8.5).

Ex. 8.5. *Pelléas et Mélisande,* Act IV (excerpt)

This procedure is frequent in Debussy's lyricism. Just previously we encountered it in the scene at the cave when Mélisande says "Allons nous en" [Let's go away] (example 8.6).

Ex. 8.6. *Pelléas et Mélisande,* Act II (excerpt)

And we shall observe it a little before the death of Pelléas, even more stressed (example 8.7):

Ex. 8.7. *Pelléas et Mélisande,* Act IV (excerpt)

At each occurrence it is essential that the difference be observed exactly. "J'entends un bruit de pas . . . Laisse-moi. C'est Golaud! Je crois que c'est Golaud!" [I hear footsteps . . . Leave me. It's Golaud! I think it's Golaud!] as the frightened Mélisande calls out. You can recognize Golaud surging from the shadows. And then you must hear Dufranne for your consolation, concluding the scene on the last turns of the disk in question.[19]

What other art could realize the miracle that music gives us? By the play of themes, the interlude that follows lays bare the souls of the three people we have just left. We experience again their anguish, their struggle, their illusions, their despair. All that rises, rises as the sea, and then subsides. But then the calm suddenly becomes disquieting. Golaud has led Pelléas into the subterranean passages of the castle. We do not know—he does not know himself—what he has come to do.

Every word of the poem contains a symbol, each sentence a philosophy. It is here, above all (and in analogous passages), where the most frequent error of Maeterlinck's interpreters occurs. This error consists in making much of these symbols and this philosophy, underscoring them, whereas in fact they should emerge from an interpretation devoid of hidden motives.

The orchestra offers a bit of clarity, but at first only a little. It is like a soft halo seen from a distance. Then the flutes bring some freshness, like a breath of clear air. The halo becomes clearer, it grows. And there is light, full light, and good sea air. There is fresh breeze, sunshine, which call forth the wonderful exclamation from Pelléas, "Ah! je respire enfin!" [Ah! At last I can breathe!]

Oh! here is music of the flowers arranged along the terrace, the odor of green plants and moist roses rising up! The glockenspiel sounds noon a noise as entrancing in its way as droplets of water full of light. And there are children going down toward the shore to swim. "A propos de Mélisande," Golaud says suddenly, "j'ai entendu ce qui s'est dit et ce qui s'est passé hier soir. Il ne faut pas que cela se répète." [About Mélisande. I know what was said and what happened last night. It must not happen again.]

We return to the same scene, again at night. And this is the remarkable moment when Golaud, tortured with jealousy, questions little Yniold in an attempt to *know.* Too little attention is paid to the admirable scene with which the fourth act begins. Performers don't give it the proper care. The fugitive dialogue of the two lovers standing before the closed door is riddled with performance difficulties.

This offers us a happy occasion to pay homage to another unforgettable artist who helped create *Pelléas.* We refer now to Félix Vieuille, who unfortunately has not recorded even a fragment of the score. But in my presence he offered advice about the role of Arkel to a younger colleague. I think of his words when listening to a record of the recitative of Arkel sung by M. Tubiana. At least this recording does not stop short after the question, rendering the sense meaningless, as does another of Arkel's recitatives, a musical amputation that is unacceptable.

Golaud appears. His exasperation has risen to such an extent that he bursts out at the slightest pretext:

> —Pourquoi tremblez-vous ainsi? Je ne vais pas vous tuer!
> —Pourquoi m'examinez-vous comme un pauvre?
> —Voyez-vous ces grands yeux? Ils sont plus grands que l'innocence! Ils donneraient à Dieu des leçons d'innocence!
>
> [—Why are you trembling so? I'm not going to kill you!
> —Why do you gaze at me like a beggar?
> —Do you see those big eyes? They're bigger than innocence itself! They could teach God lessons about innocence!]

And secretly, exasperated by his inability to master his admiration *and his infinite tenderness:* "On dirait que les anges du ciel y célèbrent sans cesse un baptême!" [One would say that the angels in heaven were celebrating their baptism endlessly!]

Then his terrifying, brutal anger erupts (which made many in the audience laugh in early performances), and then the intervention of Arkel, outraged, "Golaud!" How commendable Vieuille was here. Golaud, affecting a sudden calm: "Vous ferez comme il vous plaira, voyez-vous . . . et puis, je ne suis pas un espion. J'attendrai le hasard; et alors . . . Oh! alors!" [You shall do as you please, do you see . . . and then, I'm not a spy . . . I will await Chance; and then . . . oh, then!] One can never forget the last two words of Dufranne and their terrifying piano, nor the last phrase of Vieuille: "Si j'étais Dieu, j'aurais pitié du coeur des hommes!" [If I were God, I would pity the hearts of human beings!]

Next comes perhaps the most beautiful of the interludes, followed by the scene of little Yniold with the sheep, which lasts only a few minutes but which is usually cut. How many still know it?

We might pay homage publicly to Bourdin for not yielding to false traditions and for singing forte and *librement,* just as Debussy indicated, on the phrase "Je t'aime." This is because using a subito piano there is incorrect. Here again we must consider the ease adopted by certain singers. Why not also the eye turned aside or the mouth screwed up, as one might imagine grotesque performances providing?

Alas, it is getting late. Perhaps I have run on beyond your attention and patience, for both of which I thank you. Pelléas has died and Mélisande will as well soon. Poor Golaud finally discovered himself in an atrocious way, in the last explosion of his grief, in his insensate desire to know. But he will die like a blind man. And so Mélisande dies, her hands held out to her little infant. And the wisdom of the old king of Allemonde concludes the story when a bell, far off, tolls a quiet knell for Mélisande. Let us listen to Arkel: "Il faut parler à voix basse, maintenant." [We must speak in low voices now.] None dares to trouble the silence when a final harp arpeggio leads the soul of Mélisande to the paradise of the Damoiselle élue.

Faced with the greatest, the most perfect masterpiece of our beautiful music, shall we not when we come to interpret the work be, as Golaud has it, "comme un aveugle qui cherche son trésor au fond de l'océan" [as a blind man who searches for his treasure at the depths of the ocean]?

You had to have seen Debussy, simple but serious, attentive at the piano, to have understood the real mystery of the interpreter. There he sought to be admitted to the communion of souls as they create sound. There one heard Debussy playing as if to efface himself before the composer whose work he was about to perform. Little did it matter that the composer was Debussy himself. *It was as if he did not know it!* He was in the service of Music. In undertaking these discussions, I have simply tried to indicate how often we distance ourselves from that conception, which must be the ideal for any good, any true musician.

Certainly, I must acknowledge a charming phrase of Debussy's, gently consoling a friend after one of the last successes he was pleased to celebrate, telling him wistfully, "You see quite well that one mustn't love music too much!" We know ourselves so little.

Musicians, singers, conductors, and all of you artisans of recorded music who, to keep alive and unmechanical in front of the microphone—so faithful but pitiless—how much I could love you if you loved music as much as I do. Serve it well, as I strive always to serve it better. And we cannot fail to hear the results as long as we agree to the effort! All around us are never-ending discussions about world peace. Here we are, at home and in foreign countries, the finest of artisans. Let us not forget the beautiful legend of Arion, saved by the charm of his lyre and celebrated even by those who wished to kill him.

Mesdames, Mesdemoiselles, Messieurs, in these discussions I have avoided technical language to be more agreeable, perhaps, and more helpful without being frivolous. I sought to maintain the discussions within a proper frame of reference, and I hope that I have succeeded.

At the performance recognizing the fiftieth year of *Carmen,* which I had the honor of directing, Camille Bellaigue was invited to speak. He began with this sentence of Don José's: "Mais moi, Carmen, je t'aime encore!" [But Carmen, I love you still!]

I shall not take my conclusion from among the three masterpieces we have just reviewed, but from the *Ode à la musique* of Emmanuel Chabrier, who likewise loved music. And if we might, may we end with these verses:

Musique adorable. O déesse!
Mère du souvenir et nourrice du rêve.
C'est toi
Qu'il nous plût aujourd'hui d'invoquer sous ce toit!

[Adorable Music, O goddess!
Mother of memory and nurturer of the dream.
It is you
Whom we are happy to invoke here today!]

—Translated by James R. Briscoe

Chapter 9 Debussy, *Pelléas,* and Orchestral Conducting: An Interview with Pierre Boulez

James R. Briscoe

Pierre Boulez was born in 1925 in Montbrison, France. After a year of high school specializing in higher mathematics, he began intensive music study, and in 1944 he joined Olivier Messiaen's harmony class at the Paris Conservatoire. He became absorbed in serial technique and its extensions in the 1950s, as well as with elements of performer choice. In 1955 he began conducting, first at the Petit-Marigny company and then in 1956 for its successor, the Domaine Musical. He founded the Ensemble InterContemporain in Paris and figured prominently in the establishment of IRCAM (Institut de Recherche et de Co-ordination Acoustique-Musical) at the Centre Georges Pompidou. Boulez stands out as one of the foremost proponents of today's music, whose roots lie in Debussy, Stravinsky, and the Viennese school of Webern, Schoenberg, and Berg.

He began his orchestral conducting with a guest appearance with the Orquestra Sinfonica Venezuela in 1956 and continued at the major orchestras of Europe and the United States. He has performed prominently in Paris and London, especially for the BBC Symphony Orchestra, the Südwestfunk Orchestra of Darmstadt, the Concertgebouw of Amsterdam, the Los Angeles Philharmonic, the New York Philharmonic, the Cleveland Orchestra, and the Chicago Symphony Orchestra, of which he became the principal guest conductor in 1995. In his work as both conductor and scholar he has focused on the orchestral music of Debussy. He conducted *Pelléas et Mélisande* on two occasions, in 1969 at Covent Garden (a Vaclav Kaslik production) and in 1992 with the Welsh National Opera (a Peter Stein production), and he prepared, with Myriam Chimènes, the critical edition of *Jeux* for the ongoing Editions Durand/Costallat *Oeuvres complètes de Debussy.*

I interviewed Maestro Boulez for this book on 4 August 1997 in Paris. I have edited the interview slightly with his approval and annotated it where necessary.

PELLÉAS ET MÉLISANDE

James Briscoe: May we begin with *Pelléas et Mélisande*? Have you reflected further on elements of its realization since the 1992 production with Peter Stein? That is, have you imagined further directions that you will wish to take when you conduct it again?

Pierre Boulez: I think that I will never conduct it again. I made a first approach in 1969 at Covent Garden. The director was to have been Wieland Wagner, but unfortunately he died before that could occur. I was not terribly happy with the production. Therefore, I wanted to do it with a director whom I liked very much, and Peter Stein was my choice. I worked closely and in a quite satisfying way with him. The great difference for me between 1969 and 1992 concerned the circumstances regarding the director.

As you can imagine, you go forward and you do not remember exactly what you have done. But also, I did quite a lot in between those two productions, such as the *Ring* at Bayreuth, *Lulu, Wozzeck* and so on. All these were very important, and when I returned to *Pelléas* in 1992 I had quite a different approach. It was more dramatic, more theatrical in a way than before. Certainly I dared to create many more contrasts than in 1969. One remembers that, especially in France, there is the tradition of doing Debussy in a smooth way, nice and so beautiful always. I find that, on the contrary, there are indeed strong contrasts in Debussy, and especially in this period of his life, the period of *Pelléas,* the *Nocturnes,* of *La mer.* And so, in returning to *Pelléas* for the 1992 production, I discovered a very fresh Debussy. Especially was that the case in certain scenes of the opera that he wrote early, which resemble the Quartet in their youthfulness. That period between age thirty and forty I like in all composers, because it is one of discovery and evolution. After that, you find more depth but perhaps no longer as fresh an approach.

JB: You stated that you have found a basis that is "cruel and mysterious" in *Pelléas et Mélisande.* How did that inform your approach to conducting the music?

PB: Yes, certainly that is the case. If I had given a title to this opera, I would have called it *Golaud.* For me he is really the central figure. The more I became involved with this piece, the more I found the importance and definition of the character of Golaud, which is more pressing than the others. Mélisande, yes, but Pelléas is rather flat. The naïveté of Mélisande is a pseudo-naïveté—she is very tricky, on the contrary. But the character of Golaud is very conspicuous, as he goes completely mad. In the first scene he is tamed by the presence of Mélisande. But already in the second scene in which he appears, when Mélisande has lost the ring, he becomes suddenly crazy. Immediately, in the scene with the child Yniold when he is spying, he falls absolutely out of himself, perhaps fortunately for Mélisande. In the scene in the cave, he wants to terrify Pelléas. He does that, I would like to say, naturally. He does not try to make people afraid, he just *is* frightening because of this kind of temper. He goes from making an effort to be in possession of himself to experiencing an eruption of temper. Afterwards he regrets his rage, so that one is aware of an unbalanced character. It is very attractive artistically for me, because you never know when or how the disaster will happen.

He is certainly the most complex and contrasted character musically. You have a noble music, the theme of Golaud, but also there is a music that is very pathetic that belongs to him. Then too, you have the most violent music that Debussy ever wrote at the scene where he drags Mélisande by the hair but also at the scene with Yniold. The poor boy has become very frightened because his father has gone mad.

JB: What difference in conception did you bring to the two different recordings you have made?

PB: I suppose that I have not listened to the recordings side by side. Before making the second, I certainly did not listen to the first. I wanted nothing that was artificial. I wanted every difference to be organic and to draw upon my experience conducting orchestrally and in the theater. In the end, it is not for me to check to see. Therefore, if someone finds differences, that is their view. I think I was different in the two recordings—I thought differently, but I never wanted to say "I did this in the past and now I want to do this other." All that seems too tricky and artificial.

JB: Are there particular problems in the orchestration of *Pelléas et Mélisande* that you observe, aspects of orchestral balance and control; and what has been your resolution?

PB: No, definitely not. The register of Debussy in the orchestra and in the voice, where the range is concerned, is rather small. Mélisande, for example, never has to sing very loudly. Her range of phrasing and dynamic is subdued, very close to the range of speaking most of the time. Especially is that the case in the scene ending Act IV between Pelléas and Mélisande at the fountain. Both say "Je t'aime," but in a very low register. That is exactly the contrary to Wagner, where sometimes you have a problem of balance if you let the orchestra go. The only moments in Debussy where balance is dangerous are where Golaud drags Mélisande by the hair, or perhaps with the boy Yniold's voice where he is spying in the scene with the sheep. In these cases you must keep the orchestra very low.

JB: Do you think of particular productions of *Pelléas* that you know about and that departed too much from the composer's ideals?

PB: I have ideas which are very generous, shall we say, in the domain of opera and the theater. The men who wrote opera, Debussy or, shall we say, Berg in *Wozzeck,* had in their minds the theater of their period. They thought in those terms, much as Wagner imagined the theater of his time. Thus they gained an idea of theater that was more conservative, shall we say, one that was more influenced by the milieu than were the musical aspects. They are more original from the musical point of view than from the theatrical one. Therefore I think that generally one cannot be in phase with what these composers were thinking in terms of theater. All plays in the theater are like that. If we were to see a play by Shakespeare or Molière, we would be disappointed to see this type of period reconstitution.

Quite a long time ago, in the 1950s, I saw a production of Chekhov's *Cherry Orchard* by the original Stanislavsky company. But that was fifty-five years later than its period: it was not a museum piece, it was a mausoleum piece! It was completely out of touch with us. Things that might have been very interesting in a given period can be uninteresting in our own time. I think that with opera it is exactly the same. Sometimes I hear, "Let's put that back in this or that period." And yet that is to transpose mechanically and is so constraining. The originality of the production and that of the opera both are lost.

But also there is something that does not fit sometimes when you want to pull the opera too far away from its time. Then you risk being out of touch, of losing the identity of the opera. Even so, I am always looking for a solution that perhaps the composer did not think of, because he was so taken with the environment of his time.

JB: With regard to *Pelléas* but generally in Debussy, the dynamic range is quiet, relatively. Do you find that the range of sound or the intensity of sound requires reinforcement?

PB: Sometimes, yes. For instance, in the introduction of Act IV, which is with speed and movement, I provoke the dynamic. It needs energy at that point.

Sometimes I enhance the energy each time Golaud gets mad. You have to push there, since Golaud's music is generally the more contrasted. But for instance with Arkel, on the contrary, it is always a dynamic that is very noble but soft. The personality of the old man is soft.
JB: Do you find special demands, when rehearsing and performing *Pelléas,* in relating the pit to the stage?
PB: No, because when I participate in a production, I am there from the very beginning. I follow most of the rehearsals, although the director must be alone at certain times. If I am not satisfied with a solution that the director proposes, then I tell him so. I suggest that it will not fit musically with what must occur. Therefore, all these problems are solved every day, one by one.

When I begin to rehearse the opera with the orchestra, I know what the people on stage are doing. There are no surprises: I know very well what position the singers are in, why they are doing something, and so on. And with few exceptions the problems of fit are resolved by the time full rehearsals begin.
JB: Some critics suggest that *Pelléas* has gained only a specialized audience. What have you observed?
PB: I think that is not completely untrue, but perhaps the critics do not reveal the right reasons for their criticisms. Many people who go to the opera want to hear voices, voices with great range and virtuosity. Such music they hear in the Italian bel canto school or perhaps in Wagner. But with Debussy the voice is treated in a reserved way, as we have said. For them, therefore, *Pelléas* is not an opera that is appealing. As you know, Romain Rolland attended the work with Richard Strauss and recorded Strauss's reaction: "What, that's not an opera!" He could not conceive of an opera with this restricted use of the voice—what a different color and a contrast between *Salome* and *Pelléas!* Audiences get involved in the big monologue at the end of *Salome.* That's everything: like the winner of the Tour de France. They like this kind of muscular achievement.

Therefore I think that in this sense *Pelléas* will never be "popular." There is no excess. And yet, *Pelléas* has an important lesson to teach, a statement to make.

CONDUCTING AS PRACTICE

JB: You have served on the editorial committee of the ongoing *Oeuvres complètes* of Debussy, and have edited the score of *Jeux* with Myriam Chimènes. Has your approach to *Jeux* as a conductor changed because of the work on the edition?
PB: No, the edition is the result of my experience. What I was discussing with Myriam Chimènes when working with her [were] the mistakes I have found in

approaching the score, the inconsistencies that appeared. She was in charge of verifying the various editions and manuscripts to determine what score says one thing or the other. My choices were the result of working with the score, and not the contrary. My editorial work grew from my work as a conductor.

JB: Having studied the earliest recordings of the orchestral music, I find that over time tempos grew slower for Debussy. Once again, yours are animated. What is your conception of tempos in Debussy?

PB: They have certainly changed quite a lot with regard to flexibility. I cannot speak about their actual speed. When I did the first recordings in the 1960s, I had been conducting for less than ten years. I began really in 1959 to conduct the repertoire. Therefore when I recorded the orchestral works more than twenty years later in the early 1990s, I was much more experienced with the scores and with an orchestra. At that point I was much freer, and it was much easier to communicate how I conceived the music. I was of course more spontaneous and communicative with the orchestra in the recent recordings.

JB: Paul Griffiths wrote of your 1991 Debussy recordings on DGG that they show "the grand sweep and luxury texture of Boulez's current preferences." The recordings of the 1960s were "similarly brisk but with a spare, quasi-Japanese feeling. Boulez showed a willingness to sound out the weirdness in Debussy, but now [in 1991] there is a more sumptuous sort of pleasure."[1] Do you agree with that assessment of your approach to Debussy?

PB: Yes, that goes back to what I mentioned. If you are communicating more easily, one can get more from the orchestra. It allowed me to call forth a richer texture, a more varied texture. It allowed something that is more exact structurally, but also the texture is in a sense hidden. Before, in the early recordings, the structure was strong but the texture was weak. More recently, the structure remains strong but the texture is rich. So therefore, texture and structure fit together much better.

It is interesting to observe how further study allows one to be more spontaneous. Your knowledge is much deeper and your reaction is quick. You have no need to *think* anymore; you just do it.

JB: Does that attention to "sumptuous pleasure" remain, or do you still desire to "burn the mists off Debussy" as you once stated?[2] How do you reconcile those two interests?

PB: The range of the music of Debussy used to be considered small, and nice and smooth. But there is more to it than that. I am not speaking of a crudeness but of a certain violence in the music of Debussy. It is like a tiger or some other feline. He is quiet, but then all of a sudden he is *there*. For me that is the kind of very smooth but extremely quick reaction that is so difficult to master. That is what I mean when I say one must burn the mists off Debussy. One must sometimes be aggressive.

JB: The two forces of linearity and nuance—the horizontal and the detailed—seem to challenge conductors of Debussy particularly. Might you enlarge upon the comment that you gave at the 1993 conducting symposium in New York: you encouraged "a flexibility that does not destroy rhythm."[3]

PB: Yes, that's certainly right. The big difficulty concerns a flexibility or a kind of rubato. But you must pay attention to the rhythmical structure. For me, the Debussy rubato is one that is very subtle, but one in which the rhythm is certainly present. For instance, in even an early work like the *Prélude à l'après-midi d'un faune,* at the beginning you have the arabesques. They must be sudden and completely rhythmical. Otherwise the acute feeling of the music disappears.

This is extremely important. For me, in Debussy the problem is not of a local concern but a global one. Debussy never presents a kind of academic development. For example, in "Jeux de vagues," the second movement of *La mer,* there is a great deal of difficulty. One must be careful with many small details, but also one must attend to continuity. To manage this continuity alongside the many smaller aspects is the question. I find that you can achieve this only after going through the score quite a lot. Again it is a question of experience: you feel it and then you do not *think* about it.

JB: I would suggest that this point is the acid test in Debussy conducting, the matter of maintaining overall continuity while managing finesse and nuance.

PB: Absolutely, yes.

JB: What earlier or contemporary conductors of Debussy have you admired, for *Pelléas* or the orchestral music, and for what qualities?

PB: I heard *Pelléas* when I was very young, when I came to Paris in 1943. The *Pelléas* of that time was the *Pelléas* of Roger Desormière. But when you listen to that recording, you say that it is not good, first because of the quality of the recording, which is far from being perfect to our ears, but also because of the quality of the voices. They are quite different from what we are used to hearing now. I remember that Jacques Jansen [as Pelléas] and Irène Joachim [as Mélisande] were really at the top of Debussy performance at the time. But when I listen to that recording now, I am really puzzled because I cannot really join the two aspects together: what I hear on the recording now and what I *remember* having heard. Old recordings like that, especially when you attended the performances, do not allow you to join both ends together.

I was very enthusiastic at that time. But I consider that rather a historical recording with a great distance between then and now. And so, one cannot judge it as one judges a recording of today. But I don't think that recording is particularly indicative of Debussy's direct influence, it was already so distant from the composer. I doubt that Desormière heard a performance of Pelléas while Debussy was still alive. Probably the only two later conductors who heard the opera in Debussy's day were Monteux and Inghelbrecht.

JB: Do you hold Inghelbrecht, Ansermet, and Desormière to be particularly sensitive in respect to Debussy's performance values? Was there a continuing line, or a tradition from Debussy to them?

PB: Inghelbrecht for me was not as great a conductor as Desormière. Inghelbrecht was a specialist, however, although not as strong a technician. I heard Ansermet quite a lot when he was conducting in Paris. He conducted many works of Debussy very ably. I do not know if there can be a single tradition coming from Debussy. I am not really obsessed with biographies. Debussy had a very funny and complaining attitude toward conductors, and he was very inconsistent. At times he was not happy with Pierné or with Chevillard. With Inghelbrecht he was dealing with a much younger man. And so, you do not know Debussy's thoughts entirely in that regard. Wagner, for instance, was very forceful about his performers, and when he was not happy, he would say, "I want this or that." That especially concerned Richter, Levi, and Mottl. There you can be sure that there was something concrete that he wanted and found with them.

But also in this case, I think people have transformed Debussy in a mannered way. You cannot keep something on and on. Even now, you have two cases that are significant. Stravinsky recorded practically all his major works. Most of the recordings show a very strong personality but very poor conducting. You cannot take that, even with the authority of the composer, as a real model or example. And Bartók was occasionally a performer who recorded, but he did not devote himself completely to performing—there is a much different case with those who might play the sonata for two pianos fifty or sixty times. You might well listen to Bartók's recording and find some very interesting characteristics about how it might be performed, but you cannot say that it is a model forever. When a composer does so much, he only performs from time to time and does not devote himself to constant performing. If you hear, for instance, the recording of Ravel conducting the *Boléro,* you find that it is dreadful.

JB: It has seemed to me that Inghelbrecht, among all the earliest conductors,

strove to maintain Debussy's ideals perhaps the most closely. There are indications of Inghelbrecht having studied the scores with Debussy.
PB: Yes. There was another who seemed to succeed in pleasing Debussy, and that was André Caplet. Debussy wrote in his correspondence that he was very pleased with Caplet's conducting. But unfortunately he died too early to leave any recordings. But both Ansermet and Inghelbrecht began their full conducting careers too late to have that sort of interaction.
JB: Does the younger generation of conductors encounter special difficulties or shortfalls in approaching Debussy, and what advice would you offer them?
PB: The best advice I can give them is to learn the scores thoroughly. I do not think that you can transmit very much verbally. Every generation produces a strong personality among conductors, and every strong personality will find its way. The conductor can listen to concerts or recordings, but in the end you must find your own way. If you do not, then you have accomplished nothing. So therefore when I am asked, I say, "I do it this way." But if the young conductor wishes to do it another way, then do it another way. Sometimes I might well say, "Debussy does not require abruptness; instead he requires very, very refined transitions, careful cuts." As you know, that is really quite the contrary to Beethoven! Or I might say, "For me, the rubato is very subtle, very quick, like light changing rapidly." That I can give as my opinion, but I also can say that if you are consistent with another opinion, I can accept it.
JB: You have spoken of general mistakes orchestras make with certain composers. What common problems occur in Debussy, or in the preparation you encounter when you meet an orchestra?
PB: Orchestras sometimes bring certain habits that are not, in my opinion, correct. Beethoven, like Debussy, might be affected by an allargando or crescendo or slow tempo that I find upsetting to the music. For instance, when I begin with Debussy's second Nocturne, I find that it is always too quick. I remember having heard a recording of Toscanini playing the second Nocturne. He took it at such a frantic speed that I could simply not understand. Suddenly the middle became much too slow, and when the two themes returned and are superimposed, there was no unity. For me, I strive for the logic of the composer. When Debussy has a theme at one speed, and later superimposes another theme, the logic suggests that the two are at the same speed. That is a simple deduction. And so, when I hear in a performance a first theme that is very quick and the second much less quick, then I am not satisfied by the kind of approximation that occurs when they join.

The bad habits that I find consistently concern tempo. I agree completely with Wagner: the music finds its real meaning when you have the right tempo, or when the tempo will fit everything together. The right tempo is that which allows every part to relate to the global aspect.

JB: Are there basic dispositions or values within the orchestra that must be adhered to in Debussy? For example, in conversing with Célestin Deliège you observe that the number, balance, and order of instruments is different for Debussy as contrasted with Strauss and Mahler.[4]

PB: In Debussy, the mass of the orchestra is generally reduced, as compared with Strauss or even Mahler. Even when Debussy uses an orchestra that is rather large, as in *Jeux* with its four woodwinds and so on, he uses them in a very sparing way, not massively. And too, the writing for the strings is very often divisi. He was the first, really, to employ such a treatment of the strings. That makes the texture of the orchestra rich, in a way, but at the same time thinner with all the divisions. In Mahler, especially, one finds an accumulation of instruments: he would tend to use four flutes together. He often desires a single, thick line to dominate the full orchestra. But in French orchestration, one hears a different quality in Ravel and Debussy, and that is exactly the same as Roussel or Dukas. There the tendency always is to isolate, and to have the solo as a pure sound, not mixed. It is more in the tradition of Wagner to double the line, to mix it. You find that even in *Parsifal,* which is much more transparent for instance than the *Ring.* But in Berlioz you find very few doubled lines. At issue is truly a French sound, relying much more upon the soloist.

JB: You have spoken of Debussy's relatively clear forms.[5] What particular responsibilities does the conductor bear in articulating those, as, for example, with tempos?

PB: I think that one must attend to the "envelope" of the form, the curve that the form is creating with the amount of dynamic and repetition, the change of color and texture. All this creates the form, along with the thematic material of course. You must also bring out the thematic material very clearly. That is so especially when the form is complex, and uneasy to grasp for a listener. One must bring the thematic material forward very clearly, but not too obviously, either. You must hear the main theme and the environment, the theme and its reinforcement.

PROGRAMMING DEBUSSY

JB: Early in your orchestral career, Debussy and Webern, and also Berg and Schoenberg figured prominently. Of course Boulez, Stockhausen, and others appeared as well in your programs. The presence of Debussy continued right up through the 1960s and seventies but perhaps has drawn back somewhat, as your programming has become broader.

PB: I find that Debussy has the same prominence, but I am wary of always playing the same things. Therefore I have performed *Jeux,* the *Nocturnes,* and *La mer* very many times. I also have played the *Images* often, although in a way the movements "Gigues" and "Rondes de printemps" are weaker pieces, especially the latter. "Rondes" lacks strength after the beginning, when the folk song comes back time and again, and one feels that it does not hold up. But I am very fond of *Ibéria* from *Images.*

JB: How did Debussy appear to you as you planned those concerts, and does he continue to offer a bridge for listeners to the early century into the present?

PB: I do think so, although I think that there is no direct connection necessarily. Some of the works of Debussy, and certainly beginning with *L'après-midi d'un faune,* were the beginning of modernity. When you think for instance of the young Mahler or the young Strauss, who perhaps exhibit more audacity in their works, you still must find that the modernity is not there. For me, when I listen to the *Faune,* it reminds me of the first pictures of Monet. When I think of the German area, I might think of the painter Max Liebermann,[6] but then you think of the end of an era if you compare him to Monet. And when you think of Mahler, you think of the end of a tradition. And yet Debussy is the beginning. One might view two mountains, with Debussy as one and the contemporary as another. But now we are removed from both traditions, and we see not a valley between but the junction connecting Debussy with the modern.

JB: In regard to composition, you have observed an urge to return to certain works to "fix your horizon in relation to yourself."[7] Are there works by Debussy to which you have returned as a conductor, to fix your horizon?

PB: I don't think that I would discover something new at this point. But I nonetheless take much pleasure in returning to them. I can see where I am now. I still find myself saying, "Oh yes, I thought this way about a certain passage thirty years ago, but now it seems otherwise." Sometimes you are more complacent about a work, or sometimes less. Now I find that I have more and more admiration for *L'après-midi d'un faune,* but much less for "Rondes de printemps!" I was more indulgent toward that work formerly than I am now. When I was younger, *L'après-midi d'un faune* was natural for me. But now it seems not so natural, but rather a turning point in history, and thus I come to my admiration for it.

THE AUTHORITY OF THE SCORE

JB: In your conversations with Jean Vermeil, you spoke of your goal to approach the score literally. Elsewhere Peter Heyworth observes that interpretation is foreign to your approach.[8] Is that what Debussy wanted, in your view?

PB: First, I am not an objective performer. Objectivity was an obsession between the two wars. It was tied to Ravel and Stravinsky but to Debussy not at all. Ravel was certainly irritated by the excess of romanticism that he heard around him. Listen, for example, to what certain pianists were doing with Chopin—there were certain traditions of romanticism that were truly terrifying. The model conductor for Ravel and Stravinsky, in that context, was Ansermet. But for me, the score is simply a diagram. It becomes interesting only when it is distorted, but that within a certain logic. If you distort it in an absurd way, then you join the postromantic performers and lose all relationship with the text. But on the contrary, if you are in logic with the text, the performance will always be within the reach of what the composer has written. I call that interpretation.

JB: You have, for example, rethought the score of the *Images* in placing *Ibéria* at the end, instead of at the middle section between "Gigues" and "Rondes de printemps" as Debussy planned it.

PB: The order of the printed score looks more symmetrical: small piece, big piece, small piece—one, two, three. Several times I tried the printed order of "Gigues," *Ibéria,* and finally "Rondes de printemps." But in the end "Rondes de printemps" seemed like a kind of encore that is not required. It finishes in a way not at all as brilliant as the end of *Ibéria,* the middle "big piece" that is a set of three as you know. And therefore my logic is better. You begin with a first movement moderato ["Rondes de printemps"], and then "Gigues," which is a kind of slow moderato, and then you have the three tempi [the three movements of *Ibéria*] at the end. So I have "one, two, one, two, three." I find that my logic is a "concert" logic.

JB: Do you feel that you could persuade Debussy of that logic?

PB: I don't care!

JB: In another instance, you offered vowel sounds instead of the unidentified syllable or "bouches fermées" for the textless "Sirènes," movement three of the *Nocturnes.* Your defense that this poses no contradiction of the musical text seemed clear.[9] Are there other passages of the orchestral scores that suggest such adaptation?

PB: No, I find this passage to be the exception. I find that only opening the mouths, "ah, ah," to be terribly monotonous. But when you have a texture between the low and top voices, I do not choose that for the sonority. Instead, the singer opens the mouth with a forte and closes with such vowels as "o," "u." That is the necessary transition from open to closed. But I don't use "i" ["ee"] for instance, only "a," "o," "u" and never "i" or "eu." I don't use vowels that are out of this range.

JB: How then does one evaluate the composer's way of hearing his music? Can that ever be ascertained?

PB: I think it is impossible to guess what the composer wants. I have the experience of Messiaen, of Lutoslawski, of Berio, Ligeti. So I have experienced composers who have listened to performances I was involved in. Generally they might be panicked, because they are not in control of the sounds themselves: they say "you must do this or that." They are scarcely "professional" about their comments—they want this, that, or the other. You try to correct things. But only in my own works can I make the right corrections as a conductor. I suppose that that was the same with Strauss and Mahler, whose connection with the instruments was there immediately.

It also depends on the particular gift. Stravinsky was gifted with a sense of orchestral textures even without the experience of conducting. He is *there* with very good balance, with no problem at all. Schoenberg is more problematic because he was attempting more in the way of dispersing the orchestra. But he is not as sure as Mahler or Stravinsky in what he wanted to hear. For him, the color of the orchestra was a consideration: he did not attend to the distance between instruments. For instance, he will offer a phrase that begins with the trumpet, and then all the violins, and then a cello solo. Then will come a clarinet solo that will create a physical distance between the instruments. Thus there is not only a problem of masses of instruments or solos but also of space. That can be difficult to adjust and balance. For instance, op. 16 is very difficult. In the last movement, *recitativo obligato,* it is hard to create a sense of continuity. The same goes for Berg's op. 6, where the difficult matter of projecting the dynamic markings is concerned.

JB: What is the proper equilibrium between "object" and "work-in-progress" for Debussy?

PB: Each of his works is a closed world. One of course can identify an evolution in his life, and in this sense the different works share in the evolution. However, each work is defined, unto itself. The only place where one finds a sense of works as a group is the three last sonatas. One does not know what he would have done had he completed the set of six. First there was cello and piano, then suddenly flute, viola, and harp, and then violin and piano. Then there was to be the project with horn, harpsichord, and oboe, a fantastic idea.

JB: You state that, in the end, there are no rigid criteria in approaching a score. One must consider all contingencies of Debussy's time and of today. In what light does the composition as document still interest you principally?

PB: If because of acoustical conditions I have to provide a bassoon solo that must be heard against the strings, I might choose two bassoons playing mezzo-forte. That occurs for example just two bars at the very beginning of *La mer.* That is necessary in a large hall. Debussy has one bassoon playing forte. Such things sometimes must be changed somewhat.

JB: With Vermeil, you criticized that one might arrive at a "mania of doing Brahms only with catgut."[10] And yet that is happening now! Probably that is an extreme position. But are there absolute values in the performance of Debussy which, in your view, have been overcome by distortions of our own day?

PB: I have spoken against the fetishism of our day. For me it often moves out of context with history. Often instrumentalists have contributed a technique that is quite different from that of a hundred years ago. Even in my lifetime, I can make a comparison regarding the horns of forty or fifty years ago with those of today. The contrast is enormous! They have a bigger, more consistent sound, and the range is more homogeneous and so on. Any instrument offers this kind of education. Even as a listener, you would hear that former sound as artificial and not a genuine sound. One hundred years ago one could imagine only that kind of sound, appropriate for the times. Now we have another sound in mind, and to listen to the other would appear as an artistic engraving of the period.

The essence of music is more than that. If the essence lies only in that, then music is a very weak art.

DEBUSSY PERFORMANCE AND SOCIETY

JB: Do you think that finding a place in the popular media—perhaps in the movies—would benefit Debussy and the cause of contemporary music?

PB: I think that music generally would benefit from propaganda. However, I do not think of Debussy as particularly appropriate for that. He is a very reserved man, as in his music. He certainly withholds the gesture of a Puccini. He is very discreet. Even Stravinsky is much more outgoing in a way. But Debussy could benefit from such an exposure, as would all music. I find there are always works that communicate with a large group and those that communicate with fewer. For instance, I might take Beethoven, the epitome of a musician known everywhere. If you play the Ninth Symphony, everyone would flock to the performance. If the Mass, then many fewer. And if you play the last quartets, then you reduce to a few. I find that I am not at all shocked by that. One day Beethoven must express himself in a quite expansive way but on another much more for himself. Shakespeare wrote dramas that are played constantly, but he also wrote the sonnets, known by very few people. I do not find that unrealistic to expect a different appreciation from audiences.

In Debussy, the range of popularity might not be the same, but the comparison is valid. *La mer* is constantly performed, and rightly so. But if you play the Sonata for Flute, Viola, and Harp, you will reduce your audience significantly. Ravel is performed constantly and everywhere. But if you give the *Chansons madécasses,* or the *Mallarmé Songs,* then the reduction of the audience is the same. The nature of the composer's expression is reserved at times. If you play Stravinsky's *Petrouchka* or *Rite of Spring,* the audience is always there. But if you play *Oedipus Rex* or *Orpheus,* then the audience is smaller. If you play the Sixth Symphony of Schubert, very few people come to hear. What a different story with the Unfinished or the Ninth in C.

JB: What part can the music of Debussy play in the education of the young? If the Rug Concerts[11] were to be reborn, one might imagine a prominence for Debussy.

PB: Certainly he should play a part. If you consistently play two works that are always very popular, the *Nocturnes* and *La mer,* or *Ibéria,* then that will be very significant. But perhaps *Jeux* is more refined and less accessible. There are three or four works by Debussy that have to be done constantly. In fact two are so performed, *La mer* and the *Nocturnes.*

JB: As you approach audiences today, do you still find it appropriate to quote Lenin: "Not every compromise is a concession?"[12]

PB: Lenin said once, "I like the Soviets, but with electricity—I like the revolution, but with electricity."

JB: How can Debussy form a bridge to the public where modern music is concerned?

PB: He is such a major figure of modernity that he should be as popular as Monet or Cézanne. But he is not yet. Perhaps he will be one day. But it is especially through this comparison with the world of painting that the importance can be seen.

Part Four **Debussy**

Performance and Score Analysis

Chapter 10 Structure and Performance: Metric and Phrase Ambiguities in the Three Chamber Sonatas

Richard S. Parks

I have always felt a quality of impulsiveness in Debussy's music. I treasure that quality and the richness of variety it engenders, or from which it arises (I'm not sure which). This impulsiveness is manifest in dramatic changes in the sensation of motion from moment to moment as the music halts suddenly, bursts ahead, veers off in some unexpected direction, stumbling here, gliding there. Then too, I have always been struck by his music's improvisatory character, in which an exquisite orderliness is often disrupted by moments of delicious chaos. I am convinced that such impressions emanate in large measure from his singular treatment of relations in the domains of meter and phrase, areas that can pose difficulties for performers, whose security in execution and ensemble requires, in addition to technical mastery, a sure sense of how a composition's multifarious formal and rhythmic events fit together in a coherent manner as the piece unfolds.

This chapter is dedicated to my sister and favorite violist, Susan St. Amour. I would like to thank Charles M. Joseph, Catherine Nolan, and Rosemary Pilling Parks for reading a late draft of this essay and contributing many helpful suggestions. The shortcomings that remain persist despite their efforts and are, of course, entirely my responsibility.

This essay springs from my interest in these qualities and their effect upon us as listeners (by which term I mean to encompass performers, including conductors, who after all direct their efforts at producing what they hear). I shall explore these qualities by concentrating on passages that embody them, selected from the three chamber sonatas. In particular, I shall explore metric and phrase relations in ways that performers can easily replicate using cues from the scores and discuss them in ways that invite exploration through performance. Indeed, although it suffices to play through the passages in one's head I encourage players to read with their instruments close at hand and to interrupt as appropriate for conducting practical experiments along lines I shall suggest.

THE "INTERLUDE" FROM THE *SONATE POUR FLÛTE, ALTO, ET HARPE*

Composed in 1915 when Debussy was in the throes of an ineluctable cancer and yet at the height of his creative powers, this irrepressibly sunny composition exhibits the composer's consummate technical mastery in the service of his prodigious musical imagination. The second movement, entitled "Interlude," employs a recursive formal design that somewhat resembles a traditional five-part rondo, with two bodies of thematic-harmonic material which we could characterize, respectively, as "principal-theme-group" versus "secondary-theme-group." (See example 10.1a, which models the formal plan as a series of rectangles corresponding to the series of sections. The rectangles' lengths are proportional relative to the durations, measured in quarter notes, of the sections they represent.) Each section is well defined by meter and key, the principal-theme-group set consistently in F minor and triple meter, the secondary-theme-group in B major and compound duple.[1] The secondary-theme-group material is quite straightforward, but that of the principal-theme-group harbors a number of ambiguities in the realms of metric and phrase structure. In particular, there are metric conflicts where experiential meter may contradict notated meter, and phrase boundary conflicts where the end of one phrase overlaps the beginning of another; although such conflicts are ironic for the listener, akin to puns, they can be problematic for performers.[2]

Consider mm. 1–7 (see example 10.1b).[3] Although they are notated in quarter-note triple meter, several features combine to facilitate hearing mm. 1–5 in quarter-note duple meter ($\frac{2}{4}$): the agogic accents in the flute at m. 1, beat 3, at m. 2, b. 2, and at m. 4, b. 2 (circled in example 10.1b); the repeated four–eighth note motivic pattern in the harp in mm. 4–5 (bracketed in example 10.1b); and

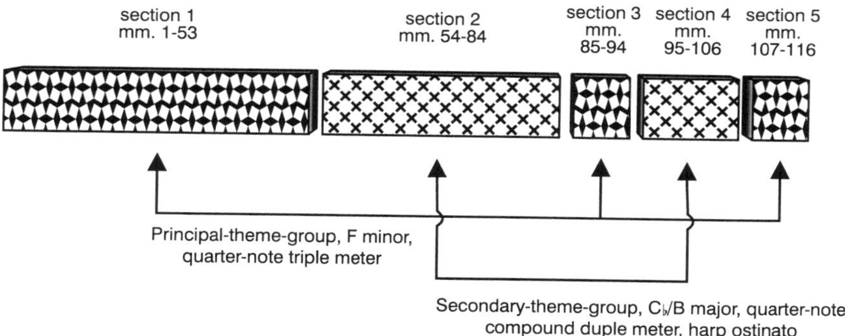

Ex. 10.1a. Overall form of the "Interlude" from the *Sonate pour flûte, alto et harpe*

the absence of articulations on the downbeats of mm. 2 and 4. At m. 6 a third iteration of the four–eighth note motivic pattern begun at m. 5, b. 3, is truncated by the strong dynamic accent that falls on the downbeat of m. 6,[4] which is reinforced by the three–quarter note motivic pattern that follows in the harp. Hence we may readily hear mm. 1–5 in $\frac{2}{4}$, but we will be hard put to resist hearing mm. 6–7 in anything other than $\frac{3}{4}$.

Performers may experience the metric nuances of mm. 1–7 by rehearsing these measures in their minds' ears while conducting: conduct mm. 1–5 in $\frac{2}{4}$, with a downbeat on b. 3 of m. 5, and then switch abruptly to $\frac{3}{4}$ for mm. 6–7. The thwarted $\frac{2}{4}$ anacrusis at m. 6 is almost palpable.

These same seven measures contain two phrases. The first culminates in m. 3, which is the locus of the upper registral extreme (g-flat^{2}),[5] the widest registral span (thirty semitones from the viola's c to the flute's g-flat^{2}), the highest registral mean-placement (the midpoint between the registral extremes straddles e-flat^{1}), a protracted metric conflict (three syncopations), and the loudest moment so far (following the crescendo from piano).

Thereafter the phrase recedes rapidly from its climax by means of an accelerating rhythmic figure and melodic descent set within a decrescendo, which combine to carry the phrase to a metrically weak conclusion on the half note c^{2} of m. 4, bb. 2–3. The entrance of the harp eclipses this conclusion, however, by commencing a new phrase at exactly the moment of the flute's arrival on its half-note goal. Or so it seems. In fact, there is no cadential or melodic closure for the first phrase, only a suggestion of cessation in the flute's relatively long duration on c^{2}. The way we really know that the first phrase has ended is because we hear a new phrase begin, in the harp. Thus the second phrase *overlaps* the first.

This phrase juncture is easy for performers to execute because in effect, the

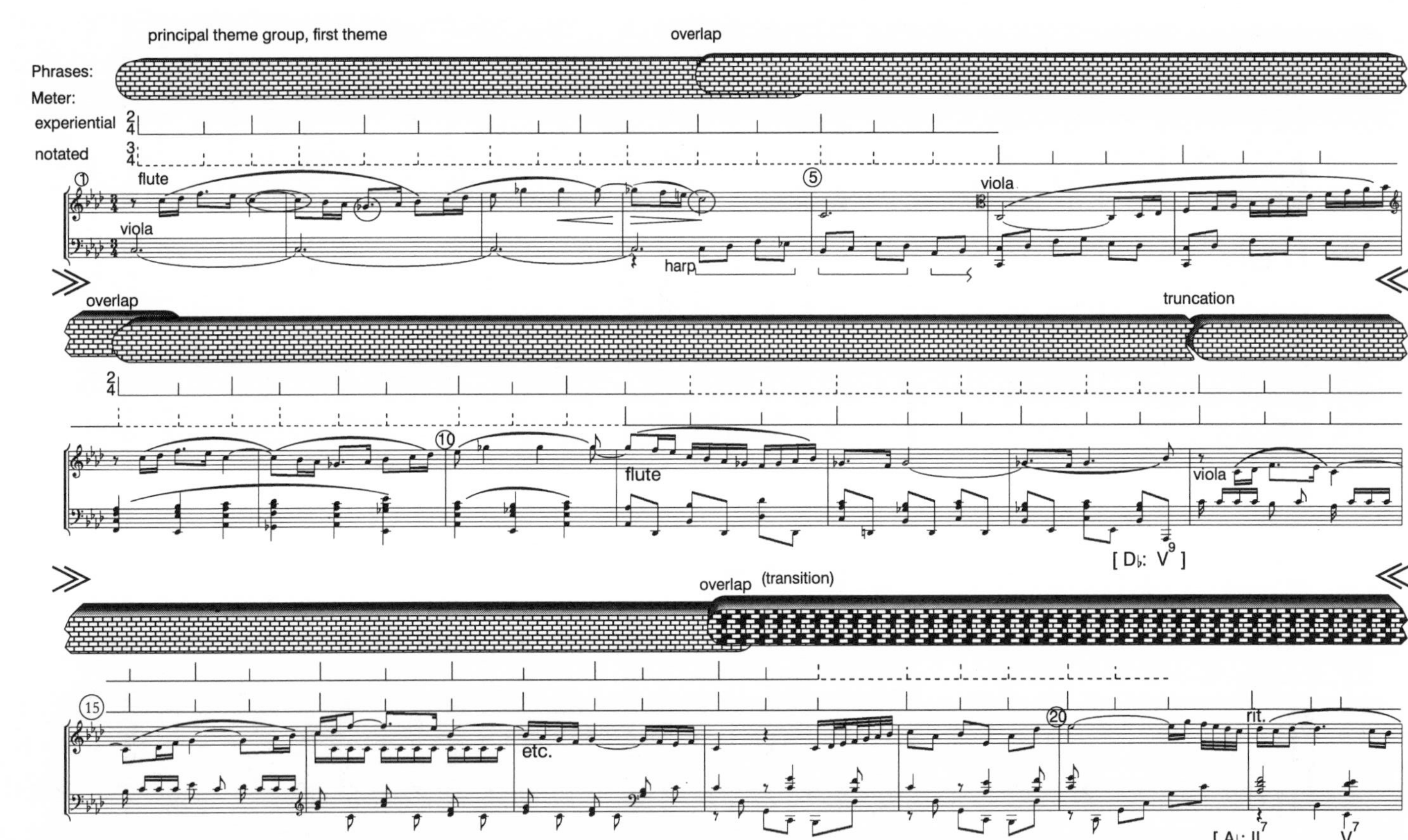
principal theme group, first theme
overlap
Phrases:
Meter:
experiential
notated
flute
viola
5
viola
harp
overlap
truncation
10
flute
viola
[D♭: V9]
overlap
(transition)
15
etc.
20
rit.
[A♭: II7 V7]

Ex. 10.1b. Phrase and metric structure for mm. 1–53 of the *Sonate pour flûte, alto et harpe,* "Interlude"

(*Example continues*)

Ex. 10.1b. (*Continued*)

two phrase boundaries are assigned to different instruments: flute and viola for the first phrase's end, harp for the second phrase's beginning. Of course, the flute and viola continue to play at the beginning of the second phrase, but for its first five quarters they merely sustain long notes, which gives them time to adjust to their role in the new phrase; meanwhile, the harp can plunge in securely to initiate the second phrase.

Identifying Metric Schemes

Before proceeding further into the "Interlude" we must consider briefly some aspects of metric structure that shape the analytical approach throughout this essay.

To be *rhythmic* merely requires that musical events possess duration. To be *metric* requires that those durations (and, therefore, the musical events that embody them) *recur* in some recognizable fashion.[6]

One way by which metric durations may emerge is *through repetitions of patterns whose overall durations are equal.* Musical patterns take many forms. Most obvious are pitch or rhythmic contours (motives), but successions of instrumental combinations or harmonies (as in cadence formulas) can also form recognizable patterns. In order to be metric, such patterns must recur within equal, overall durations. In mm. 1–7, for instance, two motivic patterns help to assert each of the metric schemes. The first occurs in the harp, mm. 4–5, as I have already noted. It comprises distinctive pitch and rhythmic contours and is immediately repeated a step lower. As its duration is two quarter notes, it reaffirms the sense of $\frac{2}{4}$ meter already established. The second pattern, in mm. 6–7 (also in the harp), again comprises pitch and rhythm and likewise is repeated immediately. Its duration, however, is three quarter notes and so it invites us to infer quarter-note triple meter: $\frac{3}{4}$.

Musical accents may also form metric patterns, provided they are separated by equal durations. Such accents are commonly classified into three types: *dynamic, agogic,* and *tonic.*[7] Dynamic accents, also known as *stress* accents, occur when one among a group of musical events receives greater acoustical weight—that is, is louder than the rest. Often performers effectuate dynamic accents by means of sharp articulations or by playing more loudly, but texture can also serve as their medium through sudden increases in the number of sounding parts, doublings, or instruments. *Agogic* accents occur when one among a succession of musical events possesses greater duration. *Tonic* accents occur when one among a series of musical events lies in a registral extreme. Conventionally, tonic accents are accorded only to the highest notes in metric groups, but here I consider both highest and lowest notes to constitute tonic accents. However, I shall distinguish the two possibilities as "tonic-high" accents versus "tonic-low." Of the three types, in general I regard dynamic accents as strong, tonic accents as weak.

Because hearing accents (especially tonic accents) engages perceptual subtleties, identifying moments of accentuation is inherently imprecise. Fortunately, such moments are often characterized by coincidences of at least two of the three accent types, which facilitates identification; better still, accents and patterns often occur together, thereby reinforcing each other and the durations they demarcate.

In sum, identifying metric groups and, by implication, the prevailing meters that underlie them entails identifying recurrent durations delineated by repeated patterns or accents.

There are seven examples of metric accents in mm. 1–7 of the "Interlude": (1) the viola's c in m. 1 (agogic); (2) the flute's c^2 tied over mm. 1–2 (agogic); (3) the flute's g-flat^1 in m. 2 (weak agogic); (4) the flute's c^2 in m. 4 (agogic), which combines with a dynamic accent caused by the harp entrance; (5) the increase in textural density coupled with three simultaneous articulations in flute, viola, and harp, which effectuates a dynamic accent at m. 5, b. 1; (6) the dynamic accent at m. 6, b. 1, wrought by four simultaneous articulations (more than occur anywhere else in the measure); (7) the dynamic accent at m. 7, b. 1, achieved by means of three simultaneous articulations (again, more than occur anywhere else in the measure). Note that the flute's agogic accent of m. 2 (g-flat^1) coincides with the registral nadir in the flute for this phrase—a tonic-low accent—so that although both types of accent here are weak, their amalgamation within a single musical event makes the overall stress on g-flat^1 clearly audible. I have not identified any accents between m. 2, b. 2, and m. 4, b. 2, nor at m. 5, b. 3, which earlier I posited was the last duple quarter-note downbeat before the change to triple meter in m. 6. By m. 2, however, we have heard two iterations of equal (half note) durations between accents, which is enough to establish a metric scheme. As for m. 5, hearing a duple downbeat on b. 3 is possible because the reiterated pattern has not yet been truncated; that event occurs on the next beat.

At this juncture a point of clarification is in order: I do not assert that meter is *established* at the beginning of the "Interlude," and certainly not that Debussy barred the passage incorrectly. Rather, I contend that the requisite features are present which *permit* one to hear $\frac{2}{4}$ for the first five measures, and I believe that hearing this metric anomaly (vis-à-vis the notated meter), including the abrupt change to $\frac{3}{4}$ meter at m. 6, both enriches one's experience of the passage and explains the sense of rhythmic awkwardness performers may encounter here during the early stages of learning the piece.

Metric Ambiguities in Measures 8–53

Because they repeat the material of mm. 1–3, mm. 8–10 are readily heard in $\frac{2}{4}$ meter (as indicated above the staff in example 10.1b). The harp part, which is new here, does not contradict a $\frac{2}{4}$ metric scheme (not even its first slur, which binds together six quarter notes) although it could as easily be heard in $\frac{3}{4}$. Measures 10–13 are less easily assigned either to $\frac{2}{4}$ or $\frac{3}{4}$. The duple metric character of mm. 8–9 encourages us to hear its continuation, but the paucity of clear accents on duple downbeats fails to reinforce such a hearing, and such accents as do occur send conflicting signals. The dotted quarter of m. 13 lies on a duple downbeat but the longest agogic accent—the half note tied to a dotted eighth—occurs on a duple upbeat (of course it also occurs on a weak beat in the notated $\frac{3}{4}$). Moreover, slurs group the quarters of m. 10 into a three–quarter note group, and the change of figuration in the harp coupled with the change of instrumental color for the principal voice (from viola to flute) both occur on a triple downbeat at m. 11. Hence mm. 10–13 can readily be heard in either duple or triple meter, but in neither unequivocally.

Measures 14–17 are rather more complicated metrically. The viola melody in mm. 14–15 can again be heard as duple (by implication from previous hearings of this material in duple settings), but harp (right hand) and flute have unequivocal triple-meter rhythmic and pitch patterns lasting three quarter notes each. (In the pitch reduction the ascending stems in the lower staff carry the $\frac{3}{4}$ rhythmic pattern.) The rhythm-pitch contour in the harp (left hand) is metrically ambiguous, susceptible of interpretation either way. In mm. 16–17 the viola's duple-metric theme passes to the flute, the harp (left hand) is triple-metric, and the viola part and harp (right hand) are metrically ambiguous.

In measures 18–21 the three–quarter notes' duration of the harp's figuration pattern combines with a dotted–quarter note agogic accent in the right hand, and half-note agogic accents in the flute in mm. 18 and 20 to delineate three–quarter note groups. As well, the *ritard* (m. 21) and its concomitant change of tempo also coincide with the notated downbeat. All of the these features conspire to convey $\frac{3}{4}$ meter. On the other hand, those same agogic accents in the flute align with possible downbeats in the duple scheme established by the recurrence of the principal theme in m. 14, with its duple-metric association. The evidence more strongly suggests $\frac{3}{4}$ meter, but $\frac{2}{4}$ cannot be ruled out.

Measures 22–29 are set unambiguously in $\frac{3}{4}$ meter, enforced by melodic patterns that align with the notated measures, coupled with the avoidance of duple-meter accents, although the melodic pattern of m. 24 adumbrates $\frac{2}{4}$.

Measures 30–45 pose no obstacles to a hearing in $\frac{3}{4}$ meter, and the unequivocally triple-meter passage of mm. 22–29 imposes an inertia that opposes alternative metric schemes; nonetheless, there are two passages that lend themselves to interpretation in $\frac{2}{4}$. Specifically, mm. 30–31 and their varied recurrence in mm. 34–35 are amenable to interpretation in $\frac{2}{4}$, mainly because of the agogic emphasis accorded g^2 at m. 30, bb. 1 and 3, and similarly at m. 34.[8] This is the pattern foreshadowed in m. 24, and listeners familiar with the piece will have no trouble hearing that measure in $\frac{2}{4}$, fleeting though the reference to duple meter is. Once established at m. 30, the duple metric scheme can be heard to continue into m. 32, but duple meter must accede to triple at mm. 32–33, owing to the three–quarter note patterns in the flute. Measures 38–39 are unequivocally triple metric because of the reiterated contour pattern in the flute (reinforced by the harp's slurs); likewise, articulation marks and contour patterns in mm. 40–45 enforce the notated $\frac{3}{4}$ meter.

Because they reprise the principal theme (in the form found at mm. 8–9, including the harp's two-measure slur) measures 46–47 strongly encourage hearing in $\frac{2}{4}$ meter. The flute part works better in $\frac{3}{4}$, however, because although it carries no accents on any downbeats (duple or triple), its rhythmic pattern of three–quarter notes' duration in m. 45 is repeated (slightly varied) in m. 46. Hence, mm. 46–47 are metrically ambiguous, although they favor $\frac{2}{4}$. In contrast, because of three–quarter note patterns in the harp and flute, mm. 48–50 favor $\frac{3}{4}$, although it remains possible to hear $\frac{2}{4}$ through m. 49. Finally, the contour patterns in mm. 51–53 favor $\frac{2}{4}$ meter. (The fermata after m. 53 accommodates the missing upbeat of the last $\frac{2}{4}$ measure.)

I have dwelt upon section 1 of the "Interlude" in order to show not only how metric ambiguities arise but also to demonstrate their rather wide range of variability, from passages such as mm. 1–5 or 37–45, where one or the other meter can be clearly heard (regardless of the notation), to those (such as mm. 14–17) that resist unequivocal association with either meter. Metric ambiguities in the "Interlude" are confined to principal-theme-group sections 1, 3, and 5. The secondary-theme-group sections 2 and 4 are solidly based in $\frac{4}{4}$ meter throughout.

Exploring Metric Ambiguities in Performance

Performers will find it useful to explore for themselves metric ambiguities of the sort discussed above, which form an important part of the composition's musical structure. Those who wish to identify possible changes in experiential meter that are obscured by notated meter should look for reiterated patterns of equal durations and series of accents separated by equal durations. It is easiest to do this with a copy of the score, as I have done in the examples, penciling in alternative meter signatures where appropriate, along with longer vertical strokes for each metric downbeat. Look for patterns in pitch contours or durations, but explore patterns in other domains as well, such as texture or instrumentation. In the harp part of mm. 18–19, for example, fluctuations in the number of sounding parts from eighth note to eighth note vary according to the following series: ⟨111333111333⟩. The texture pattern that emerges meshes readily into $\frac{3}{4}$ meter (as ⟨111333/111333⟩), but does not comfortably map onto $\frac{2}{4}$ (as ⟨1113/3311/1333⟩). In these measures the viola's consistent texture of two sounding parts has no effect on the harp's metric scheme, nor does the flute's single-part texture.

Performers can compare and rehearse passages in both notated and experiential metric schemes to assimilate the ambiguities into their stores of musical imagery. I believe that performers should endeavor to become comfortable with the ambiguities rather than overcome them, preserve rather than efface them, strive for metric flexibility and the ability to switch gracefully from apparent duple to triple and back again as appropriate, and to independently project conflicting metric schemes in ensemble against the pervasive ground of the notated $\frac{3}{4}$ meter.

Identifying Phrase Boundaries

Let us now turn to consider some aspects of phrase structure that relate to the discussion of phrase boundaries. In general it is clear throughout the "Interlude" where each phrase begins. If phrase material is new, usually the beginning is marked by a distinctive melodic-harmonic contour, texture, figuration, or instrumental assignment, all features which conspire to signal to the listener that a fresh musical idea has begun. Reprises or repetitions of material define the beginnings of phrases even more clearly because we recognize immediately the beginning of a phrase we have heard before.

Phrase endings are another matter. Often the conclusion we expect of one phrase (from cues like harmonic cadential progressions, melodic cadential voice-leading, and the tendency for concluding metric-rhythmic figures to expend their momentum on the downbeats of last measures) will be thwarted by the "premature" commencement of the next. In such situations, and they are common in the "Interlude," we can identify phrase endings by default since if a new phrase has begun the previous one must have ended. But merely to acknowledge that one phrase must have ceased because another has begun fails to capture the complexity of experiencing phrase structure in this movement. Often the aforementioned cues *do* reach their expected conclusions—a dominant harmony proceeds to its tonic, voice-leading connections are made, the rhythmic momentum of a line or complex of parts expends itself into a downbeat or long duration—but the concluding events occur at the same moment as the initiating events of the new phrase, hence the durations of those concluding events can only be conjectural; the new phrase *overlaps* the old. Also one experiences both conclusion and initiation simultaneously, which is a very different and much more complex sensation from that of experiencing conclusion and initiation in turn.

Overlaps can elicit different effects. Sometimes the two phrases simply share an event: the old phrase's conclusion is the new phrase's initiation; and we recognize that the material on the cusp functions both ways. This kind of overlap is called *elision.* In Debussy's music, however, overlaps often entail a *truncation* of the old phrase in order to make way for the new, as though, prematurely, the new phrase abruptly pushes aside the old. There is another possibility that I call *bifurcation,* where the beginning of the next phrase branches out from but does not curtail the phrase in progress. We shall see an example of bifurcation later in the "Interlude."

Phrase Ambiguities in Measures 8–53

We have already examined the first overlapping phrase juncture at m. 4, as illustrated in example 10.1b.[9] The second phrase proceeds similarly, insofar as momentum increases throughout mm. 4–7 pointing toward the downbeat of m. 8. The sources of this momentum include the stepwise motions in the viola and harp [right hand], which are directed, respectively, at c^2 and c, as well as the rapid, stepwise ascending sixteenth notes which hurtle toward the downbeat. In addition, there is, in the key of F minor, the minor-dominant harmony's impulse (from m. 7) toward the tonic (at m. 8). But while these dynamic goals are achieved on the downbeat of m. 8, once again the dramatic change of texture in the harp, which signals the commencement of the next phrase restating the opening theme in the viola, thwarts the effect of conclusion. Hence the boundaries of the second and third phrases also overlap.

The restatement in the third phrase beginning at m. 8 has a new continuation in m. 11. From m. 9 onward, the consistent use of G-flat coupled with the bass line's chromatic, stepwise ascent (from D-flat to D-natural to E-flat) and subsequent downward leap (to A-flat) imply a local shift to the key of D-flat major. The harmony and voice-leading in these measures signals culmination in an authentic cadence, for which the last sonority of m. 13 functions as a dominant-ninth chord, but the resolution to tonic never occurs; instead, m. 14 brings another reprise of the opening theme and with it the modal dominant of F minor. Hence the third phrase is effectively *truncated,* one harmony (and measure) short of where we anticipate its conclusion will occur.

Phrases 4–9 all entail overlapping boundaries. The fourth phrase's conclusion at m. 18, b. 1, is stymied by the entry at that moment of the fifth phrase, which serves as a transition to the second theme of the principal-theme-group. This fifth, transitional phrase comes closest so far to achieving closure, by means of a perfect-authentic cadence begun in m. 21 (A-flat: II^7–V^7–I), descending stepwise voice-leading that resolves both sevenths, and a prominent *ritardando* coupled with rhythmic attenuation. But even this conclusion is foiled, at m. 22, b. 1, by the change of figuration, resumption of movement, and new melodic contour that signals the onset of the second theme of the principal-theme-group.

At m. 26 repetition signals the beginning of the seventh phrase at exactly the moment of resolution of the authentic cadence (in A-flat major) that would define the end of the sixth phrase. At m. 30, before the seventh phrase can complete its course, marked changes of texture, figuration, and instrumentation indicate a new phrase, and at m. 34, changes in texture, instrumentation, and loudness that accompany the reiterated second theme of the principal-theme-group announce the start of the ninth phrase, obscuring the perfect-authentic cadence begun in m. 33 that would signal the end of the eighth.

The tenth phrase (mm. 38–41) truncates its antecedent, as does the eleventh, although the effects are different. At m. 38 the tenth phrase gently interrupts the ninth just as the latter is dissolving. It arrives as though in the nick of time, and presses forward in an *animando* as if to regain lost momentum. In contrast, the abruptness with which the eleventh phrase interrupts the tenth (at m. 42) is startling, and would be brutal were it not for the sudden reduction in texture from six busy, sounding parts to one pianissimo sustained half note in the viola.

So far I have identified two sources of ambiguity in phrase structure: consequent phrases whose fore-boundaries overlap rendering their antecedents' endings equivocal, and antecedent phrases whose endings are truncated to make way for their consequents. There is a third kind of phrase ambiguity, for which the term *bifurcation* seems most apt. It occurs twice in close proximity in the first section of the "Interlude," first in mm. 46–47, and again in m. 49.

In mm. 46–48 the viola and harp initiate a new phrase that reprises the material of mm. 8–10 almost exactly, but for the first two bars the flute carries a continuation of the material from the preceding mm. 44–45. Thus the phrases overlap but in a different manner from previous examples because here the continuation in the flute of material from the preceding phrase is not merely implicit, eclipsed or obscured by the onset of the new phrase, but explicit, jutting two measures into the new phrase. In m. 49 the flute initiates the final phrase of the section, but this time the harp and viola cling to the phrase begun in m. 46. In mm. 48–51 we must divide our attention between both phrases until the viola and harp finally concede to the flute the brief flourish that closes the section.

Like metric conflicts, phrase boundary conflicts are manifest in many guises. Simple overlap, truncation, and bifurcation are three ways of characterizing the devices by which closure is averted; but in fact every juncture is different, and players and listeners must respond accordingly. In the first fifty-three measures of the "Interlude" there is not a single phrase save the last that concludes unequivocally before the next one begins. In every case something intervenes to keep the piece moving. Constant motion is the central feature of this piece. Nonetheless, *there are phrases,* thirteen by my count, averaging almost exactly four bars each over fifty-three measures, and so the piece is far from being an unbroken stream of events. This kind of phrase structure provides a means whereby listeners as well as performers have opportunities to breathe at intervals that feel quite natural, but each must be a "catch" breath to balance the need for punctuation with the impulse to motion.

Exploring Phrase Ambiguities in Performance

Performers who wish to continue exploring phrase structure in the remainder of the "Interlude" can begin by identifying the phrases as I have done above. Although the task poses some problems, they are not especially difficult. The criteria I have used for identifying phrases and their boundaries are as follows:

1. Look for discontinuities caused by *clearly discernible changes* in such things as tempo, character of thematic-harmonic material, accompanimental figuration, instrumental assignment, key, or meter.
2. Look for discontinuities caused by intrusive references to previous material—*repetitions,* say—and by pauses.
3. Look for *harmonic closure* in the form of authentic cadences (often with modal dominants).
4. Concentrate on locating the beginnings of phrases because it is easier to identify beginnings than endings, which may be obscured by overlappings.

It is perhaps easiest to mark phrase boundaries on the score and then rehearse the phrases one at a time before reassembling them to experience the complexities of their interactions. Performers should feel a sense of breathlessness at having to constantly press ahead as one phrase supplants another before the latter has quite finished. The beginnings of phrases should always be played securely, solidly; the ends will take care of themselves.

THE "PASTORALE" OF THE *SONATE POUR FLÛTE, ALTO ET HARPE*

In the "Interlude" we examined ambiguities that arise because repeated durations, which separate accents or span motivic patterns, allow us to hear metric schema that are at odds with the notated meter. In the first movement, ambiguities arise for different reasons. Here the problem is a sparsity of regular durations generated by reiterated patterns or accents, or, alternatively, an abundance of regular durations confounded by a dearth of clear grouping cues.

All of the distinct categories of thematic-harmonic materials used in the "Pastorale's" eighty-three measures are exposed in the first thirty bars, which can be further divided into four subsections consisting of mm. 1–17, 18–20, 21–25, and 26–30. The latter three subsections are relatively straightforward in terms of phrase and metric structure. Only mm. 1–17 are metrically problematic, and so I shall concentrate upon them.

Metric and Phrase Ambiguities in Measures 1–3

The very first measure of the "Pastorale" begins with six perfectly regular sixteenths in the harp (see example 10.2a). Clearly, given the tempo (*lento, dolce rubato*), these sixteenths are too quick to represent measures or beats (hence they cannot in themselves constitute metric units), and so they must be grouped together in some way. The $\frac{9}{8}$ signature indicates a compound meter that implies subdivision into three dotted–quarter note durations, or sextuplet-sixteenths. But the tie on the last sixteenth denies us the articulation at the second metric subdivision that would confirm the notated meter, and, similarly, the tie on the last eighth of the second subdivision's triplet-eighths denies us the articulation at the third subdivision. Nor does the series of thwarted subdivision beats end here, for although the harp (left hand) articulates the first subdivision of the second measure by plucking g-flat, the tied-over c^2 in the flute masks the downbeat; so also does the tie on the third eighth of the flute's triplet obscure the

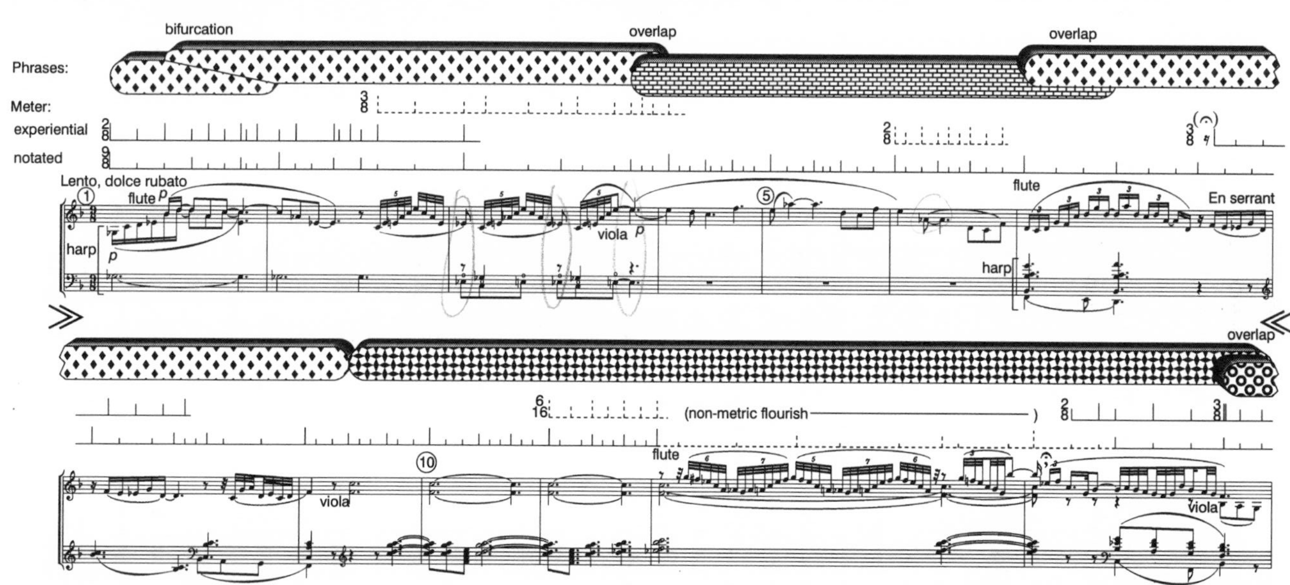

bifurcation
overlap
overlap
Phrases:
Meter:
experiential
notated
Lento, dolce rubato
flute
harp
viola
flute
harp
En serrant
overlap
(non-metric flourish)
flute
viola
viola

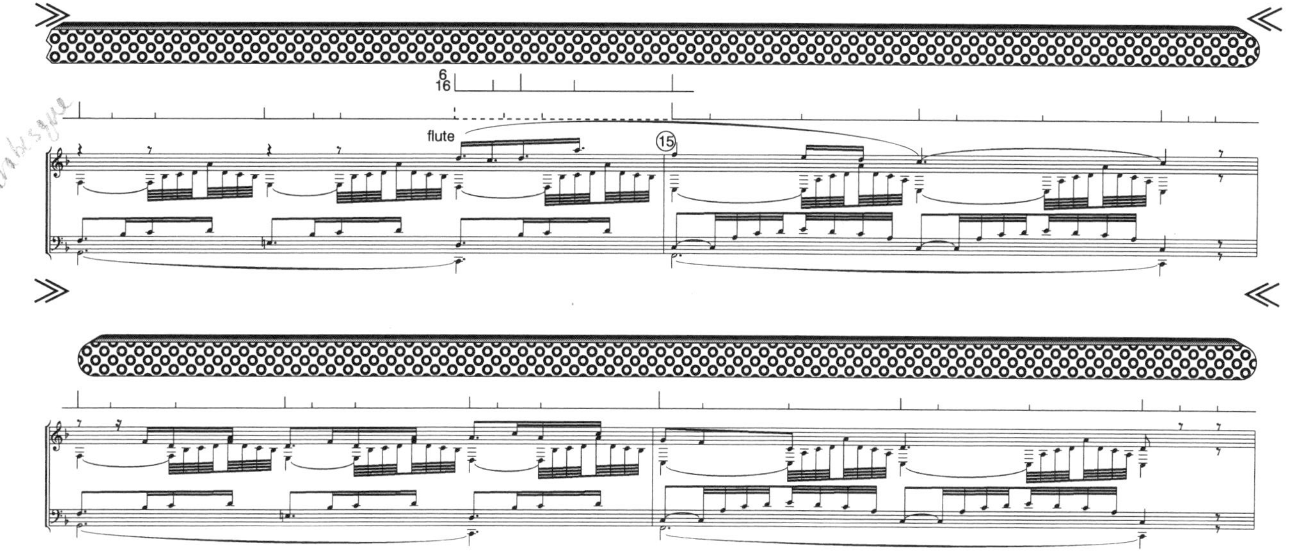

Ex. 10.2a. Phrase and metric structure for mm. 1–17 of the *Sonate pour flûte, alto et harpe,* "Pastorale"

beginning of the second subdivision of m. 2 and, similarly, the eighth rest somewhat obscures the beginning of the third subdivision (although it is articulated by the harp's g-flat).

The effect of these missing or equivocal articulations—not a single subdivision in the first two measures is articulated in the melodic line, nor is the downbeat of m. 2 unequivocal—is to deny us the regular, articulated durations that would make the compound triple meter intelligible. At the same time, the three ties in the treble part that obscure the notated metric subdivision accents also create agogic accents whose onsets imply possible alternative metric unit boundaries (even though subsequently they are not confirmed) that are wholly at odds with the notated metric subdivisions: the tied d^2 in m. 1, the tied c^2 in mm. 1–2, and the tied e-flat^1 in m. 2. Add to this the entrance of the flute doubling the harp in the midst of the first metric subdivision of m. 1, a change of timbre that implies a boundary of some sort (perhaps of metric unit, perhaps of phrase), and we have a concatenation of conflicting cues calculated to confound the surest sense of meter!

Phrase and metric structures are inextricably linked in this passage. Obviously, the harp initiates the first phrase, but the flute's entrance intrudes as though initiating a new phrase for which the harp's sixteenth notes are merely introductory, a false beginning. In this intrusion of one phrase into the space of another, the phrase structure of mm. 1–3 is similar to the bifurcations which occur at the end of the passage just examined in the "Interlude."

Metric and Phrase Ambiguities in Measures 3–17

In the third measure, but only for the first two-thirds of the bar, the harp and flute align to articulate eighth-note durations, which we may hear as triplet-eighth metric subdivisions; thereafter, the ties in both flute and harp across the third subdivision obscure that metric unit; nor does the entrance of the viola help project the latter, since it merely sneaks in, piano. In fact, the flute's slurs encourage the player to project three–eighth note metric units that are misaligned by one beat from the notated meter (shown above mm. 2–3 in example 10.2a as a $\frac{3}{8}$ scheme).

The viola solo continues to perpetrate metric ambiguities through ties across triplet-eighth subdivisions (thrice, on e^2, a-flat^2, and a-flat^1, respectively) and their concomitant agogic accents. In m. 6, especially, the long durations engender confusing metric signals. (Should we hear this measure in $\frac{2}{8}$ as shown in example 10.2a?)

In mm. 7–9 articulations at each metric subdivision generally support the notated metric scheme, although in m. 7 the tie on a^1 and the sixteenth rest that follows, coupled with the slight *ritardando* indicated by the *en serrant,* slightly blur the onset of the last metric subdivision. Still, from the end of m. 7 through m. 8 the interplay between flute and harp allows us to hear the onsets of the brief flute gestures as initiations of metric subdivisions, for which the harp's dotted-quarter figures serve as concluding articulations, in which case the experiential metric scheme is misaligned with the notated meter by one sixteenth note—but only for a measure, because the regular rhythm of all parts at the end of m. 8 clearly confirms the notated meter.

It is up to the performers to decide how readily we will hear this conflict since they may choose either to exploit or suppress it. If the flute enters securely but a tad late on each of the sixteenth-note passages and the harp strives to place its notes at the beginning of m. 8 precisely in rhythm with the flute, the meter will be ambiguous. If both flute and harp are scrupulously accurate with their entrances and the flute plays each of its gestures with a slight crescendo from a soft beginning, it will be much easier to hear the notated meter.

In mm. 9–11 the notated meter is not clouded by ties crossing over subdivisions since either viola or harp has an articulation at the beginning of every metric subdivision. Here what slightly obscures the notated meter is the absence of articulations *within* metric subdivisions; only twice are there such articulations, at the beginnings of mm. 10 and 11, and because the second of these is a duplet instead of a triplet, there arises the conjectural experiential scheme of $\frac{6}{16}$ shown in example 10.2a.

The flute's flourish at m. 12 is nonmetric, or, rather, it sounds stilted if played so that its metric character is made audible. Not until m. 13 does the notated meter reemerge, and then not unequivocally until the last metric subdivision of the measure, where we hear the viola's triplet-eighths imitate those of the harp. In the middle of the measure, because of the flute's dotted rhythm following the fermata we could as easily hear a $\frac{2}{8}$ metric scheme, as shown in the example.

Measures 14–17 clearly evince the notated $\frac{9}{8}$ meter throughout (although, as shown, the duplets in the flute in m. 14 briefly invite us to hear a scheme of $\frac{6}{16}$).

There is little to say about phrase structure for mm. 3–17. Most phrase boundaries overlap (as shown n the example), with exceptions at m. 9, b. 3, and at the end of m. 15, where abutting phrases are discrete.

Exploring Metric and Phrase Ambiguities in Performance

These seventeen measures set the tone for the movement as a whole. The absence of clear metric patterns contributes to a strong impression of the music emerging quietly, tentatively, as if from nowhere. The whole movement has a strongly improvisatory character, as though comprised of a series of fragments composed on the spot by players who proceed in fits and starts as ideas materialize and dissipate. It is a favorite illusion of Debussy's, which we encounter often in his works.[10] Performers can minimize this quality by means of an aggressively dry approach that maintains a meticulously regular beat throughout and observes rubatos and fermatas with restraint. In this fashion metric ambiguities will be reduced to merest nuances, but it will require a heavy commitment to rehearsing details of ensemble.

Alternatively, we can embrace the metric and phrasing ambiguities, emphasizing them to the point of blatancy. Such a strategy would strive for secure and confident entrances and conspicuous, even exaggerated, rubatos and pauses. As mentioned earlier, all of the distinct categories of thematic-harmonic materials are exposed in mm. 1–17, 18–20, 21–25, and 26–30. It is instructive to rehearse these passages by playing phrases repeatedly, as separate entities, focusing by turns upon experiential versus notated metric structures. Performers should identify metric and phrase conflicts beforehand as part of their preparation, treating disagreements as sources of alternative hearings that uncover more facets of the composition's rich store of relations.

Vif et joyeux, Measures 26–27

Before leaving this movement I would like briefly to discuss the flourishlike entries in the viola at mm. 26–27, which can pose ensemble problems (see example 10.2b). Although the difficulties here do not result entirely from metric or phrase boundary conflicts, they do arise from rhythmic-metric considerations since in each case the flute and harp join the viola on a metrically unaccented beat (the third of three sextuplet-sixteenth groups in each $\frac{18}{16}$ measure), which can feel very awkward. I would suggest rehearsing these two bars as if each were split into two $\frac{12}{16}$ measures further subdivided into sixteenth-note triplets, as shown above the notated metric scheme in the example. In such a scheme the fermatas imply a duration that approximates the two additional beats required by the paired measures in $\frac{12}{16}$. The viola enters immediately after b. 1 of the first

Ex. 10.2b. Metric structure for mm. 26–27 of the *Sonate pour flûte, alto et harpe,* "Pastorale"

measure and the flute and harp enter on b. 1 of the next, four beats later; the scheme is repeated for m. 27. The passage is much easier to hear this way—and the ensemble will be much more precise after rehearsing it thus—than if the ensemble attempted to enter together on the third sextuplet group of a triple-meter measure of $\frac{18}{16}$.

THE "ALLEGRO VIVO" OF THE *SONATE POUR VIOLON ET PIANO*

Measures 1–14

Like the beginning of the *Sonate pour flûte, alto et harpe,* the character of the first fourteen measures of the *Sonate pour violon et piano* is improvisatory, tentative, and contemplative. But unlike the former, where that character set the tone for the entire first movement, the corresponding material in the violin sonata merely serves as an introduction for the main body of a work that is more conventionally expository, more straightforward in metric and phrase structure. Nevertheless, this opening passage harbors obscurities in the domains of meter and phrase that resemble those we have examined at the beginning of the flute, viola, harp sonata. Phrase and metric relations interact closely to create a complex rhythmic fabric that precludes unambiguous apprehension of either domain.

The piece begins with sustained triads in the piano, each of two measures' duration, after which the violin enters with a series of half notes (see example 10.3).[11] Given the rapid tempo (dotted half note = 55) it seems reasonable to hear the first four bars as a half-phrase, to be completed by a repetition adding

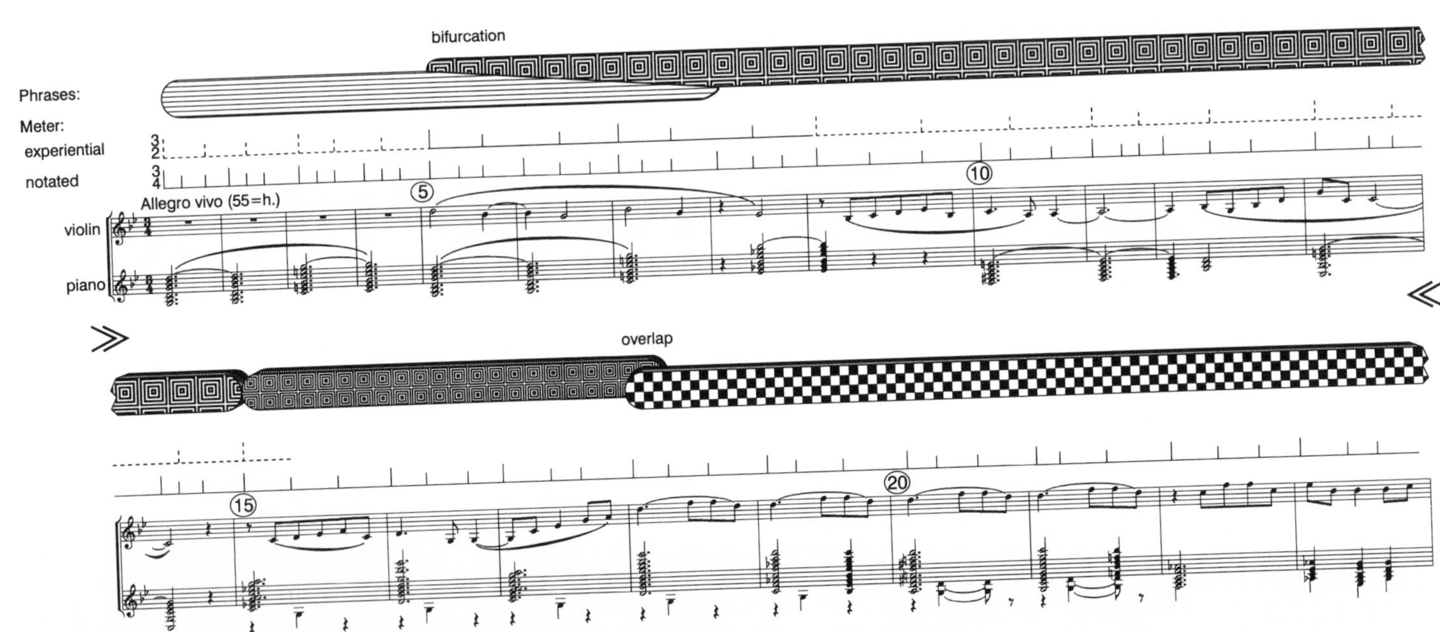
bifurcation
Phrases:
Meter:
experiential
notated
Allegro vivo (55=h.)
violin
piano
5
10
overlap
15
20

Ex. 10.3. Phrase and metric structure for mm. 1–63 of the *Sonate pour violon et piano,* "Allegro vivo"

(*Example continues*)

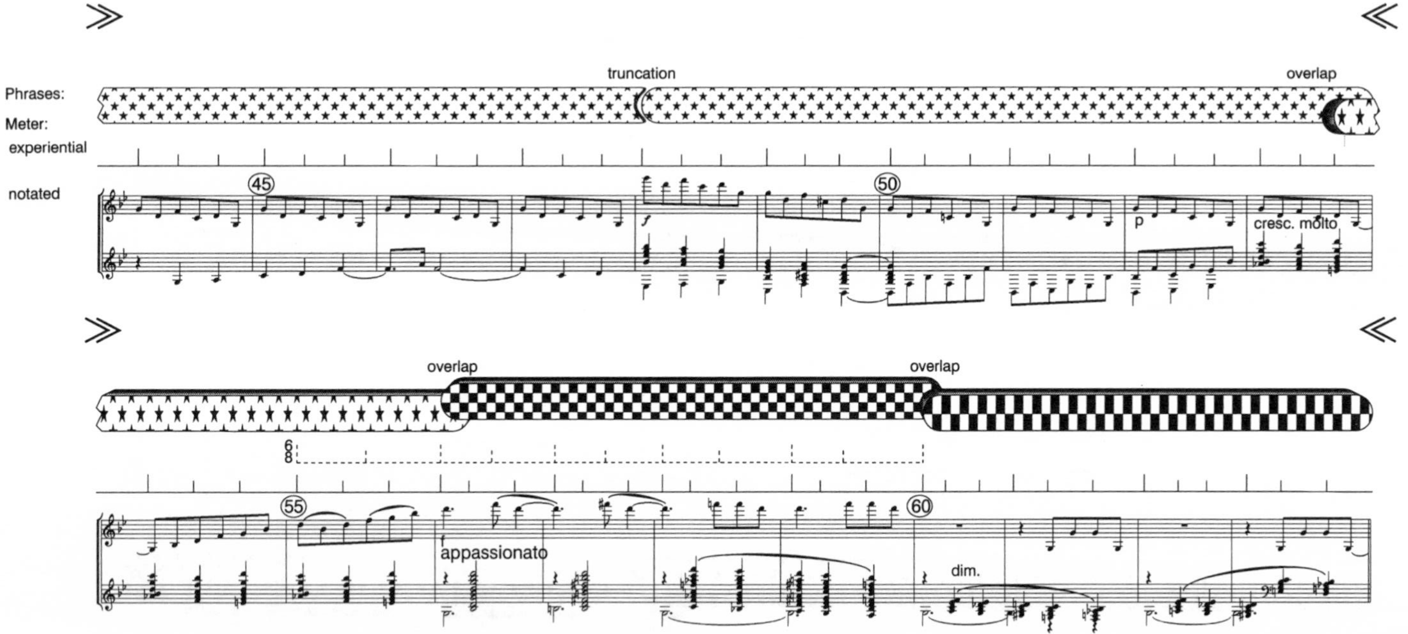

Ex. 10.3. (*Continued*)

four more measures. And indeed, mm. 5–7 do repeat their counterparts in mm. 1–3; however, the violin's entry promulgates a departure from the material of the original half-phrase that transforms mm. 5–8 from a repetition-consequent of mm. 1–4 into an antecedent half-phrase for a consequent phrase that spans mm. 9–14. Thus we may hear the violin at m. 5 as an intrusion into the midst of a regular eight-measure phrase, bifurcating the latter into one branch in the piano that ends in a stub at the end of m. 7, and another that continues on through m. 14 (in the violin, which the piano joins in m. 8). The effect is disconcerting. On one hand, we get to breathe twice in mm. 8–9, at the quarter rest and after the E-flat minor chord is struck; on the other, both breaths feel more like gasps, from which the music lurches forward to propel us through m. 14.

The rapid tempo also affects the metric scheme, for while the notated meter is $\frac{3}{4}$ (for which the designated metric duration is the quarter note) it is almost impossible not to hear quarter notes as submetric durations that conjoin to form metric durations, that is, comprising quarter-note triplets within some sort of compound meter such as $\frac{6}{4}$ (in which the dotted half is a metric subdivision). But that is not the only possible metric interpretation, for quarter notes could also form duplets, which is what occurs when the violin enters in mm. 5–8. And since quarter-note triplets are never confirmed by grouping cues in mm. 1–4, the experiential metric scheme for mm. 1–8 must be $\frac{3}{2}$ (as affirmed by the violin's half notes in mm. 5–8). A $\frac{3}{2}$ metric scheme also reinforces a hypermetric phrase structure that pairs $\frac{3}{4}$ bars to produce the bifurcated phrase structure shown above the metric scheme. This scheme is viable through m. 14 since we may experience the agogic accents in both violin and piano as easily in $\frac{3}{2}$ as in the notated $\frac{3}{4}$ (although the rhythm in m. 12, which groups together the last two quarters of that measure, favors $\frac{3}{2}$). For many measures thereafter, quarter notes are unequivocally grouped in threes by melodic patterns and figurations in violin and piano.

Of course, performers who take their metric cue from the *visual* grouping of quarters into triplets in the score may certainly *impose* a metric scheme of quarter-note triplets onto mm. 1–8, in which case mm. 5–8 contain hemiola, and m. 8, b. 2, contains an odd accent. But I believe an account that contrasts the *possibility* of triplet-quarter $\frac{3}{4}$ measures with a *realization* that groups duplet quarters into $\frac{3}{2}$ hypermeasures is richer, more interesting, and better fits the pliable phrase structure in which the first phrase is interrupted, after two measures of $\frac{3}{2}$, by the superimposition of a phrase of five measures (of $\frac{3}{2}$), a hearing in which mm. 9–14 are metrically ambiguous.

Measures 15–63

In my survey of phrase structure for mm. 1–63 I count ten more phrases in addition to the two already discussed, providing a total of eleven junctures between twelve adjacent phrases.[12] We have seen that the first juncture (at m. 5) eschews closure for the antecedent phrase by means of bifurcation. Of the remainder, nine more forestall closure through overlaps or truncations so that only once during these sixty-three measures (at m. 15) is there a real sense of partition in the otherwise constant flow of events from the movement's inception. In other words, like the first large section of the "Interlude" from the flute, viola, harp sonata, the first main division of the violin sonata is one long span, punctuated mainly by catch-breaths, with room for a full expiration only at the end of m. 14.

The juncture at m. 18 (which has a counterpart at m. 56) is achieved by the onset of new material brusquely flopped onto the still-unfinished phrase begun in m. 15. Similarly, although somewhat less abruptly, the junctures at mm. 34, 42, and 48 entail sudden juxtapositions of new phrases onto (or into) old, except that instead of new thematic-harmonic materials, the onsets of the new phrases at these three measures are marked by continuative thematic-harmonic materials set in strikingly different textures and registers.

The smoothest overlapping junctures occur at m. 53, b. 3, and m. 60, where consequent phrases seem to grow naturally out of their antecedents. At mm. 53–54 pronounced changes in figuration in the piano, and contour in the violin, signal a new phrase; at m. 60 there is a pause in the violin before the arrival of a new melodic gesture in m. 61. Both times there are marked changes in texture, loudness, and register, but they precede the actual junctures by an entire measure.[13] Perhaps the most interesting junctures occur at mm. 24 and 28, where extraordinarily long agogic accents on f-sharp[1] interrupt phrases to signal new ones.

There are few conflicts between experiential and notated meter in mm. 15–63. Exceptions are mm. 34–37 and 55–59. The first of these passages evinces conflicts among different strata embodied within the two instrumental parts. Certainly, hearing mm. 34–37 in $\frac{3}{4}$ poses no difficulties since there are articulations on every quarter note in both violin and piano, but the slurs in the violin suggest a bipartite division of mm. 34 and 36 and the undifferentiated eighth notes of mm. 35 and 37 do not obstruct such an interpretation. At the same time, the slurs and descending half-note durations in the piano group the two pairs of $\frac{3}{4}$ measures into two $\frac{3}{2}$ measures with half-note beats. The conflicting metric accents across three metric strata impart a churning, dancelike effect.

In mm. 55–59 the slurs and ties in the violin part allow for an interpretation of these measures in $\frac{6}{8}$ meter after the manner of mm. 34–37, although since only the violin part of m. 55 displays slurs that actually conflict with $\frac{3}{4}$, and in the absence of explicit corroboration in the piano's figuration, the more likely interpretation is $\frac{3}{4}$ with hemiola in m. 55.

Implications for Performance

Following the pensive, somewhat hesitant beginning of mm. 1–14, the first movement of the violin sonata plunges ahead, inducing a vital sense of continuing momentum throughout, not unlike (although more intense than) the "Interlude" from the flute, viola, harp sonata. By maintaining a measured physical tension underneath a relaxed easy facility, players who apprehend the inherent contradictions among phrase boundaries and metric schemes can leap from one musical idea to the next and will achieve the rhythmical eddying that mitigates these coruscating showers of musical diamonds.

THE "SÉRÉNADE" FROM THE *SONATE POUR VIOLONCELLE ET PIANO*

Measures 1–18 and 31–41

The Cello Sonata contains numerous passages evincing convoluted metric and phrase structures. We shall look at two: one that encompasses the first eighteen measures of the "Sérénade" and another that occurs a bit further in, beginning at the *Vivace* in m. 31.

Of the junctures that occur between each pair of the "Sérénade's" first six phrases, nearly all (there is one exception) overlap by means of simple elisions in which a note or chord embodies dual functions, serving as a closing element of the given pair's antecedent and the initiating element of the consequent (see example 10.4). At m. 8 the arrival on the cello's harmonic e^2 completes the metric impulse toward the downbeat that is initiated by the sixteenths at the beginning of m. 7, an impulse enhanced by four features at the end of that measure: a dramatic ascent, a crescendo, a strummed trichord, and a *sforzando* chord in the piano. But the terminus of that impulse also serves to initiate the next phrase by embodying a host of features that sharply disrupt continuity and mark it as the first element in a new event, including radical changes in instrumental color (bowed harmonic sans vibrato instead of *pizzicato* natural string with vibrato), register placement (from an axis about g-sharp before the juncture to c-sharp^2

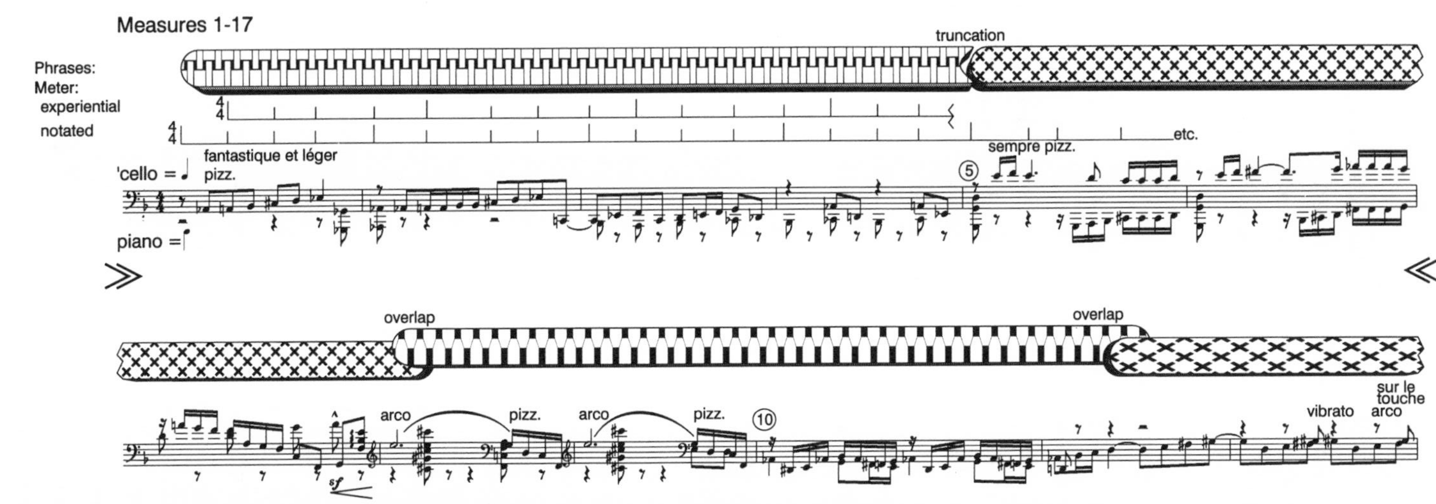
Measures 1-17
Phrases:
Meter:
experiential
notated
truncation
etc.
'cello =
piano =
fantastique et léger
pizz.
sempre pizz.
5
overlap
overlap
arco
pizz.
arco
pizz.
10
sf
vibrato
sur le touche
arco

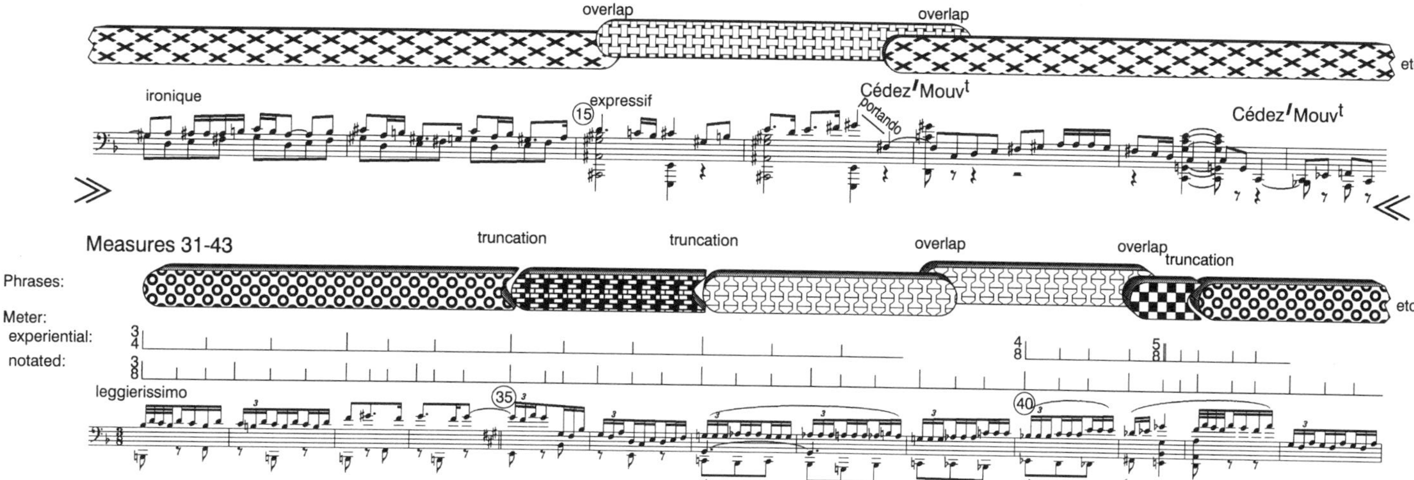

Ex. 10.4. Phrase and metric structure for mm. 1–18 and 31–43 of the *Sonate pour violoncelle et piano,* "Sérénade"

after it—the compass of register remains about the same at around two octaves), thematic character (from active sixteenths and eighths to the sustained dotted half), and accompanimental figuration (from chords articulated upon each quarter-note beat to chords struck only on weak beats 2 and 4). The near-literal repetition of the next measure immediately affirms continuity for this new, consequent phrase.

Subsequent phrase junctures elide similarly. At m. 15 sharp contrasts in the cello part's expressive character and in the piano accompaniment's figuration, texture, register compass, and register placement distinguish this moment as the beginning of another new phrase even as it fulfills the metric impulse of the preceding phrase. At mm. 11 and 17 the moments that serve as phrase junctures are more subtle, in part because changes are less marked but also because in both cases ties in piano (m. 11) or cello (m. 17) render equivocal the exact moment of the new phrase's inception. It is only after a few more eighths allow us to recognize the whole-tone melodic contour in the piano that we can identify the first of these junctures as signaling new material, and the second as a varied repetition.

The exceptional phrase juncture mentioned at the outset of this discussion is the one that falls at m. 5. There the overlap is forced when the antecedent phrase's metric and thematic-harmonic material is truncated by the sudden onset of the consequent's fresh melodic gesture, in which experiential and notated metric schemes become unequivocally congruent for the first time. This feature provides us with a convenient segue by which to turn from phrase boundaries to meter, about which I wish to discuss two features.

The first occurs right here, at the beginning. For while the notation is clear enough and presents no problems of execution or ensemble, there is a subtle ambiguity in the first four measures wrought by the cello's agogic and tonic stress on E-flat at the end of m. 1 and by the syncopated agogic C-natural at the end of m. 2; both events make weak metric accents of each measure's last quarter-note beat, to which the preceding notes sound anacrustic. Hence it is easier for listeners and performers to hear (as opposed to what they would see in the score) the first two measures as though the bar lines are displaced by one beat. Nothing in mm. 3–4 contradicts such a hearing, and indeed the cello vociferations in m. 4 reinforce it since they effectively accent the beats on which they fall. Only in m. 5 is this alternative metric scheme dispelled by the declivitous piano chord on the first beat, which is indubitably a downbeat.

The second metric ambiguity occurs at m. 31 and consists of a grand hemiola engendered by the piano's figuration, which joins pairs of 3/8 measures to form 3/4 measures (see the last system in example 10.4). Although the figuration explicitly encourages this experiential metric scheme for only six measures (mm. 31–36), the long slurs over mm. 37–38 coupled with the repeated pairs of triplet-sixteenths in the cello do not contradict the scheme and thereby allow it to continue. It is only in m. 39 that articulation and pitch contour favor hearing in $\frac{3}{8}$. In mm. 40–41 these same features in cello and piano are sufficiently contradictory to confound an unequivocal hearing since they allow at least one irregular metric interpretation, as suggested by the two metric schemes sketched over the staff in example 10.4.

Implications for Performance

Of all the examples discussed, these last two from the Cello Sonata are the least recondite. Both metric anomalies are obvious burlesques. Performers can lapse into playing the beginning of the "Sérénade" as though the measure lines were moved one beat to the right and wrench themselves back to the notated bar lines at m. 5, which will heighten this gaucherie for themselves and the audience. The metric pun at m. 31 is subtler. Although the piano accompaniment is easily heard in $\frac{3}{4}$, the cello is sometimes amenable to such a hearing (for example, mm. 37–38), but more often it better fits the notated $\frac{3}{8}$ (for example, mm. 31–35, although even then it permits itself to be fitted to a metric framework of $\frac{3}{4}$). If well executed (the piano as though in $\frac{3}{4}$, the cello more neutrally), the result will convey a certain awkward ponderosity.

A sense of burlesque pervades the "Sérénade." It is implicit in the frequent swings of mood indicated by instructions in the two quoted excerpts—*fantastique et léger* (m. 1), *ironique* (m. 13), *expressif* (m. 15), and *leggierissimo* (m. 31), and in the frequent disruptions of tempo (for example, the two *cédez mouvt.* indications at mm. 16–17 and 17–18). These features combine with the metric and phrase-boundary anomalies to suggest an exaggerated style characterized by dramatic use of rubato, accent, and changes in articulation, loudness, and color.

In closing I must reiterate that I do not suggest for any of the examples I have discussed that metric ambiguities arise from either confusion or carelessness in notation on the part of the composer. On the contrary, I believe the notated metric schemes are entirely correct and reflect viable meters throughout. Rather, what I wish to convey is how Debussy plays with meter, how a given metric scheme can be obscured by accents, articulations, and melodic-harmonic patterns whose durations do not coincide with those of the metric units—either measures or beats.

Likewise, I do not wish to imply that Debussy's handling of phrase boundaries is in any sense inattentive, for I am convinced of quite the opposite. I believe that his careful use of overlapping and bifurcation is calculated to allow performers (and listeners) their necessary, regular breathing, at the same time that it prevents losing momentum and helps maintain a sense of constant tension. The predominance of overlapping, truncated, and bifurcated phrase boundaries accounts for the sense of momentum and intensity that is characteristic of Debussy's later works.[14] So also do the contrary anomalies between meter as felt and meter as read account for the sense of purposeful hesitation, at times almost like stumbling, that attends this music.

I cannot overemphasize for performers the importance of devoting a significant portion of preparation and rehearsal to a close reading of phrase and metric structures. It will not always be necessary to dissect entire pieces; usually it will suffice to identify the main categories of musical materials and concentrate on representative passages from each, until there emerges a sense of Debussy's compositional voice in these subtle, exquisite jewels that he crafted during his last, troubled years.

Chapter 11 Timbre, Voice-leading, and the Musical Arabesque in Debussy's Piano Music

Jann Pasler

We often think of Debussy's harmonic language, especially his "impressionist" sonorities, as the key to understanding his music. In his own day, critics often contrasted his style with that of contemporaries at the Schola Cantorum, a private school that emphasized counterpoint, Gregorian chant, and the study of early music. But Debussy was also interested in musical line—which he referred to as the "musical arabesque"—and in "arabesques intertwining to produce *melodic harmony.*"[1] Writing in the *Revue blanche* (1 May 1901), he explains:

> The primitives—Palestrina, Vittoria, Orlando di Lasso, etc.—had this divine sense of the arabesque. They found the basis of it in Gregorian chant, whose delicate tracery they supported with twining counterpoints. In reworking the arabesque, Bach made it more flexible, more fluid, and despite

This chapter is dedicated to my mother, who instilled in me a love of Debussy's music, and to my teacher, Pierre Sancan of the Paris Conservatory, who helped me to decipher its complexities, enigmas, and lyricism. I am grateful to Roy Howat and Marianne Kielian-Gilbert for commenting on an earlier version of this chapter and to Editions Durand et Costallat for permission to reproduce the musical examples.

> the fact that the Great Master always imposed a rigorous discipline on beauty, he imbued it with a wealth of free fantasy so limitless that it still astonishes us today. . . .
>
> In Bach's music, it is not the character of the melody that affects us, but rather the curve. More often still it is the parallel movement of several lines whose fusion stirs our emotions—whether fortuitous or contrived.[2]

The following year, in *Musica* (October 1902), he suggests that such curves are a source of beauty in music: "We can be sure that old Bach, the essence of all music, . . . preferred the free play of sonorities whose curves, whether flowing in parallel or contrary motion, would result in an undreamed of flowering . . . of beauty. That was the age of the 'wonderful arabesque,' when music was subject to the laws of beauty in the movements of Nature herself."[3]

Another music that impressed him by both its roots in nature and the importance it ascribed to musical line was Javanese music. Debussy first heard it at the Universal Exhibition of 1889. In this tradition, various instruments perform different elements of a "balungen," or melodic framework, at varying rates. In the transcriptions of two Javanese gamelan pieces for Western instruments by his friend Charles Koechlin, published in 1910, there are up to twelve different versions of the balungen proceeding simultaneously, some of them with interlocking patterns.[4] Debussy, who borrowed this procedure in works like "Sirènes" from *Nocturnes,* waxes poetic on the subject in a 1913 essay: "Their school consists of the eternal rhythm of the sea, the wind in the leaves, and a thousand other tiny noises, which they listen to with great care. . . . Javanese music obeys laws of counterpoint that make Palestrina seem like child's play."[5]

Such statements suggest that what attracted Debussy to these three traditions—the sixteenth-century "primitives," Bach, and Javanese music—was what results from a multiplicity of simultaneous lines. The "twining counterpoints," "the parallel movement of several lines whose fusion stirs our emotions," "curves, whether flowing in parallel or contrary motion," were all synonymous with what he referred to as the musical arabesque. Rather than the emotive power of a single line, as in a melody, it was lines in relationship to other lines and in constant metamorphosis that he understood as synonymous with musical beauty.

Debussy's lines take many forms and vary in length, extending several measures or arising as a function of short, self-contained motives—the building blocks of his experiments in musical form. Along with relying on the tonal (or modal) implications of their pitches, the construction of these lines reflects a variety of principles—melodic, timbral, and abstract linear—all of which contribute to a constant renewal of balance and equilibrium in Debussy's music. Some lines appear as sensuous melismas and sweeping arpeggios, as in early works like *Arabesques* for piano (1888–91) and *Suite bergamasque* (1890–1905). These are delicately balanced waves of sound arching several octaves within a single measure. Their recurrent proportions, together with any harmonic drive inherent in their pitches, give shape to the music's momentum. In later works like the *Etudes* (1915–16), similar lines in sixty-fourth notes coalesce into sound-color, their overall timbre becoming more important than their directionality. Other lines in his music result from the shape and direction of a series of chords, especially those moving in parallel motion, such as those in "Canope" and the opening of "La terrasse des audiences du clair de lune" from *Préludes,* Book II (1911–13). Some also arise from a succession of notes in the same register, though the space between them may permit other notes or intersecting lines, as in the étude "Pour les arpèges composés." When they are based on a melodic series, certain lines, as in this étude, even tolerate octave displacements of their pitches without losing their integrity.

Performing Debussy's music is a challenge in part because it is often ambiguous where lines begin and end and which line should have priority at any one moment. This is especially true when, as in the beginning of his first *Arabesque,* the same notes serve a variety of functions—part of the propelling motion of the flowing arpeggios, the horizontal articulation of a harmonic sequence, and the linear movement of a melody. As David Lewin suggests, even when the lines move in parallel motion as in a series of parallel chords, we should question the conventional practice of "balanc[ing] and regulat[ing] the voices equally, or else bring[ing] out one of them uniformly as a tenor or cantus firmus throughout."[6] When the same measure is repeated, as is often the case throughout Debussy's oeuvre, we should also question whether Debussy intended these measures to be performed identically. In this chapter, I suggest that the performer study what comes before and after such passages to understand the overall linear momentum, for sometimes the same lines or combination of lines serve different functions from one measure to the next and thus should be performed differently.

In Debussy's late piano music, the density of material and the frequent juxtapositions of contrasting ideas make it particularly difficult to determine the various lines and their function. Although he sometimes uses three staves to help clarify the lines, the relation between them in preludes like "La terrasse" is ever-changing—a demanding feat for the performer. Double-bar lines may mark moments of transition or junctions in the music, but what should move into the foreground, what into the background, is not at all evident. This is no accident.

Like the Javanese who appeared to him to "learn music as easily as one learns to breathe," Debussy liked to say that "real music is never 'difficult.'" And yet, as in the highly complex counterpoint of his Southeast-Asian model, he recognized a necessary paradox: "The beauty of a work of art is something that will always remain mysterious. . . . At all costs let us preserve this element of magic peculiar to music."[7]

Although scholars have tended to undervalue the music's counterpoint when analyzing Debussy's music,[8] in this chapter I argue that the articulation of Debussy's musical lines is crucial. Without sacrificing a work's mystery and magic, a performance attuned to the metamorphoses of the musical arabesque can clarify the musical form. This orientation is not to deny the harmonic goals and structure of the music. Here, however, I wish to draw attention to the textural and registral aspects embedding the lines, the dynamics that support the waves, the special touch that connects notes distant from others or that differentiates two lines within the same register. Performers exert substantial control over such matters. Their careful use of timbres, in articulating the linear structure of a work, can knit together the succession of disparate ideas, especially at interlocking junctions. Thus though a work may seem discontinuous, the performer can reveal threads of continuity and a listener who might otherwise be put off by its constant changes can be drawn into its charm.

A good place to begin this discussion is with music that involves repetition, whether of a short section or an entire measure. It is important for the performer to study these repetitions carefully, for they are not always what they seem. The *Suite bergamasque* is full of such examples, often using measure-pairs. In the "Prélude" (example 11.1), mm. 1–2 return as mm. 7–8, mm. 11–12 are identical to mm. 13–14, m. 20 is the same as m. 24, mm. 20–24 closely resemble mm. 36–40, and so on. The equivalence of mm. 1–2 and mm. 7–8 (the "A" measures) is reinforced by the two measures that follow each pair (the "B" measures). However, though the soprano of mm. 3–4 and mm. 9–10 is identical, the harmonic context of the accompanying chords implies a different performance. In m. 3, the g^1 is a 9–8 suspension leading to f^1, reinforcing the F major and B-flat harmonies in the bass. In m. 9, the same g^1 is the fifth of a C minor chord while the f^1 is the fifth of the b-flat in the bass, or, heard in another way, both present parallel sixths above the bass (b-flat–a). In the second case then, the g^1 and f^1 should be played as equal in importance.[9]

Nicolas Ruwet has argued that the function of repeated passages is often to establish a formal equivalence between elements. As in classical music, this re-

Ex. 11.1. "Prélude" from *Suite bergamasque*, mm. 1–27 (*Example continues*)

sults in a "play of symmetries and asymmetries."[10] With its series of two-measure groups (mm. 1–10), the opening of this "Prélude" constitutes a kind of AB-CAB′ (with C as the change of rhythm and direction in mm. 5–6). Its structure implies that what follows will complete the phrase with another two-measure unit, one resembling C. However, while mm. 11–12 start out as they do in the beginning of C, they proceed in a totally new way. Instead of resolving the structural implications of mm. 1–10, mm. 11–12 frustrate our expectation with a drive upward, underlined by a crescendo. This is cut off by the repetition of these measures in mm. 13–14, prolonging the suspense created by the lack of closure. The

Ex. 11.1. (*Continued*)

long descending line in the five measures which follow, balancing the insisting ascents of mm. 11–14, suggests that mm. 15–19 are the consequent of an elongated asymmetrical coda. To understand form in Debussy's music, this passage suggests that the performer look not just at what is repeated but also at the context for any repetition, especially the drive and directionality of its lines.

The second kind of repetition in this work is more typical of what Ruwet calls a "dialectic of the repeated and non-repeated," that is, returning to an idea to alter it subtly and create "complex relationships over time."[11] To understand this and project it, the performer must be acutely aware of the composer's timbral notations. Measures 20–25 from the same "Prélude," for example, use the same musical idea over and over (mm. 20 and 24 are identical, and m. 21 differs only in its last beat).[12] The return of this material in mm. 36–41 suggests an ABA structure for this, the second part of the piece (example 11.2). However, the dot over the first note e^3 in m. 36 complicates this scenario. Like a Janus figure, it signals both an ending and a beginning, for it completes the line of rising staccatos in m. 35 and it marks the return of the material from m. 20. The dot also causes a displacement of the beginning of the breath group from the high e^3 to the lower b^2. This foreshadows other differences in the second A section.

Making audible subtle variations in repeated sections is important, for they

Ex. 11.2. "Prélude" from *Suite bergamasque,* mm. 34–44

often help draw the listener's attention to other changes. Those in mm. 36–40 give the section not only a different sound from that of mm. 20–25 but also a different function. Whereas mm. 20–25 start out very static, turning around A minor, but end in a state of disequilibrium underlined by two crescendos, mm. 36–40 do the reverse. A crescendo comes earlier in this section (m. 37), balanced by the displaced swell of m. 38. Debussy also follows the analogous crescendo of m. 40 with two decrescendos in m. 41. Reinforcing this relaxation of the momentum, the line itself changes from the rising fourth in the soprano of m. 25 (e^3–a^3) to a descending octave (e^3–e^2) in preparation for the two-measure coda ending this section of the piece. Such timbral indications give shape to the work and ensure the balance of ebb and flow so important in Debussy's music.

Passages like these make it clear that Ruwet's conclusions, as valid as they may be in a structuralist analysis of the music, depend on the performer to articulate difference or similarity from one passage to the next. Not all variations are of pitch; many affect only the dynamics of a repeated idea, or the kind of touch making the sound. Those we have discussed so far are notated in the score for the performer to interpret.

In "Clair de lune," the third movement of the *Suite bergamasque,* more difficult questions arise when this varied repetition is accompanied by a more complex melodic texture with few performance indications in the score. A circular rhythmic-melodic motive spanning two measures dominates the middle of the work, recurring six times (mm. 27–28, 31–32, 35–36, 39–40, 43–44, and 47–48) before returning at the end of the piece. Its repetitive nature creates a tension that is released in long arching arpeggios and a variety of consequents, propelling the music forward. But in the "Calmato" section, which involves almost exact repetition in mm. 43–44, 45–46, and 47–48, for the first time there is a countermelody to this motive in the tenor and then the bass (example 11.3). Its relationship to the returning motive in the upper voices is not altogether clear.

The performer has two choices here: he or she can underline the overall harmonic motion of the passage from A-flat in mm. 43–46 to g-flat in mm. 47–50, in preparation for the return of the original theme on F minor in m. 51. This means performing the section as a series of measure-pairs: m. 44 like m. 43, m. 46 like m. 45, and m. 48 like 47, with mm. 49–50 as a long pedal. One need only decide how to weigh and timbrally distinguish the three voices and keep this relation constant within each measure-pair. Such a performance underlines the balanced proportions of this passage. Alternatively, the performer can focus on the succession itself, that is, the flow from one measure-pair to the next, and show how the melodic motion of the various parts contributes to the final ar-

Ex. 11.3. "Clair de lune," from *Suite bergamasque,* mm. 41–53

rival on f¹ in m. 51. This means articulating subtle differences within the repeating measures, perhaps emphasizing one voice and then another, in order to reinforce connections with the surrounding measures.

Deciding which voice to emphasize and how to shape the three of them is not easy. Studying the character of each, where it comes from, and what it leads to can resolve this dilemma. Though they begin on a major second, d-flat¹/e-flat¹, the upper-note chords in the soprano of m. 43 are also the end of a previous line, the descending thirds of mm. 41–42. They should be played accordingly, with the other two chords in the measure as an extension of the e-flat^1. The principal line of the passage is in the tenor, the new countermelody. It too begins one measure before, in m. 42 on a, resolving to a-flat in the implied D-flat tonality of the "Calmato." The most independent of the lines, it drives the music forward with its upward ascent.

As for the next measure, looking ahead to what follows suggests that one not perform it exactly as m. 43. Because the tenor line no longer has the same drive in m. 45 and the E-flat chord on the last eighth beat of m. 44 is the beginning of an arch upward in the soprano of the next measure, the relation between the voices could change at some point within m. 44. Playing the tenor line in m. 44 more quietly than in m. 43, or with a slight diminuendo, gives attention to the E-flat chord and what follows without necessarily increasing its volume.

A related but somewhat different situation arises in mm. 45–46. At the beginning, the soprano chords are clearly in the foreground and the major second on which they end maintains a certain tension. Their reiteration in m. 46 can be played as an echo. Emanating from the lowest note of the soprano chords and later disintegrating into arpeggios, the tenor here becomes a middle-ground accompaniment. What is interesting in the passage comes at the end of m. 46. After a series of sweeping arpeggios, the bass returns to an oscillation around a-flat. This prepares the g-flat on which the tenor's countermelody will return in m. 47, only in the bass. Playing both the soprano and tenor lines slightly diminuendo at the end of m. 46 then allows the listener to focus on the bass which will initiate this return.

With the tenor's melody in the bass, mm. 47–48 are a variation of mm. 43–44 but on G-flat major (functioning as ii$^6_5$ to a half-diminished vii^7 in D-flat). To underline this similarity, the performer might want to repeat the shape given to mm. 43–44: that is, first focus on the principal line in the bass, then in the course of m. 48, shift emphasis to the upper voice melody to prepare for the climactic leap upward to the high e-flat^3 in m. 49 and the return of F (f^1 and f^3) in m. 51. In this way, the performer can support the harmonic structure of the section while helping the listener hear the changing function of the various lines and their complex interconnections.

The musical arabesque becomes more complex in Debussy's later piano pieces, where there are often fewer clues for disentangling the multiple lines. "La terrasse des audiences du clair de lune," from *Préludes,* Book II, is characterized by perpetual metamorphosis from one relatively self-contained idea to another.

There is repetition in the work, and certainly motivic recurrence, but its structure is not part of a "dialectic of the repeated and the non-repeated." To effect movement between the music's various "terraces," the performer must decipher the voice-leading, the key to the work's continuity.

Understanding the repetitions at the end of "La terrasse" provides a way to approach the work. It is not immediately evident why mm. 34 and 35 are identical (see example 11.4). They are not preceded or followed by other measure-

(*Example continues*)

Ex. 11.4. "La terrasse des audiences du clair de lune," *Préludes,* Book II, mm. 1–45. Revised version (1985) by Editions Durand et Costallat, Paris; reproduced with the generous permission of the publishers.

Ex. 11.4. (*Continued*)

pairs and do not underline a binary phrase group (as in the *Suite bergamasque*). Study of the surrounding music suggests an interpretation. Two measures earlier, in m. 32, there are two lines in contrary motion—one rising from d-sharp^2 in the middle register, the other, in the same rhythms, descending from d-sharp^3 in the upper register. In m. 33 these lines merge into a single line on D-sharp (doubled in three registers) and continue in a series of octaves on A-sharp and

Ex. 11.4. (*Continued*) (*Example continues*)

E-sharp. The slight crescendo at the end of m. 33 followed by the diminuendo in m. 34 suggests that the performer connect the octaves in m. 33 to those that follow in the next measure on G-sharp, F-sharp, and C-sharp, though they are here embedded in a thicker, more complex texture. In other words, the upper octaves in m. 34 are the final notes of the counterpoint begun in m. 32 and should

Ex. 11.4. (*Continued*)

be played accordingly. Emerging from the shadows of the upper-voice octaves and overlapping with their range, is another line in this measure made up of sixteenth-note octaves oscillating around B. Although it is background to the upper-octave line in the beginning of the measure, in the middle it can begin to take on its own momentum.

Although m. 35 repeats m. 34, what follows suggests that the lines in m. 35 do

Ex. 11.4. (*Continued*) (*Example continues*)

not serve the same function. No longer are the upper-voice octaves needed to complete the previous counterpoint. They can be played as an echo, a lingering resonance of the preceding idea. Of more importance here are the inner voices, for the music collapses to their line in m. 36, recalling the descending octaves of mm. 2 and 5. It is this line that is resolved by the cadence on B to F-sharp in the

Ex. 11.4. (*Continued*)

bass of m. 37. The subsequent importance of the inner-voice line in m. 36 thus argues for emphasizing it in m. 35.

If the performer uses dynamics, touch, or tone color to change the foreground-background relation between the voices in these measures, this instance of repetition can serve as a pivot, a means of shifting attention gradually between the counterpoint begun in m. 32 and the descending line that leads to the work's tonic, F-sharp, in m. 37. Unlike the traditional transitions of nineteenth-century music, what happens here is not a smooth connection between the ideas, but rather their superimposition or overlapping within the repeated measures. Elsewhere I call this kind of movement in Debussy's music "conjunct transformation" because it involves a change of function of some pivotal point, as opposed to "disjunct transformation,"which is change brought about by a discontinuous and unmediated change.[13] With such a technique, the composer does not attempt to reconcile the differences between his ideas or to find some point in common but simply to mutate from one to the next. Such repeated gestures guide the listener through the structural changes taking place in the music.

In the two measures which follow, repetition has another purpose, equally dependent on the performer's articulation of timbral differences. Because they are the same except for octave displacements, at issue here is which note to emphasize, if any, within the repeating octaves and chords. The voice-leading of the surrounding music again makes plausible a certain interpretation. The descending augmented fourths and minor sixths in the inner-voice octaves of m. 36 suggest that in m. 37 the performer emphasize the *upper* notes of the bass octaves which continue this pattern of movement. In the nine-voice chord, the placement of the descending melisma in the middle range suggests that the performer emphasize the lower voices from which it emerges. It is important to prepare the listener's ear for this melisma, for here is the first time in the work that a long descending glissando comes on the beat. This gesture functions like a big exhale. It relaxes some of the tension built up by the work's many rich complexities.

The same ideas in m. 38 serve to prolong the arrival on the tonic. With the melisma up an octave, the balance of the sound shifts to the outer registers, as if both to reinforce the closure of the previous section and to create a frame for what will come in m. 39. If the performer emphasizes the outer registers then, the descending line of the melisma will lead the listener's ear again to F-sharp, this time in the middle register. The rest of the piece is essentially one long pedal on F-sharp major, the F-sharp approached by a variety of ingenious aural routes in each register of the piano.

Elsewhere in the piece, the greatest challenge is to make sense of the constant registral shifts. The first thing to ascertain is what is primary and what subsidiary, which notes carry the lines and which are ornamental color. The opening motive, for example, begins in the middle register. The descending melisma and the octaves that resolve to c-sharp^7 in m. 3 ornament the middle register by leading to it or circling within it. This suggests a rationale for playing the more problematic chordal doublings in mm. 3–4. If the main line is in the middle register, then the upper doubling on every other beat of the b-flat^7 chord should be played as ornamental to the middle register b-flat^7 chords, not a shift of the line up two octaves. The staccatos on these doublings three times in m. 4 support this interpretation. They signal that the right-hand doublings should be played lighter than those an octave lower. As such, they are a kind of color resonating over the lower notes.

What is primary and what subsidiary in this music is ever changing, as the next measures make clear; it is for the performer not only to articulate this but, even more important, to clarify the moments of transition. For example, the ornamental glissando of m. 2 changes roles when extended two octaves in m. 6. Here it serves to connect the upper and lower registers and guides the listener's ear to the D-sharp in the bass and the subsequent modulation in m. 7.

Thick chords, such as those of mm. 7–9, raise other issues which only questions of balance and the form of the section as a whole can answer. Are there separate lines within their eight-note texture? Since their rhythms and melodic shape are related to those of m. 1, do they initiate another six-measure section, an ABAC, or do they close the previous section, an ABA, as the double-bar lines in mm. 8 and 9 might indicate? What we have seen at the end of the piece suggests an approach. As one might want to shift emphasis from the inner voices of the chord and bass octaves of m. 37 to the outer ones in m. 38, here likewise, with a similar registral expansion of previous material, one might want to emphasize the outer registers, the upper notes of the chord and the lower notes of the bass octaves. The voice-leading also suggests that one might emphasize the right-hand notes, for the B-flat major chord on which the progression ends in m. 8 only resolves smoothly in these voices (in the left hand, all voices drop augmented fourths or fifths). That Debussy leaves time for the sound to dissipate after the strange movement from D-sharp to C-sharp to B-flat, articulated in the bass and reinforced in the other voices, suggests that this is the end of a section.

Emphasizing the outer registers of mm. 7–8 has other formal ramifications as well. This interpretation suggests a formal extension over time of the kind of resonance Debussy creates in doubling a chord an octave higher, such as on the upbeats of mm. 3–4. Like an echo in an upper register not of a note or chord but of an entire section, these measures add a new timbral as well as harmonic color to the opening motive. Heard later in the work (for example, at mm. 25ff and 39ff), they frame what we have heard from another perspective, thereby also coloring our memory.

What follows in mm. 10–12 reinforces this sense of closure in m. 9, for though these measures are structurally ambivalent, they function as an extended transition. The transition begins with the B-flat chord repeated "marqué" in m. 9, a short measure in $\frac{3}{8}$ surrounded by double-bar lines. With it, Debussy shifts interest back to the middle register. This chord, serving as a pivot, should be played as both emanating from the previous chord and a way to draw attention to the middle range, where a new idea begins in m. 10. With its alternating chords that gradually rise, outlining a minor seventh (f^1/e-flat^2), mm. 10–11 resemble mm. 3–4, whose chords leap c-sharp^1/b-flat^1, a diminished seventh. Both sections begin on chords that resolve movement from the previous measures, and both stay largely in the middle register. However, the insistent return to f and f^1 in mm. 10–12, preceded by very quick melismas that reinforce the arrival on e-flat^1 and e-flat^2, does not culminate in a nice archlike swell, as in m. 4. Instead, mm. 10–12 are a structural elongation of the pitch f. In them, François Delalande sees the "staircase" patterns of chordal ascent as less important than a conelike aural shape that decreases to a point at the f in mm. 10–12.[14] This short section is thus interesting in its ironies. Debussy lightens up the tone (*léger*) and enlivens the tempo (*un peu animé*), but for music whose rate of change slows down.

That momentary stasis (rather than harmonic movement) brings about the movement from the first to the second section of the work is reiterated by a second pivot, the second f in m. 12. No longer the goal of the measure, as in mm. 10 and 11 (though prepared by a crescendo on the descending melisma), and no longer a dominant of B-flat which effects a circular return to the same material, the f stands alone in the middle of this measure. Its function is signaled by the absence of dynamic shape on the preceding melisma, its *più pp* dynamics, its elongation by an eighth note, and its enharmonic change to e-sharp. As the beginning of a crescendo on e-sharp^7, it signals a return to the first chord of the piece, with d^1-sharp instead of d^1. However, because counterpoint emerges as significant in the next section, the rising arpeggios of m. 12 are not just a line leading to the chords of m. 13 but, more important, a subtle introduction to the notes with which the next section's counterpoint begins, d-sharp^1, d-sharp^2, and d-sharp^3.

With such procedures in mind, it is far easier to plan a convincing performance of the most difficult part of the work where, with five separate lines and five sections separated by double-bar lines, the arabesque is at its most complex. The first of these, mm. 13–14 completed by the $\frac{3}{8}$ measure that follows, introduces the first contrary motion in the prelude (which returns in mm. 32–33). Moving chromatically in both directions around D-sharp on three octaves, the duet's two lines are equally important here, though to balance the upward arching curves of mm. 10–11, one might want to emphasize the downward arching curve of the soprano octaves. This duet, filling out the upper half of the middle register, initiates a movement that culminates in m. 20.

As the dance expands to all registers in the next section, mm. 16–20, the texture expands to five threads—the soprano octaves on C-sharp, those a bit lower oscillating around F-double sharp, the repeating major seconds b/c-sharp^1, the tenor line beginning on e-sharp, and the gonglike repeated CCC-sharp in the bass. Here the challenge is to distinguish these lines and their constant flux into and out of the foreground. Because the C-sharp octaves in the right hand conclude the previous counterpoint in both the soprano and alto and remain static, in performance one might play them in a gradual diminuendo in m. 16. In the foreground of mm. 16–19, another duet in largely contrary motion gradually emerges between the middle-register octaves and the rising tenor line. Beginning at f-double sharp^1 and f-double sharp^2 in the soprano and at e-sharp in the tenor, these both start somewhat lower than the inner-voice lines of m. 13. Foreshadowing the rhythms and contour of the inner-voice line in mm. 34–36, the octaves on F-double sharp in m. 16 begin as an alternative resolution of the counterpoint in mm. 13–15. Together with the repeating b/c-sharp^1 seconds accompanying them, they call for a different timbre than the other voices and, at first, no dynamic shape. Like the tenor that constantly turns back on itself before attaining its goal in the "Calmato" of "Clair de lune," this tenor line adds forward momentum to the passage and should be played accordingly. When the inner octaves move into conjunction with it in m. 17 (e/f-double sharp^1 to f-sharp/g-sharp^1 and e/f-double sharp^1 to f-sharp/f-double sharp^1), these octaves begin to come into the foreground.

In m. 19, however, the relation between the voices changes as they prepare another shift to the outer registers in m. 20, this time with the texture changed to a lyrical melody with accompaniment. Although this passionate arrival in m. 20 may seem out of context, the performer can prepare the listener for it. Playing the notated *tenuto* on the C-sharp octaves in the soprano of m. 17 suggests that these octaves may later reemerge in importance. As they take on the rhythmic and melodic shape of the inner-octave line in m. 19, they move into a duet in parallel motion with the inner-voice line to lead the listener's ear to the high f-sharp^2 and f-sharp^3 in m. 20. The inner-octave line also changes in character as its rhythms slow to eighth notes and its final notes G/E/E-sharp reiterate those in the opening chord progression.[15] With no low bass, the prolonged chord in the left hand takes on a pedal function in preparation for the descent to the low G-sharps in m. 20.

Linear complexity returns in the next double-bar section, mm. 21–24, as Debussy begins another wave of movement to the outer registers, this time starting almost an octave lower than in m. 13 and pushing somewhat higher. This again starts in the middle register, beginning with a leap downward in all parts. Although the same rhythmic patterns continue in the soprano, the abruptness of the gesture is startling. To bridge this discontinuity, one could perform the tenor in a crescendo over the soprano chords at the end of m. 20, for it is this line rising an octave from g-sharp to f^1 that prepares the e^1 on which the right hand of m. 21 begins. This voice-leading implies that the performer should emphasize the lower notes of the right-hand chords throughout m. 21. The contrary motion between them and the upper notes of the left-hand chords, equally important in this measure, serves to focus attention again on the middle register, especially as the two lines converge on the same d^1 there. As at the end of m. 15 and in m. 33, this convergence of lines from contrary motion clears a space for other lines in turn to emerge in importance.

Throughout this section, Debussy uses the contrary motion of chromatic lines to create tension and drive his music upward. Along the way, he positions rests in the bass to draw attention to dramatic leaps in the upper voices. Just as in m. 8, when a rest interrupts the soprano to draw attention to movement in the bass, one on the fifth eighth beat of m. 21 exposes the soprano's first arch upward of a fourth. This rest also draws attention to the subsequent two-note incipit in the bass. In m. 22 then, the performer may want to shift emphasis to the lower voices of the left-hand chords. Rests in the bass of m. 24 also expose a particularly important moment—the convergence of the upper lines in the rhythmic and harmonic conjunction of the right- and left-hand chords. At this point, the right-hand chords should be in the foreground to lead the movement to the upper register.

In the section which follows, mm. 25–27, for the first time the middle register recedes entirely into the background as Debussy inverts the registral relation with which the piece began. Now in the outer registers and moving entirely together, both hands play a lilting tune built of the rhythmic-melodic motive introduced in m. 16 and derived from the first measure of the piece. This is the first time the outer registers share the principal line; with its ABA shape, it is the first melody in the piece that feels complete. On the upbeats, both hands also play the accompaniment, a short arching line of triads around E-flat.

At the apex of the work, mm. 28–31, emphasis again returns to the middle register, this time to initiate another form of consolidation. In mm. 29 and 31, there is only one line—all parts join in the homophonic texture of the chordal progression. Debussy effects the transition to this unusual moment by changing the function of the registers themselves—not surprisingly, by means of a repeated gesture and two *tenuto* marks, recalling those of m. 17. The outer chords resolve the main line of mm. 25–27 and should be played as such. The rising octaves and G^7 begin as subsidiary. When the gesture is repeated, however, the outer chords should recede in importance and let the rising octaves draw attention to the G^7, for it begins the chordal progression that follows. Here all voices come together not in doubled triads, as in m. 7, but in doubled seventh chords (ten-note clusters). These fill out the middle register completely, becoming the most dense section of the piece. This is the only time the music expands from piano to forte. It comes at the work's Golden Section (the end of m. 28), a perfectly proportionate moment for the work's climax, after which the dénouement begins with a return to the pianissimo counterpoint of mm. 13–14, the middle register, and lines that lead to the tonic.[16]

In "La terrasse," as in many of Debussy's works, it is not incidental that most of the piece is to be played in the range between pianissimo and piano. Most crescendos, such as those of mm. 21–24, culminate in a return to piano or pianissimo. Debussy even writes "subito pianissimo" after the slightest of crescendos, as in m. 13, and at moments of arrival, like mm. 13 and 25. Varied voicings of a chord and the timbral differences needed to distinguish the different threads of the musical arabesque are much more difficult when playing loudly. During the only forte passage of this work, mm. 29–31, subtlety is not an issue, for the line does not shift between various ideas and registers but is maintained entirely within the chordal succession.

Although there is much more that could be said about this fascinating prelude, this analysis has tried to show how important the performer's role is. He or she is responsible for not only maintaining a quiet dynamic level but also clarifying moments of transition, often signaled by repeated gestures, and articulating varying relations between the registers of the piano. This is the key to projecting the work's form. As we have seen, at the beginning and end of "La terrasse," the focus is on the middle register. Movement from or within the other registers can be played as a kind of resonance ornamenting the center, giving it a harmonic foundation, or emanating from it, whether this resonance appears as upper-octave doublings of chords or the variation of some idea over time. The middle of the work, by contrast, consists of three linear gestures that gradually move outward from this center. In each case, the contrary motion of a duet creates tension to propel the expansion to other registers and prepares a different relation between them, one suggested by the interdependence of the lines. Climaxes, or moments of arrival in this music, occur when the linear complexity drops out, and what appears is either a simple melody and accompaniment (in mm. 20 and 25–27), everything condensed into one line—albeit one full of unresolved dissonances (at the Golden Section)—or, at the end, two pitches, F-sharp and C-sharp, dispersed into every register.

Debussy's "Pour les arpèges composés" from his *Douze études pour le piano,* Book II (1915), poses additional problems for the performer and listener because of the nature of line within arpeggios and the extreme density of ideas characteristic of Debussy's late works. First, as in much of Bach's music for solo instruments, Debussy expects the performer to articulate more lines than the musical texture seems to call for (example 11.5). In m. 2, for example, he adds stems down on certain notes of the right hand, beginning with b-flat^2, and notates their rhythms as different from the stream of sixteenth notes in the arpeggiated line. In spite of the time interval between the notes, this is the principal line of mm. 1–6. The dots over the arpeggiated notes in the left hand instruct the pianist to find a third timbre in counterpoint to the right hand's flowing arpeggios and the sustained notes of the main line. In m. 3, a fourth and fifth line enter: one on AA-flat in the bass followed by the rising fifth, D-flat and A-flat; the other in the middle register on the third beat, another b-flat/a-flat with stems down.

Debussy surprises us with a *rinforzando* on this third beat and makes us question the function of the b-flat/a-flat. The notes continue the pattern of descending arpeggios in the right hand but, with their stems down, one might ask, Should the performer play them as an echo of the principal line, two octaves lower? We have seen similar repetition in other pieces, but in none of them was the second gesture to be played louder than the first. This b-flat/a-flat flow naturally from the arpeggiated line and thus one could play them as its conclusion, but this does not explain Debussy's emphasis on them. After the lovely airiness of the upper register arpeggios, the idea could be to shift attention to the middle register. Yet in m. 4 and m. 7, this *rinforzando* does not lead to an new idea there; in both measures, the main line returns to an outer register. Unlike in "La terrasse," then, the music which immediately follows does not imply one kind of performance over another.

Only study of the rest of the piece explains this puzzling timbre. The b-flat/a-flat are in fact the cell from which the rest of the work expands. The melodic line itself juxtaposes them in the first measure, with b-flat^2 the first note and a-flat^2 the last one. Likewise, the work as a whole begins on B-flat and ends on A-flat. Moreover, the metric placement of the notes in the first measure suggests a

Ex. 11.5. "Pour les arpèges composés" from *Douze études pour le piano,* Book II, mm. 1–16. Revised version (1991) by Editions Durand et Costallat, Paris, reproduced with the generous permission of the publishers.

rhythmic analogue to this relation, for b-flat^2 and f^2 fall on the strong part of the beat and e-flat^3, c^3 and c^2, and a-flat^2 on the weak part. On the second beat of the second measure, this ordering inverts, with the arpeggios beginning on a-flat^2 and ending on b-flat^1. This foreshadows the shift of B-flats to offbeats later in the work, such as in mm. 59 and 61, when thirty-second note B-flats propel motion to dotted eighths on A-flat. In the penultimate measures (mm. 62–63),

Ex. 11.5. (*Continued*)

Debussy displaces the opening motive to the second beat, leaving A-flat on the first beat as the work resolves to its tonic.[17]

To understand the accent in m. 3, then, one might also look later in the piece. As in the *Suite bergamasque,* there are subtle but important variations of mm. 1–6 in their return in mm. 50–57 (see example 11.6). The most important is one

Ex. 11.6. "Pour les arpèges composés" from *Douze études pour le piano,* Book II, mm. 50–57. Revised version (1991) by Editions Durand et Costallat, Paris, reproduced with the generous permission of the publishers.

that seems to have escaped most pianists. The high b-flat^2 at the beginning of mm. 52 and 56 does not have a stem up connecting it to the main line as before. One might argue that this is a mistake in the score and perform the passage exactly as in m. 3.[18] But if the pianist leaves a sort of void in the main line at this point—not stressing the upper b-flat^2 of the arpeggios—the b-flat two octaves lower at the end of mm. 52 and 56 becomes the completion of the soprano line. This b-flat/a-flat, then, is not an echo of the upper line but a two-octave displacement of it. As in other works, Debussy here uses repetition to shift attention to another register, where static pitch oscillations slow time down, and cadences to C major in m. 53 and to G-flat $^{13}_{9}$ in m. 57 prepare for the end of the piece.

The challenge for the performer of this piece is to follow the musical line as it wanders over the keyboard, conveying structural movement as well as the sonorous opulence of the arpeggios. Focusing on two things will help. First, Debussy often notates his long melismas of sixty-fourth notes with a note-size smaller than normal, something he calls "la petite note" at the end of "La terrasse." These are to be played "lightly" (as in "La terrasse"), that is, as horizontal blocks of sound rather than as principal or even subsidiary lines. For example, in mm. 7–11, 20–24, and 46–47, there is only one line, that of the low bass, the notes with stems down. In such passages, one should take care to articulate and shape the main line, which is notated with normal-sized notes, and play the smaller notes as harmonic color.

This is not to imply that all quick notes are ornamental in Debussy's music and that only longer ones make up the musical line. Quite the contrary. As the piece proceeds, very quick notes in this étude also serve three other functions. Some are part of the main lines. In mm. 12–15 (as in mm. 21–24, 27–28, 32, 39, 46–47, 59, and 61), the stems down on certain thirty-second notes connect them to the dotted eighths and the principal line of the passage. Debussy uses these short notes to propel the line forward, to give it a bit of a snap. It is thus necessary to differentiate them from the ornamental melismas which may precede or follow them. In unusual cases, short notes serve to lead to new ideas in subsequent measures (as at the end of mm. 27, 28, 37, and 39). Debussy stresses the importance of performing them as part of the main lines by noting precise performance instructions like *staccato marcato* in mm. 27 and 37 and crescendos in mm. 38 and 39. Thirty-second notes and sixty-fourth notes may also constitute subsidiary or transitional lines that lead the listener's ear from one register to another (such as in m. 26).

Second, Debussy's frequent use of octave displacement does not necessarily imply discontinuities in his musical lines.[19] Although the opening section (mm. 1–6) presents five distinct lines—some of them in the same register, others defined by their different registers—all five employ many of the same pitches. That the middle register line, the bass, and the oscillating arpeggios all end on A-flat at the end of m. 6 makes the leap down to the low AA-flat in the bass not as surprising as the registral shift of two octaves might otherwise appear. If the performer imagines the pitch movement as if within one register, leaps in the principal line of more than an octave, from a-flat to AA-flat in m. 6 to m. 7, from D-flat to f in m. 10, and elsewhere, are much easier to follow. The lines are sweeping, yes, often spanning two or more octaves, but in terms of pitch-class movement (that of notes with octave and enharmonic equivalence), they may span only a second (as from the low D-flat in m. 10 to c^1 in m. 11, or from the f^1 in m. 18 back to the low E-flat in m. 20).

Keeping in mind the various functions served by the short notes and the role of movement through pitch-class successions will help the performer make sense of the complex middle section of this étude (mm. 25–45). Here the rapid succession of contrasting motivic ideas, coupled with the constantly shifting registers, dynamic levels, and harmonies, challenge a listener's desire for continuity. Three things help to structure this section: first, the periodic return of the bass, second, the alternation of staccatos and accented notes, and third, the nature of the principal lines. The low E anchors the section, as does the eventual movement in the bass to F-sharp, B and B-flat, and finally A-flat in m. 50. It is interesting, however, that despite their importance, most of these bass notes have relatively short note-values and are marked with staccatos. In other words, despite the importance of the tonal alternation between E major and an ambiguous A-flat major/F minor throughout this section, the bass movement may be largely secondary to other linear elements.

Staccatos and accents on virtually every note of mm. 25–45 help clarify the principal lines because, as in the first third of the work, staccatos often indicate subsidiary notes and lines (except where noted above), while accented notes delineate principal ones (see example 11.7). The rhythm of their alternation accustoms us to this timbral hierarchy, bridges the shift from one idea to the next, and creates for the music a timbral analogue for the melodic alternation of B-flat/A-flat and the harmonic one in this section of E major and an ambiguous A-flat major/F minor. Their alternation also creates a context for playful associations between timbre and meter. For example, in mm. 25–28 the interaction of staccatos and accents with the various dynamic levels results in a rhythmic alternation of short and long notes within each measure. As the section proceeds, the accented notes keep the performer focused on the main line, thereby rendering of ambiguous importance notes with metrical and harmonic weight, such as the arrival on B and E in the bass on the first downbeat of mm. 31 and 34, both marked with staccatos. Debussy's metric placement of staccatos on the short-note upbeats within the main lines (especially on the last beats of mm. 27, 28, 37, and 39 and every other eighth beat within the "Giocoso" section) clues us into how larger units may relate to one another, especially those with the same pitches. In the two identical measures, mm. 27–28, for example, the bass notes of the first have staccatos, those of the second are legato; likewise, in m. 35 the

Ex. 11.7. "Pour les arpèges composés" from *Douze études pour le piano,* Book II, mm. 25–35. Revised version (1991) by Editions Durand et Costallat, Paris, reproduced with the generous permission of the publishers.

low F-sharp is sustained, and in m. 36 the same has a staccato. This articulates an upbeat-downbeat or downbeat-upbeat relation between the measure-pairs. The presence of staccatos throughout the last measures of this section, mm. 39–44, reinforces the sense that the modulation to B major is a transition, a structural upbeat if you will, to the legato passage, mm. 46–49, that prepares the return of the opening material in m. 50.

Paying close attention to these differences in articulation helps the listener stay focused on the principal lines whose progressions are often quite simple. Despite other movement up and down two octaves, the principal line of mm. 25–28 remains in the middle register, centered around the middle c-sharp^1 with which the section begins. Beginning a half-step lower on c^1, the "Giocoso" section continues this line, but at a brisk pace and ornamented with only a few short graces. So do the registrally wide chords of the "Scherzandare" with the initial B in the right hand acting as a typical Debussyan pivot. (This completes the bass movement of "Giocoso" section and introduces the lowest note of the left-hand chords which follow.) Even the C-sharp/G-sharp chords of m. 32 can be played as the continuation of this line if one emphasizes the upper f-sharp^1 of the right-hand chords in m. 31, followed by the lower notes of the chords which follow (c-sharp^1 and g-sharp^1). Similar movement links this passage to the return to the "Giocoso" music after the rest in m. 32. Its pitch-class relations are conjunct in both hands. (The right-hand chord's g-sharp^1 leads naturally to the right hand's grace notes on g^1, and then f and e, an octave lower, and the left-hand chord's c-sharp^1 leads to the left hand's D/C-sharp/C/BB/BB-flat two octaves below.) The rest of this section, mm. 33–39, can be played likewise, as can the end of the work, mm. 58–61. By paying attention to timbral detail and the voice-leading and by rethinking the octave displacements of the musical line, it is thus possible to clarify for the listener this sequence of ever-changing ideas.

Much of Debussy's music plays with lines in this way, with shapes submerging into other shapes and colors emerging out of and disintegrating into other colors. This is not unlike the role Debussy conceived for music in the shadows of his opera *Pelléas et Mélisande.* Although its surface is full of discontinuities—in part because of the very process of repetition and the movement from one idea to the next—changes in his music are rarely abrupt. Debussy once said that he never wanted to hear the stitches in it. The performer can support this aesthetic by shifting weight gradually from one line to another, even in the middle of a measure, as the relative importance of one line emerges and another retreats, and by using timbral articulation (touch, dynamics, tone quality) in as many ways as possible to differentiate the lines of ever-changing hierarchical relation.

A number of techniques can help the performer resolve similar problems in other Debussy pieces. First, study any repetition in the music very carefully, looking for slight variations in the notated score from one instance of an idea to the next, and question whether there is a possible change in the overall function of the repeated section. Second, listen to the preceding and succeeding measures of any such section to understand any connections between the repeated material and where it may be coming from or leading to. Sometimes this may entail looking later in the piece. Third, ascertain where each musical line begins and ends, especially if the line is within or overlaps the beginning or ending of another section. Fourth, decide which line is most important at any given moment, what function it serves in that role, and which lines or voices are subsidiary. Notice that often when contrary lines come together on the same pitch or pitch-class, other lines are beginning to emerge in importance; find some way of making this audible. Fifth, take great care to control the dynamic level and the performance of all dynamic markings in such a way that it is possible to differentiate with subtle timbral shadings all the various voices and lines of the work. Sixth, look for any analogues to the notated timbral distinctions in the melodic, harmonic, rhythmic, metric, or formal relations within the work. And seventh, keep in mind the overall structural shape of the piece such that its various sections are balanced and the performance results in a coherent sense of form.

I have examined these pieces in some detail not only because they raise interesting questions about the significance of timbre in performing Debussy's piano music. This method of analysis helps us to understand why Debussy laid such emphasis on curves and arabesque in his music, why he once defined musical charm as the *mise en place* of a composer's ideas, and why he was preoccupied with "what should precede and what should follow" at any given moment of his work.[20] It acknowledges the diverse functions of repeated material in Debussy's music and the role of timbre in articulating his structures. In some cases, it even proposes that his love of resonance, or repeating an idea in the outer registers, had an effect on his conception of musical form. These, I would argue, are important secrets of his musical logic.

Notes

CHAPTER 1: DEBUSSY ON PERFORMANCE

Epigraph: Karl Lahm, "Erinnerungen an Claude Debussy," *Melos* 21/11 (November 1954): 314–15, reprinted in Roger Nichols, *Debussy Remembered* (London: Faber and Faber, 1992), 122–23.

1. Jos van Immerseel's claim that an 1897 Erard was "the unquestioned choice" for a recording of Debussy on a historic piano is not an entirely convincing argument when seen against testimonies of Debussy's own playing and his preference for the muted sound of a Blüthner with the lid closed, even in recital. The Erard has very characteristic harmonics and different tones in different registers: the opposite of the more homogeneous sound of the Blüthner. The Channel Classics compact disc *Claude Debussy: Préludes and Images* (CCS 4892, 1993) is nonetheless revealing, as are the notes.
2. See Debussy, *Early Recordings by the Composer: The Condon Collection* (Bellaphon 690 07 011, 1992). This compact disc includes the composer's piano rolls made in 1913 on the Duo-Arte system replayed and re-recorded on a new piano, as well as early recordings of Debussy made by various pianists from 1910 to 1923.
3. Robert Philip, *Early Recordings and Musical Style* (Cambridge: Cambridge University Press, 1992), 234.
4. Mahler, quoted in N. Bauer-Lechner, *Erinnerungen an Gustav Mahler* (Vienna, 1923; Eng. trans., London, 1980), 46, quoted in Philip, *Early Recordings,* 8.
5. Philip, *Early Recordings,* 8.

6. "Vous savez mon opinion sur les mouvements métronomiques: ils sont justes pendant une mesure, comme 'les roses, l'espace d'un matin.'" Debussy to Jacques Durand, 9 Oct. 1915, in *Lettres de Claude Debussy à son éditeur,* ed. Jacques Durand (Paris: Durand, 1927), 158. All translations Richard Langham Smith's unless otherwise indicated.
7. Debussy's spell on *La revue blanche* began in April 1901, but his announcement of an article called "De l'inutilité de Wagnérisme" in *L'idée libre* of 10 September 1893 suggests that he had had the idea of writing about musical matters for some time previously.
8. "Je ne suis pas plus avancé que toi sur la partition de *Messidor* parce que la vie est courte et qu'il vaut mieux aller au café ou regarder les images; puis comment veux-tu que des gens aussi laids que Zola et Bruneau soient capables d'autre chose qu'un effort vers le médiocre?" Debussy to Pierre Louÿs, 9 Mar. 1897. In *Correspondance de Claude Debussy et Pierre Louÿs,* ed. H. Borgeaud (Paris: José Corti, 1945), 92, reprinted in Debussy, *Correspondance, 1884–1918* [hereafter cited as *Correspondance* (1993)], ed. François Lesure (Paris: Hermann, 1993), 196–97.
9. Presumably your second half of beer. "Remarques-tu que ce Charpentier prends les 'cris de Paris' qui sont délicieux de pittoresque humain, et comme un sale prix de Rome, il en fait des cantilènes chlorotiques, sous des harmonies dont je dirai qu'elles sont parasites, pour être poli. . . . Et on appelle cela de la Vie! Ciel de Dieu, j'aime mieux mourir tout de suite.—Ce sont des sensations qui sentent cette 'gueule de bois' particulière au 'vingtième demi.'" Debussy, *Correspondance* (1993), 136–137, 155.
10. On the contrast between Maeterlinck's and Zola's aesthetics see chapter 1 of Roger Nichols and Richard Langham Smith, Claude Debussy: "Pelléas et Mélisande," Cambridge Opera Handbook (Cambridge: Cambridge University Press, 1989).
11. One of the best of these is Edward Lockspeiser's article "Debussy's Concept of the Dream" in *Proceedings of the Royal Musical Association* 89 (1962–63): 49–61. Jarocinski's *Debussy: Impressionism and Symbolism* (English trans. Rollo Myers, London: Eulenberg, 1976), while throwing up many interesting ideas, is typical of much writing on the composer in failing to center on Debussy's own ideas as he expressed them.
12. The interview originally appeared in Maurice Emmanuel, *Pelléas et Mélisande* (Paris: Mellottée, 1926). This quotation is from 35–36. Lockspeiser included a translation and commentary in *Debussy, His Life and Mind,* vol. 1 (London: Cassell, 1962), 204–8.
13. "Je crois que jamais je ne pourrai enfermer ma musique dans un moule trop correct. Je me dépêche de vous dire que je ne parle pas de la forme musicale, c'est simplement à un point de vue littéraire. J'aimerai toujours mieux une chose où, en quelque sorte, l'action sera sacrifiée à l'expression longuement poursuivie des sentiments de l'âme"; "Des personnages dont l'histoire et la demeure ne seront d'aucun temps, d'aucun lieu," Debussy to Eugène-Henri Vasnier, 4 June 1885, cited in Debussy, *Correspondance* (1993), 33.
14. "Par moments, vous avez pu tellement vous abstraire de toute influence extérieure que cela devenait surnaturel, et la façon dont vous avez su dire: 'Tout ceci sera quand il viendra' est une des émotions musicales les plus fortes que j'aie jamais ressentie, c'est vraiment quelque chose de sûrement inoubliable," Debussy to Blanche Marot, 24 May 1900. Cited in Debussy, *Correspondance* (1993), 158.
15. Debussy expands upon this in an article on Mary Garden: "La réalisation scénique d'une oeuvre d'art, si belle soit-elle, est presque toujours contradictoire au rêve intérieur qui,

tour à tour, la fit sortir de ses alternatives de doute et d'enthousiasme," "Mary Garden," *Musica,* Jan. 1908, reprinted in Claude Debussy, *Monsieur Croche et autres écrits,* ed. François Lesure, expanded and enlarged edition (Paris: Gallimard, 1987), 200.

16. "Je voulais à la musique une liberté qu'elle contient peut-être plus que n'importe quel art, n'étant pas bornée à une reproduction plus ou moins exacte de la nature, mais aux correspondances mystérieuses entre la Nature et l'Imagination," "Pourquoi j'ai écrit 'Pelléas,'" note written to Georges Ricou, Secretary General of the Opéra-Comique, in April 1902, published in *Comoedia,* 17 October 1920, and reprinted in *Monsieur Croche,* 62.

17. "Soit qu'il collabore avec Baudelaire, avec Verlaine, avec Mallarmé, ou qu'il tire de son propre fonds le sujet de ses ouvrages, le compositeur s'affirme avant tout soucieux d'éviter ce qu'on pourrait nommer la traduction directe des sentiments. Ce qui l'attire, chez les poètes que nous venons de nommer, c'est précisément leur art de tout transposer en images symboliques, de faire vibrer, sous un mot, des résonances multiples. . . . La plupart de ses compositions sont ainsi des symboles de symboles, mais exprimés en une langue par elle-même si riche, si persuasive, qu'elle atteint parfois à l'éloquence d'un verbe nouveau," Paul Dukas, "'Nocturnes' de Debussy," *Revue hébdomadaire,* February 1901, reprinted in *Les écrits de Paul Dukas sur la musique* (Paris: Société d'Editions Françaises et Internationales, 1948), 529–33.

18. "Une espèce de collaboration à peu près unique"; "Mais, d'être une intelligence au service d'une infinie compréhension, est un luxe qui vous est familier"; "Je puis avouer que je ne pense plus, ou presque plus, musicalement, tout en étant profondément persuadé que la Musique reste à jamais le plus beau moyen d'expression qui soit"; "une pauvreté extrême, une incapacité notoire à s'évader de la table de travail; c'est toujours éclairé par la lampe triste, jamais par le soleil," Debussy to Paul Dukas, 11 February 1901, reprinted in Debussy, *Correspondance* (1993), 161.

See Debussy's article on Dukas's "Variations on a Theme of Rameau," which openly takes the line that Dukas's music was too "worked out." "Il y a bien des moments où Rameau lui-même ne serait pas fichu de retrouver son thème parmi tant de festons et d'astragles. . . . et pour dire au fond de ma pensée; j'aime mieux Dukas sans Rameau," "A la société nationale," *Gil Blas,* 30 March 1903, reprinted in *Monsieur Croche,* 137.

19. "Il suffirait que la musique force les gens à *écouter,* malgré eux, malgré leurs petits tracas quotidiens [. . .] qu'ils pensent avoir rêvé, un moment, d'un pays chimérique et par conséquent introuvable," Debussy to Dukas, 11 February 1901, reprinted in Debussy, *Correspondance* (1993), 162.

20. "Il ne s'occupe nullement des chanteurs et leur lance des accords dans les jambes, sans le moindre souci de la vertu harmonique de ces derniers"; "vous aviez su éveiller la vie sonore de Pelléas avec une délicatesse tendre qu'il ne faut plus chercher à retrouver, car il est bien certain que le rythme intérieur de toute musique dépend de celui qui l'évoque, comme tel mot dépend de la bouche qui le prononce. . . . Ainsi telle impression de Pelléas se doublait de ce que votre émotion personnelle en avait pressenti, et lui donnait par cela même, de merveilleuse 'mise en place,'" Debussy to Messager, 9 May 1902. In *L'enfance de "Pelléas": Lettres de Claude Debussy à André Messager,* ed. Jean-André Messager (Paris: Dorbon-ainé, 1938), 15–17, and reprinted (text slightly different) in Debussy, *Correspondance* (1993), 172–73.

21. "Ce que vous me demandez est d'ailleurs difficile à résoudre! On ne peut démontrer la valeur exacte d'un rythme, pas plus qu'on n'explique l'expression diverse d'une phrase! Le meilleur, à mon avis, est que vous vous en remettiez à votre sentiment personnel," Debussy to Manuel de Falla, 13 January 1907. Reprinted in Debussy, *Correspondance* (1993), 222.
22. Recorded in May 1904 and available on compact disc: EMI Références CHS 7 61038 2.
23. On the question of agogic accents see Philip, *Early Recordings,* 41 ff.
24. Philip, *Early Recordings,* has detailed this in chapter 2: *Tempo rubato.*
25. Roy Howat has rightly commented that the 1904 recordings in general show a sparing use of rubato. He also points out that criticism of these early recordings is necessarily speculative: Debussy may not have been playing well. All one can do is be guided by one's musical judgment: this recording seems convincing and the bars in question do not seem "sloppy"—for a long time the word commonly used by those who despised the performance practices of this era. See Roy Howat, "Debussy and Welte," *Pianola Journal* 7 (1994): 3–18. The article is less concerned with performance practice than with the information gleaned from Debussy's recordings which poses or resolves editorial problems.
26. "Ici comme dans la plupart des oeuvres modernes, les interprètes gagneraient souvent à *dire* parfois le texte, *avant* d'y ajouter la mélodie debussyste destinée à le poétiser ensuite," D.-E. Inghelbrecht, *Comment on ne doit pas interpréter "Carmen," "Faust," et "Pelléas"* (Paris: Heugel, 1933), 59.
27. "Il ne suffira pas à la chanteuse de nous transmettre seulement le mot et la note. Par la fixité de son regard, elle mettra à profit le précepte si clairvoyant de Faure, relatif aux influences physiologiques, pour triompher de certaines difficultés d'interprétation," Inghelbrecht, *Comment on ne doit pas interpréter,* 60.
28. Debussy, "Mary Garden."
29. "Vous et Veuille êtes presque les seuls qui aient conservé la compréhension de l'art que j'ai essayé de faire dans *Pelléas;* c'est pourquoi je vous demande de continuer à défendre cette oeuvre que d'autres ne me semblent plus autant aimer. Dans le cinquième acte, il me semble que les mouvements sont un peu languissants? Puis, je vous prie, exagérez plutôt la triste et poignante tristesse de Golaud, . . . donnez bien l'impression de tout ce qu'il regrette de n'avoir pas dit, de n'avoir pas fait . . . et tout le bonheur qui lui échappe à jamais," Debussy to Hector Dufranne, 26 October 1906, in Debussy, *Correspondance* (1993), 219.
30. Ninon Vallin, "O Klod Debussi," *Sovetskaya Muzyka,* January 1936, translated in Nichols, *Debussy Remembered,* 182.
31. See François Lesure, *Claude Debussy* (Paris: Klincksieck, 1994), 390 and 400, and Lockspeiser, *Debussy,* vol. 1, footnote to page 65.
32. Betty Bannerman, ed., *The Singer as Interpreter: Claire Croiza's Masterclasses* (London: Gollancz, 1989), 108–9.
33. "L'échelle de ses nuances allait du *triple piano* au *forte* sans jamais arriver à des sonorités désordonnées où la subtilité des harmonies se fût perdue": Marguerite Long, "Les nuances," in *Au piano avec Claude Debussy* (Paris: Julliard, 1960), 37. "The nuance, to Debussy, was everything," E. Robert Schmitz, "A Plea for the Real Debussy," *The Etude,* December 1937, 781–82, quoted in Nichols, *Debussy Remembered.*

34. Claire Croiza underlines this: "Above all do not confuse tempo with nuance—the one has nothing to do with the other. Never make a *rallentando* on a *pianissimo* or hurry a *crescendo* when only a change of nuance is indicated," Bannerman, *Singer as Interpreter,* 39.
35. On Debussy's preference for the Blüthner piano, see Maurice Dumesnil, "Coaching with Debussy," *Piano Teacher* 5 (September–October 1962): 10–13, reprinted in Nichols, *Debussy Remembered,* 158–163, and Roy Howat, "Debussy's Piano Music: Sources and Performance," in *Debussy Studies,* ed. Richard Langham Smith (Cambridge: Cambridge University Press, 1997), 78–107. Ninon Vallin quotes Debussy as saying "Before I put in an accent or nuance, I sometimes brood over it for several days, thinking about the precious words which form the text of my songs," Vallin, in Nichols, *Debussy Remembered.*
36. I have deliberately avoided extensive quotes from Marguerite Long's readily available and crucial *Au piano avec Claude Debussy* which most readers will know.
37. Schmitz, in Nichols, *Debussy Remembered,* 168.
38. Dumesnil, in Nichols, *Debussy Remembered,* 159.
39. Croiza, in Bannerman, *The Singer as Interpreter,* 38–39.
40. "Un pianiste, venu lui jouer certaine de ses oeuvres, à tel passage s'arrête et lui dit, 'Maître, à mon avis, là, c'est *libre*. . . ' Et Debussy fulminant: 'Il y a des gens pour écrire la musique, des gens pour l'éditer, et ce monsieur pour faire ce qu'il veut . . . une interprète fidèle me suffit,'" Long, *Au piano avec Claude Debussy,* 27.
41. Dumesnil, in Nichols, *Debussy Remembered,* 159.
42. See note 2, above, for details.
43. "Les mains ne sont pas faites pour être en l'air, sur le piano, mais pour *entrer dedans,*" Long, *Au piano avec Claude Debussy,* 22.
44. Dumesnil in Nichols, *Debussy Remembered,* 159.
45. Roy Howat, personal communication.
46. "Le *rubato,* lié à l'interprétation de Debussy à celle de Chopin. Chez l'un et l'autre des deux musiciens, ce *rubato* reste délicat, difficile à obtenir tel qu'il a été voulu, c'est à dire 'imbriqué' dans l'exactitude rigoureuse. Tel, encore une fois, le flot captif de ses berges. *Rubato* ne veut pas dire altération de ligne, de mesure, mais de nuance et d'élan," Long, *Au piano avec Claude Debussy,* 45.
47. Philip quotes the work of John McEwen in the 1920s who measured the perforations on piano rolls of celebrated pianists, proving incontestably that none of them made up for robbed time. Philip, *Early Recordings,* 45.
48. Recorded 5 June 1928 and 2 June 1930, respectively. Both reissued on *Cortot Plays Debussy and Ravel,* Biddulph LHW 006, 1991.
49. See Philip, *Early Recordings,* page 52, for a transcription of Paderewski's subtle attenuations in Chopin's Mazurka in C-sharp minor, Op. 63 no. 3.

CHAPTER 2: SYMBOLISM AND PERFORMANCE

1. Degas, in Paul Valéry, *Degas Danse Dessin* (Paris: Gallimard, 1946), 129.
2. Charles Baudelaire, "L'invitation au voyage," *Les Fleurs du Mal,* no. 53. In *Oeuvres complètes* (Paris: Bibliothèque de la Pléïade, 1975), I:53.

3. Paul Verlaine, "Art poétique (Jadis et Naguère)," *Oeuvres poétiques complètes* (Paris: Bibliothèque de la Pléïade, 1968), 326.
4. Stéphane Mallarmé, "Sur l'évolution littéraire," *Oeuvres complètes* (Paris: Bibliothèque de la Pléïade, 1945), 869.
5. René Ghil, "Le traîté du verbe," cited in Stefan Jarocinski, *Debussy: impressionnisme et symbolisme* (Paris: Editions du Seuil, 1970), 53.
6. Paul Sérusier, cited in Jarocinski, *Debussy: impressionnisme,* 54.
7. Claude Debussy, *Correspondance, 1884–1918* [hereafter cited as *Correspondance* (1993)], ed. François Lesure (Paris: Hermann, 1993), 49.
8. Henri Bergson, *Les deux sources de la morale et de la religion* (Paris: Presses Universitaires de France, 1982), 42.
9. Debussy, in Robert de Flers, "*Pelléas et Mélisande,*" *Le Figaro,* 16 May 1902, reprinted in Claude Debussy, *Monsieur Croche et autres écrits,* ed. François Lesure (Paris: Gallimard, 1987), 276.
10. Lalo, in Debussy, *Correspondance* (1993), 207.
11. Debussy, *Correspondance* (1993), 207–8.
12. "Entretiens inédits d'Ernest Guiraud et de Claude Debussy, notés par Maurice Emmanuel," *Inédits sur Claude Debussy* (Paris: Publications Techniques, 1942), 31.
13. Jane Bathori, *Sur l'interprétation des mélodies de Claude Debussy* (Paris: Editions Ouvrières, 1953), 8.
14. In her book *Au piano avec Claude Debussy* (Paris: Julliard, 1960), Marguerite Long insisted repeatedly on the necessity of performing Debussy's rhythms rigorously as notated.
15. Plato, *Laws,* para. 665. In *Greek Musical Writings,* ed. Andrew Barker (Cambridge: Cambridge University Press, 1984), I:149.
16. "Debussy Discusses Music and His Works," *New York Times,* 26 June 1910, reprinted by David Grayson in *Cahiers Debussy* 16 (1992): 25–26.
17. Debussy, in Henry Malherbe, "M. Claude Debussy et *Le Martyre de Saint Sébastien,*" *Excelsior,* 11 February 1911, reprinted in Debussy, *Monsieur Croche,* 325.
18. Claude Debussy, *Lettres à deux amis* (Paris: José Corti, 1942), 130, and *Correspondance* (1993), 298.
19. Bergson, *Deux sources,* 268.
20. Léon Vallas, *Claude Debussy et son temps* (Paris: Albin Michel, 1958), 205.
21. Debussy, *Lettres à deux amis,* 121, and Debussy, *Correspondance* (1993), 265.
22. These binary and ternary rhythmic patterns are what Ernest Ansermet calls "existential cadences" in traditional music, an upbeat followed by one or two downbeats, or a downbeat followed by one or two upbeats. This fundamental, understood rhythm gives a feeling of continuity to the musical discourse. Ernest Ansermet, *Les fondements de la musique,* rev. ed. (Neuchâtel: A la Baconnière, 1987), 137–43.
23. Claude Debussy, *Lettres inédites à André Caplet (1908–1914),* ed. Edward Lockspeiser (Monaco: Editions du Rocher, 1957), 46, and *Correspondance* (1993), 264.
24. Debussy, in M. D. Calvocoressi, "An Appreciation of Contemporary Music," *The Etude,* June 1914, reprinted in Claude Debussy, *Debussy on Music,* collect. and introd. François Lesure, trans. and ed. Richard Langham Smith (New York: Knopf, 1977), 320.

CHAPTER 3: *PELLÉAS ET MÉLISANDE* IN PERFORMANCE

1. A single exception may be noted concerning the principles adopted here. One must mention Act III scene 4, mm. *46*3–4 (rehearsal 46, mm. 3–4), where the cue is "Parce qu'elle ne peut pas être ouverte." It is printed thus in the pocket score as well as in the vocal score and is probably an error, to be replaced by Maeterlinck's original reply "Parce qu'on ne veut pas qu'elle soit ouverte." This serves to assure the connection with Golaud's cue that follows, "Qui ne veut pas qu'elle soit ouverte?" as well as that of measures *49* 7–9: "Mais pourquoi ne veulent-ils pas que la porte soit ouverte?"
2. See, among others, *Claude Debussy, Esquisses de "Pelléas et Mélisande" (1893–1895),* ed. François Lesure (Geneva: Minkoff, 1977), as well as Louis-Marc Suter, "Quelques aspects du rythme dans la musique de Claude Debussy," *Revue internationale de musique française* 2/5 (June 1981): 23–30. See also David A. Grayson, "The Interludes of *Pelléas et Mélisande*." In *L'oeuvre de Claude Debussy.* Actes du Colloque International, University of Geneva March 1989, *Cahiers Debussy* 12–13 (1990), 100–22.
3. See, among others, David A. Grayson, *The Genesis of Debussy's "Pelléas et Mélisande"* (Ann Arbor: UMI Dissertation Services, 1994), 209–10. For most of the questions relating to Debussy's "drame lyrique," one may profitably consider this writing as well as two others: Roger Nichols and Richard Langham Smith, *Claude Debussy: "Pelléas et Mélisande,"* Cambridge Opera Handbook (Cambridge: Cambridge University Press, 1989), and Maurice Emmanuel's essential work, *"Pelléas et Mélisande" de Claude Debussy* (Paris: Mellottée, 1933).
4. Pierre Boulez brings up this problem in *Conversations de Pierre Boulez sur la direction d'orchestre avec Jean Vermeil* (Paris: Plume, 1989), 75–76.
5. Claude Debussy, *Lettres, 1884–1918,* ed. François Lesure (Paris: Hermann, 1980), 51.
6. Debussy, *Lettres, 1884–1918,* 10.
7. Debussy, *Lettres, 1884–1918,* 55.
8. Debussy, *Lettres, 1884–1918,* 83.
9. The cough corresponds to the pizzicati of measure 3 *7* and is found in the vocal score but not the pocket score.
10. In the pocket score the pause is not found over the quarter rest following Pelléas's question.
11. The sense of the pause is different in such places from those in examples 3.5 and 3.7, where it is placed on a figure of silence.
12. The pause (a fermata over the bar line) is found in the pocket score but not in the piano-vocal score: clearly there was an omission in the piano-vocal score.
13. On this version, see note 2, above.
14. I indicate seventeen or eighteen measures, for if there is a general relation between the pocket score and the piano-vocal score regarding the interlude in its entirety, the two versions present differences that are not negligible: a) measures 2–1 *34* of the pocket score are not transcribed in the piano-vocal score; b) in the pocket score scene 3 begins at measure *34* 1, whereas it begins only at measure *34* 2 in the piano-vocal score; c) at measure *32* 1, the piano-vocal score clarifies "Toujours *pp* (mais dans une sonorité claire)."

15. See as well Pierre Boulez, *Points de repère* (Paris: Bourgois/Seuil, 1981), where the text in question is taken from pages 419–32.
16. Cachemaille sang Golaud for the recording made under the direction of Charles Dutoit (see discography) and on 4 May 1995 in Paris under the same conductor.
17. Very recently we have been confirmed in this point of view through reading a remark addressed by Ernest Ansermet to his friend and philosophy teacher Jean-Claude Piguet. While Ansermet was in New York to conduct several performances of *Pelléas* at the Metropolitan Opera in November 1962, the centenary year of Debussy's birth, he wrote to his penfriend in Lausanne on 9 November: "And my work has been exciting. Because once they are on stage and in action, singers take liberties; the point is to hold them so as to make their short phrases link up in an unbroken tempo and [to make the] harmony always coincide with melody, and besides the orchestra [must] be transparent. At the third performance, they took it a little too easy and I was having a new *Pelléas*," from *Correspondance Ansermet—Piguet (1948–1969)*, ed. Claude Tappolet (Geneva: Georg, 1998), 148. These few sentences give evidence to how much the lack of observance of the proper rhythm of *Pelléas* can alter not only the musical phrase and the resulting relationship between the vocal line and its instrumental support but above all the very spirit of the work.
18. The present chapter was virtually complete when a study by Eric Gaudibert appeared, "Essai sur les différentes catégories du silence musical," *Dissonance (La nouvelle revue musicale suisse)* 45 (August 1995): 15–17. The article is based upon examples taken from the work of different composers. The author suggests ideas about "silence dramatique," "interrogatif," "pathétique," "intégré," "ponctuel," "vacant," and "entretenu." The categories of silence I have discussed regarding Debussy's lyric drama only, and regarding psychological moments both diverse and peculiar to this masterpiece, belong to another point of view and thus do not share the nomenclature of Gaudibert. Furthermore, a silence may be at the same time "dramatic," "interrogatory," "filled with pathos," and so on.

CHAPTER 4: DEBUSSY AND ORCHESTRAL PERFORMANCE

Because of the general availability of Debussy scores, discussions of scores and tempi will not be accompanied by music examples. However, having the scores at hand while reading this chapter is recommended.

1. Pierre Boulez, *Relevés d'apprenti,* ed. Paule Thévenin (Paris: Seuil, 1966), 33. This and all subsequent translations from the French are by the author unless indicated otherwise.
2. *Debussy Letters,* select. and ed. François Lesure and Roger Nichols, trans. Roger Nichols (Cambridge: Harvard University Press, 1987), 259.
3. Claude Debussy, *L'enfance de "Pelléas": Lettres de Claude Debussy à André Messager,* ed. Jean-André Messager (Paris: Dorbon-Ainé, 1938), 19.
4. Debussy, *L'enfance de "Pelléas,"* 53.
5. Long, quoted in Roger Nichols, *Debussy Remembered* (London: Faber and Faber, 1992), 176.
6. Leinsdorf, quoted in Elliott W. Galkin, *A History of Orchestral Conducting: In Theory and Practice* (New York: Pendragon, 1988), 661.

7. Toscanini, quoted in B. H. Haggin, *Contemporary Recollections of the Maestro;* reprint of *Conversations with Toscanini* (1959) and *The Toscanini Musicians Knew* (1967) (New York: Da Capo, 1989), 30.
8. Ibid.
9. Haggin, *Contemporary Recollections,* 40.
10. Ansermet, quoted in Harold C. Schonberg, *The Great Conductors* (New York: Simon and Schuster, 1967), 333.
11. Claude Debussy, *Lettres, 1884–1918,* ed. François Lesure (Paris: Hermann, 1980), 235.
12. Debussy, quoted in Léon Vallas, *Claude Debussy et son temps* (Paris: Editions Albin Michel, 1958), 297.
13. Debussy, *Lettres, 1884–1918,* 166.
14. Debussy, *Lettres, 1884–1918,* 28.
15. Claude Debussy, *Correspondance, 1884–1918* [hereafter cited as *Correspondance* (1993)], ed. François Lesure (Paris: Hermann, 1993), 152.
16. Debussy, *Correspondance* (1993), 212.
17. Debussy, *Correspondance* (1993), 163.
18. Debussy, *Correspondance* (1993), 264.
19. Debussy, *Correspondance* (1993), 200.
20. Quoted in Marie Rolf, "Debussy's *La Mer:* A Critical Analysis in the Light of Early Sketches and Editions" (Ph.D. diss., University of Rochester, 1976), 309.
21. Debussy, quoted in Nichols, *Debussy Remembered,* 185.
22. Debussy, *Correspondance* (1993), 232.
23. Laloy, quoted in Vallas, *Claude Debussy et son temps,* 298.
24. Radot, quoted in Rolf, "Debussy's *La Mer,*" 330.
25. Vallas, *Claude Debussy et son temps,* 297.
26. Van Rees, quoted in Nichols, *Debussy Remembered,* 232.
27. Gui, in Nichols, *Debussy Remembered,* 226.
28. Wood, in Nichols, *Debussy Remembered,* 219.
29. Claude Debussy, *Debussy on Music,* collect. and introd. François Lesure, trans. and ed. Richard Langham Smith (New York: Knopf, 1977), 117.
30. Debussy, *Debussy on Music,* 39, originally in *La revue blanche,* 1 June 1901.
31. Debussy, *Debussy on Music,* 189–90.
32. Debussy, *Debussy on Music,* 15.
33. Germaine and Désiré-Emile Inghelbrecht, *Claude Debussy* (Paris: Costard, 1953), 288.
34. Debussy, *Correspondance* (1993), 209.
35. Debussy, *Debussy on Music,* 164.
36. Debussy, *Lettres, 1884–1918,* 188–89.
37. Debussy, *Correspondance* (1993), 231.
38. Debussy, quoted in Vallas, *Claude Debussy et son temps,* 209.
39. Debussy, quoted in Rolf, "Debussy's *La Mer,*" 310.
40. Désiré-Emile Inghelbrecht, trans. *The Conductor's World* [*Le chef d'orchestre et son équipe,* by G. Prerauer and S. Malcolm Kirk] (London: Peter Nevill, 1953), 105.
41. Inghelbrecht, *Conductor's World,* 67.
42. Jann Pasler, "Paris: Conflicting Notions of Progress," in Jim Samson, ed., *Music and So-*

ciety: The Late Romantic Era; From the Mid-Nineteenth Century to World War I (Englewood Cliffs, N.J.: Prentice Hall, 1991), 390.

43. *Debussy Letters,* 316.
44. Debussy, *Correspondance* (1993), 114.
45. Debussy, *Debussy on Music,* 189.
46. Debussy, *Correspondance* (1993), 337.
47. Piero Coppola, *Dix-sept ans de musique à Paris, 1922–1939,* preface by Aloÿ Fornerod (Lausanne: Librairie F. Rouge, 1944), 62.
48. Debussy, quoted in Nichols, *Debussy Remembered,* 149.
49. Inghelbrecht, *Conductor's World,* 117.
50. Norman Del Mar, *Anatomy of the Orchestra* (Berkeley: University of California Press, 1981), 50.
51. Daniel J. Koury, *Orchestral Performance Practices in the Nineteenth Century* (Ann Arbor: UMI Press, 1986), 294.
52. See Joan Peyser, ed., *The Orchestra: Origins and Transformations* (New York: Scribner's, 1986), 149 and 163.
53. Inghelbrecht, *Conductor's World,* 4–5.
54. Debussy, *Debussy on Music,* 144.
55. Debussy, *Debussy on Music,* 94.
56. Debussy, *Correspondance* (1993), 138.
57. Debussy, *Debussy on Music,* 127.
58. Especially see Stefan Jarocinski, *Debussy: Impressionism and Symbolism* (London: Eulenberg Books, 1976), and François Lesure, *Claude Debussy avant "Pelléas," ou Les années symbolistes* (Paris: Klincksieck, 1992) on Debussy and symbolism.
59. Louis Laloy, *Debussy* (Paris: Aux Armes de France, 1944), 71.
60. Debussy, *Correspondance* (1993), 106.
61. Laloy, *Debussy,* 75–76.
62. D'Udine, quoted in Vallas, *Claude Debussy et son temps,* 214.
63. Calvocoressi, quoted in Rolf, "Debussy's *La Mer,*" 315.
64. Ibid., 331.
65. Laloy, *Debussy,* 88.
66. Laloy, quoted in Vallas, *Claude Debussy et son temps,* 336.
67. Ibid., 335–36.
68. Robert Charles Marsh, *Toscanini and the Art of Conducting* (New York: Collier, 1962), 109.
69. *Debussy Letters,* 58.
70. Debussy, *Correspondance* (1993), 210.
71. Laloy, quoted in Vallas, *Claude Debussy et son temps,* 304.
72. Both quotations in Rolf, "Debussy's *La Mer,*" 318–19.
73. Smith, in Debussy, *Debussy on Music,* xii.
74. Debussy, *Correspondance* (1993), 338.
75. Inghelbrecht, *Claude Debussy,* 289.
76. Ibid.
77. Ibid.

78. Present location not traced; reproduced on the record jacket of LP Ducretet Thomson 320C 152, with Inghelbrecht and the Orchestre National performing the *Prélude à l'après-midi d'un faune.*
79. Désiré-Emile Inghelbrecht, *Mouvement Contraire,* vol. 1: *Vers le temps heureux* (Paris: Domat, 1947), 146.
80. Inghelbrecht, *Claude Debussy,* 288.
81. Ansermet, quoted in Robert Chesterman, ed., *Conversations with Conductors* (New York: Robson, 1976), 93. The interview took place in 1968.
82. Ibid., 78.
83. Ansermet, quoted in François Hudry, *Ernest Ansermet, pionnier de la musique* (Lausanne: L'aire musicale, 1983), 85.
84. Chesterman, *Conversations,* 86.
85. Cited in Claude Tappolet, *Lettres de compositeurs français à Ernest Ansermet (1911–1960)* (Geneva: Georg, 1988), 139–40.
86. Gustave Doret, *Temps et contretemps: Souvenirs d'un musicien* (Fribourg, Switzerland: Editions de la Librairie de l'Université, 1942), 379.
87. Simon Trezise, *Debussy: "La mer"* (Cambridge: Cambridge University Press, 1994), 29.
88. Doret, *Temps et contretemps,* 94.
89. Katims, in Haggin, *Contemporary Recollections,* 229.
90. Ansermet, in Chesterman, *Conversations,* 99.
91. Thomson, quoted in Galkin, *History of Orchestral Conducting,* 629.
92. Letter of 9 October 1915 to Jacques Durand, quoted in Durand, ed., *Lettres de Claude Debussy à son éditeur* (Paris: Durand, 1927), 158.
93. Manuscript letter of 11 April 1908, owned by the Harry Ransom Humanities Research Center, University of Texas at Austin.
94. Cited in Rolf, "Debussy's *La Mer,*" 153 (citing Jean Barraqué, *Debussy* [Paris: Seuil, 1962], 154 (citing Laurence David Berman, "The Evolution of Tonal Thinking in the Works of Claude Debussy," Ph.D. diss., Harvard University, 1965), and 166.

CHAPTER 5: DEBUSSY AND EARLY DEBUSSYSTES AT THE PIANO

1. "Debussy à travers le Journal de Madame de Saint-Marceaux, 1894–1911," *Cahiers Debussy* 3 (1976): 10. This and all subsequent translations from French are mine. Madame de Saint-Marceaux was a well-known patroness of the arts who regularly held *salons* at her home. This was where Ravel met Colette and Fauré's music was regularly performed. The exact title of this movement from *Images* II is "Et la lune descend sur le temple qui fut."
2. Marguerite Long, *Au piano avec Debussy* (Paris: Julliard, 1960), 13.
3. This compact disc was produced by Kenneth K. Caswell in Austin, Texas, for research purposes. It is the result of thirty years of trial and error, as well as a keen mechanical and musical mind which sought to make all the fine-tuned adjustments necessary to produce a representative recording of Debussy's Welte rolls. Several pianos were restored before this recording was made on the chosen Feurich. I am indebted to Don Manildi at the International Piano Archives at the University of Maryland for making this disc available

to me, and to Mr. Caswell for subsequently forwarding to me my personal copy. The music on this compact disc includes: "Danseuses de Delphes," "La cathédrale engloutie," "La danse de Puck," "Minstrels," "Le vent dans la plaine," "La plus que lente," "La soirée dans Grenade," the entire *Children's Corner,* and *D'un cahier d'esquisses.* Also, four songs with Debussy accompanying Mary Garden: "Mes longs cheveux," "Green," "L'ombre des arbres," and "Il pleure dans mon coeur." The old 1950s Columbia and Telefunken records of these rolls did not do justice in any way to Debussy's playing.

4. Alfredo Casella, "Claude Debussy," *Monthly Musical Record* 63 (1933): 2.
5. Long, *Au piano avec Debussy,* 27.
6. François Lesure, "Une interview romaine de Debussy (Février 1914)," *Cahiers Debussy* 11 (1987): 4.
7. Marguerite Vasnier, "Debussy à 18 ans," *La revue musicale,* 1 May 1926, 17.
8. John R. Clevenger, "Achille at the Conservatoire, 1872–1884," *Cahiers Debussy* 19 (1995): 3–35.
9. *La revue musicale,* 1 May 1926, 6.
10. Ibid., 10.
11. Fargue and Garden, quoted in Roger Nichols, *Debussy Remembered* (London: Faber and Faber, 1992), 49–50 and 72.
12. *Claude Debussy: Lettres, 1884–1918,* compiled and presented by François Lesure (Paris: Hermann, 1980), 189.
13. I indicate metronome markings for rough reference, to give the reader an approximate idea of the overall pace. They are obviously not to be taken literally as no performance would ever match any metronome beat for more than a few measures. See Debussy's comment on the subject in his letter to Durand of 9 October 1915, quoted below.
14. Long, *Au piano avec Debussy,* 108.
15. Casella, "Claude Debussy," 1.
16. See Marcel Dietschy, "Debussy trahi par les virtuoses," *Revue musicale suisse* 116 (January–February 1976): 48–52. This comparative article concerning eleven recordings of *Children's Corner* describes in exhaustive detail individual performances. The eleven pianists compared are Arturo Benedetti Michelangeli, Jörg Demus, Philippe Entremont, Jacques Février, Samson François, Peter Frankl, Walter Gieseking, Monique Haas, Werner Haas, Claude Helffer, and Noël Lee.
17. See Dietschy, "Debussy trahi," 48–52. In this article, Roy Howat describes other, more subtle divergences between the printed score and Debussy's performances.
18. Charles Burkhart, "Debussy plays "La cathédrale engloutie' and Solves Metrical Mystery," *Piano Quarterly* 65 (Fall 1968): 14–26.
19. Critical edition by James R. Briscoe of Debussy, *Preludes for Piano, Books 1 and 2* (New York: Schirmer, 1991).
20. Roy Howat, "Debussy and Welte," *Pianola Journal* 7 (1994): 3.
21. *Debussy Letters,* select. and ed. François Lesure and Roger Nichols, trans. Roger Nichols (Cambridge: Harvard University Press, 1987), 305.
22. *Debussy Letters,* 301–2.
23. Maurice Dumesnil, "Coaching with Debussy," *Piano Teacher* (Sept.–Oct. 1962), pt. I, p. 13.

24. Ibid.
25. The 1995 recording of the complete piano works of Debussy by Philippe Cassard is exceptional not only because of this young French pianist's undeniably genuine artistry but also in large part because of Cassard's choice of instrument, a 1898 concert grand Bechstein he discovered in a private home outside Paris. I believe that the sound quality of that particular instrument reflects more closely Debussy's ideal than other modern recordings. Cassard explains why: "Debussy's work for the piano was ideally suited to this piano's wide range of colors and tones, note attacks, vibrations, and lyrical potential. Each register was clearly and precisely defined. The high notes had a certain mineral luster to them. The medium range was dense, smooth, and naturally cantabile. From the deep, resonant bass notes, multiples harmonics arose and intertwined" (from the notes of his compact disc, Audivis, France, 1995).
26. Alfred Cortot, *La musique française de piano,* rev. ed. (1930–32; Paris: Presses universitaires de France, 1981), 44.
27. Casella, "Claude Debusssy," 1.
28. Dumesnil, "Coaching with Debussy," 10.
29. Claude Debussy, *Correspondance, 1884-1914* [hereafter cited as *Correspondance* (1993)], ed. François Lesure (Paris: Hermann, 1993), 356.
30. Alfredo Casella, *Music in My Time: The Memoirs of Alfredo Casella,* trans. and ed. Spencer Norton (Norman: University of Oklahoma Press, 1955), 126.
31. Dumesnil, "Coaching with Debussy," 10.
32. François Lesure, *Claude Debussy, biographie critique* (Paris: Klincksieck, 1994), 263 and 317–18.
33. Louis Laloy, *La musique retrouvée* (Paris: 1928), 120.
34. George Copeland, "Debussy, the Man I Knew," *Atlantic Monthly,* January 1955, 38.
35. Claude Debussy, *Douze Etudes,* Premier Livre (Paris: Durand, 1916), 1.
36. Claude Debussy, *Etudes pour le piano,* Facsimile of the autograph sketches (1915), with an introduction by Roy Howat (Geneva: Minkoff, 1989), [10] and [43].
37. *Debussy Letters,* 301.
38. Debussy, *Etudes pour le piano,* 14.
39. Gabriel Fauré, letter to Debussy, 25 April 1917, quoted in *Revue de musicologie.* Special issue, ed. François Lesure (Paris, 1962), 75–76.
40. Letter to Gabriel Fauré, *Claude Debussy: Lettres, 1884–1918* (1980), 277.
41. Igor Stravinsky, *An Autobiography* (New York: Norton, 1962), 49.
42. Harold Bauer, *Harold Bauer, His Book,* (New York, 1948), 82. Ravel dedicated "Ondine" from *Gaspard de la nuit* to him.
43. *Claude Debussy: Lettres, 1884–1918* (1980), 193.
44. Ibid., 283.
45. *Debussy Letters,* 330.
46. Ibid., 153.
47. Quoted in Charles Timbrell, "Claude Debussy and Walter Rummel: Chronicle of a Friendship," *Music and Letters* (Aug. 1992): 399. Most of the information about Rummel comes from this source and Timbrell's first article on Rummel in *Cahiers Debussy* 11 (1987): 24–33.

48. Quoted in Nichols, *Debussy Remembered,* 245.
49. *Claude Debussy: Lettres, 1884–1918* (1980), 282.
50. I am indebted to Don Manildi at the International Piano Archives at the University of Maryland for making the Rummel recordings available to me, as well as recordings by Ricardo Viñes, George Copeland, and E. R. Schmitz.
51. The premiere of these Preludes has previously been erroneously attributed to Viñes, Debussy, and Jane Mortier.
52. Marcel Dietschy and Edward Lockspeiser erroneously credit the premiere of all twelve Etudes to Rummel. According to Charles Timbrell, a review of the concert in *Musical America* with the program listed proves them wrong, as only four Etudes were mentioned (without specifying which ones). Furthermore, George Copeland performed two Etudes a month earlier at Aeolian Hall in New York (see below), possibly "robbing" Rummel of two premieres.
53. Quoted in Charles Timbrell, "Claude Debussy and Walter Rummel," 402. The letter is in a private collection.
54. Quoted in Roy Howat's introduction to the *Douze Etudes,* 9.
55. Quoted in Charles Timbrell, "Claude Debussy and Walter Rummel," 403.
56. Madame Gaston de Tinan, "Memories of Debussy and His Circle," *Recorded Sound* 50 (1973): 160; Pasteur Vallléry-Radot, "Mes souvenirs sur Claude Debussy," quoted in Nichols, *Debussy Remembered,* 204.
57. Quoted in Cecilia Dunoyer, *Marguerite Long: A Life in French Music* (Bloomington: Indiana University Press, 1993), 59. The autograph letter is housed at the Bibliothèque Musicale Gustav Mahler in Paris.
58. *Claude Debussy: Lettres, 1884–1918* (1980), 279.
59. Long, *Au piano avec Claude Debussy,* 37.
60. Emma Debussy, quoted in Dunoyer, *Marguerite Long,* 72. The autograph letters from Emma Bardac to Long are housed at the Bibliothèque Musicale Gustav Mahler.
61. Ibid., 75.
62. Ibid., 79.
63. Samazeuilh, quoted in Dunoyer, *Marguerite Long,* 77–78. From *Le ménestrel,* December 12, 1919.
64. E. Debussy, quoted in Dunoyer, *Marguerite Long,* 78.
65. Quoted in Nichols, *Debussy Remembered,* 148. From *Segalen et Debussy* (Monaco, 1962).
66. Quoted in Edward Lockspeiser, *Debussy: His Life and Mind,* vol. 2 (Cambridge: Cambridge University Press, 1978), 35.
67. Nina Gubisch, "Le journal inédit de Ricardo Viñes," *Revue internationale de musique française* (June 1980): 221.
68. Letter to Georges Jean-Aubry, quoted in *Oeuvres complètes de Claude Debussy,* série 1, vol. 3 (Paris: Durand-Costallat, 1991), avant-propos, xiv.
69. Claude Debussy, *Debussy on Music,* collect. and introd. François Lesure, trans. and ed. Richard Langham Smith (New York: Knopf, 1977), 164.
70. Quoted in Nichols, *Debussy Remembered,* 182.
71. Copeland, "Debussy, the Man I Knew," 37.
72. Copeland, "Debussy, the Man I Knew," 38.

73. E. Robert Schmitz, "A Plea for the Real Debussy," *The Etude* (December 1937): 782.
74. Madame Gaston de Tinan, "Memories of Debussy and His Circle," 159.
75. Long, *Au piano avec Claude Debussy,* 36.
76. Casella, "Claude Debussy," 1.
77. Louisa Liebich, "An Englishwoman's Memories of Debussy," *Musical Times,* 1 June 1918, 250. Liebich's husband, Franz, was a pianist who studied with Debussy and premiered the Prelude "La fille aux cheveux de lin."
78. Letter to Robert Godet, 14 October 1915. *Claude Debussy, Lettres* (1980), 264.
79. Copeland, "Debussy, the Man I Knew," 38.

CHAPTER 6: DEBUSSY, THE DANCE, AND THE *FAUNE*

1. Claude Debussy, "Impressions sur la Tétralogie à Londres," *Gil Blas,* 1 June 1903, reprinted in *Monsieur Croche et autres écrits,* ed. François Lesure (Paris: Gallimard, 1971), 183–84. Translation by Stephanie Jordan.
2. See, for example, his letter of 8 July 1910, in *Debussy Letters,* select. and ed. François Lesure and Roger Nichols, trans. Roger Nichols (London: Faber and Faber, 1987), 221; *Le Matin,* 15 May 1913, in Claude Debussy, *Debussy on Music,* collect. and introd. François Lesure, trans. and ed. Richard Langham Smith (New York: Knopf, 1977), 291; letter to Diaghilev, 20 May 1917, quoted by Robert Orledge in *Debussy and the Theatre* (Cambridge: Cambridge University Press, 1982), 174.
3. Debussy, *Le Matin,* 15 May 1913, in *Debussy on Music,* 291.
4. Igor Stravinsky, *Chronicle of My Life* (London: Victor Gollancz, 1936), 64.
5. Reported in the *Daily Mail,* 21 February 1913, quoted by Richard Buckle, *Diaghilev* (London: Weidenfeld and Nicholson, 1979), 244.
6. Interview in *La Tribuna,* 23 February 1914, quoted by Jean-Michel Nectoux in *Afternoon of a Faun: Mallarmé, Debussy, Nijinsky,* ed. Nectoux (New York: Vendome Press, 1987), 32, 35.
7. For details of this career, see Orledge, *Debussy and the Theatre,* part 2: "The Ballets."
8. Fokine, letter to the *Times,* 6 July 1914, quoted by Cyril Beaumont, *Michel Fokine and His Ballets* (London: C.W. Beaumont, 1935), 147.
9. Hugo von Hofmannsthal and Richard Strauss, *Correspondence Between Richard Strauss and Hugo von Hofmannsthal,* (London: Collins, 1961), 150. Hofmannsthal's letter to Strauss was dated 1912.
10. For a summary of the Dalcroze method and of its early development, see Selma Odom, "Wigman at Hellerau," *Ballet Review* 14/2 (Summer 1986): 41–53.
11. See Marie Rambert, *Quicksilver* (London: Macmillan, 1972), 51.
12. For instance, Theo Hirsbrunner, "Debussy's Ballett *Khamma,*" *Archiv für Musikwissenschaft* 36/2 (1979): 119.
13. Letter to D'Annunzio, 30 November 1910, in *Debussy Letters,* 219.
14. Letter to D'Annunzio, February 1911, in *Debussy Letters,* 237.
15. Letter to Durand, January 1912, in *Debussy Letters,* 255.
16. Bronislava Nijinska, *Early Memoirs,* ed. and trans. Irina Nijinska and Jean Rawlinson (London: Faber and Faber, 1981), 113, 122.

17. Nijinska, *Early Memoirs,* 444.
18. Ann Hutchinson Guest and Claudia Jeshke, *Nijinsky's "Faune" Restored,* (Philadelphia: Gordon and Breach, 1991); Jill Beck, ed., "A Revival of Nijinsky's Original *L'Après-midi d'un faune,*" *Choreography and Dance* 1/3 (1991), entire issue.
19. Ann Hutchinson Guest, "Nijinsky's *Faune,*" *Choreography and Dance* 1/3 (1991): 21.
20. Charles Tenroc, "Nijinski va faire dans *l'Après-Midi d'un Faune* des essais de chorégraphie cubiste," *Comoedia,* 18 April 1912, 4.
21. Rambert, *Quicksilver,* 54.
22. Michel Fokine, *Memoirs of a Ballet Master,* trans. Vitale Fokine, ed. Anatole Chujoy (London: Constable, 1961), 209.
23. Hofmannsthal, quoted in the *Standard,* 15 February 1913, reprinted in Nesta Macdonald, *Diaghilev Observed by Critics in England and the United States, 1911–1929* (New York: Dance Horizons, 1975), 79–80.
24. Richard Buckle, *Nijinsky* (London: Weidenfeld and Nicolson, 1971), 241; Buckle, *Diaghilev,* 185.
25. Edwin Denby, *Dance Writings* (London: Dance Books, 1986), 498.
26. Debussy, interview in *La Tribuna,* 23 February 1914, quoted by Nectoux, *Afternoon of a Faun,* 35.
27. Auguste Rodin, "La rénovation de la danse," *Le Matin,* 30 May 1912, quoted by Nectoux, *Afternoon of a Faun,* 51.
28. For instance, Carl Van Vechten, in *The Dance Writings of Carl Van Vechten,* ed. Paul Padgette (New York: Dance Horizons, 1974), 77.
29. Buckle, *Nijinsky,* 239.
30. Lydia Sokolova, *Dancing for Diaghilev* (London: John Murray, 1960), 40.
31. Ibid.
32. Jill Beck, "Recalled to Life: Techniques and Perspectives on Reviving Nijinsky's *Faune,*" *Choreography and Dance* 1/3 (1991): 72.
33. Debussy, "Pourquoi j'ai écrit Pelléas," in *Debussy on Music,* 74–75.
34. Joan Ross Acocella, "The Reception of Diaghilev's Ballets Russes by Artists and Intellectuals in Paris and London, 1909–1914," Ph.D. diss., Rutgers University, 1984, 219.
35. Camille Mauclair, *La revue,* 1 August 1910, quoted by Deirdre Priddin, *The Art of the Dance in French Literature* (London: A. and C. Black, 1952), 106.
36. Debussy, *Le Matin,* 15 May 1913, in *Debussy on Music,* 292.
37. Courtney's review of 14 October 1908, quoted by Orledge, *Debussy and the Theatre,* 130.
38. Roger Shattuck, *The Banquet Years* (New York: Knopf, 1955), chap. 11: "The Art of Stillness."
39. For instance, Geoffrey Whitworth, *The Art of Nijinsky* (1913; repr. New York: Benjamin Blom, 1972), 83; and Eugene Belville, "Les arts décoratifs au théâtre—La Saison russe—Nijinsky chorégraphe—Pénélope—Les Nocturnes de Debussy," *Art et industrie* (September 1913): 362.
40. Thomas Munro, "*The Afternoon of a Faun* and the Interrelation of the Arts," *Journal of Aesthetics and Art Criticism* 10 (1951): 102–3.
41. Nijinsky in *Pall Mall Gazette,* 15 February 1913, quoted by Macdonald, *Diaghilev Observed,* 79.

42. Nijinska, *Early Memoirs,* 315.
43. Charles Tenroc, "Nijinski va faire dans "L'après-midi d'un faune' des essais de chorégraphie cubiste," *Comoedia,* 18 April 1912, 4.
44. Acocella, "Reception of Diaghilev's Ballets Russes," 147.
45. Hugo von Hofmannsthal, "Nijinsky's *L'Après-midi d'un Faune*" (1912), quoted in Nectoux, *Afternoon of a Faun,* 53.
46. Bertolt Brecht, *Brecht on Theatre: The Development of an Aesthetic,* ed. and trans. John Willett (London: Methuen, 1964), 38.
47. See Roger Copeland, "Merce Cunningham and the Politics of Perception" (1979), in *What Is Dance?* ed. Copeland and Marshall Cohen (Oxford: Oxford University Press, 1983), 307–24.
48. Romola Nijinsky, *Nijinsky* (1933; repr. London: Sphere Books, 1970), 125.
49. Munro, "*Afternoon of a Faun,*" 103–5.
50. Jacques Rivière, "*Le Sacre du printemps*" (1913), in *What Is Dance?* 118.
51. Ibid., 116.
52. Quittard, *Le Figaro,* 17 May 1913, quoted by Buckle, *Nijinsky,* 289.
53. See W. A. Propert, *The Russian Ballet in Western Europe, 1909–1920* (London: Bodley Head, 1921), 77–78; and Valentine Gross, "Impressions sur le ballet *Jeux,*" *Comoedia Illustré,* June–July 1913.
54. Debussy, letter to Gabriel Pierné, 4 February 1914, quoted in Orledge, *Debussy and the Theatre,* 171.
55. Letter to Robert Godet, 9 June 1913, in *Debussy Letters,* 272.
56. Author's interview with Millicent Hodson, 31 March 1995. The reconstruction of *Jeux* premiered 9 May 1996 at the Teatro Filarmonico of the Arena di Verona.
57. Letter to André Caplet, 25 August 1912, in *Debussy Letters,* 262.
58. The *Times,* 26 July 1913, quoted by Macdonald, *Diaghilev Observed,* 102.
59. See Ann Cooper Albright, "The Long Afternoon of a Faun: Reconstruction and the Discourses of Desire," *Dance Reconstructed Conference Proceedings,* Rutgers University, 1992, 219–22.

CHAPTER 7: THE HISTORY OF (RE)INTERPRETING DEBUSSY'S SONGS

1. For example, see Dale Harris, "The Lost Art of French Vocal Style," *High Fidelity Magazine,* April 1972, 102.
2. See Richard Langham Smith, "Debussy: Songs, Claudette Leblanc, Valerie Tryon" [Review], *Musical Times* 134 (1993): 528.
3. I am grateful for the technical assistance of Willie Strong at Yale University, Brian Hart at Northern Illinois University, and David Lasocki at the Indiana University Music Library. I also thank Dina Kuznetsova, who inspired several of the ideas behind this study.
4. In addition to studying the recordings, I have consulted these primary sources on interpretation (listed chronologically): Nellie Melba, *The Melba Method* (New York: Chappell-Harms, 1926); Jane Bathori, *Sur l'interprétation des mélodies de Claude Debussy* (Paris: Editions Ouvrières, 1953); Pierre Bernac, *The Interpretation of French Song* (London: Victor Gollancz, 1970); Maggie Teyte, [A Collection of Loose Leaves with Hints for Vocal

Students], written in the 1970s and published by Gary O'Connor in *The Pursuit of Perfection* (London: Victor Gollancz, 1979).

5. The discography at the end of the chapter lists all the recordings discussed here. Elsewhere I identify recordings merely by performer(s) and—if necessary—date.
6. Poulenc's recording of the *Ariettes oubliées* with Lucienne Tragin (1943) adopts tempi comparable to those of Garden/Debussy. His recordings with Pierre Bernac (1950) and Claire Croiza (1930) similarly favor a quick pace.
7. Reprinted in Richard Hudson, *Stolen Time: The History of Tempo Rubato* (Oxford: Clarendon Press, 1994), 191.
8. For a full reference, see the previous note.
9. Hudson encapsulates this development in his introduction, pages 1–3.
10. Hudson, *Stolen Time,* 340–55 (see especially 352).
11. By "scooping" I mean that Garden begins her attack slightly below the indicated pitch. Although this usually caps an ascending leap, Garden sometimes scoops notes in a descending line (at the word "pleure," discussed below).
12. That "*pleu*-re" falls on the highest note of the song (G-sharp, reached in m. 14 as well) may suggest a practical motive behind Garden's scooping. The next note (on "pleu-*re*"), however, lies a whole step lower; in dropping below that F-sharp in order to scoop up to it, Garden evidently follows expressive rather than practical dictates.
13. Will Crutchfield quotes Domenico Corri from 1810 advising singers to do this ("An Open Ear," *Opera News* 52/2 [1987]: 20).
14. Debussy attempts to lead her to the correct note by playing an unnotated E-sharp under "L'om-*bre*."
15. For the majority of points related to recording technology, I take as my starting point Crutchfield, "Open Ear." Having acknowledged that debt here, I shall limit my citations to other studies that contribute to the discussion.
16. Electric replaced acoustic recording technology in 1925.
17. An additional implication, that Garden and others incorporated such sounds in live performances, is problematic for reasons I shall explore momentarily.
18. J. B. Steane, *The Grand Tradition: Seventy Years of Singing on Record* (Portland, Ore.: Amadeus Press, 1994), 10. See also Crutchfield's discussion of Busoni, "Open Ear," 22.
19. Nellie Melba, *The Melba Method* (1926), reprinted in William Moran, *Nellie Melba: A Contemporary Review* (Westport, Conn.: Greenwood Press, 1985), 414.
20. See Debussy's articles of 1901 and 1903 on music in the open air, reprinted in *Debussy on Music,* collect. and introd. François Lesure, trans. and ed. Richard Langham Smith, trans. Richard Langham Smith (Ithaca: Cornell University Press, 1988), 40–42, 92–94. Later I quote Debussy vilifying the phonograph for making music accessible to the masses.
21. Crutchfield postulates lack of eye contact as a source of some "musical mishaps" captured by early recordings ("Open Ear," 22).
22. For example, her *Bilitis* take but 7 minutes, 3 seconds, as contrasted to Teyte's own fairly brisk 8 minutes, 16 seconds.
23. Translation of first line: "They seem not to believe"; translation of second line: "The great, slender fountains among the statues."

24. Translation: "Your lovely eyes are weary, poor lover / Rest a while without opening them again."
25. Alone of Debussy's singers, Croiza goes out of her way to draw out the sound of the language; she regularly initiates sound ahead of both the notated beat and pitch (as with the "r" of "Reste" in "Le jet d'eau," m. 6). The possibility that she influenced Bernac and Souzay (the latter one of her students), whose diction I address below, should not be overlooked.
26. Bernac, *Interpretation of French Song*, 204–5. Durand republished "La grotte" under the title "Auprès de cette grotte sombre," in *Le promenoir des deux amants*, 1910.
27. Translation: "The shadow of this vermillion flower / And of the bending reeds / Seem to be there amid / The dreams of the sleeping water."
28. It is instructive to compare Teyte's delivery of the word "sommeille" to Souzay's in 1961: Souzay whispers the word suggestively, while Teyte's gentle portamento conveys falling asleep.
29. The Canadian Gauthier auditioned with Debussy for the part of Yniold in a Covent Garden production of *Pelléas* (which was ultimately canceled). The French Gerville-Réache created the role of Geneviève in *Pelléas*. Another Canadian, Edvina, sang Mélisande during Debussy's lifetime. Although the Swiss Panzéra, a French-song specialist, did not make his début until 1919 (a year after Debussy's death), I single him out as important for two reasons: first, his Parisian education (at the Conservatoire) leaves open the possibility that he familiarized himself with the style of Debussy's preferred singers and could even have known Debussy. Second, of all the singers listed in this paragraph, he comes the closest to Teyte's quick pace, restrained expression, and modest rubato.
30. One other clarification: I have used these interpreters to reach general conclusions; I do not seek to characterize them individually.
31. It should go without saying that these generalizations overlook such inevitable divergences as Muzio's heavily rolled "r"s and other peculiarities related to accent. I discuss more significant divergences momentarily.
32. Debussy, trans. Felix Aprahamian, reprinted in Roger Nichols, *Debussy Remembered* (London: Faber and Faber, 1992), 179.
33. I paraphrase Vallin's summary of Debussy as a vocal coach: "He hardly ever made any remarks, he only insisted that the performer should look closely at what he had written," Henry Thompson, trans.; reprinted in Nichols, *Debussy Remembered*, 182.
34. See Nichols, *Debussy Remembered*, 150. For a similar anecdote, recounted by violinist Arthur Hartmann, see *Debussy Remembered*, 206.
35. Teyte's aphorisms regarding tradition, dating from the early 1970s, appear in Garry O'-Connor, *The Pursuit of Perfection: A Life of Maggie Teyte* (London: Victor Gollancz, 1979), 275–76.
36. Vallin and Croiza also frequently leave the score behind, changing note values, inserting ritards, and even removing beats from measures (Vallin seems to have worked this out in advance with conductor Gustave Cloëz in "Air de Lia," as they both shortchange m. 61 by an eighth note). Only Bathori demonstrates fidelity of a literal nature; her restraint does indeed evoke Debussy's insistence on "no romantic shudder," and her uncompromisingly fast tempi reflect his advice to her regarding "Mandoline": "It should go twice as fast." See Nichols, *Debussy Remembered*, 179.

37. As recalled by Louisa Liebich, reprinted in Nichols, *Debussy Remembered,* 202. An anecdote underlines how unlikely it was that Debussy actually expected this sort of fidelity: Melba echoes Debussy's sentiments in 1926, when advising her students to "show respect to the *Composer* by singing what he has written, down to the last double dotted demi-semiquaver" (*The Melba Method,* reprinted in Moran, 415). But in her own recording of "En sourdine" (*Fêtes galantes* I), she alters the even rhythm of the sixth measure (the second eighth note becomes a sixteenth, the third a dotted eighth, perhaps to capture the mottled light filtering through branches), raises a D-sharp to E (at "Et quand, sol-*len*-nel," mm. 33–34), and scoops liberally (a practice she forbids to her students on account of its inaccuracy).
38. Pianist Maurice Dumesnil records Debussy's low opinion of pedal indications: "'Pedaling cannot be written down,' he explained. 'It varies from one instrument to another, from one room, or one hall, to another.' So he left it to his interpreters," reprinted in Nichols, *Debussy Remembered,* 163. Debussy's comment on the ineffectiveness of metronome marks reveals a similar attitude: "You know what I think about metronome marks: they're right for a single bar, like "roses, with a morning's life.' Only there are 'those' who don't hear music and who take these marks as authority to hear it still less!" Letter to Jacques Durand (9 October 1915); published in *Debussy Letters,* select. and ed. François Lesure and Roger Nichols, trans. Roger Nichols (Cambridge: Harvard University Press, 1987), 305.
39. Oboist François Gillet relates this anecdote regarding Debussy and Chevillard, reprinted in Nichols, *Debussy Remembered,* 183.
40. In his article entitled "Taste" of 1913, Debussy writes of preserving the magic and mystery of music and warns against "people who are only preoccupied with the formula that will yield them the best results," in Debussy, *Debussy on Music,* 277–80.
41. From an article of 1913, reprinted in Debussy, *Debussy on Music,* 288.
42. Debussy criticizes Guy Ropartz's *Symphony on a Breton Chant* on these grounds in an article of 1903, concluding, "He should have respected [the chant] like the true Breton he is" (in Debussy, *Debussy on Music,* 128).
43. Although in this case Teyte falls into a smooth progression toward faster tempi, keep in mind the more relevant perspective set forth earlier, whereby she, Bathori, Vallin, and Croiza consistently outpace their contemporaries.
44. One could make that point on a purely musical level simply by noting that precision infiltrates late twentieth-century recordings of nearly all repertoires. One could also view precision in broader, societal terms, as embodying the ideal of objectivity underlying the Cold War.
45. Descriptions of Debussy's meticulousness in his later life are ubiquitous; the anecdote about a thread on the carpet is Teyte's (in Nichols, *Debussy Remembered,* 181). Regarding the other references in the preceding sentence: "pedantic and precise": Teyte, ca. 1908 (in *Debussy Remembered,* 89); "controlled and clean": recalled by Victor Segalen, 1908 (*Debussy Remembered,* 147); "nothing shimmering": quoted by Monteux, ca. 1912 (*Debussy Remembered,* 186).
46. Debussy drops this comment on the subject of the conductor Artur Nikisch: "I would

take as an example [of bad taste] his performance of the Overture to *Tannhäuser*, where he makes the trombones play with portamenti more suited to that lady in charge of the sentimental songs at the Casino de Suresnes" (in Debussy, *Debussy on Music*, 39).

47. See the comparison of Garden to von Stade regarding the first line of "Green," above.
48. Robin Bowman, "Mélodies en exile," *Music and Musicians* 25 (1977): 36.
49. Teyte sings detached notes at "et puis voici mon coeur *qui ne bat que* pour vous" (mm. 11–12).
50. Cited earlier in relation to Muzio, Sayaö, and Bathori.
51. Nordica adds these "la"s as well (in 1911).
52. Earlier I noted the appearance of interpretive guides to Debussy's songs appearing around mid-century. In more modern times, Wallace Berry's book *Musical Structure and Performance* (New Haven: Yale University Press, 1989) offers analytical criteria as replacements for intuition in performing these songs (among other works). The explanation of uniformity proffered here should not be taken as the only one; the mid-century proliferation of classical recordings on long-playing records surely prompted this development as well.
53. This way of thinking depends on the fashionable view that attempts at authentic performance practices inevitably tell us more about the age that produces them than about the age they purport to restore.
54. All three selections reissued on compact disc, EMI CHS 761038 2.
55. All Melba recordings listed in this appendix have been reissued on compact disc, RCA Victor Gold Seal 09026-61412-2.
56. Reissued on Discophilia KG-G-3.
57. Both songs reissued on Town Hall 003.
58. Reissued on Rococo Records 5254.
59. Reissued by Yale University Library: *Treasures from the Yale Collection of Historical Sound Recordings*, Yale Historical Sound.
60. Reissued on EMI, Le voix de son maître; Références 2C 151-73.084–5.
61. Reissued on compact disc, Romophone 81008-2.
62. All Bathori recordings reissued on EMI Angel GR-2141.
63. Both Croiza recordings (1930 and 1932) reissued on Emi Angel GR-2221.
64. Both Vallin recordings (1928 and 1930) reissued on compact disc, Pearl GEMM CD 9948.
65. Reissued on compact disc, Romophone 81015-2.
66. All songs reissued on EMI CHS 761038 2.
67. Reissued on compact disc, Library of Congress (*Historic Performances from the Library of Congress*).
68. All three previous songs (1938 and 1940) reissued on RCA Camden CBL 101.
69. Reissued on EMI CHS 5 65198 2.
70. Reissued on EMI CHS 5 65198 2.
71. Reissued on EMI C 04712538.
72. Both songs have been reissued on EMI CHS 5 65198 2.
73. Reissued on Odyssey Y 33130
74. Reissued on compact disc, EMI France CDM 7 64096-2–64098-2.

CHAPTER 8: HOW NOT TO PERFORM *PELLÉAS ET MÉLISANDE*

This excerpt has been translated and reproduced with the kind permission of Editions Heugel, Paris.

1. Jean-Baptiste Faure (1830–1914) was a baritone celebrated in the title role of Mozart's *Don Giovanni* and as Mephistopheles in Gounod's *Faust.*
2. Arthur Nikisch (1855–1922), an Austro-Hungarian violinist and conductor, held posts at the opera at Leipzig, the Leipzig Gewandhaus Orchestra, and symphony orchestras in Boston, Budapest, and Berlin. Nikisch toured to Paris in 1901 with the Berlin orchestra, receiving an appreciative review from Debussy. Further see François Lesure, ed., *Claude Debussy: Monsieur Croche et autres écrits* (Paris: Gallimard, 1987).
3. André Messager (1853–1929) studied at the Ecole Niedermeyer with Fauré and Saint-Saëns. Early in his career he was known as an organist and light-opera composer, but he later concentrated on opera administration at the Opéra-Comique, the Opéra, and Covent Garden. He encouraged Debussy and conducted the premiere of *Pelléas et Mélisande* in 1902 at the Opéra-Comique.
4. Inghelbrecht's remarks here are parallel with those of Louis Laloy, in "Exercice analytique sur les quatres premières mesures de *Pelléas,*" which appeared first in 1902 but was reprinted in Laloy's book *La musique retrouvée* (1928; Paris: Desclée de Brouwer, 1974). It is quite possible that Inghelbrecht knew this important writing.
5. Here Inghelbrecht reveals a particular understanding of Debussy's thought on performance. Inghelbrecht could probably not have known the composer's 1908 conversations with Victor Segalen, in which Debussy stated, "Split up the woodwinds . . . so that their entries don't sound like somebody dropping a parcel" (quoted in Roger Nichols, *Debussy Remembered* [London: Faber and Faber, 1992], 149). But Inghelbrecht could well have recalled their discussion of the point in his and Debussy's sessions on performing the scores.
6. Hector Dufranne sang the role of Golaud at the premiere of the opera on 30 April 1902.
7. Mary Garden created the role of Mélisande at the opera's premiere.
8. The Belgian poet and playwright Maurice Maeterlinck (1862–1949) wrote the play *Pelléas et Mélisande* in 1893.
9. The reference is to the title character in Debussy's Poème lyrique for soprano, female chorus, and orchestra of 1887–88. Further on the "Blessed Damozel" of Dante Gabriel Rossetti and the important relationships of Debussy's work, see Richard Langham Smith, "Debussy and the Pre-Raphaelites," *Nineteenth-Century Music* 5/2 (Fall 1981): 95–109.
10. The reference is to the title character of Jules Massenet's opera of 1892.
11. Rose Féart sang certain of Debussy's songs with his sanction, if not particular enthusiasm, as well as the role of Mélisande at Covent Garden in 1909.
12. Jean Périer created the role of Pelléas at the 1902 debut.
13. Roger Bourdin first took the role of Pelléas in a 1927 revival, alongside the original singers Mary Garden, Hector Dufranne, and Félix Vieuille.
14. At the time of Inghelbrecht's writing in 1933, no complete recording had been issued. According to the discography by Malcolm Walker in Roger Nichols and Richard Langham Smith, *Claude Debussy: "Pelléas et Mélisande,"* Cambridge Opera Handbook (Cambridge: Cambridge University Press, 1989), three extended excerpts had been recorded.

Excerpts appeared in 1924 and 1927 under the direction of Piero Coppola (EMI 520/2; DA677; W614/7 and EMI D2083/6; E603/5, respectively). The singers in both were Brothier (Mélisande), Panzéra (Pelléas), Vanni-Marcoux (Golaud), and Tubiana (Arkel). A third recording of excerpts under the direction of Georges Truc appeared in 1928 on Columbia 68518/23, with the singers Nespoulos (Mélisande), Maguenat (Pelléas), Dufranne (Golaud), Narçon (Arkel), and Croiza (Geneviève). Inghelbrecht was especially displeased by the Truc recording, although he referred to the "available recordings" at times in disparagement. In this essay, he also merged his experience and judgment of live performances with that of the recordings.

15. Emmanuel Chabrier and Jules Massenet were among the composers who set the libretti of the writer Mendès (1841–1909). Mendès wrote the first full-length biography of Richard Wagner and collaborated with Debussy on the opera project *Rodrigue et Chimène,* left unfinished in 1891.
16. This reference is obscure. Apparently Debussy's widow, Emma, had authorized certain emendations to the voice lines in the opera.
17. The draftsman and artist T. A. Steinlen.
18. The tenor Maguenat apparently, noted above in the 1928 recording.
19. The recording in question is the one conducted by Georges Truc in 1928.

CHAPTER 9: AN INTERVIEW WITH PIERRE BOULEZ

1. Paul Griffiths, "Body Language" reprinted in Jean Vermeil, ed., *Conversations with Boulez: Thoughts on Conducting,* trans. Camille Naish (Portland, Ore.: Amadeus Press, 1996), 140.
2. Boulez, in William Glock, ed., *Pierre Boulez: A Symposium* (London: Eulenberg; New York: Da Capo, 1986), 30.
3. Boulez, in Griffiths, "Body Language," 139.
4. Celestin Deliege, *Pierre Boulez: Conversations with Celestin Deliege* (London: Eulenberg, 1976), 20.
5. Deliege, *Pierre Boulez,* 18.
6. Max Liebermann (1835–1927), German painter and etcher born in Berlin and educated in Weimar and Paris.
7. Boulez, in Deliege, *Pierre Boulez,* 49.
8. Peter Heyworth, "The First Fifty Years," in Glock, *Boulez: A Symposium,* 25.
9. Vermeil, *Conversations with Boulez,* 58.
10. Ibid., 38.
11. A series of informal concerts for young audiences given by Boulez in New York.
12. Boulez, in Glock, *Boulez: A Symposium,* 22.

CHAPTER 10: STRUCTURE AND PERFORMANCE

1. Debussy notates the harp passages in C-flat major because it is natural for the harpist to think of lowering the pedals for the diatonic C major scale to C-flat, but the flute and viola parts are written in B major.

2. By "experiential meter" I mean the meter that a listener may infer from the sound of a passage in contrast to the meter that one sees in the score according to the way a passage is barred and beamed. I mean "puns" in the sense that a given passage is susceptible to different metric interpretations, depending upon whether the listener attends the effects of the rhythms as events in themselves or imposes upon them the metric context provided by the score's notation.
3. Example 10.1a and all remaining examples are laid out as follows. The contents of the score are reduced to a single system that contains the materials paramount for this discussion including outer voice parts, a token of the prevailing texture and figuration, and cues for changes in instrumentation but that omits many details, such as most dynamics and slurs as well as many doublings and even whole voice parts. Most readers will wish to have the scores at hand for the passages discussed throughout this essay since the pitch reduction is intended to serve merely as a mnemonic. Immediately above the system there appears a horizontal axis which is intersected by vertical strokes corresponding to strong and weak beats in the notated meter: longer strokes for downbeats, shorter strokes for weak beats. Sporadically superimposed over this scheme are alternative metric schema that contradict the notated meter, which can be heard for reasons I shall explain shortly. Highly plausible metric schema are drawn with solid lines; those that are obscure or problematic use broken lines. Superimposed on yet another horizontal axis above the metric schema is a series of filled oblongs that model the phrases and their junctures, which I shall discuss. Each system is separated from its successor by chevrons that appear at left and right margins.
4. The accent is achieved by four simultaneous articulations. (The flute is omitted from the pitch reduction at m. 6.)
5. In this study references to specific pitches will employ a commonly used system in which middle C through B above are represented as $c^1 \ldots b^1$, C through B an octave above by $c^2 \ldots b^2$, etc. The octave from C below middle C through B above are represented by c . . . b, the octave below that by C . . . B, etc.
6. Interesting questions arise in the notion of metric ambiguity. Can meter as experienced contradict meter as notated? How do we determine plausible metric schemes? For that matter, what is meter? Obviously I cannot resolve the deeper issues here; instead I shall proceed from the assumption that experiential meter *can* contradict notated meter and propose a few practical guidelines for identifying experiential metric schemes. Readers who wish to pursue questions of meter in more depth might begin with the following: William E. Benjamin, "A Theory of Musical Meter," *Music Perception* 1/4 (1984): 355–413; Wallace Berry, "Metric and Rhythmic Articulations in Music," *Music Theory Spectrum* 7 (1985): 7–33; William Rothstein, *Phrase Rhythm in Tonal Music* (New York: Schirmer, 1989); Norman Wick, "A Theory of Rhythmic Levels in Tonal Music" (Ph.D. diss., University of Wisconsin, 1986).
7. These commonly accepted classifications raise a number of refractory issues, which I shall not pursue here. Interested readers could consult Hasty and Roeder, who enumerate some of the problems and discuss relevant literature. Christopher Hasty, "Rhythm in Post-Tonal Music: Preliminary Questions of Duration and Motion," *Journal of Music*

Theory 25/2 (Spring 1981): 183–216; John Roeder, "A Calculus of Accent," *Journal of Music Theory* 39/1 (Spring 1995): 1–46.

8. The g^2 falls on the same beats in mm. 28–29, of course, but there the reiterated contour pattern of three–quarter notes' duration overwhelms any impulse to group the quarter notes in pairs.
9. As explained in note 3, phrases are depicted in each example as filled oblongs located on a horizontal axis that lies above the metric schema and graphically models overlapping, truncated, and bifurcated phrase boundaries.
10. "Pour les agréments" and "pour les notes répétées" from the *Douze Etudes* come immediately to mind, for example, as well as the flute solo that introduces the *Prélude à l'après-midi d'un faune,* or the "laughter" figure at rehearsal no. 61 of "Le matin d'un jour de fête" from *Ibéria,* in the *Images pour orchestre.*
11. There is a wonderful essay by David Lewin that posits a connection between this first gesture in the piano and a new motive that appears "out of the blue," as it were, in the violin's gesture at m. 61. David Lewin, "Some Instances of Parallel Voice-Leading in Debussy," *Nineteenth-Century Music* 11 (1987): 59–72.
12. Although for the reasons given I believe that the phrase scheme I have just described is the most persuasive, it is certainly possible to formulate plausible alternatives; in particular my phrases 1, 2, 4, 6, 7, and 8 could be partitioned into shorter phrases of three or four bars each. A performance based upon a smaller normative phrase duration would project a more agitated, impetuous style compared with the determined but more leisurely bustle of my longer phrase durations.
13. At m. 53 there is expansion from three parts or voices to six, from piano through a crescendo molto, and in the bars that straddle the juncture from a range and tessitura that spans two octaves in a low-medium register (B-flat to g^1) to two and a half octaves placed about two octaves higher (g–d^3). At m. 60 the new phrase is marked by compression from eleven voices or parts to six, from forte toward pianissimo through a diminuendo, and from a range and tessitura that spans almost five octaves about c-sharp^1 as an axis (G_1–f^3), to less than three octaves about c as an axis (G_1–f^1).
14. These qualities are in fact common in late works by many composers, especially from the early nineteenth century onward. Beethoven, Schubert, Chopin, Brahms, Wagner, Franck, and Mahler spring immediately to mind as examples of composers whose mature works maintain a constant tension and sense of momentum throughout by blurring phrase boundaries and occasionally confounding notated metric schemes. As original as is Debussy's compositional language, this is one feature that it shares with those of his antecedents and contemporaries. All of this is, of course, a topic for some other essay.

CHAPTER 11: TIMBRE, VOICE-LEADING, AND THE MUSICAL ARABESQUE

1. Debussy uses this expression to describe the effect achieved by a Palestrina mass he heard performed in the church of Saint-Gervais in 1893. It is in a letter to Prince Poniatowski, cited in his *D'un siècle à l'autre* (Paris, 1948) and in Claude Debussy, *Debussy on Music,*

collect. and introd. François Lesure, trans. and ed. Richard Langham Smith (New York: Knopf, 1977), n. 1, p. 31.

2. Claude Debussy, "Good Friday," *La revue blanche* (1 May 1901), in *Debussy on Music,* 27. Debussy goes on in this review to contrast this music with "that silly wailing you find in opera" and to describe it as "preserv[ing] a sense of nobility . . . it forces one to respect if not to adore [it]." Such an attitude suggests additional links with those at the Schola Cantorum. Founded in 1896 as an alternative to the Conservatoire (which prepared students to write operas), many of its faculty (and students) had aristocratic sympathies.
3. Claude Debussy, *Musica* (October 1902), in *Debussy on Music,* 84.
4. Charles Koechlin's transcriptions, "Gamelang Palag" and "Gamelang Salandro," premiered in Paris at the Société Musicale Indépendante on 4 May 1910; the latter was published in the journal *S.I.M.* (15 October 1910), 548–63. "Gamelang Salandro" is for piccolo, flute, violin, celesta, xylophone, organ, harp, piano, timpani, and gong.
5. Claude Debussy, *S.I.M.* (15 February 1913), in *Debussy on Music,* 278. See also Richard Mueller, "Javanese Influence on Debussy's Fantaisie and Beyond," *Nineteenth-Century Music* 10 (1986): 157–86.
6. David Lewin, "Parallel Voice-Leading in Debussy," in *Music at the Turn of the Century,* ed. Joseph Kerman (Berkeley: University of California Press, 1990), 60.
7. Debussy, *S.I.M.* (15 February 1913), in *Debussy on Music,* 279.
8. *Analyse Musicale* (June 1989) contains studies of "La terrasse des audiences du clair de lune" by Theo Hirsbrunner, Allen Forte, Marcel Mesnage, Eugene Narmour, Fred Lerdahl, Gino Stefani, Luca Marconi, Eero Tarasti, François Delalande, and Michelle Biget.
9. I am grateful to Pamela Madsen and Marianne Kielian-Gilbert for pointing out these harmonic subtleties.
10. Nicolas Ruwet, "Notes sur les duplications dans l'oeuvre de Claude Debussy," *Revue belge de musicologie* (1962): 57–70.
11. Ibid., 59, 70. André Schaeffner traces Debussy's interest in this kind of repetition to Russian composers. See his "Debussy et ses rapports avec la musique russe," in *Musique russe,* ed. Pierre Souvtchinsky, vol. 1 (Paris: Presses Universitaires de France, 1953), 95–138.
12. In some editions, there is a misprint in the lowest note of the first chord in m. 21. It should be an A, as in the previous measure and m. 37.
13. Jann Pasler, "Debussy, Stravinsky, and the Ballets Russes: The Emergence of a New Musical Logic" (Ph.D. diss., University of Chicago, 1981), 371–77. Here I argue that playing with figure-ground, or foreground-background, is one of Debussy's primary means of creating "conjunction" from one idea to another in his music. By contrast, most instances of overlap in Stravinsky's early ballets induce disjunct transformation, or "disjunction" rather than "conjunction," because the overlapping ideas are not pivots but figures in their own right.
14. François Delalande, "'La terrasse des audiences du clair de lune': un essai d'analyse esthétique," *Analyse Musicale* (June 1989): 80, 82.
15. Roy Howat notes that this line, G/E/G/E/E-sharp, comes note for note from the piece's opening melisma (letter to the author, 15 September 1996).
16. Of the eighty-nine dotted quarter notes in the work, the Golden Section lies at the end of the fifty-fifth beat, the last beat of m. 28. Howat points out, furthermore, that this

whole section, mm. 16–31, sits symmetrically at the center of the piece, with twenty-eight dotted quarter notes on either side (ibid.).

17. On an even larger structural level, the movement of B-flat to A-flat major in this étude could be seen as leading to the A major of the subsequent étude, "Pour les accords." The A-flat of the F minor chord with which this étude begins serves as a pivot, returning attention to the middle register. In this étude, the main line stays solidly rooted in this register, the octave reiterations in the outer registers always remaining subsidiary.
18. In this case, consulting Debussy's autograph manuscript does not resolve the question. There is no stem up on the b-flat^2 in mm. 3 and 52 of the manuscript, but there is one on this same note in m. 6. It is possible that Debussy clarified his intentions on the proofs, on which the printed score is based.
19. In "Parallel Voice-Leading in Debussy," Lewin points out that it is not always obvious wherein lies the "continuous musical impulse" of Debussy's music. In the piano part of Debussy's Violin Sonata, he suggests that the line jumps from one voice to another within a sequence of parallel chords.
20. Debussy, *S.I.M.* (15 March 1913), in *Debussy on Music,* 283–84.

Bibliography

Acocella, Joan Ross. "The Reception of Diaghilev's Ballets Russes by Artists and Intellectuals in Paris and London, 1909–1914." Ph.D. diss., Rutgers University, 1984.

Ansermet, Ernest. *Les fondements de la musique.* Rev. ed. Neuchâtel: A la Baconnière 1987.

Bannerman, Betty, ed. *The Singer as Interpreter: Claire Croiza's Masterclasses.* London: Gollancz, 1989.

Barraqué, Jean. *Debussy.* Paris: Seuil, 1962.

Bathori, Jane. *Sur l'interprétation des mélodies de Claude Debussy.* Paris: Editions Ouvrières, 1953.

Bauer, Harold. *Harold Bauer, His Book.* New York: Norton, 1948.

Bauer-Lechner, Natalie. *Erinnerungen an Gustav Mahler.* Leipzig: Tal, 1923. English translation: *Recollections of Gustav Mahler,* trans. Dika Newlin; ed. and annot. Peter Franklin. London: Faber and Faber, 1980.

Beaumont, Cyril. *Michel Fokine and His Ballets.* London: C.W. Beaumont, 1935.

Beck, Jill. "Recalled to Life: Techniques and Perspectives on Reviving Nijinsky's *Faune.*" *Choreography and Dance* 1/3 (1991).

Beck, Jill, ed. "A Revival of Nijinsky's Original *L'Après-midi d'un Faune.*" *Choreography and Dance* 1/3 (1991). Special issue.

Belville, Eugène. "Les arts décoratifs au théâtre—La saison russe—Nijinsky chorégraphe—Pénélope—Les Nocturnes de Debussy," *Art et industrie* (September 1913).

Benjamin, William E. "A Theory of Musical Meter." *Music Perception* 1/4 (1984): 355–413.

Bergson, Henri. *Les deux sources de la morale et de la religion.* Paris: Presses Universitaires de France, 1982.

Berman, Laurence David. "The Evolution of Tonal Thinking in the Works of Claude Debussy." Ph.D. diss., Harvard University, 1965.

Bernac, Pierre. *The Interpretation of French Song.* London: Victor Gollancz, 1970.

Berry, Wallace. "Metric and Rhythmic Articulations in Music." *Music Theory Spectrum* 7 (1985): 7–33.

Berry, Wallace. *Musical Structure and Performance.* New Haven: Yale University Press, 1989.

Borgeaud, Henri, ed. *Correspondance de Claude Debussy et Pierre Louÿs.* Paris: José Corti, 1945–92. Reprinted in Debussy, *Correspondance, 1884–1918,* ed. François Lesure. Paris: Hermann, 1993.

Boulez, Pierre. *Conversations de Pierre Boulez sur la direction d'orchestre avec Jean Vermeil.* Paris: Plume, 1989.

Boulez, Pierre. *Points de repère.* Paris: Bourgois/Seuil, 1981.

Boulez, Pierre. *Relevés d'apprenti,* ed. Paule Thévenin. Paris: Seuil, 1966.

Bowman, Robin. "Mélodies en exile." *Music and Musicians* 25 (1977).

Briscoe, James R. *Debussy: Preludes for Piano, Books 1 and 2.* Critical edition. New York: Schirmer, 1991.

Buckle, Richard. *Diaghilev.* London: Weidenfeld and Nicholson, 1979.

Buckle, Richard. *Nijinsky.* London: Weidenfeld and Nicolson, 1971.

Burkhart, Charles. "Debussy Plays 'La cathédrale engloutie' and Solves Metrical Mystery." *Piano Quarterly* 65 (Fall 1968): 14–26.

Casella, Alfredo. "Claude Debussy." *Monthly Musical Record* 63 (1933): 2.

Casella, Alfredo. *Music in My Time: The Memoirs of Alfredo Casella,* trans. and ed. Spencer Norton. Norman: University of Oklahoma Press, 1955.

Chesterman, Robert. *Conversations with Conductors.* New York: Robson Books, 1976.

Clevenger, John R. "Achille at the Conservatoire, 1872–1884." *Cahiers Debussy* 19 (1995).

Cooper Albright, Ann. "The Long Afternoon of a Faun: Reconstruction and the Discourses of Desire." *Dance Reconstructed Conference Proceedings,* Rutgers University, 1992.

Copeland, George. "Debussy, the Man I Knew." *Atlantic Monthly,* January 1955, 38.

Copeland, Roger. "Merce Cunningham and the Politics of Perception." 1979. Reprinted in *What Is Dance?* ed. Roger Copeland and Marshall Cohen. Oxford: Oxford University Press, 1983.

Coppola, Piero. *Dix-sept ans de musique à Paris, 1922–1939.* Preface by Aloÿ Fornerod. Lausanne: Librairie F. Rouge, 1944.

Cortot, Alfred. *La musique française de piano.* 1930–1932. Rev. ed. Paris: Presses Universitaires de France, 1981.

de Tinan, Madame Gaston. "Memories of Debussy and His circle." *Recorded Sound* 50 (1973).

Debussy, Claude. *Correspondance, 1884–1918,* ed. François Lesure. Paris: Hermann, 1993.

Debussy, Claude. *Lettres, 1884–1918,* comp. and annot. François Lesure. Paris: Hermann, 1980.

Debussy, Claude. *Debussy on Music: The Critical Writings of the Great French Composer,* collect. and introd. François Lesure as *Monsieur Croche et autres écrits;* trans. and ed. Richard Langham Smith. New York: Knopf, 1977. Rev. and enlarged ed. Ithaca: Cornell University Press, 1988.

Debussy, Claude. *Douze Etudes,* Premier Livre. Paris: Durand, 1916.

Debussy, Claude. *Etudes pour le piano.* Facsimile of the autograph sketches (1915), with an introduction by Roy Howat. Geneva: Minkoff, 1989.

Debussy, Claude. *Lettres à deux amis: Robert Godet et Georges Jean-Aubry.* Paris: José Corti, 1942.

Debussy, Claude. *Lettres inédites à André Caplet (1908–1914),* ed. Edward Lockspeiser. Monaco: Editions du Rocher, 1957.

Debussy, Claude. Notes to *Early Recordings by the Composer.* The Condon Collection. Germany: Bellaphon 690 07 011, 1992.

Debussy, Claude. Notes to *Préludes* and *Images.* Channel Classics CCS 4892, 1993.

Debussy, Claude. *Oeuvres complètes.* Paris: Durand and Costallat, 1985–.

"Debussy à travers le journal de Madame de Saint-Marceaux, 1894–1911." *Cahiers Debussy* 3 (1976).

"Debussy Discusses Music and His Works." *New York Times,* 26 June 1910. Reprinted by David Grayson in *Cahiers Debussy* 16 (1992).

Debussy Letters, select. and ed. François Lesure and Roger Nichols; trans. Roger Nichols. Cambridge: Harvard University Press, 1987.

Delalande, François. "'La terrasse des audiences du clair de lune': Un essai d'analyse esthétique." *Analyse Musicale* (June 1989).

Deliège, Célestin. *Pierre Boulez: Conversations with Celestin Deliege.* London: Eulenberg, 1976.

Del Mar, Norman. *Anatomy of the Orchestra.* Berkeley: University of California Press, 1981.

Denby, Edwin. *Dance Writings.* London: Dance Books, 1986.

Dietschy, Marcel. "Debussy trahi par les virtuoses." *Revue musicale suisse* 116 (January–February 1976): 8–52.

Doret, Gustave. *Temps et contretemps. Souvenirs d'un musicien.* Fribourg, Switzerland: Editions de la Librairie de l'Université, 1942.

Dukas, Paul. "*Nocturnes* de Debussy." *Revue hébdomadaire,* February 1901. Reprinted in *Les écrits de Paul Dukas sur la musique.* Paris: Société d'Editions Françaises et Internationales, 1948.

Dunoyer, Cecilia. *Marguerite Long: A Life in French Music.* Bloomington: Indiana University Press, 1993.

Durand, Jacques, ed. *Lettres de Claude Debussy à son éditeur.* Paris: Durand, 1927.

Emmanuel, Maurice. *"Pelléas et Mélisande."* Paris: Mellottée, 1926.

Fokine, Michel. *Memoirs of a Ballet Master,* trans. Vitale Fokine; ed. Anatole Chujoy. London: Constable, 1961.

Galkin, Elliott W. *A History of Orchestral Conducting: In Theory and Practice.* New York: Pendragon, 1988.

Gaudibert, Eric. "Essai sur les différentes catégories du silence musical." *Dissonance: La nouvelle revue musicale suisse* 45 (August 1995): 15–17.

Glock, William, ed. *Pierre Boulez: A Symposium.* New York: Da Capo, 1986.

Grayson, David A. "The Genesis of Debussy's *Pelléas et Mélisande.*" Ph.D. diss., Harvard University, 1983.

Grayson, David A. "The Interludes of *Pelléas et Mélisande.*" In *L'Oeuvre de Claude Debussy.* Actes du Colloque International, University of Geneva, March 1989.

Gross, Valentine. "Impressions sur le ballet *Jeux.*" *Comoedia Illustré* (June–July 1913).

Gubisch, Nina. "Le journal inédit de Ricardo Viñes." *Revue internationale de musique française* (June 1980).

Guest, Ann Hutchinson. "Nijinsky's *Faune.*" *Choreography and Dance* 1/3 (1991).

Guest, Ann Hutchinson, and Claudia Jeshke. *Nijinsky's "Faune" Restored.* Philadelphia: Gordon and Breach, 1991.

Haggin, Bernard H. *Contemporary Recollections of the Maestro.* Reprint of *Conversations with Toscanini* (1959) and *The Toscanini Musicians Knew* (1967). New York: Da Capo, 1989.

Harris, Dale. "The Lost Art of French Vocal Style." *High Fidelity,* April 1972.

Hasty, Christopher. "Rhythm in Post-Tonal Music: Preliminary Questions of Duration and Motion." *Journal of Music Theory* 25/2 (Spring 1981): 183–216.

Hirsbrunner, Theo. "Debussy's Ballett *Khamma.*" *Archiv für Musikwissenschaft* 36/2 (1979): 105–21.

Hofmannsthal, Hugo von, and Richard Strauss. *Correspondence Between Richard Strauss and Hugo Von Hofmannsthal.* London: Collins, 1961.

Howat, Roy. "Debussy and Welte." *Pianola Journal* 7 (1994): 3–18.

Hudson, Richard. *Stolen Time: The History of Tempo Rubato.* Oxford: Clarendon Press, 1994.

Hurdy, François. *Ernest Ansermet, pionnier de la musique.* Lausanne: L'aire musicale, 1983.

Inédits sur Claude Debussy. Paris: Les Publications Techniques, 1942.

Inghelbrecht, D.-E. *Comment on ne doit pas interpréter "Carmen," "Faust," et "Pelléas."* Paris: Heugel, 1933.

Inghelbrecht, Désiré-Emile. *Mouvement contraire,* vol. 1: *Vers le temps heureux.* Paris: Domat, 1947.

Inghelbrecht, Désiré-Emile, *Le chef d'orchestre et son équipe,* trans. G. Prerauer and S. Malcolm Kirk as *The Conductor's World.* London: Peter Nevill, 1953.

Inghelbrecht, Germaine, and Désiré-Emile Inghelbrecht. *Claude Debussy.* Paris: Costard, 1953.

Jarocinski, Stefan. *Debussy: Impressionnisme et symbolisme.* Paris: Editions du Seuil, 1970. English translation: *Debussy: Impressionism and Symbolism.* Trans. Rollo Myers. London: Eulenberg, 1976.

Koury, Daniel J. *Orchestral Performance Practices in the Nineteenth Century.* Ann Arbor, Mich.: UMI Press, 1986.

Laloy, Louis. *Debussy.* Paris: Aux Armes de France, 1944.

Laloy, Louis. *La musique retrouvée.* 1928. Paris: Desclée de Brouwer, 1974.

Lesure, François. *Claude Debussy, biographie critique.* Paris: Klincksieck, 1994.

Lesure, François. *Claude Debussy avant "Pelléas," ou Les années symbolistes.* Paris: Klincksieck, 1992.

Lesure, François. "Une interview romaine de Debussy." 1914. *Cahiers Debussy* 11 (1987).

Lesure, François, ed. *Claude Debussy, Esquisses de "Pelléas et Mélisande" (1893–1895)*. Geneva: Minkoff, 1977.

Lewin, David. "Parallel Voice-Leading in Debussy." In *Music at the Turn of the Century*, ed. Joseph Kerman. Berkeley: University of California Press, 1990.

Lewin, David. "Some Instances of Parallel Voice-Leading in Debussy." *Nineteenth Century Music* 11 (1987): 59–72.

Liebich, Louise. "An Englishwoman's Memories of Debussy." *Musical Times*, 1 June 1918.

Lockspeiser, Edward. *Debussy: His Life and Mind.* 2 vols. London: Cassell, 1962–78.

Lockspeiser, Edward. "Debussy's Concept of the Dream." *Proceedings of the Royal Musical Association* 89 (1962–63): 49–61.

Long, Marguerite. *Au piano avec Claude Debussy.* Paris: Julliard, 1960.

Macdonald, Nesta. *Diaghilev Observed by Critics in England and the United States, 1911–1929.* New York: Dance Horizons, 1975.

Marsh, Robert Charles. *Toscanini and the Art of Conducting.* New York: Collier Books, 1962.

Mauclair, Camille. *La Revue*, 1 August 1910. Reprinted in Deirdre Pridden, *The Art of the Dance in French Literature.* London: A. and C. Black, 1952.

Melba, Nellie. *The Melba Method.* 1926. Reprinted in William Moran, *Nellie Melba: A Contemporary Review.* Westport, Conn.: Greenwood Press, 1985.

Messager, Jean-André, ed. *L'enfance de "Pelléas": Lettres de Claude Debussy à André Messager.* Paris: Dorbon-ainé, 1938.

Mueller, Richard. "Javanese Influence on Debussy's Fantaisie and Beyond." *Nineteenth Century Music* 10 (1986): 157–86.

Munro, Thomas. "*The Afternoon of a Faun* and the Interrelation of the Arts." *Journal of Aesthetics and Art Criticism* 10 (1951).

Nectoux, Jean-Michel. *Afternoon of a Faun: Mallarmé, Debussy, Nijinsky.* New York: Vendome Press, 1987.

Nichols, Roger. *Debussy Remembered.* London: Faber and Faber, 1992.

Nichols, Roger, and Richard Langham Smith. *Claude Debussy: "Pelléas et Mélisande."* Cambridge Opera Handbook. Cambridge: Cambridge University Press, 1989.

Nijinska, Bronislava. *Early Memoirs*, ed. and trans. Irina Nijinska and Jean Rawlinson. London: Faber and Faber, 1981.

Nijinsky, Romola. *Nijinsky.* 1933. London: Sphere Books, 1970.

O'Connor, Garry. *The Pursuit of Perfection: A Life of Maggie Teyte.* London: Victor Gollancz, 1979.

Odom, Selma. "Wigman at Hellerau." *Ballet Review* 14/2 (Summer 1986): 41–53.

Orledge, Robert. *Debussy and the Theatre.* Cambridge: Cambridge University Press, 1982.

Pasler, Jann. "Debussy, Stravinsky, and the Ballets Russes: The Emergence of a New Musical Logic." Ph.D. diss., University of Chicago, 1981.

Pasler, Jann. "Paris: Conflicting Notions of Progress." In Jim Samson, ed., *Music and Society: The Late Romantic Era; From the Mid-Nineteenth Century to World War I.* Englewood Cliffs, N.J.: Prentice Hall, 1991.

Peyser, Joan, ed. *The Orchestra: Origins and Transformations.* New York: Scribner's, 1986.

Phillip, Robert. *Early Recordings and Musical Style.* Cambridge: Cambridge University Press, 1992.

Propert, W. A. *The Russian Ballet in Western Europe, 1909–1920.* London: Bodley Head, 1921.

Rambert, Marie. *Quicksilver.* London: Macmillan, 1972.

Rodin, Auguste. "La rénovation de la danse." *Le Matin,* 30 May 1912.

Roeder, John. "A Calculus of Accent." *Journal of Music Theory* 39/1 (Spring 1995): 1–46.

Rolf, Marie. "Debussy's 'La Mer': A Critical Analysis in the Light of Early Sketches and Editions." Ph.D. diss., University of Rochester, 1976.

Rothstein, William. *Phrase Rhythm in Tonal Music.* New York: Schirmer, 1989.

Ruwet, Nicolas. "Notes sur les duplications dans l'oeuvre de Claude Debussy." *Revue belge de musicologie* 16 (1962): 57–70.

Schaeffner, André. "Debussy et ses rapports avec la musique russe." In *Musique russe,* ed. Pierre Souvtchinsky, vol. 1. Paris: Presses Universitaires de France, 1953.

Schmitz, E. Robert. "A Plea for the Real Debussy." *Etude* (December 1937): 781–82.

Schonberg, Harold C. *The Great Conductors.* New York: Simon and Schuster, 1967.

Shattuck, Roger. *The Banquet Years.* New York: Knopf, 1955.

Smith, Richard Langham. "Debussy and the Pre-Raphaelites" *Nineteenth-Century Music* 5/2 (Fall 1981): 95–109.

Smith, Richard Langham. "Debussy: Songs, Claudette Leblanc, Valerie Tryon." [Review]. *Musical Times* 134 (1993): 528.

Smith, Richard Langham, ed. *Debussy Studies.* Cambridge: Cambridge University Press, 1997.

Sokolova, Lydia. *Dancing for Diaghilev.* London: John Murray, 1960.

Steane, J. B. *The Grand Tradition: Seventy Years of Singing on Record.* Portland, Ore.: Amadeus Press, 1994.

Stravinsky, Igor. *An Autobiography.* New York: Norton, 1962.

Stravinsky, Igor. *Chronicle of My Life.* London: Victor Gollancz, 1936.

Suter, Louis-Marc. "Quelques aspects du rythme dans la musique de Claude Debussy." *Revue internationale de musique française* 2/5 (June 1981): 23–30.

Tappolet, Claude. *Lettres de compositeurs français à Ernest Ansermet (1911–1960).* Geneva: Georg, 1988.

Tenroc, Charles. "Nijinski va faire dans *l'Après-Midi d'un Faune* des essais de chorégraphie cubiste." *Comoedia,* 18 April 1912, 4.

Trezise, Simon. *Debussy: "La Mer."* Cambridge: Cambridge University Press, 1994.

Timbrell, Charles. "Claude Debussy and Walter Rummel: Chronicle of a Friendship." *Music and Letters* (August 1992).

Timbrell, Charles. "Walter Rummel." *Cahiers Debussy* 11 (1987): 24–33.

Valéry, Paul. *Degas Danse Dessin.* Paris: Gallimard, 1946.

Vallas, Léon. *Claude Debussy et son temps.* Paris: Editions Albin Michel, 1958.

Van Vechten, Carl. *The Dance Writings of Carl Van Vechten,* ed. Paul Padgette. New York: Dance Horizons, 1974.

Vasnier, Marguerite. "Debussy à 18 ans." *La Revue musicale,* 1 May 1926.

Whitworth, Geoffrey. *The Art of Nijinsky.* 1913. New York: Benjamin Blom, 1972.

Wick, Norman. "A Theory of Rhythmic Levels in Tonal Music." Ph.D. diss., University of Wisconsin, 1986.

Contributors

Claude Abravanel is the director of the Archives of Israeli Music and a teacher at the Rubin Academy of Music and Dance in Jerusalem. He was born in 1924 in Switzerland and studied piano under Dinu Lipatti and Yvonne Lefébure, and composition with Arthur Honegger. He is the author of *Claude Debussy: A Bibliography.*

James R. Briscoe is professor of musicology at Jordan College of Fine Arts, Butler University, in Indianapolis. He is the author of *Claude Debussy: A Guide to Research, Historical Anthology of Music by Women,* and the *Contemporary Anthology of Music by Women*. His critical editions of Debussy include the *Preludes* (Schirmer, 1991) and *62 Songs* (Leonard, 1993).

Cecilia Dunoyer is professor of piano at Pennsylvania State University. She has received international awards and concertized extensively in the United States, Mexico, and Europe, including debut recitals in Paris and Vienna in 1987. Highlights of her 1995–96 recital season included a series devoted to Fauré's music, all-Debussy recitals, and appearances with major orchestras. She is the author of *Marguerite Long: A Life in French Music.*

Stephanie Jordan is professor of dance studies at Roehampton Institute, London. Her books include *Striding Out: Aspects of Contemporary and New Dance in Britain* and *Parallel Lines: Media Representations of Dance* (coedited with Dave Allen). She is also a dance critic.

Richard S. Parks is professor of music theory at the University of Western

Ontario. For many years he maintained a busy schedule as a freelance trumpet performer and recitalist. He is the author of *Eighteenth-Century Counterpoint and Tonal Structure* and *The Music of Claude Debussy.*

Jann Pasler is professor of musicology at the University of California, San Diego. A pianist, musicologist, and documentary filmmaker, she has published widely on contemporary music in France and America, modernism, and cultural life. In progress is her *The Mechanisms of Musical Life and Compositional Choice, 1870–1914.*

Richard Langham Smith is reader in music at the University of Exeter. A student of Wilfred Mellers and Edward Lockspeiser, he has written extensively on French music, including translations of Debussy's articles, published as *Debussy on Music,* and the Cambridge Opera Handbook of *Pelléas et Mélisande.* His edition of Debussy's *Rodrigue et Chimène* formed the basis for the reconstructed opera performed at the Opéra de Lyon in 1993, now released as a compact disc on Erato.

Louis-Marc Suter is professor of musicology at the University of Bern. He is the author of a book on music in Yugoslavia, the catalogue raisonné of the work of Norbert Moret, and a book compiling diverse studies of that composer.

Brooks Toliver is professor of music history at the University of Akron. His publications include "*Leaves of Grass* in Claude Debussy's Prose" and "Improvisation in the Madrigals of the Rossi Codex." Current projects include studies of irony in Debussy's *Gigues,* the aesthetics of the late Verdi in *Otello,* and nature in late nineteenth-century tone poems.

Index